YUGOSLAVIA AND ITS HISTORIANS

Yugoslavia and Its Historians

Understanding the Balkan Wars of the 1990s

Edited by

NORMAN M. NAIMARK

and

HOLLY CASE

Stanford University Press, Stanford, California

Stanford University Press
Stanford, California

© 2003 by the Board of Trustees of the
Leland Stanford Junior University.
Printed in the United States of America
on acid-free, archival-quality paper.

Library of Congress Cataloging-in-Publication Data

Yugoslavia and its historians : understanding the Balkan wars of the
1990s / edited by Norman M. Naimark and Holly Case.
    p. cm.
Includes bibliographical references and index.
    ISBN 0-8047-4594-3
    1. Yugoslavia—History. 2. Yugoslavia—Historiography. 3. Balkan
Peninsula—Politics and government—20th century. 4.
Nationalism—Balkan Peninsula. I. Naimark, Norman M. II. Case, Holly.
DR1246 .Y83 2003
949.6'007'20497—dc21   2002015102

Original Printing 2003
Last figure below indicates year of this printing:
12   11   10   09   08   07   06   05   04   03

Designed by Eleanor Mennick
Typeset by Classic Typography in 9.5/12.5 Trump Mediaeval

To Uncle Wayne

Contents

Acknowledgments

The editors are grateful for the help and encouragement we have received from numerous colleagues and friends while bringing this volume to publication. We wish to thank Stanford's Department of History and its Center for Russian and East European Studies for supporting the conference from which the book originated. We are grateful for the leadership of Nancy Kollmann and for the essential logistical contributions of Mary Dakin and Rosemary Schnoor. The Robert and Florence McDonnell Chair in East European Studies provided support for the conference and volume; we are beholden to the McDonnell family for their generosity and for their commitment to the East European field. Norris Pope of Stanford University Press was an enthusiastic supporter of this project from its inception. Thanks are also due to John Lampe of the University of Maryland for his careful and constructive reading of the manuscript. Dušan Djordjevich of Stanford's History Department provided the editors invaluable help in correcting parts of the text. Holly Case was an indispensable partner in this endeavor; her historical erudition and linguistic acumen made this a much better book.

An earlier version of Gale Stokes' contribution also appeared as "Containing Nationalism: Solutions in the Balkans," in *Problems of Post Communism* 46, no. 4 (July-August 1999), 3–10. Thanks to Ivo Banac of Yale University for allowing us to use his map of Bileća Rudine.

This book is dedicated with love and admiration to Professor Wayne S. Vucinich, who has communicated the history, the fascination, and the dignity of the peoples of the Balkans to so many of his students and colleagues.

Contributors

WENDY BRACEWELL is senior lecturer in history and director of the Centre for South-East European Studies at the School of Slavonic and East European Studies, University College London. She was adopted as a Vucinich niece as an undergraduate at Stanford after showing an interest in Balkan languages, and was subsequently enticed into pursuing research on frontier society and border warfare in the graduate program. Most subsequent writing, whether on sixteenth-century border raiders (*The Uskoks of Senj: Piracy, Brigandage and Holy War in the Sixteenth-Century Adriatic* [1992]), on gender and nationalism, or on definitions of "South-East Europe," reveals the influence of the Vucinich School.

HOLLY CASE is a Ph.D. candidate in East European history at Stanford. She is at work on her dissertation on ethnic relations in wartime Cluj.

DUŠAN J. DJORDJEVICH is a Ph.D. candidate in history at Stanford, completing his dissertation on the national question in late interwar Yugoslavia. He is co-editor of *Political and Ideological Confrontations in Twentieth-Century Europe* (1996).

THOMAS A. EMMERT (Stanford Ph.D., 1973, under Wayne S. Vucinich) is professor of history at Gustavus Adolphus College in St. Peter, Minnesota, where he teaches courses on Russia, the Ottoman Empire, and the Balkans. He is the author of *Serbian Golgotha: Kosovo, 1389*, editor with W. S. Vucinich of *Kosovo: Legacy of a Medieval Battle*, and is completing a one-volume *History of Serbia* for the Studies of Nationalities series at Hoover Institution Press.

JOHN V. A. FINE is professor of history at the University of Michigan, Ann Arbor. He teaches and writes on Byzantium and the modern and medieval Balkans. Professor Fine is the author of *The Bosnian Church*; *The Early Medieval Balkans*; *The Late Medieval Balkans*; and (with Robert J. Donia) *Bosnia-Hercegovina: A Tradition Betrayed*.

CHARLES JELAVICH is professor of history, emeritus, at Indiana University. He received his AB (1944), MA (1947), and Ph.D. (1949) from the University of California at Berkeley. In 1986–87, Professor Jelavich was president of the American Association for the Advancement of Slavic Studies. He is author of *Tsarist Russia and Balkan Nationalism; South Slav Nationalisms: Textbooks and Yugoslav Union before 1914;* co-author of *Russia in the East, 1876–1880; The Education of a Russian Statesman: Memoirs of Nicholas Karlovich Giers; The Establishment of the Balkan National States, 1804–1920;* editor of *Language and Area Studies: East Central and Southeastern Europe;* and co-editor of *The Balkans in Transition.*

BARIŠA KREKIĆ is professor of history, emeritus, at the University of California at Los Angeles. He received his Ph.D. at the Serbian Academy of Arts and Sciences in 1954. Professor Krekić conducted post-doctoral studies at the Sorbonne in Paris, 1957–58, and has taught at Belgrade and Novi Sad Universities in Yugoslavia, at Central European University in Budapest, at Indiana and Stanford Universities, and, since 1970, at the University of California, Los Angeles. He is the author of five books and numerous articles published in the United States and Europe. His main research topic is the history of late medieval and Renaissance Dubrovnik (Ragusa) and Venice.

NORMAN M. NAIMARK is Robert and Florence McDonnell Professor of East European Studies at Stanford. His latest book is *Fires of Hatred: Ethnic Cleansing in Twentieth-Century Europe* (Harvard University Press, 2001).

ANDREW ROSSOS is professor of history at the University of Toronto. Over the years his research has ranged from Russian-Balkan relations to Czech historiography to the Macedonian question. His studies on Macedonian history have appeared in *Slavonic and East European Review* (1991), *Slavic Review* (1994), *National Character and National Ideology in Interwar Eastern Europe* (I. Banac and K. Verdery, eds., 1995), *Journal of Modern History* (1997), and, most recently, *East European Politics and Societies* (2000). He is now preparing a volume, *Macedonia and the Macedonians: A History*, for the Studies of Nationalities series published by the Hoover Institution Press.

GALE STOKES is Mary Gibbs Jones Professor of History and interim dean of humanities at Rice University. He is the author of *The Walls Came Tumbling Down: The Collapse of Communism in Eastern Europe* (winner of the Vucinich Prize for the best book on Eastern Europe and

Eurasia for 1993); *From Stalinism to Pluralism: A Documentary History of Eastern Europe since 1945;* and *Three Eras of Historical Change in Eastern Europe.* Professor Stokes has also written monographs on Serbian history and recently published a Western Civilization textbook. He has won several teaching awards at Rice and has appeared in national forums such as the *McNeil/Lehrer News Hour,* National Public Radio, the *Washington Post,* and CNN.

ARNOLD SUPPAN is professor of East European history at the University of Vienna and president of the Austrian Institute of East and Southeast European Studies. Born in 1945 in Carinthia, Professor Suppan received his Ph.D. from the University of Vienna in 1970, where he has taught since 1971. He has also been a visiting professor at the universities of Klagenfurt, Leiden, and Fribourg and at Stanford. His main publications are *Innere Front: Militärassistenz, Widerstand und Umsturz in der Donaumonarchie, 1918* (1974); *Die österreichischen Volksgruppen* (1983); *Ostmitteleuropa am Wendepunkt, 1938* (1988); *Jugoslawien und Österreich, 1918–1938* (1996); and *Zwischen Adria und Karawanken* (1998).

WAYNE S. VUCINICH is Robert and Florence McDonnell Professor of East European Studies, emeritus, at Stanford University. Among his books are *Serbia Between East and West; The Ottoman Empire;* and, most recently, *Ivo Andrić Revisited* (editor). He has served as president of the American Association for the Advancement of Slavic Studies and is at present general editor of the Studies of Nationalities series published by Hoover Institution Press.

LARRY WOLFF is professor of history at Boston College. He received his AB from Harvard in 1979 and his Ph.D. from Stanford in 1984. He is the author of *The Vatican and Poland in the Age of the Partitions; Postcards from the End of the World: Child Abuse in Freud's Vienna; Inventing Eastern Europe: The Map of Civilization on the Mind of the Enlightenment;* and *Venice and the Slavs: The Discovery of Dalmatia in the Age of Enlightenment.*

Preface

NORMAN M. NAIMARK

The idea behind this volume derives from a fairly straightforward observation: that much of the recent history of Yugoslavia has been written and rewritten by journalists and political analysts looking for the origins of the wars that have plagued the Balkans over the past decade. If history is a conversation between the past and the present—to use E. H. Carr's famous formulation in *What is History?*[1]—then over the course of the 1990s the conversation became one-sided, with the present overwhelmingly dominant. The healthy balance between past and present was upset to the point where the past became almost unrecognizable. The notion of a Balkan world of perpetual violence, cultural marginality, and "ancient hatreds" dominated public discourse about the war and was legitimized by a raft of newly published histories. The most influential of these studies was Robert D. Kaplan's *Balkan Ghosts,*[2] which, according to numerous reports, had a profound impact on the Clinton administration's understanding of the war in Yugoslavia.[3]

In some ways, scholars can be grateful for the work done by journalists, writers, diplomats, and policy analysts.[4] The shelves of bookstores, only fifteen years ago bereft—with few exceptions—of new, serious studies of the South Slavs and their history, are now bursting with fresh publications, so many that it has been hard to keep up with all of them.[5] Moreover, human rights organizations, the United Nations, the European Union, and many other government and intergovernmental organizations, as well as nongovernmental organizations (NGOs), sponsored (and continue to sponsor) the publications of books on the former Yugoslavia that analyze the origins of the war. Much like the Vietnam War, when Americans learned for the first time about Saigon and Hanoi, not to mention Haiphong and the Mekong Delta, the public has learned the geography of conflict in former Yugoslavia. Few students in the 1980s could identify on the map the locations of Vukovar, Sarajevo, or Priština. They now have some idea of the physical, cultural, religious, and linguistic landscape of the region.

Journalists also performed the invaluable service of bringing the war into American homes, through television, newspapers, and magazines. It is hard to imagine the crescendo of concern in the West about the bloody conflict in Bosnia-Herzegovina independent of Christiane Amanpour's passionate CNN reports from the region.[6] Roy Gutman's *Newsday* articles, which won a Pulitzer Prize, brought the term "ethnic cleansing" to the attention of the Western public and revealed the horrors of the detention camps, like Omarska, in Bosnia.[7] A courageous young journalist by the name of David Rohde helped to break the story about the massacres in Srebrenica in the summer of 1995, and also wrote a Pulitzer Prize–winning book on the subject.[8] And journalists wrote articles and books that filled in the many shades of meaning to ethnic conflict by providing intimate portraits of the people involved.[9] Sometimes, those portraits were of the main culprits, Milošević, Tudjman, and others; sometimes they were of the common folk caught up in the whirlwind of hatred.

Professional historians of Yugoslavia were strangely silent about the war and the breakup of the country, especially at the beginning. Some might think of Noel Malcolm as the exception that proves the rule. Though trained as an historian, Malcolm worked as a journalist and wrote for the *Spectator* and the *Daily Telegraph*. His readable and elegant, if still somewhat partisan, studies of Bosnia and Kosovo have provided a positive model for far-reaching insights into the histories of the peoples and locales of former Yugoslavia.[10] Shocked both by the rapid disintegration of the country and the virulence of the fratricidal struggles, most historians of the region retreated from active commentary on events. Those with an interest in the history of Serbia, in particular, found it hard to understand the aggressiveness of Belgrade's policies. Former colleagues and friends in Serbia had become propagandists for Milošević's wars; it became much harder to carry on serious research in the Yugoslav archives. Those who worked on the history of Croatia were not anxious to be associated with the greater Croatian designs of the Tudjman regime. The few historians who knew something about Bosnia-Herzegovina published what they could, but the products were very desultory. Anyone who identified with Yugoslavia and the increasingly unpopular appellation "Yugoslav" tended to withdraw from the debate altogether. Although this silence gradually changed over the decade of the 1990s, individuals who knew the most about the history and culture of the peoples of the region still remained remarkably restrained about commenting on its past, present, and future.[11]

The four wars of Milošević—against Slovenia, Croatia, Bosnia-Herzegovina, and finally against Kosovo—came to an end only with the bombing of Serbia, the removal of Milošević from power, and the development of a Serbian reform-oriented regime. NATO forces control the most unsettled areas of former Yugoslavia; UN, European Union, and the Organization for Security and Cooperation in Europe (OSCE) officials manage the political and economic life of Bosnia and Kosovo. Attempts by Albanian insurgents to destabilize Macedonia and gain acceptance for their demands for autonomy within the Macedonian state were firmly rejected by the West. Despite occasional explosions and shooting incidents, the Macedonian government has proceeded to implement the Ohrid Agreement of August 2001, calling for a restructuring of Macedonian-Albanian ethnic relations. With Slobodan Milošević facing charges of crimes against humanity and genocide before the Hague Tribunal, Serbian politics has the chance to evolve in a more firmly democratic direction. The Montenegrin separatist movement has been relegated to an oppositionist role since the Belgrade Agreement of March 14, 2002, which fostered the maintenance of a Serbian and Montenegrin Union. Political developments in both Montenegro and Albania remain under the watchful eyes of European Union and NATO officials. There is a minimum of violent conflict in Bosnia and Kosovo, where the major problems continue to be corruption, poverty, unemployment, and ethnic discrimination. The shocking lesson of the War of Yugoslav Succession—that "it's never over when you think it's over"—still holds. With that said, the possibilities of peace in the Balkans are at their greatest now, the summer of 2002, than they have been since the spring of 1991. Confidence in the future has slowly returned to the region; a symbol for that process is the rebuilding of the elegant Turkish "Old Bridge" over the Neretva river in Mostar, a historical landmark that was wantonly destroyed during the war.

With the potential of a genuine peace in the Balkans, this appears to be a particularly good time to ask historians to reflect on the meaning of their own work for understanding the present and future of the lands of former Yugoslavia. At a symposium at Stanford in the spring of 2000, dozens of scholars from the United States and abroad gathered to share their work and their thoughts on the war. Many of the participants were former students and colleagues of Wayne S. Vucinich, the doyen of Balkan history in the United States. In his eighty-ninth year, Professor Vucinich continues to encourage his students, some themselves now close to retirement age, to write and rewrite the history of the South

Slavs. His life-long devotion to patient and conscientious scholarly inquiry remains an inspiration to generations of Balkanists.

The logic of this book follows from the flow of the symposium and its discussions. In the first chapter, Dušan Djordjevich from Stanford University reviews the recent historiography of Yugoslavia and its successor states, with special attention to the many ways in which the war itself has influenced scholarship and journalism about the region. In the next two chapters, Wendy Bracewell from the University of London and Larry Wolff from Boston College explore dimensions of the image of the Balkans that suffuse Western thinking about the peoples of the region. Bracewell looks at the myths and realities surrounding the *hajduks*, the infamous Balkan "bandits." Wolff, in a preview of his new book on Venice and Dalmatia, analyzes the encounters between the Venetians and the so-called "Morlacchi," in Venetian eyes wild and primitive Slavic inhabitants of the Dalmatian hinterlands. In Chapter 4, Bariša Krekić from UCLA draws from a long career of research on the history of Dubrovnik to construct a wistful portrait of the calculated and reasoned diplomatic practices of the Ragusan patricians of the ancient republic. In the final chapter of Part I, Wayne Vucinich contributes a piece on transhumance from his major anthropological and autobiographical study of his home region of Bileća Rudine. Here, Vucinich retraces the annual summer trek of villagers and their livestock from Bileća Rudine into the surrounding mountains and home again. Although the subject matter is quite personal, the backdrop to Vucinich's story is that of a region struggling with the legacies of war, ultra-nationalism, collectivization, and the demographic changes that accompany these phenomena, while attempting to preserve a traditional lifestyle.

Charles Jelavich from Indiana University leads off Part II, which deals more directly with politics and the dissolution of Yugoslavia, with a chapter on South Slav education and its historical inability to foster a Yugoslav identity. Arnold Suppan from the University of Vienna follows in Chapter 7 with an analysis of the complicated and troubled history of "Yugoslavism" in the twentieth century. Andrew Rossos (University of Toronto) presents us in Chapter 8 with a timely overview of the history of the Macedonian question and its critical linkages with stability in the Balkans. In Chapter 9, Thomas Emmert (Gustavus Adolphus College) looks at the problems of Serbian identity over the past decade, in the process helping us understand the future of a post-Milošević Serbia.

The book concludes with broad-ranging and speculative chapters by two of this country's leading historians of the South Slavs, John Fine from the University of Michigan and Gale Stokes from Rice University. Fine's provocative contribution centers on the notion that if there were no Yugoslavia, one would have to invent one. He rejects the inevitability of the demise of the Yugoslav state; he places much of the onus for the wars in the region on the Slovenes and Croats; and he envisions the recreation of a Yugoslavia in the future. Stokes's chapter on the future of the region makes almost exactly the opposite point. Stokes sees no alternative to the remapping of former Yugoslavia along ethnic lines. Borders will have to be changed and populations will have to be transferred to create ethnically homogeneous states. Otherwise, he maintains, there will be endless friction and warfare. That two such distinguished historians of the Yugoslav past could come to such different conclusions about the future should be of no surprise to scholars of the region. Historians are not exempt from the passions and partisanship that have dominated discussions about the war. This book shows, however, that those passions can illuminate a still little-known past and, in turn, create a better understanding of the present and future.

PART I

Images of the Past

1 Clio amid the Ruins

Yugoslavia and Its Predecessors in Recent Historiography

DUŠAN J. DJORDJEVICH

> What seest thou else
> In the dark backward and abysm of time?
> —Shakespeare, *The Tempest*, I.ii.49

Past Political

Exit into History, The Rebirth of History, Return to Diversity, The Haunted Land, Balkan Ghosts. . . . Since 1989, "past as prologue" has been a dominant motif in accounts of contemporary Eastern Europe, as these titles of some of the most popular books on the subject indicate. There are several reasons for this. One is the notion that people of the region are unusually preoccupied with their histories, real and imagined, and tend to view the present in terms of the past. This tendency seemed especially significant with the new freedoms and uncertainties of life after communism. Outside observers, too, looked to precommunist Eastern Europe for clues to the new era, as awareness grew of persistent, historically charged local conflicts previously subordinated, in fact or perception, to superpower rivalry. Moreover, the fall of the Wall happened to roughly coincide with a "turn to history" in various social sciences against their commonly ahistorical stance since the 1950s.[1]

For those who write and teach about the history of Eastern Europe, these developments would seem to be a boon. And to an extent they have been, at least in terms of heightened interest in the region's past among social scientists and lay audiences. At the same time, however, there has been dismay in the profession at the often crude manner in which history has been interpreted and used.

Nowhere has this been more true than in the case of the former Yugoslavia. When fighting broke out, there was little knowledge of the country's history among Western publics, especially in North America, and thus a marked inability or reluctance to interpret the state's disintegration on its own terms. Instead, simple messages from more familiar history—the Sarajevo assassination as catalyst of world war; the Munich Pact as appeasement; Vietnam as quagmire—were put forward as dubious guides. The dominant "ice-box" model of East European communism has meant that Titoist Yugoslavia is all but ignored; instead, Tito's death and the collapse of communism are claimed to have reanimated a more essential historical pattern, often reduced to serial slaughters and vague, intractable, age-old "Balkan" antagonisms, more often referred to (especially by critics) as "ancient ethnic hatreds." Masquerading as historical explanations, such claims are in fact profoundly dismissive of the need for historical knowledge; a turn *from*, not *to* history. So a good deal of scholarly energy is spent combating this type of simplistic conventional wisdom. Unfortunately, these efforts have had limited effect on popular understanding, and they may have actually impoverished academic discourse: denunciation of the ancient-hatreds thesis and similar breezy reductionisms has become almost *de rigueur* in scholarly texts, where the author is usually preaching to the converted.

At stake of course is not simply historical understanding for its own sake. Behind the ancient-hatreds thesis, there often is, or is seen to be, an argument against outside involvement and in favor of ethnic partition. At the other extreme, interpretations that dismiss the force of history altogether and focus solely on contemporary elites can serve the cause of intervention of one kind or another. Dueling historical analogies are even more clearly tied to rival policies.[2]

Political passions surrounding rival interpretations run as high in academia as anywhere else. This stems in part from historians' awareness that they are inescapably participants in politically charged, competing visions of the future as well as of the past. More simply, it has also been true that in East European studies (as in other fields, to be sure), "special pleading, based on national self-images and stereotypes, can infuse even works of scrupulous scholarship and high erudition," as the British historian of Yugoslavia Mark Wheeler has written. So it is perhaps not surprising that Yugoslavia's violent collapse has led to a high degree of polarization and frequent recriminations among those who study the region.[3]

Unsurprising, perhaps, but regrettable. Too rarely will Yugoslav specialists of different political persuasions appear together at a conference or in a book, addressing each other's arguments directly, respectfully, and productively. Too often, criticism and debate revolve implicitly or explicitly around the question: Which side are you on? Of course, focusing on the moral and political assumptions, motivations, or implications of scholarship is perfectly legitimate. Even the most politically charged fields, however, can and should be subject to more academically grounded evaluation as well, as shown by the valuable reflections in recent years on the historiography of Russia and the Soviet Union.[4]

The historiography of the South Slavs might have seen similar assessments, had Yugoslavia's breakup been more consensual and less subject to debate over international policy. As it is, the field is overdue for a checkup. There has been an overwhelming flood of publications since the early 1990s.[5] Most of the new books will have short shelf lives, but the number of valuable, serious works has been rising steadily. Some of the historical writing is based on new archival research (mostly conducted during the 1980s, a period of generally freer research environments that ended with the disruptions and destruction of the 1990s). Much more is primarily synthetic or interpretive in nature.

In this chapter, I survey recent work on the modern history of the Yugoslav lands, hoping to make a contribution toward evaluating the state of the field and to encourage discussion of its needs and achievements in the wake of the country's collapse. A few notes on the chapter's scope: I emphasize general trends in the historiography of Southeast Europe at the expense of a more comprehensive bibliography and closer examination of the monographic literature on South Slav history. The focus is on the nineteenth century and first half of the twentieth, excluding for the most part the large and growing body of work on Socialist Yugoslavia, not to mention its breakup. Finally, I cover only English-language texts, mainly North American and British publications that have appeared since 1990, thus leaving out much important work by both native and foreign scholars. In exchange for these omissions, the boundaries make for a more manageable and coherent survey.

Seeing Ghosts

Much more pervasive and influential than scholarly writing, of course, has been the presentation of history by journalists, diplomats, and others from outside the academy. Including these works would make for a different kind of essay. But they relate to an issue important to the present discussion: the marginalization of scholarship.

In 1993, National Public Radio correspondent Sylvia Poggioli wrote:

When I arrived in Belgrade in October 1988 for my first assignment in Yugoslavia, I brought with me the latest Western publications on Yugoslav political developments. When war broke out two and a half years later I realized
those books were outdated and useless and I had to begin a difficult search
for old and out of print books on Balkan history, on the Ottoman and Austro-
Hungarian empires, and on the Catholic-Orthodox schism—long forgotten
subjects which had suddenly re-emerged as the signposts needed to understand what was happening now.[6]

Exaggerated as this is—journalists would have done well to turn to a
number of newer books on these not-quite-forgotten subjects and to read
some of those "useless" ones more carefully—it is hard not to sympa-
thize. Even though Yugoslavia received more attention than most other
East European countries, the historian Ivo Banac had reason to lament
that the study of South Slav history in the West suffered from "scholarly neglect" and "was on the whole neither profound nor substantial."
Among its most important shortcomings was the one Poggioli encountered: topics of superficial importance were often chosen over more fundamental issues. It is easy of course in hindsight to see that we could
have used a few more good books on, say, national self-determination at
the expense of a few on workers' self-management. But such problems
were also clear at the time to perceptive observers—as when, thirty years
ago, Stevan Pavlowitch remarked: "It could be an amusing relaxation to
compile a kind of *anti*-bibliography on Yugoslavia."[7]

One reason for the misplaced emphases was, as John Lampe has written, the fact that "most scholars who enlisted in the Western army of
Yugoslav specialists, the present author included, simply assumed that
the country would and should continue to exist."[8] Sympathy for Yugoslavia's experiments in socialism, federalism, or both certainly played a
role in encouraging wishful thinking. Beyond that, as Mark von Hagen
reminds us, academic agendas and assumptions for many years reflected
"the ideology of the reigning cold-war-era social science school of 'modernization,' which posited the eventual disappearance of ethnic and national difference as societies became more urbanized, industrialized and
literate."[9] If few Yugoslav specialists expected the actual disappearance
of national difference, many did focus on economic and social forces
generally seen as counterweights to, perhaps even solvents of, the cen-
trifugal effects of "narrow nationalisms."

It is possible that the real and perceived inadequacies of the scholarly
literature have made nonacademic publishers even more inclined than

usual to prefer the breezy to the bookish. This may help explain, for instance, the depressing choice of Robert Kaplan of *Balkan Ghosts* fame to compile "A Reader's Guide to the Balkans" for the *New York Times Book Review*.[10] It is also true, however, that a number of prominent scholars of the region have appeared regularly in newspapers and journals of opinion in Britain and the United States; others could but choose not to.[11]

More disconcerting is the fact that even many academic publishers prefer authors willing and able to present Yugoslavia's tangled pasts in colorful, undemanding, and unambiguously "relevant" terms. Noting that academic presses have been "looking beyond the specialty monograph and the 'tenure book' to secure a larger share of the publishing market," Robert Baldock, an editor at Yale University Press, writes that editors are making a virtue of necessity by turning in particular to journalists, who are producing "works of major scholarship" by combining academic research with their "fieldwork" as reporters. The results can in fact be impressive, as in his primary example, Anatol Lieven's highly regarded book, *The Baltic Revolution*. Lieven calls upon Czeslaw Milosz's nostalgia for the days when "a reporter, sociologist and a historian used to coexist within one man," and he combines those roles admirably.[12]

Unfortunately, Baldock's other examples, British journalists Marcus Tanner and Tim Judah, do not transcend their professions in their histories of (respectively) Croatia and the Serbs. The books offer introductions to certain important moments in each nation's historical memory, but the authors' approach to history is parochial, romantic, and determinist, and as a result they fail to meet the acute need for good, accessible surveys of their subjects. It is equally disheartening that a leading intellectual journal such as *Daedalus* would invite Tanner and Judah to contribute articles on Croatian and Serbian history. The essays distill the most objectionable aspects of the books, while lacking their chief virtues (useful if patchy historical narrative and some keen reporting). Only the former Yugoslavia gets amateur treatment in this theme issue on Europe, and the two essays seem quite out of place alongside pieces by such scholars as Szporluk, Malia, Khazanov, and Schnapper.[13]

Academics have responded in various ways to their marginal presence and influence. One of the more fruitful responses has been: If you can't beat 'em, historicize 'em. As K. E. Fleming notes, the field of Balkan studies has long been characterized by a "bifurcation" between a small group of academic specialists and a larger number of "semi-scholarly" authors who dominate public discussion whenever a crisis brings attention to the otherwise obscure region.[14] The history of how perceptions of "the Balkans" have thus been shaped and used has become an important topic of research in recent years. This work is largely carried out within postmodern and postcolonial theoretical frameworks and is especially indebted to Edward Said's seminal study of orientalism, but it also calls upon earlier literatures on topics such as ethnic stereotyping.

Eastern Europe emerged relatively early as a rich vein for these explorations of symbolic geography and images of the Other.[15] The crisis in Yugoslavia then brought special scrutiny to ways of "imagining the Balkans."[16] The best studies in this genre have certainly contributed to our understanding of political cultures and international relations within and outside the region, by studying how, in Todorova's words, difference "is interpreted and harnessed in ideological models."[17]

It should be noted, however, that some influential historians worry about the trend toward studying the representation of groups and regions, rather than the things themselves. Gale Stokes asks:

How might it be possible to write about difference? Is there any way to use terms like "The West," "Balkan," "Central Europe," or "Southeast Europe" sensibly, without being accused of implicitly "privileging" something? Or is there another way of speaking in broad terms about regional differences that is more sensitive, more indicative of an author's realization that these terms contain multitudes?

An even more skeptical Tony Judt complains: "Between 'invention,' 'imagination,' 'representation,' and the invocation of 'Otherness,' the story of the West's failure to see Eastern Europe as it was and as it is runs the risk of sinking under the weight of overtheorized scholarly suspicion."[18]

This is not the place to go further into these important if sometimes dispiritingly divisive debates over the merits of postmodern approaches and their concern with breaking down "essentialist" generalizations. I note instead an exemplary aspect of Todorova's book: she devotes an erudite and insightful chapter to the obvious question, which, as Stokes and Judt imply, is too often ignored or dismissed by the "imagologists": Is there, after all, any there there? She finds that there is, that the region is distinguishable primarily by Ottoman rule and its various legacies. Over the past century and more, however, these legacies have faded, becoming less relevant to understanding political and social developments than the changes and challenges of modernity, to which Balkan states have responded in ways comparable to other agrarian societies. Thus the Balkans have been losing their "balkanness."[19]

Todorova's argument underscores the need to resist attributing time-less qualities to cultures and traditions. Historical context is also stressed in a widely cited article by Paschalis Kitromilides, in which he argues that conditions in the eighteenth century—relatively stable frontiers, freedom of movement, fluid linguistic boundaries—were conducive to the existence of a shared mentality and identity among the Orthodox population of the Ottoman Balkans. By the end of the century, however, social upheavals, a growing sense of backwardness, and the spread of European ideas led Christian elites to turn to the pre-Ottoman past and to vernacular languages as new sources of separate and divisive national identities.[20]

Kitromilides seems to equate the breakup of a common *identity* with the impossibility of a common *mentality*. In contrast, a number of scholars insist that an Eastern Orthodox mentality lived on as a powerful underlying influence on culture and politics. This reflects a more general renewed interest in the significance and staying power of religious and civilizational fault lines. Yugoslavia's breakup, and the fact that the exit from communism has seemed particularly problematic in Serbia, Romania, and Bulgaria (not to mention Russia, Ukraine, and Belarus), has certainly given new life to the old argument that (nominally) Orthodox societies are maladapted to Western values and institutions—Samuel Huntington's claims about the civilizational divide between Western and Eastern Christianity being just the best-known example. He and some other advocates of this idea surely delight in outraging anti-essentialist sensibilities (Michael Radu, for instance, declares that "Orthodox political culture has not changed much since the days of Leo VI [886–912]"[21]). But the claim is advanced more seriously in recent works by two prominent social scientists who specialize in Eastern Europe. George Schöpflin argues that Western Christianity since the Reformation has stressed the role of individual conscience, reciprocity, and mutual obligation; Orthodoxy and Islam, on the other hand, "privilege the collective over individual responsibility, encode a strong sense of hierarchy, pronounce non-negotiable truth claims, offer weak cognitive models of change and radical rather than incremental change."[22]

Andrew C. Janos makes similar arguments in his important new book, *East Central Europe in the Modern World*. Janos is sensitive to contingency and agency but attributes much greater importance to structure, to the "same stubborn facts" that the region's "ever-changing political regimes" have had to face over the last 150 years or so. ("To historians, the message of the book is best summarized . . . : The more things change, the more they stay the same.") Christianity's continental

divide is one of these stubborn facts. Among its implications for Eastern Europe: "Because it was rooted in the communalism and paternal-
ism of Byzantine Orthodoxy, communism resonated far more positively
in the Orthodox societies of the southeast, than in the legalistic, contract societies of the northwest tier."[23]

This claim has been made and disputed for decades (more in the historiography of Russia than of the Balkans). Plausible at first blush, such
assertions of "resonance" between disparate phenomena often remain
just that: vague assertions rather than careful arguments. Janos for instance states that his "proposition may be validated" by looking at the
level of dissent in different regions: in a few sentences on Yugoslavia, he
finds greater opposition to communist rule in Slovenia and Croatia than
in the southeastern republics. (Belgrade is an exception attributable to
its character as a "microcosm of the larger [Yugoslav] society.")

This is unlikely to persuade the skeptic, and it certainly begs the
question of distinguishing correlation from causation. Such claims are
often too nebulous to really lend themselves to testing, but there can be
much value to theoretically informed, empirical studies that explicitly
address them. On Orthodoxy, Todorova's and Kitromilides's recent work
suggest potential avenues of research, as does that of the late Romanian
historian Alexandru Duțu. He acknowledges the persistence of "com-
munitarian" values and social models in Balkan Orthodox societies, in
contrast to the Western "contractualist model," but questions the extent to which this distinction can "shed light on complex political phenomena" in the modern era.[24]

Duțu deals primarily with Romania, Kitromilides with Greece. There
has been comparatively little work of similar sophistication on the influence of South Slavic religious cultures on modern politics and society.[25]
Among other things, such research would help determine how much one
should disaggregate generalizations about religious communities.[26]

Modernities

In treating the modern Balkans as a unified historical subject,
there is a more common and compelling theme than Orthodox mentality: nation- and state-building against the backdrop of great-power rivalry and Ottoman crisis.[27] This traditional framework, with its heavy
emphasis on politics, diplomacy, and ideology, remains more common
than alternative approaches, due in part to the stubborn fact that "political innovations came to the Balkans in the nineteenth century before
the advent of social and economic change," as Gale Stokes puts it.

Writing in the early 1980s, Stokes lamented the fact that "this inconvenient transformation of the superstructure before the base" meant that "West European historians with an interest in socio-economic modes of explanation have taken little notice of the Balkans."[28] Since then, however, the pendulum has swung toward political and ideological explanations of modernity, and the Balkan case has seemed less marginal. It has become common to see in the post-Ottoman Balkans a classic, perhaps the original case of "dependency"—not so much Wallersteinian economic dependency as political dependency, defined by Kenneth Jowitt as "a consequence of the premature but imperative adoption of a political format for which the appropriate social base is lacking."[29] With variations in emphasis, this approach characterizes recent work by Stokes, Schöpflin, Janos, and Kitromilides, among others. They stress that the new Balkan states adopted the organizational and ideological forms of the dominant powers in order to press political claims and gain aid and prestige in the international system. But imitation of the modern, liberal, class-based nation-state, which had arisen organically in Western Europe, was superficial in the Balkans and did not alter the patrimonial power structures of traditional status society; instead, Stokes writes, it "permitted the committed few simply to substitute themselves for the departed upper classes of Ottoman times."[30] Economic development was undercut by the costs of maintaining a modern state apparatus and, as Janos stresses, by the "international demonstration effect," which led the new class of "political entrepreneurs to use the institutions of states to accomplish what they had not been able to accomplish as economic entrepreneurs: to raise their standard of living to the level enjoyed by the middle classes of the advanced societies of the Occident."[31]

Another view, recently expressed forcefully by Diana Mishkova, challenges this dependency approach. Superstructure may have preceded base in Balkan societies, but even their Western models developed under greater state influence than older modernization theories allowed.[32] In the Balkans as elsewhere, state-led nationalism and administrative modernization were not distractions from or obstacles to economic development; on the contrary, these integrative forces from above were the prerequisites for development. More than mere façades, Western political institutions did in fact serve to undermine old patterns of authority and patrimony.[33]

There are echoes here of the controversies surrounding the notion of Germany's *Sonderweg*. What were the "special paths" to modernity of states and societies east and south of Germany? Do deviations from Western paths explain underdevelopment and illiberalism? Answers as sophisticated and fruitful as the best contributions to the debate about Germany are much needed. In a recent notable example, Gary B. Cohen explicitly applies some of the ideas of the *Sonderweg* discussions to the historiography of late imperial Austria, suggesting that emphasis on "the failure of parliamentary liberalism, rising national and class conflicts, and growing governmental paralysis" needs to be revised to account for evidence of "the capacity of the state to accommodate modern modes of popular political engagement."[34]

At issue in part are definitions of modernity. Some argue that one should distinguish Westernization from modernization and think instead in terms of "multiple modernities."[35] In this view, modernization is "a set of events whose coming to pass takes place in contingent, infinitely variable ways," as Vicente Rafael has recently put it.[36] Applying this increasingly popular anti-Eurocentric outlook in practice, however, presents difficulties. Schöpflin for instance acknowledges the possibility that the Balkans can have its own model of modernity, but adds that "it will have to be constructed on the basis of South-East European thought-styles and thought-worlds, practices, and traditions rather than by a mass importation of ideas and patterns from elsewhere. If this means giving greater salience to ethnicity or hierarchy or whatever, so be it."[37] As he implies, Balkan elites did in fact look northwestward for models of modernity. This is one reason why most historians of Europe continue to use the continent's northwest corner as the standard for socioeconomic and political development, with, in Martin Malia's terms, "a whole spectrum of West-East *Sonderwege*" dividing leader from follower societies.[38]

Whatever one's conceptual model, many conclusions must remain provisional until more basic empirical work is done on the history of modernization in the former Yugoslav lands. On issues of politics and ideology, Stokes's writing on Serbia stands out, serving as a case study on the growth of political classes in place of Western-style bourgeoisies.[39] Also notable is his article "The Social Origins of East European Politics," a rare exercise in comparative history of societies within the region, where he argues among other things that the earlier political mobilization of Serbia's peasants accounts for their docility relative to the socioeconomically similar Bulgarian peasantry.[40]

Many aspects of economic history, especially before 1945, remain terra incognita. Particularly neglected are the South Slav lands of the Habsburg Empire. Although Habsburg economic history has been the subject of growing scholarly interest, the literature concentrates on the Empire's more advanced northwest provinces.[41] Now that the bias toward treating national states as the basic unit of research has turned in favor of Croatia and Slovenia, we can expect more study of their pasts, involving greater attention to the work of native economic historians and efforts to disaggregate the data within which the new states' economic histories have been hidden.[42]

Economic history of the post-Ottoman Balkans has benefited from pioneering studies by several working historians, notably John Lampe.[43] Over the last two decades, Michael Palairet has also published a number of important studies, particularly on Serbia. His interpretations often challenge conventional wisdom and spark fruitful debate: Palairet's insistence on the lackluster growth of the Serbian, Montenegrin, and Bulgarian economies before World War I, for example, are cited by dependency-theory advocates in arguing that institutional modernization did not result in sustained economic development.[44]

Future work on all aspects of modernization in these lands will benefit from two recent books abounding with useful information and interpretations. Traian Stoianovich's *Balkan Worlds* is the culmination of decades of research into the economic, social, and intellectual history of Southeast Europe. The *longue durée* of this *Annales* devotee extends back to Paleolithic times, but much of this sprawling work concerns contact with the modern West and the resulting rapid change and complex set of disruptions to long-established patterns in Balkan, particularly South Slav, societies. Even when idiosyncratic, Stoianovich's interpretations are thoughtful and suggestive, applying theory and method from a variety of disciplines and schools of thought. More focused but similarly rich is John Allcock's *Explaining Yugoslavia*. A historical sociologist, Allcock offers measured judgment on various scholarly debates while exploring the processes of economic, demographic, political, and cultural change in the former Yugoslavia and its modern predecessors, through the present day.[45]

The number of occasions when Stoianovich and Allcock must resort to speculation indicates the scarcity of good secondary sources on many subjects, most glaringly in social history. One indication of the problem is how little follow-up there has been to the issues explored by Jozo Tomasevich in his seminal 1955 study, *Peasants, Politics, and Economic Change in Yugoslavia*, which remains the indispensable source on many aspects of rural society in the nineteenth and early twentieth centuries.[46] East European studies were not much affected by the turn to social history in the 1960s and 1970s. By contrast, the current emphasis on nations and nationalism accords well with today's general preoccupation with cultural history, indeed with cultural explanations of virtually every phenomenon. So there is a danger that leap-frogging the social-history phase enjoyed by other regions will leave many gaps in the historiography of South Slav societies. With due attention to the new insights of post-modern and anthropologically informed approaches, historians of the Yugoslav lands must not neglect the question that "defines the central mission of European social history," according to Charles Tilly:

> How did Europeans live the big changes? In different European regions and eras, what were the connections—cause, effect, or correlation—between very large structural changes such as the growth of national states and the development of capitalism, on the one hand, and the changing experiences of ordinary people, on the other?[47]

One subject that has never ceased to attract interest is the history of the family in this part of the world.[48] In general, though, while contemporary societal issues in the former Yugoslavia are attracting considerable scholarly interest, their historical development receives scant attention. Recent events, for example, have led to examination of the contemporary role of gender in nationalism and of wartime violence against women, but historical research, whether in the form of the "old-fashioned" history of women or of newer approaches to the study of gender, is sorely lacking.[49] And while a number of scholars have written on Yugoslav popular culture of the last two or three decades, few have looked at its earlier history. Little for instance is known about the broad reception of nationalist and other political and cultural ideas, so a study such as Jeffrey Brooks's *When Russia Learned to Read*, about actual reading habits attending the rise of literacy in different parts of the former Yugoslavia, would be a valuable start toward balancing the heavy emphasis on high culture.[50] Foreign researchers studying these and many other issues will benefit from the important and increasingly sophisticated work on social history being conducted by native scholars.[51]

Empires and Nations

The Yugoslav wars have of course the dubious distinction of having introduced the expression "ethnic cleansing" into the popular vocabulary, and they have been perhaps the primary stimulus behind a burgeoning literature on the comparative history of nationalist homogenization, partition, forced migration, and related issues. Reference is often made to previous episodes of ethnic cleansing involving the peoples of former Yugoslavia, but there has been little new research, despite the fact that the existing literature is spotty and often tendentious, leaving many hotly contested issues that careful studies could help resolve.

One long-neglected subject that has become the subject of empirical and interpretive work is the ethnic cleansing of Muslims from the former Balkan provinces of the Ottoman Empire.[52] This work is part of an important trend of the last decade, the comparative history of the functioning and collapse of multinational polities, especially Yugoslavia, the Soviet Union, and the Ottoman and Habsburg empires.[53]

These studies reflect one of the more notable developments of recent years: conscious efforts to challenge the nation-state's dominance as the preferred unit of scholarly analysis. Such efforts are not entirely new, but they have gained momentum from postmodern approaches that "emphasize multiplicity and fragmentation, diversities and contingencies, uneven diffusions and incomplete projections" of nations and states, in Celia Applegate's description.[54] They also reflect the antinationalist climate of academia in the West—not least in response to the depredations of the Yugoslav wars. Applegate writes about a corresponding increase in European regional history, but one still finds little of this with regard to the former Yugoslavia.[55] Instead, there is greater attention paid to the history and fate of ethnic and religious groups that became anomalous in the age of Balkan nationalism, including Jews, Roma, Vlachs, and especially Muslims.[56]

There is a notable change in attitudes toward Ottoman history. It has long been true, in the words of historian Çaglar Keyder, that "accounts of the decline and fall of the Ottoman Empire vie on an ideological battlefield, with political commitments largely determining the reasons one offers for the collapse."[57] The turn against nationalist accounts of the Turkish yoke means that the field of Ottoman studies is increasingly subject to the kinds of lively discussions about the merits and viability of the Empire that have taken place in Habsburg studies since 1918. Keyder for instance offers an "'optimist's' reading of imperial history," arguing that reforms could have prevented the Empire's collapse. These will probably remain rarer than optimistic readings of Habsburg history. But overall one finds a shift in "blame" from the legacies of Ottoman rule to the practices of nationalists in accounting for underdevelopment, corruption, intercommunal conflict, and other societal ills in the post-Ottoman Balkans.[58]

It remains largely true, however, despite the growing number of pleas and efforts to move beyond the nation-state, that "the faculty of attained statehood is an indispensable condition of historiographical legitimacy," as Geoff Eley has written.[59] Thus, for example, Bosnia-Herzegovina's independence gave it historiographical legitimacy, but one which, like the embattled state itself, was contested from the start. So it is not surprising that the first important post-Yugoslav surveys of Bosnia's past, by Noel Malcolm and by Robert Donia and John Fine, also serve as passionate defenses of their subject's legitimacy as "a coherent entity for centuries," which "has shown over these centuries that pluralism can successfully exist even in a Balkan context," in John Fine's words.[60] There have also appeared valuable surveys of the history of Bosnian Muslims and studies of the development of their identity and political life.[61] The Croat and Serb communities of Bosnia and Herzegovina have not received much separate treatment.[62]

I will briefly address some aspects of the new historiography of the other successor states, before moving to histories of Yugoslavia itself. Slovenia, considerably less contested than Bosnia, has been a considerably less popular historical subject, despite its (generally overlooked) importance to understanding Yugoslavia. One noteworthy collection that "grounds the foundation of the new state firmly in a national history" is *Independent Slovenia*, which includes several essays by Slovene and American historians that stress in particular Slovenes' experiences in Yugoslavia and their shifting attitudes toward the Yugoslav state and idea.[63] Processes of nation-building at the local level and along the Slovene-German linguistic frontier have been the subject of a number of interesting articles belonging to the genre of historical and anthropological studies of "ethnic groups and boundaries."[64]

A few scholars have recently addressed similar issues of national differentiation among Orthodox and Catholic inhabitants of the Habsburg Military Frontier.[65] In general, however, Croatia has received surprisingly little attention, in part surely because the conflict in Bosnia overshadowed the Croatian war of 1991 as well as its sudden resolution in 1995. In addition to shedding light on recent events, new historical research on Croatia could illuminate neglected aspects of Habsburg history, and could both benefit from and contribute to recent approaches to the study of nations and nationalism. Two important works of a more traditional nature have appeared: Ivo Goldstein has contributed the first adequate survey of Croatia in English, while Mark Biondich's study fills another of the more glaring gaps in English-language historiography of Eastern Europe: the story of Stjepan Radić, the Croat Peasant Party, and their roles in Croatian political and national movements in the early twentieth century.[66]

Overall, the quantity and quality of new historiography on Serbs and Serbia are disappointing, especially considering how frequently but superficially Serbian history is called upon by social scientists, journalists, and all parties to the conflict in explaining contemporary developments. Efforts to reinterpret or fill gaps in the literature are often subject to obtrusive, distorting agendas of apology or condemnation.[67] No new, adequate, book-length survey of either the Serbs or Serbia has appeared; twenty-five years after its publication, Michael Boro Petrovich's *History of Modern Serbia, 1804–1918*, regretfully out of print, remains the essential work in English.[68]

Several books and articles do contribute usefully to the literature on Serbian politics and nationalist movements in the (long) nineteenth century.[69] The prominent role of the Kosovo epics and myths in contemporary Serb nationalism has been studied from various angles, some of which illuminate the historical development of the cult of the Battle of Kosovo.[70] In fact, for all the importance of the Kosovo legend, there has been perhaps too much stress placed on it and too little scrutiny of other stories Serbs tell themselves and of other vital elements of Serbian identities and political cultures. The role of World War II has received some attention, as noted below, but historical memories of World War I, of the "golden age" of 1903–1914, and of the uprisings of 1804–1815, to take three crucial episodes, have been largely overlooked.[71]

The history of Kosovo itself was largely overlooked, as well, until very recently. What scholarly consideration Kosovo did receive in the 1980s and 1990s focused on contemporary politics, as does most of the deluge of published analysis since 1999. Two surveys of Kosovo's history have appeared in English, both in 1998. Noel Malcolm's is both the more academically substantial and the more polemical. In his historiographical discussions and debunking of myths, he is also debunking Serbian claims to the territory and clearly hoping to reverse Eley's dictum by granting Kosovo "historiographical legitimacy" in advance, and in support, of its statehood. Malcolm's attention to premodern history is most welcome. Miranda Vickers's book, more balanced but less sophisticated, concentrates on the twentieth century.[72]

Montenegro has been all but totally ignored. But if Eley's dictum holds, this may change.

As for Macedonia, it "has evidently lost none of its power to excite," as Mark Mazower writes.[73] Not only has Macedonian history been subject to controversies and polemics even greater than those associated with other parts of the Balkans; it has also been the subject of some of the richest scholarship to emerge from the ruins of Yugoslavia. As the site of multiple contests over territory and identity, Macedonia is an excellent if complex case for exploring the construction of identity. There have been useful reviews of competing claims to the territory;[74] accounts of the "Macedonian question" in international affairs;[75] and studies, notably in an ethnographic vein, of the formation of Macedonian identity.[76]

Yugoslavia: Chaotic Gaps

The "first" Yugoslavia (1918–1941) has long suffered from historiographical neglect, which is just beginning to be remedied. Foreign scholars should benefit from opened archives and a significant amount of new research on this period in the former Yugoslavia. Among newer works, Biondich's book on the Croat Peasant Party stands out. Culture and the intelligentsia have also been subjects of growing interest.[77] On interwar Yugoslavia's foreign relations, there has been some research on relatively narrow topics, but the most important study in English remains Jacob Hoptner's forty-year-old book on the state's efforts to navigate the turbulent seas of prewar European rivalries.[78]

In his 1971 history of Yugoslavia, Stevan Pavlowitch titled the chapter on the Second World War, "The Chaotic Gap." The same phrase could describe the historiography of the war. Few periods of such importance have been so insufficiently and haphazardly covered, not to mention mythologized and politicized. That we have no general history is understandable, given the complexity and diversity of the divided country's experiences during the war.[79] There first needs to be much more archival research, detailed studies, and smaller surveys of the various satellite states and occupation regimes—as seen from below as well as above.[80]

The best-covered topic has long been British policy and the Partisan-Chetnik dispute. Several recent works, most notably Simon Trew's book, successfully step into this controversial arena.[81] Much remains to be learned on the Partisan[82] and Ustaša[83] movements. Recent events have prompted some scholars to examine collective memories and commemorations of the Second World War, an avenue worth pursuing: Yugoslavia is a prime candidate for greater inclusion in the flourishing field of historical memory, particularly of war.[84]

Three post-Yugoslav biographies of Tito have appeared in English. There is still much to learn and write on the Communist Party.[85] On the postwar period, the recent trend has been "the effort to trace an emerging civil society in Yugoslavia, focusing particularly on the inter-action between social forces and state structures and actors."[86] A wel-come exception to the general neglect of social history, these studies demonstrate the limits of the party-state's ability to impose its will even in its most "totalitarian" phase, although they also reveal the lim-ited strength of civil society.[87]

The Future of the Past

This trend, along with several others discussed in this chapter, represents an effort to bring Yugoslav studies out of its traditional ex-ceptionalism and into dialogue with the larger debates and theories that frame and animate the study of modern Europe and beyond. Such efforts can be seen as one of the post–Cold War peace dividends, as Russian and East European studies become more engaged with issues of common intellectual concern to colleagues across disciplinary and geographic boundaries, who are themselves increasingly intrigued by "our" part of the world. Most South Slav and Balkan specialists welcome these de-velopments, though one also encounters fears that the field may be swamped by ephemeral fashions and inapplicable models.[88]

A greater danger, however, comes from the temptations of newly ac-quired hindsight. One must guard against taking shortcuts to the end of the story and its lessons, against making the outcome seem inevitable, against excessive concern with legitimizing or condemning certain his-torical processes.

It is true, with all due care not to read the present onto the past, that a certain teleology has become inevitable in historians' narratives. What Jonathan Schell writes of the Soviet Union applies also to Yugoslavia: "It is understandable that contemporaries are usually startled by events, but historians have no right to present surprise endings to the tales they tell. Their new job will be to retell the story of the Soviet Union in such a way that the sudden collapse at the end makes sense." History is in-evitably and properly a constant dialogue between past and present. The historian does well, however, to bear in mind that this dialogue will be different in the future. On history's larger stage, consider Schell's sobering reminder: "The story of the Cold War that was the scene of history's only nuclear arms race will be very different from the story of the Cold War that turned out to be only the first of many interlocking nuclear arms races in many parts of the world."[89] In their own ways, the futures of Bosnia and Kosovo, Macedonia and Montenegro will change our views of their pasts.

Or take the events in Serbia in the fall of 2000. Many, perhaps most scholars expressed skepticism about the prospect of political change in Serbia, until the moment Milošević was actually ousted from power. Historians led the way. Three weeks before the election, for example, Charles Ingrao dismissed Vojislav Koštunica's candidacy as a "mirage": unfair electoral conditions aside, Milošević enjoyed the "passive support of a silent majority of Serbs," among whom "mass ignorance" due to functional illiteracy and nationalist mythology "virtually foreclose the ability to question the veracity of government propaganda or to critically analyze evidence." And just a few months earlier, John Allcock wrote:

In all areas [of former Yugoslavia] except Serbia, it is possible to see ways in which modernising coalitions might be put together which could manage the processes of restructuring and reorientation. A precondition of this is often the splitting or displacement of dominant, traditionalist, nationalist parties—especially the HDZ in Croatia and the SDA . . . in Bosnia-Herzegovina. Only in Serbia does the configuration of parties not hold out such a possibility, even in the event of the displacement of Milošević from the leadership of the SPS. . . . The bleakness of the future of Serbian politics, therefore, cannot be attributed only to "nationalism," but substantially also to the failure of any alternative, modernising vision.

I mention this not to take historians to task for failed predictions, but to point out that they sometimes reflect a way of thinking about history that may (or may not) need to be revised. For example, although one cannot yet render many verdicts on Serbia's new, at least rhetorically modernizing coalition government, it is possible that one currently popular framework for understanding modern Serbian history—decades of elite ambivalence toward modernity culminating in a wholesale "flight from modernization" in the 1980s and 1990s—will seem to lose some of its explanatory power.[90]

So a key challenge historians face in the post-Yugoslav moment is, broadly stated, to "restore an important sense, missing in much of the popular literature, of the dynamic interactions of agency, structure, and historical contingency," as Barkey and von Hagen write about the study of multinational empires.[91] And it is contingency, the least glamorous of the trio, that is perhaps most liable to be neglected in the rush to make sense of events.

These events have brought an unprecedented and invaluable injection of fresh ideas, energy, and interest to Balkan studies. But the accompanying sense of passionate urgency, however appropriate in the face of the horrific Yugoslav wars, has not always been conducive to producing the most thoughtful and enduring scholarship. History-in-the-making may slow down (a relief, one hopes, to those who have had to live it); for history-on-the-page to progress, it is necessary to begin evaluating the needs and achievements of the field, its new directions, unfortunate detours, and roads not taken, after an extraordinary and tragic decade.

2 "The Proud Name of Hajduks"

Bandits as Ambiguous Heroes in Balkan Politics and Culture

WENDY BRACEWELL

The term *bandit*—or *hajduk* or *haidut* or *klepht* or other, similar terms—has become a key word in the dictionary of Balkanisms, evoking connotations (depending on perspective) of struggle against oppression, thirst for liberty, and heroic masculinity or alternatively of lawlessness, primitivism, and violence. The association of *bandit* and *Balkan* does not necessarily derive from any particular Balkan propensity for banditry (though the phenomenon was endemic in parts of the Balkans into the twentieth century); nor because banditry achieved an apotheosis in the Balkans (*pace* Eric Hobsbawm, who adopted the Balkan term *hajduk* to represent the most institutionalized and conscious form of social banditry).[1] After all, the phenomenon of rural lawlessness was equally ubiquitous and equally long-lasting in other parts of Europe where political and economic conditions permitted or provoked it, particularly in the circum-Mediterranean.

The idea that the bandit is a particular specialty of the Balkans might be better traced in Western representations of the region from the Enlightenment anthropology of Alberto Fortis, who included an account of hajduks in his description of the customs of the Dalmatian Morlacchi; through innumerable travelers' tales of frightening encounters on lonely mountain roads and novelists' fictions, from Eduard About's burlesque *Roi des Montagnes* (1857) to Karl May's Balkan desperados; to journalistic exposés or popular histories, especially those purporting to explain the violence of warfare in the region to the Western reader. Recent studies, inspired in part by postcolonialist approaches, have touched upon the ways some such writers used the image of the bandit to characterize Balkan society and culture as backward and lawless, at the same time affirming Western order and rationality (while suppressing any acknowledgment of analogous deficiencies in their own societies).[2] But such approaches, by focusing solely on Western images, ignore the part played by the people of the region in inventing and manipulating the myth of the Balkan bandit. This was not simply a projection from the outside, however much it may have served outside interests. Indeed, it might be argued that the Western image of the Balkan bandit developed in good part through appropriating and reworking local narratives. After all, eighteenth-century Western fantasies of Balkan brigands were also fed by the biography of the hajduk Stanislav Sočivica written by Ivan Lovrić of Sinj as part of his riposte to Fortis, and translated and republished a score of times across Europe—though in contexts giving it a rather different effect than Lovrić had intended.[3] Much the same could be said of the ways the image of the bandit as a romantic hero, as opposed to a common outlaw, was developed by Balkan national revivalists, sometimes inspired by Western models as much as by local legend, and then adopted (or mocked) by Western observers.

The role of the bandit-hero in Balkan political discourses is not a new subject. A number of folklorists and historians, from both inside and beyond the region, have analyzed popular traditions dealing, among other things, with banditry; how they were collected, edited, and anthologized; and the political uses to which they have been put.[4] The Balkan bandit is an excellent example of a national symbol used to encapsulate and communicate political meanings to naturalize present ideological understandings through reference to the nation's history. He has served both as a symbol of the nation and its struggle for freedom and as a device for marking the boundaries between one national community and another. As such, he can tell us something about the societies that have created and used such symbols. But particularly in the context of the recent wars on the territory of the former Yugoslavia, cultural analyses of politics are too often homogenized and oversimplified, with the bandit myth presented as a coherent narrative (the bandit as an ideal hero; the embodiment of national and social liberation) and as part of a single (national) political culture. The figure of the bandit has in practice been ambiguous and contradictory, open to very different uses. This account of the bandit as national hero explores the shifting ways bandits have been construed as political symbols, with particular attention to the ambiguities and contradictions in Balkan national narratives of the bandit, and how these shifts have opened space for alternative definitions and political counter-narratives. The point is to offer a more differentiated account of the bandit in national ideologies and to suggest that these

ideologies and national cultures may be less monolithic than they sometimes are made to seem.

The single term *bandit*—or its Balkan synonyms—collapses together
a great variety of activities. *Bandit* was used to designate all sorts of people outside the law: escaped serfs, demobilized soldiers, men caught up
in blood feuds, refugees, or any number of others; *banditry* included—
besides semi-organized rural depredations—institutionalized practices
of livestock raiding in pastoral societies, the irregular warfare of imperial frontiers, the depredations of private retainers employed by local
strongmen, or the actions of nationalist militias supported, openly or
not, by states. A good deal of this context was stripped away in the oral
tradition that accumulated around the figure of the bandit. On the one
hand, singers and storytellers tended to bleach out historical specificity,
mixing characters belonging to different periods and *milieux*. On the
other hand, they had a lively interest in moral complexity: the bandit of
oral tradition is far from being a straightforward hero. Popular tradition
included a whole range of assessments of the bandit from the epitome
of a hero, a paragon of masculinity, brave, honorable, and just, to the
cruel, capricious personification of disorder and violence, not to mention treatments of the bandit as comic or deluded. Even in the epic tradition, often advanced by nationalist ideologues as evidence of an un-
complicated popular approbation for bandit heroism, much of the drama
hinges on the moral dilemmas faced by a protagonist negotiating the often contradictory requirements of honor, heroism, and manliness.

But this multiplicity of meanings tended to narrow or to be suppressed
as bandits were incorporated into the narratives of national history in
the course of the nineteenth century. National awakeners, looking at
their past under foreign rule, needed to show that rule as illegitimate,
demonstrate a continuity of resistance to foreign domination, and present their own nation as permanently unreconciled to foreign rule. Bandits could be made to suit these purposes very well, and throughout the
region bandits were reinterpreted in nationalist historiography as pre-
cursors of national liberation, guerrilla fighters who set the stage for the
national revolts; as consciousness-raisers, keeping alive the sense of a
separate national identity; and even as state-builders, who both participated in the wars of liberation and bequeathed the new states their traditions of egalitarianism and sense of justice.[5] At the same time, oral
tradition was collected, edited, and anthologized to supplement histories that were often sparse or unsatisfactory. Epic songs with bandit heroes were grouped together as a separate category or subcategory (usually within the genre of heroic songs), placed within an overall scheme

of "cycles" that incorporated them into a teleological narrative of national loss and redemption (for the South Slavs beginning with the Kosovo "cycle," proceeding through the hajduk epics, and ending with songs of the liberation from Ottoman rule), and selected to de-emphasize those with nationally ambiguous plots or characters (bands that raided co-nationals and "Turks" alike, for instance). History and tradition, suitably nationalized, were promoted as edifying narratives in which readers could not only recognize themselves as part of a national community with a shared heroic past but could also themselves learn how to be (properly) national, with all the virtues of the bandit heroes of old—patriotism, self-sacrifice, heroism.

Serbian national narratives provide a good illustration of the pattern described here. Serbian hajduks were heroes: they had played the role of a national elite when Ottoman conquest had left the Serb people leaderless; they had defended the Serbs against Ottoman oppression; they had kept alive a sense of national consciousness under foreign rule; they had not only set the stage for national liberation but had also contributed to it in the Serbian Revolt of 1804. The hajduk tradition was put at the center of the Serbian national mission: the preservation of the Serbian nation, the overthrow of foreign rule, the establishment of an independent state, and the unification of all Serbs. Serbian writers quoted the derogatory comment attributed to Lajos Kossuth, the Hungarian patriot, who in 1848 had remarked that the Serbs thought that they were a nation, but in reality they were "nothing but a pack of hajduks"—but they made this epithet into a badge of honor, since it was such men who had succeeded in building a Serbian state.[6] To cite just one author, writing in the 1930s about Serbian hajduks: "it was in connection with [the hajduk] struggle that there came into being our army, in the first place the infantry; but also our state, and ultimately even the democratic organization of our society and polity" and "today's very developed national sense and political maturity . . . among the Serbian part of our people, can in good part be understood as an inheritance from the one-time hajduk struggles for the liberation of our nation."[7] At about the same time, a work promoting the use of the folk tradition as a source of national pedagogy explained why hajduk epics should be taught in schools: "they create in the souls of their listeners an ideal of heroes; a desire for freedom and justice, love towards their native soil and their people, preparing them to lay down their lives too on the altar of liberty, when needed."[8]

But putting such men at the foundations of the national state idea could pose problems of legitimacy as well as decorum, as Kossuth's remark about the Serbs as a pack of bandits hinted. The usual response was to differentiate between ordinary robbers, out for personal gain, and nationally motivated hajduks. In writing about the Serbian revolt, Karadžić took this tack, stressing that the term should be translated into German as "*Helden,*" not as "*Räuber.*"[9] But Karadžić's celebration of the Serbian hajduk in his *Dictionary* is also shot through with references to the gap between the ideal of resistance to Ottoman rule and the reality of banditry in Serbia, attempting to reconcile the heroic myth of the bandit with the more sordid reality. (As well as giving anecdotes of hajduk violence and cruelty, greed, and cowardice, he concludes a discussion of hajduk honor with the somewhat ambivalent comment that "a true hajduk will never kill a man who has done nothing to him, unless a friend or ally urges him on."[10]) Ultimately, the only certain hero was a dead hero—preferably one who had been safely martyred in the defense of the nation. Problems arose when the same sort of men continued to carry out precisely the same sort of bandit action after independence, though now defying not Ottoman authority but the authority of the newly independent national state.

The issue was not just how to deal with rural lawlessness or assertions of power by private militias, though all the newly independent Balkan states faced these dilemmas.[11] The persistence of banditry also threatened to undermine the national meanings attributed to the bandit heroes of national liberation—and in the process to call into question the heroism and self-sacrifice of the national liberation struggle and the image of the nation-state as the embodiment of popular aspirations for liberty and justice. If the patriot-liberators *were* nothing but "a pack of hajduks," the state they had created would have lost a part of its sacred aura. Hence the need to draw semantic distinctions between heroic, nationally conscious hajduks or klephts, and lawless, venal robbers. The Serbian journalist and former Radical Pera Todorović, reporting on a trial of bandits in the Čačak district in 1896, attempted to specify the difference in the following way:

Hajduk! Once a proud and holy title, on which the Serb prided himself—now our shame and our general misfortune! The old hajduks were guarantors of faith and liberty, defenders and protectors of the weak Serbian orphans against Turkish violence; but today's outlaws (*razbojnici*), who claim the proud name of hajduks, take necklaces from the necks of women, steal and carry girls off to the woods, even demand ransoms from their parents . . . . Today's outlaws are unjustly given the name of hajduk![12]

The distinction between the patriot-bandit of the national revolt and the ordinary bandit acting on his own account against the authority of the state was elaborated most clearly in Greek political discourse (especially in the aftermath of the Dilessi affair—the abduction and murder of a number of foreign travelers in 1870). Patriotic commentators emphasized that this sort of contemporary banditry had nothing to do with historic klephtism, and emphatically nothing to do with the essence of the Greek character—if not actually committed by foreign nationals (Albanians, Vlachs), it was at most the sad legacy of four hundred years of Ottoman misrule.[13]

Still, contemporary bandits—allied to images of the mountain freedom-fighter against national oppression—had distinct utility for the state when it came to recruiting fighters across official frontiers in "unredeemed" national territory. This was hardly an innovation; bandits had often been recruited into the irregular Ottoman, Habsburg, and Venetian forces, thus controlling potential rebels and turning them to the purposes of state-building.[14] From the emergence of the new Balkan nation-states in the nineteenth century, the development of professional armies was paralleled and supplemented by the indirect exercise of violence through state-sponsored nationalist organizations, volunteer bands, insurrectionary networks, and veterans' units. In territories such as Macedonia, for example, in the late nineteenth or early twentieth centuries, governments, politicians, and journalists hailed raiding and insurgency as a continuation of the hajduk struggle, and thus as a spontaneous uprising of heroic individuals fighting against alien oppression and for the national cause—even when it was the neighboring Serb, Greek, and Bulgarian governments recruiting, organizing, training, arming, and funding paramilitaries for guerrilla actions in neighboring states.[15] These irredentist bands deliberately adopted the vocabulary of traditional banditry, bandit tactics, even traditional bandit dress, in order to clothe what was essentially state-sponsored terrorism in the familiar and acceptable garb of individual, heroic, and spontaneous struggle against alien oppression, while their sponsors could both disclaim responsibility and (in the tradition of earlier state-bandit alliances) attempt to benefit from otherwise potentially disruptive men.

The fact that all the Balkan peoples shared a heritage of banditry did not mean that the phenomenon necessarily served as a means of integration. On the contrary—to be national heroes, bandits had to have a recognizable national character, belonging to one group and not to another. This led to bitter squabbles over which nation could claim which bandits. Was Starina Novak, the hero of many epic songs, a Serb or was he really a Bulgarian or a Romanian?[16] Was a certain Panos (also called Bano, Babo, Yabo, or Tabo) active in the seventeenth century a Greek, a

Bulgarian, an Albanian, even a Macedonian?[17] The character of banditry could be used as a diacritic marking not just national boundaries but also moral, cultural, and political ones. In the aftermath of the Balkan Wars and the First World War, one Greek analysis implied that the contemporary political alignment between Greece and Serbia rested on profound cultural similarities not shared by Bulgaria: according to the author, Bulgarian oral poetry, "in the absence of any other sort of hero, exalts the haiduts, otherwise known as brigands, who have absolutely no connection with the Serbian hajduks or the Greek klephts. The latter are national heroes, after a historical model; the Bulgarian haiduts are common-law criminals, devoid of personality and lacking even the virile audacity of ordinary brigands."[18]

In the period up to the Second World War, when the precise contours of Serb, Croat, and Yugoslav national ideologies were hotly discussed, often in terms of national character or "ethnopsychology," bandits provided one possible key to national character and thus national belonging. For the geographer Jovan Cvijić, a proponent of a Serbocentric Yugoslavism deriving its force from "Dinaric patriarchal culture," hajduks were the quintessential representatives of the Serb state-building tradition, with their military virtues, their heroism, and their ardent sense of national mission. Cvijić did not explicitly equate hajduks with Serbs; but the way that he linked the hajduks so closely to Serbian culture, even in areas outside the Serbian heartlands, left the impression that not only were the hajduks the most outstanding exemplars of Serb virtues but also that all hajduks were in fact Serbs.[19] It was their heroic and masculine virtues that had fed the Serbian national mission, and it was these virtues that would guarantee a Serbian leading role in the new state. But other interpretations of the character and meaning of the hajduk contribution to state-building were also advanced. In contrast to the Serb flavor of Cvijić's Yugoslavism, Vladimir Dvorniković made a great effort to ensure that all the South Slav elements were mixed up into his recipe for integration. He, too, put Dinaric patriarchal culture as exemplified by the hajduks at the center of a Yugoslav national entity, but without associating the phenomenon of heroic banditry with any one nation. Thus, for example, he stressed the role of Vlachs and Albanians in hajduk bands and immediately balanced a reference to the influence of the (Serbian) Kosovo tradition upon the hajduks with the suggestion that the hajduks were also influenced by the example of the medieval Croatian bans.[20] For Dvorniković, hajduks were a symbol of Yugoslav integration, but one that the Yugoslavs could all share in equally.

Other national ideologues accepted the theory of a common Dinaric culture associated with bandits but saw nothing positive in it as a state-building ideology. For Ivo Pilar, Serbian national character (derived from Vlach pastoralism) had a very different connotation from that given it by Cvijić. "The national meaning of 'Serb' preserves very well the no-madic and bandit-like character of mountain pastoralists, and it is so obvious that it is easy to recognize it, particularly in their social and po-litical behavior as a mass. . . . Everywhere that Serbs appear as a mass, the motive of their actions is very frequently that of seizing the belong-ings of others"—as befits their bandit natures.[21] So yes, the Serbs *are* hajduks: banditry is part of their racial and cultural inheritance, and it does shape their national character and mission, but here the equation is pejorative. And it is implied that these patterns are foreign to the Croats—just one aspect of a dichotomy between Serbs and Croats that Pilar saw as invalidating any attempt at political integration.

The Croatian sociologist Dinko Tomašić developed this idea in the interwar period and after the war, setting an idealized peasant "zadruga culture" of the Croatian plains (to which banditry was allegedly foreign) in opposition to a Dinaric culture that gloried in violence and celebrated the hajduk. Serb predominance in the Yugoslav state could thus be ex-plained by the predatory "power-seeking" and tribal violence epito-mized by the Dinaric hajduk.[22] Such Croatian opponents of Yugoslav-ism could easily agree that hajduks were more a Serbian phenomenon than a Croatian one. They agreed with Kossuth that the Serbs were "a pack of hajduks." And the lesson, drawn quite explicitly, was that such a people had no natural or moral right to a leading role in a common state. But such a stance required that the Croats suppress (or relinquish) their own local traditions of hajduks and uskoks. An alternative was to claim these bandit traditions but to differentiate between Serb and Croat heroes, usually on the basis of their moral character. The introduction to one interwar collection of Croatian heroic songs argued, for instance, that Croatian hajduk songs showed a higher, more Christian moral stan-dard than other (implicitly Serbian) songs about hajduks. "Mijat Tomić is the prototype of Croatian national heroism and the representative of a quite specific type of national individuality" that characterized the Croats, who "ascribed to him spiritual distinctions, which the majority of other hajduks lack," although "singers from other areas, for other au-diences, may give Mijat quite different characteristics, such as they give their ordinary hajduks."[23] Here, a differentiation between a Croatian haj-duk and hajduks celebrated by other nations becomes not only a key to

Croatian national specificity but also a means of claiming national and ethical superiority. Even their bandits could be used to confirm Croatian claims to be a part of European civilization, shaped by Catholic tradition, distinct from their neighbors—and the political implications that sprang from these understandings led to division, not integration, between these two peoples.

Incorporating the bandit into national discourses involved persistent ambiguities and contradictions, and these were constantly argued. Were bandits good or bad, state-building or state-resisting, ours or theirs, a bond between peoples or a boundary? But one constant was that any national narrative that idealized the bandit was creating a rod for its own back. The notion that it was the bandit who was best equipped to distinguish between oppression and justice made it possible to turn this symbol against the state and to contest the moral and national legitimacy of the established order by using its own rhetoric. Opposition politicians, popular uprisings, individual rural law-breakers—even literary movements—also made good use of the bandits' associations with mountain freedom and national purity, heroic resistance to alien authority and atavistic violence. By "claiming the proud name of hajduks" they cast doubt on the credentials of the state in standing for the nation, claiming the right to defend themselves against the cynical manipulations of urban politicians who were betraying the village and the nation. Even the most banal rural depredations could evoke something of a patriotic aura by claiming the mantle of the heroic bandit; Cretan sheep-thieves, for example, emphasizing their superior Greekness against the Turk-like authority of Athens.[24] But such rhetoric could be found right across the political and intellectual spectrum. Thus, for example, in the interwar period, Bulgarian leftists used hajduk themes to evoke the anticapitalist struggle;[25] far-right movements such as the Croatian Ustaša and the Serbian Zbor drew on these models in their opposition to liberalism and communism;[26] avant-garde and traditionalists alike joined in opposition to "decadent" European humanism and rationalism, hailing instead the Balkan heroism and unspoiled "barbarism" personified by the bandit.[27]

Bandit imagery had obvious utility in the resistance movements of World War II, which drew on the imagery of the hero-bandit for a good deal of their self-presentation, ritual, and popular propaganda—thus, for example, the Četnik movement, rooted in the insurrectionary četas of the period before World War I; or the Yugoslav Partisans; or the Greek guerrillas of the German occupation and civil war.[28] And in response, their opponents denigrated such movements as nothing but bandits (so that, for example, the nationalists labeled their opponents in the Greek civil war as *listosimmoritai* or "brigands," and the civil war itself as *simmoritopolemos* or "war against the bandits").

For the Yugoslav Partisans, common traditions of banditry could be used to evoke national "brotherhood and unity" (though these sentiments were somewhat difficult to reconcile with the anti-Muslim implications of the heroic epics).[29] Thus Vladimir Nazor's Partisan diary contains a lengthy dream-evocation of bygone Bosnian hajduks who transcend time and national boundaries to inspire their latter-day descendants in the struggle against alien oppressors. They include Mijat Tomić for the Croats, Mali Radojica for the Serbs, and Djerdjez-Alija (a Muslim hero, indeed, but not a hajduk at all, though Nazor failed to mention this fact in filling out his national key).[30] The image of the hajduk could also help link the idea of a common national liberation struggle to that of communist-led social liberation. One of the most anthologized hajduk songs in postwar Yugoslavia concerned Maleta the hajduk, who woos a reluctant bride by announcing, "I do not slaughter the young lambs, nor the shepherds in the woods; nor do I plunder the villagers in the village; rather I plunder the city dwellers in the city, who plunder the villagers in the village" (this after slaughtering her wedding party and bridegroom). A typical editorial comment, from a textbook of 1955, applauded "the ideological maturity of Hajduk Maleta, who has identified the phenomenon of social differentiation among the hajduks, and finds the most correct path, the only progressive path in his period, and that is the struggle against usurious capital which has penetrated the village. The hajduk has been transformed from a rebellious, avenging warrior against the Turk into a special form of social protest, struggling for more just social relations."[31]

Hajduks were reinvented as premature partisans, lacking only a political commissar to explain that national liberation and social revolution went hand-in-hand, and that the hajduk struggle was also the struggle of the working people of all the other nations and nationalities of Yugoslavia and the rest of the Balkans—a theory elaborated at length in a postwar history of partisan warfare published by one Yugoslav general-turned-historian.[32] And just as bandit violence was excused by the circumstances of their struggle, so too the bloodshed of war and revolution was both vindicated and idealized. Not only did the end justify the means, the means themselves acquired a certain heroic glamour through association with the hajduk tradition, which could excuse and even glorify acts of cruelty and vengeance, the rejection of all external authority coupled with unforgiving discipline, extremes of self-sacrifice, and the merciless condemnation of weakness under torture. War memoirs, in particular, demonstrate the ways that the vocabulary of epic heroism could sanitize excesses of violence—as well as hinting at persistent doubts about the toll in blood exacted by licensing bandit terror.[33]

The postwar socialist states preserved this ideal of the bandit unchallenged, promoting the image of the heroic rebel in school texts, anthologies, and speeches (while at the same time quelling any attempt at popular rebellion against state authority). But just as communists had borrowed the rhetoric of epic banditry to legitimate their revolutionary aspirations in World War II, so anticommunist and nationalist ideologues adopted the vocabulary of epic banditry to use against their enemies, eventually undermining and capturing the tropes preserved and nurtured in official discourse—most vividly in the Yugoslav wars. One example will serve to show how such images and language could be used to claim the moral and national high ground against the authority of the state. In 1991, at the beginning of the armed conflict, the Belgrade journal *Duga* published a long eulogy for Djordje Božović Giška, an underworld figure and the commander of the paramilitary Serbian Guard, who had been killed by a sniper while in Croatia, fighting at the head of a Serbian paramilitary band. The piece combined gangster imagery with evocations of historic and folkloric bandits, comparing Giška to Hajduk Veljko, the self-willed hero of the nineteenth-century Serbian Uprising, and eulogizing him with lines from one of the most familiar set-texts in school anthologies: "he could overtake and run away, and stand his ground in a terrible place; he feared nothing save death and dishonour."[34] Treating Giška as a latter-day hajduk made this paramilitary and member of Belgrade's criminal underworld out to be a heroic throwback, a spontaneous rebel, motivated above all by love of his nation and a hatred of state tyranny (in this case depicted as both anti-Serb and communist) and a representative of true Serbdom, while at the same time obscuring the paramilitaries' economic interests, the political connections that supported them, or indeed any official role in recruiting or equipping the paramilitary units, and glossing over the widespread refusal of Serb conscripts to respond to mobilization. The use of hajduk imagery connected the contemporary maneuvers of some nationalists as part of a centuries-long struggle of the whole Serb people for freedom and independence; made rebels and heroes of their fighters (regardless of covert state support for their activities or of their less altruistic motives); stigmatized the federal and republican governments as antinational ("worse than the Turks"); and converted paramilitary violence and looting into epic acts, giving it a sort of folkloric legitimacy. The rhetoric was hardly new; neither were the purposes.

The persistence of this sort of language, as much as the programs it has underpinned, has contributed to arguments that "Balkan violence" and more particularly the bloody horrors of the Yugoslav wars can be explained in terms of a specific regional culture or mentality, usually ultimately derived from a premodern tribal social organization in which violence, the cult of heroism, and the bandit played an important role.[35] Such interpretations are often both static, disregarding the sweeping social changes that have transformed the region over the past century, and essentialist, ignoring important differences among the people so labeled (and not least the fact that the so-called "Balkan" conflict has been limited so far to the former Yugoslav space).

Other cultural interpretations of the wars have focused more closely on the power of myth, and particularly on the "cult of the hajduk." More than a hundred years ago in a study of Balkan hajduks, a German writer, Georg Rosen, pointed to the celebration of the bandit as a key characteristic of the Balkan peoples, remarking that "other countries are also plagued with such robbers . . . but the Spaniard or the Italian would never dream of priding himself on his brigands nor would see in them the very backbone of his nationhood."[36] More recent critiques have also identified as something specifically Balkan a political culture built around specific symbols such as the bandit, which structures collective action and (especially in the former Yugoslavia) has shaped the violence of war. The German Slavicist Reinhard Lauer, for example, has singled out the promotion of the myth of the heroic and patriotic hajduk in history and folklore, listing the extremes of violence and looting depicted in hajduk epics, and concluding that "this catalog of motifs comes close to the war crimes which are being reported daily. . . . It has been fatal that no one troubled himself to disarm the explosive charge of inhumanity hidden in these songs. Rather the opposite: the songs were relished." He explains the bloody realities of the Yugoslav conflict as "the literal conversion of myths into action."[37] In other words, warfare is simply the continuation of epic poetry by other means. It is certainly pertinent to ask why the myth of the bandit has such resonance; and it is useful to be reminded that these myths and symbols can have an effect on the ways that we make sense of the world. However, in such interpretations they seem to take on a life of their own, regardless of who uses them and for what purpose. Trapped in an all-encompassing culture of patriotic violence, the people of the Balkans (or of the former Yugoslavia or, most frequently, the Serbs) have no choice but to act out its unchanging scripts—at best failing to confront the possibility of choice ("relishing" rather than "disarming" their myths).[38]

Other scholars, while recognizing the ways that myths and symbols can be constitutive of reality, have focused on the creation and use of such symbols as communication devices. The "cultural matrix," to use Ivo Žanić's term, provides a reservoir of images such as the heroic bandit to be incorporated into political discourse. Ideologues—whether politicians, journalists, or novelists—use such symbols to convey messages and to mobilize action, relying on a collective emotional response rooted in a common cultural tradition. Such an approach opens the way to a less determinist notion of political discourse and of culture in general, highlighting the fractured, ambiguous, or contradictory nature of symbols, as well as the conflicting interests of those who employ them. Bandits offer a particularly compelling illustration of this, since each manifestation of the bandit as symbol generates its own opposite and counterpart. Ivo Žanić has illustrated the way that opposing state, national, and religious traditions among the South Slavs engendered complementary bandit imagery—the heroic, Turk-defying patriot of the Serbs (and, to an extent, the Croats) set against the lawless brigand of the Bosnian Muslim epics (or of official state discourses)—and the ways these contrary perceptions entered political discourse in the 1990s.[39] But even within a single tradition the bandit could have contradictory meanings: even the hajduk of the epic songs is not always a positive figure (thus one epic laments, "from one side the Turks attack, from the other the mountain hajduks; there is no salvation for the poor"). But it is also worth pointing out that beyond the popular tradition of banditry, each use of the bandit myth for political purposes has provoked a similar counter-narrative. Romantic evocations of the bandit as a hero, defending his people against oppression and fighting for a national ideal, provided the background against which iconoclastic novelists could dismantle the romantic myth of the hajduk. To give an example from nineteenth-century Serbia, we might read Svetolik Ranković's *Mountain Tsar*, in which the main character becomes a hajduk through a mixture of misplaced hero-worship and discontent, and sinks into murder and senseless crime. Far from embodying freedom or justice, the depredations of the hajduk band only subsidize the comfortable urban existence of their patron.[40] Such fictions were a parallel to more explicit political critiques of the bandit myth and the national ideologies that sustained it, with their own visions of the nation and its mission or role. Again, to single out only one Serbian example, at the beginning of the century Jovan Skerlić, a literary critic and political writer, identified the cult of the hajduk and the idealization of atavistic violence and lawlessness as one of the key myths of Serbian national romanticism—part of a broader tendency to promote rural virtue over urban degeneracy, and national purity over "the rotten West"—and criticized it as an obstacle to modernization and progress in Serbia and as providing the basis for demagogic politics. Against the idea that the hajduk represented a quintessentially "national" hero, Skerlić suggested that the bandit image had been imported by way of Byron and Schiller, and only then dressed up in Serbian folk costume to serve nationalist purposes.[41] Other examples from literature, criticism, and pedagogy, and from across the region, could be multiplied— a necessary correction to Lauer's accusation that no one thought to question the implications of such myths.[42] More recently critics have pointed out that an exaltation of violence and direct individual action neither produced model citizens nor encouraged democratic political struggle, while a version of national history that glorified only heroes of armed struggle devalued peaceful development and promoted war.[43] One might also point to the feminist critique of heroic Balkan masculinity, identifying the way the glorification of the warrior-hero perpetuates patriarchal power structures in both the public and private spheres.[44]

Neither the popular tradition nor the political discourses that have drawn upon it are single, coherent, and or unambiguous. Even the official or dominant national narrative of the bandit-hero was shot through with contradictions, and these left it open to reinterpretation, challenge, or inversion. For some the bandit was a symbol of mountain purity against the pollution of the city, the armed hero against the corrupt capitalist, native virtue against the decadent West. But all these images could be reversed; so the bandit might be made to stand for the primitive, barbaric violence of the countryside against Western, urban multiculturalism, democracy, and modernity. Various groups could choose different aspects of the bandit myth to build distinct narratives for specific purposes; no one version of the bandit held absolute sway, just as no one interpretation of what it meant to be "national" did. The variety of strategies for the use of the bandit should make us skeptical of the ways in which people responded to such manipulations. Although shared myths (and a shared culture) may provide the conceptual wherewithal for communication and for collective action, they do not necessarily dictate a single, predetermined reaction. Rather than a script to be followed word for word, bandit myths—with all their ambiguities and contradictions—might better be understood as providing the material for scenarios by which people stage their own dramas, shaped not just by the cultural and political context but also by their own specific interests and intentions. This points up the final ambiguity of the bandit as hero: he expresses something of shared culture or tradition while being at the same time constantly reinvented for individual purposes. Though myths of the bandit may help us grasp the rhetoric of manliness, nationalism, and war, neither they nor the notion of a "common culture" offer an ultimate explanation of the roots of violence, nor do they offer a substitute for individual responsibility. The bandit can be both a symbol of the Balkans and a warning against the dangers of accepting him as an embodiment of Balkan realities.

3 The Rise and Fall of 'Morlacchismo'

South Slavic Identity in the Mountains of Dalmatia

LARRY WOLFF

Introduction: "The Most Primitive Population"

In 1797 there appeared in Venice an article entitled "Il Morlacchismo d'Omero," that is, concerning the *morlacchismo* of Homer. The concept of *morlacchismo* was created in the eighteenth century, within the Venetian state, with reference to a particular part of the population of Dalmatia, the pastoral people who lived in the mountains and were known under the name of *Morlacchi*. This designation was most commonly used by Dalmatians of the Adriatic coast to describe pejoratively the inland population of the Dinaric Alps, and in the eighteenth century the name *Morlacchi* acquired a broad currency and important significance in Venice and even throughout Europe. Indeed the name was meaningful enough to become the basis for the abstract noun *morlacchismo*. The article about the *morlacchismo* of Homer was written by a Dalmatian from the coastal town of Split, Giulio (or Julije) Bajamonti, and, unusually, he wrote about the Morlacchi not to distinguish them from himself, a cultivated urban intellectual, but rather to recognize his own relation to them, to people he perceived as primitive Slavs. Indeed it was their primitive customs that made him think of the Morlacchi in connection with the heroic characters of Homer: "The thought has come to me to make him become a Slav. I see no other means by which to understand that this divine genius belongs to me. I thus want to make myself related to him in a certain manner."[1] Bajamonti's *morlacchismo*, as formulated in 1797, signified a Slavic character and served as a marker for the relation among Slavic peoples.

The Morlacchi did, in fact, speak a Slavic language, but Bajamonti was more concerned to demonstrate that the concept of *morlacchismo* was fundamentally a matter of customs. "I intend to establish that the Homeric poems are in Morlacchi taste," Bajamonti explained, "and that the Morlacchi would find in them the manners and customs of their country."[2] Homeric verse was in Morlacchi taste, because the Morlacchi recited the oral epics of the South Slavs, and it was from the Morlacchi that such poetry first came to the attention of the Enlightenment in Europe. Their customs were reflected in their poems and also in Homer's poems to the extent that the customs of the Morlacchi, like those of the warring Greeks and Trojans, appeared similarly primitive from the perspective of the eighteenth-century Enlightenment. *Morlacchismo*, as an abstract noun, thus represented a specifically primitive Slavic character, distilled in the Dalmatian mountains. Throughout the eighteenth century, official Venetian perspectives had emphasized this primitive character of the Morlacchi, which served as the basis of a civilizing imperial mission in Dalmatia. Bajamonti, however, coined the term *morlacchismo* and affirmed his own relation to the Morlacchi at the very moment when the Venetian state, with its trans-Adriatic empire, was about to cease to exist, abolished by Napoleon in 1797. That term summed up a profuse eighteenth-century imperial Adriatic discourse that was about to lose its fundamental political importance. Not only the concept of *morlacchismo*, but the Morlacchi themselves, were so inextricably bound to the political existence of Venetian Dalmatia that 1797 may be taken as the moment at which they began their slow descent into ethnographic oblivion. *Morlacchismo* lost its meaning without Venice, and the Morlacchi themselves have become extinct, vanished from the correlative spheres of ethnography and lexicography.

In the early twentieth century the Serbian ethnographer, Jovan Cvijić, discussing the Adriatic variety of the Dinaric type, mentioned the Morlacchi in a footnote, and identified them as Slavicized Vlachs: "In the course of my voyages in the Dalmatian Zagora, people have often remarked to me upon the difference between the Dinaric immigrants and ancient Slavic population on the one hand, and the Slavicized Vlachs or Morlachs on the other. These latter, according to my informers, constituted the most primitive population, moreover very rare."[3] Wayne Vucinich has pointed to the importance of the pastoral *katun* community for understanding Vlachs, Slavicized Vlachs, and therefore Maurovlachs or Morlacchi as well; he has also emphasized the importance of perspective in designating the Morlacchi, "a name which the Venetians and the coastal inhabitants used for the Slav population of the hinterland." Vucinich has suggested that "the term has no ethnic significance," and Wendy Bracewell has further clarified its nonethnic connotations for the Venetians: "The word they use denote the peasant and nomadic stock-herding population of the hin land, living outside the confines of the coastal cities and their immeui ate environs, was Morlach." Predrag Matvejević has indicated that the names "Vlach" and "Morlach" possessed a "polysemantic quality," and he has noted their "multifarious uses" in specifying populations.[4] The Morlacchi included, confessionally, both Orthodox and Catholics, and they have presumably been sorted into Serbs and Croats under the influence of modern nationalism in the nineteenth and twentieth centuries. Ethnographic descent is a problematic concept, but in terms of geographical terrain, the Krajina Serbs, who were "ethnically cleansed" from Croatia in 1995, were living in the same inland areas where Morlacchi once lived in the eighteenth century.

It was the Paduan philosophe Alberto Fortis, who made the Morlacchi famous all over Europe in the age of Enlightenment with his anthropological study of their customs. Fortis casually considered them to be a "nation," though writing in 1774 he barely contemplated the modern meaning of national identity: "I believe that I owe to the nation, by whom I was so well received and humanely treated, a most ample Apologia, writing about that which I personally saw of their inclinations and customs."[5] Fortis also found that they did not necessarily call themselves Morlacchi but rather Vlachs, and he freely translated the names as equivalents. Boasting of his own prowess at climbing in the mountains, Fortis reported the reaction of the Morlacchi:

My own savage self-esteem was much flattered by the surprise of those men, born and hardened to the effort, at my agility in climbing and descending the cliffs. I heard one of them exclaim with extreme satisfaction: "Gospodine, ti nissi Lanzmanin, tissi Vlah!" "Sir, you are not a cowardly Italian (*Italiano-poltrone*), you are a Morlacco!" I confess to you that I was more appreciative of that peroration than I could ever be of the mostly insincere praises of men in the great world.[6]

In this case they called themselves Vlachs, which Fortis translated or interpreted as Morlacchi. These Morlacchi constituted the curious phenomenon of a "nation" identified more from without than from within, a national identity externally ascribed rather than internally assumed. Yet for Bajamonti in 1797 the concept of *morlacchismo* served as the vehicle by which he recognized himself as a Slav. The decline and disappearance of *morlacchismo* in the nineteenth and twentieth centuries occurred alongside the development of modern national designations and identities among the South Slavs. The reclassification of the Morlacchi thus offers some insight into the crystallization of alternative terms for denominating the peoples of Southeastern Europe.

"In Morlacchia"

With the inland extensions of the borders of Venetian Dalmatia, after the settlements of Carlowitz and Passarowitz in 1699 and 1718, Venetian administrators placed new emphasis on the increased inland populations, precisely those who were labeled as Morlacchi. During the eighteenth century they were always perceived as an administrative problem. Zorzi Grimani, who governed Dalmatia as Provveditore Generale in the 1730s, distinguished them to the coastal Dalmatians and described the Morlacchi as "by nature ferocious, but not indomitable."[7] In the 1740s the Provveditore Generale Paolo Boldù softened the distinction between coastal and inland Dalmatians. "Obstinate is the aversion of even the coastal subjects to every other application except that of the flocks, and the labor of arms," he recorded in a spirit of administrative frustration. "Also lazy by nature, especially the Morlacco . . . and incapable of discipline. . . ."[8] Boldù thus emphasized that the coastal Dalmatians and inland Morlacchi were closely related, inasmuch as "even" the former were averse to labor, while the latter were simply "especially" lazy. In this sense the term *Morlacco* seemed to signify not so much a specific part of the Dalmatian population but rather a particular aspect of that population, that is, its economic inaptitude. Administrative concern about the Morlacchi was, at first, focused on the problem of whether they could be disciplined; later in the eighteenth century, after the emergence of an anthropological discourse, the problem was restated as a more modern imperial dilemma of whether the Morlacchi could or should be civilized.

Though administrative discussion of the Morlacchi involved comments on their customs, focused anthropological study dated from the publication of Fortis's *Viaggio in Dalmazia* in 1774, his account of his recent voyage in Dalmatia, with a special section on "The Customs of the Morlacchi." Though "anthropology" did not acquire its modern meaning until some years later, with the publication of *Anthropologie, ou Science Générale de l'Homme* by Alexandre-César Chavannes in 1788, Fortis's scientifically conceived study of customs must be considered a pioneering work in the founding of the field. At the same time his interest in the poetry and dances of the Morlacchi make Fortis also a founding figure in the field of folkloric studies. The Morlacchi, the Slavs, and Eastern Europe more generally were not, however, the incidental objects of the Enlightenment's disciplinary diversification but rather the first framing of these subjects, indeed the "discovery" of Eastern Europe by the Enlightenment was fundamentally anthropological and folkloric in its conception. The Morlacchi, though the signification of the term may appear somewhat insubstantial as one puzzles over their identity, were in fact a more concrete subject than either the "Slavs" or "Eastern Europe," concepts that were just receiving their modern elaboration within the Enlightenment; in fact, the customs of the Morlacchi were a crucial point of reference for identifying both the ethnographic unity of the Slavs and the geographical domain of Eastern Europe.

For Fortis the term *Morlacchi* did indeed possess an ethnic significance. "The origin of the Morlacchi," he wrote, "is involved in the darkness of barbarous centuries, together with that of so many other nations resembling them in customs and in language in such a manner that they can be taken for one sole nation, vastly extended from our sea to the glacial ocean." This was the "nation" of the Slavs, extending geographically from the Adriatic to the Arctic, and thus delineated by Fortis well before Herder's related observations on the same subject; in the fourth part of the *Philosophie der Geschichte* in 1791, Herder described the "Slavic peoples" as ranging "from the Don to the Elbe, from the Baltic to the Adriatic," and thus inhabiting "the most monstrous region of earth which in Europe one Nation for the most part inhabits still today."[9] Fortis positively reevaluated the customs of the Morlacchi, which had been previously seen as almost altogether negative, that is, administratively problematic, in the judgment of the Provveditori Generali; he admired the "moral and domestic virtues" of the Morlacchi, in the spirit of Rousseau's admiration for the noble savage, and even saluted them as "spirits uncorrupted by the society that we call civilized." Fortis declared that "the innocent and natural liberty of the pastoral centuries are maintained still in Morlacchia."[10] Yet "Morlacchia" was not so much a precise geographical place as an unfixed philosophical space, a kind of Arcadia. This Rousseauist appreciation of the Morlacchi was even more pronounced in the sentimental novel, *Les Morlaques*, published in 1788 by the Venetian writer Giustiniana Wynne, Countess of Orsini Rosenberg. She described an almost idyllic pastoral society of Morlacchi, awakened to a sense of Slavic ethnicity by the reports of Russian military campaigns against the Ottoman Empire in Southeastern Europe. "You are a Slav," pronounced the fictional Morlacchi patriarch in the novel, thus nationally consecrating his young grandson.[11] Fortis's account of the Morlacchi, translated into French, English, and German, together with Wynne's novel, composed in French, brought the Morlacchi to the attention of the international Enlightenment.

The Morlacchi were thus identified as Slavs, but they were also seen as a very particular sort of Slav. At carnival in Venice in 1793 there was performed a play about the Morlacchi, called *Gli Antichi Slavi*, "the ancient or old-fashioned Slavs." Fortis believed that the Morlacchi, because they preserved their primitive customs, were still living the life of "the pastoral centuries," and the dramatist Camillo Federici followed this same line of reasoning in representing the Morlacchi as the ancient Slavs, an ancient community surviving into the present by preserving their old-fashioned customs. The plot of the play involved a romantic rivalry between an old-fashioned Slav in the mountains, that is, a Morlach, characterized by primitive manners and a ferocious attachment to his sword, and a new-fashioned Slav from the Dalmatian coast with Italian clothes and Italian manners. The Dalmatian heroine had to choose between them in a dilemma that metaphorically reflected the Enlightenment's conception of Eastern Europe: lands and peoples faced with the all-important alternatives of barbarism and civilization. "If you call yourself a Slav, put your valor to the test," cried the old-fashioned Slav, issuing an old-fashioned challenge, but at the end of the drama he conceded the superiority of his civilized rival, and the heroine unequivocally favored the man with Italian manners, providing a denouement that made perfect sense to the audience in Venice.[12] In the last years of the Venetian republic, Federici's play thus posed the question of what it meant to call oneself a Slav and proposed a civilized alternative to the identity of old-fashioned Slavs.

Some years later, however, the play was reconceived as a ballet and performed in Bergamo in 1802 under the title, *Le Nozze dei Morlacchi* (The Marriage of the Morlacchi). The plot was the same, but the denouement was different. This time, under the poetic influence of Romanticism and without the civilizing agenda of the Venetian republic, the well-mannered coastal Slav ceded the hand of the heroine to the old-fashioned inland Slav, the Morlach, and the contented lovers lived primitively ever after.[13] For several decades into the nineteenth century the ballet continued to be performed, with the title later simplified as *I Morlacchi*, the Morlacchi, no longer emphasizing their ethnographic significance as primitive Slavs. In 1812, *I Morlacchi* was performed at carnival in Novara, with new choreography by Antonio Biggiogero, and a geographical note that "the action is supposed to occur in Morlacchia on the border of Turkish Bosnia." In 1830 *I Morlacchi* was performed in Bologna, together with a Rossini opera *La Donna del Lago*, and in 1831 the ballet was staged in Milan on the same program with a drama about Peter the Great.[14] In the nineteenth century, in the aftermath of anthropological discovery and sensation, the Morlacchi became a folkloric curiosity, an exotic entertainment, an exercise in the choreography of barbarism, on the way to eventual effacement and oblivion.

"Morlacchi (That Means Serbo-Croatian)"

Federici's drama belonged to the final decade of the Venetian republic, but the subsequent ballet developed in the post-Venetian context of Napoleonic Italy. Dalmatia itself was incorporated into the Napoleonic province of Illyria and governed by Marshal Auguste-Frédéric-Louis Marmont. The celebrity of the Morlacchi in the late Enlightenment was such that Marmont could still recycle Venetian wisdom about their "poverty and laziness." He purposefully employed them in public works: "When an enlightened government possesses a country of poor and barbarous peoples, it must hasten to have executed, by corvée, the great works of public utility. It thus advances the epoch of their wealth and civilization." France hastened to adapt the Venetian civilizing mission in Dalmatia, vaunting the values of the Enlightenment and clarifying the relation between "civilized" government and "barbarous" peoples. Marmont recognized the inhabitants of the Dalmatian mountains as "the descendants of the ancient Slavs," still living primitively like their ancestors.[15] He, too, discerned in the customs of the Morlacchi the anthropological origins of the Slavs of Eastern Europe.

An anonymous French traveler, visiting Napoleonic Illyria, published in Turin his *Souvenirs d'un Voyage en Dalmatie*, giving only his initials C. B. on the title page. He included anthropological information about the Morlacchi and endorsed the civilizing concerns of Marshal Marmont. C. B. praised the Napoleonic government for planting mulberry trees and regretted that "the Morlaque, who seems to enjoy the state of barbarism in which he is plunged, and to find therein a sort of misunderstood liberty, uproots them by night as soon as they are planted, and thus opposes himself to the progress of his own civilization."[16] The catalog of the defects of Morlacchi character echoed the eighteenth-century concerns of the Venetian Provveditori Generali:

Lazy with delight, ignorant and stubborn beyond all expression, credulous and superstitious in consequence, dirty to excess, thieves by habit and by circumstance, brigands by heroism and by superstition, declared enemies of economy, of agriculture, of laws, of subordination, of order, and of all that could hinder the indolent and unbridled life in which they love to wallow: in a word, savages.[17]

Yet C. B. relished their barbarism sufficiently to hope that they would preserve their customs and their costumes, that they would not become, in an original French coinage, *démorlaquisé*. Rather, a beneficent government would have to try "to tame them little by little, to render them susceptible to a more refined civilization."[18] The anonymous traveler tried to reconcile the sentimental and civilizing perspectives on the Morlacchi when he proposed a policy of civilization that would nevertheless preserve them from the condition he insightfully discerned as *démorlaquisé*. That was, in fact, precisely the condition that awaited the Morlacchi, destined gradually to disappear as a recognizable community.

The cultural significance of the term *Morlacchi* was already being effaced at the end of the Napoleonic interlude with the poetic annunciation of a modern national consciousness among the South Slavs. In 1814 Vuk Karadžić published in Vienna his *Mala prostonarodna pjesnarica*, a small volume of simple folk poems. He included in the collection the poem called "Hasanaginica," which had first been published forty years before by Fortis in *Viaggio in Dalmazia* as the "Mourning Song of the Noble Wife of Asan Aga." Fortis presented it as a specimen of a hitherto altogether unknown oral literature, the poetry of the Morlacchi, transcribed in Slavic and Italian; probably he received the transcription from his friend Giulio Bajamonti of Split, who would later take an interest in the relation between Slavic and Homeric verse.[19] The poetry of the South Slavs was to become an important folkloric field, whether pursued as a national project by someone like Vuk Karadžić in the nineteenth century or as an academic project by scholars like Milman Parry and Albert Lord in the twentieth century. The field originated, however, in the eighteenth century with philosophes like Fortis and Bajamonti, who presented their literary discovery not as the poetry of the South Slavs but rather as the poetry of the Morlacchi. In the 1770s Goethe promptly rendered into German the "Hasanaginica" that he found in Fortis and recognized it as Morlacchi poetry—*aus dem Morlackischen*—and Herder then included that German version, specified as *Morlackisch* by origin, in his collection of *Volkslieder*. However, when Karadžić published the "Hasanaginica" in 1814 and sent a copy of the volume to Goethe, it was inscribed thus: "A Slav sends to the greatest German, alongside the original of the 'Mourning Song of the Noble Wife of the Hero Asan Aga,' also the first publication of Serbian folksongs." When Goethe then reflected on the subject later in the 1820s, the critical cultural classification was no longer "Morlackisch" but rather, in a modern national attribution, "Serbische Lieder," Serbian songs.[20] The "Hasanaginica" had already been, in some sense, *démorlaquisé*.

Karadžić, in fact, never found an authentic reciter to perform the poem orally for him, so he had to rely on Fortis's transcription and eventually made alterations that had the effect of creating a more Serbian version. This Serbian appropriation of the "Hasanaginica" would not go uncontested, and by the beginning of the twentieth century Camilla Lucerna, from Zagreb, was insisting that the dialect of the poem was Croatian, while observing that its subject concerned Moslem Slavs. "So it is incorrect to designate the poem as Serbian, as in Vuk's misleading procedure," concluded Lucerna. Yet equally emphatically she rejected the notion that the poem could be attributed to the Morlacchi: "There is no Morlacchi language, no Morlacchi people." She preferred to label the poem as simply "South Slavic."[21] Thus, in the age of modern nationalism, the "Hasanaginica" continued to provoke classificatory concern, following from its discovery in the age of Enlightenment as a masterpiece of the Morlacchi.

Dalmatia was ruled by the Habsburgs from the downfall of the Napoleonic empire until the collapse of the Habsburg Monarchy itself at the end of World War I. Lucerna's emphatic declaration that the Morlacchi people did not exist, published in Habsburg Croatia in 1905, was consistent with other perspectives on Habsburg Dalmatia that evolved within the monarchy during the century of Viennese rule. Most important was the linguistic classification of nationality according to the state census by which the South Slavic population of Dalmatia could only identify itself as Serbo-Croatian. The eighteenth-century recognition that the "nation" of the Morlacchi spoke a Slavic language that related them to a broader Slavic domain was applied in the nineteenth century in such a fashion as to make that nation officially disappear, absorbed into a broader national category. The administrative categories of the modern imperial state contributed to this absorption, while modern national movements among the South Slavs exercised a similarly effacing influence upon the Morlacchi, who were confronted with the increasingly articulate affirmations of Serbian, Croatian, or Yugoslav nationalism.

In 1892 there was published in Vienna a large, handsome, heavily illustrated book about Dalmatia as part of a series entitled *Die österreichisch-ungarische Monarchie in Wort und Bild*, the Austro-Hungarian Monarchy "in word and image." As a collaborative work of scholarship, including Dalmatian contributors, the perspective involved provincial views integrated into an overall imperial representation. Among the images were photographs of the Morlacchi, labeled as such, but the text called into question the validity of the label.

In a natural history of the Dalmatians descent is all the less acceptable as a basis for classification, as with regard to the Morlacchi the scientific struggle still fluctuates, since some want them to be viewed as Romans (Mavrovlachos,

that is, black Latins), and others as true Serbs. Since, however, the Morlacchi conform almost completely (*nahezu vollkommen übereinstimmen*) to the
Serbo-Croatian majority of the inhabitants of Dalmatia, in body size, as well
as in eye, hair, and skin color, and no less in the form of the skull, here the
more notable differences between the inhabitants of the Dalmatian mountains and the coast will be incidentally (*gelegentlich*) indicated.[22]

The text thus emphasized racial resemblance even though the images
made a case for distinctive costume. The Morlacchi were ethnographically reconceived in complete conformity to the Serbo-Croatian majority, a grouping that also, of course, corresponded to the linguistic category of the Habsburg census. In 1892 Fortis was still being cited for his
pioneering contribution to the study of South Slavic folk poetry: "In the
book *Viaggio in Dalmazia* (Venice, 1774) Fortis published several spec-
imens of Morlacchi (that means Serbo-Croatian) songs."[23] The paren-
thetical redefinition—"*einige Proben morlackischer (das heisst serbisch-
kroatischer) Lieder*"—effectively eliminated the Morlacchi from the
anthropological equation. It was impossible to mention Fortis without
mentioning the Morlacchi, but they were named only to be dismissed as
an anachronistic folkloric classification, irrelevant to the official modern
summation of Dalmatia. Lucerna, who affirmed that there were "no
Morlacchi people," blamed Fortis for the currency of the name: "Though
he was not the first to use this dubious designation, it was really launched
with the success of his work."[24] For those who believed in the objective
character of ethnography and nationality at the turn of the century, the
Morlacchi did not really exist. They were merely an imaginary community.

"Barbaric Gorgeousness"

In a guide to Dalmatia, published in Vienna in 1899, there was a
short section on *Morlaken*, with the warning that this "nickname" might
not be well received by the subjects themselves. They would prefer to
be designated "as Croat or Serb, or else as Dalmatian," since *Morlaken*
was "used for a long time in the sense in which the Greeks once spoke
of Scythian or Sarmatian," that is, to signify barbarians. That said, the
guide then went on to designate them as *Morlaken*, while explaining
their primitive customs, exotic costumes, and lack of economic sense.[25]
Thus, even when the designation was discounted as an ethnographically
meaningless "nickname," it still served as a signature for primitive customs and economic underdevelopment. If the Morlacchi survived into
the nineteenth century as the exotic subject of a ballet about barbarism,

at the beginning of the twentieth century they played the part of a folk-loric tourist attraction. The memoirs of travelers, sometimes including photographs, testified to the persistence of the Morlacchi phenomenon. In 1908 Maude Holbach published *Dalmatia: The Land Where East Meets West*; in 1910 Frances Kinsley Hutchinson reported on the new automobile tourism in *Motoring in the Balkans: Along the Highways of Dalmatia, Montenegro, the Herzegovina and Bosnia*; in 1914 Alice Lee Moqué enthusiastically contributed *Delightful Dalmatia*.[26] All three English and American women regarded an encounter with the Morlac-chi as a thrilling touristic treat for the traveler in Dalmatia. They all cited as their cicerone in Dalmatia the three-volume guide to its archi-tectural monuments by Thomas Graham Jackson, published in 1887, and his expertise seemed to shape their reactions to the Morlacchi.[27]

"The huts in which the Morlacchi live are the same as those described by Fortis," wrote Jackson, more than a hundred years after the publication of *Viaggio in Dalmazia*. He went on to describe the Morlacchi women as "half-savage looking creatures," wearing "embroidered leggings that give them the appearance of Indian squaws," while the Morlacchi men wore "rags and tatters." The festive adornments of coins and beads only added "a deeper tinge to their barbarism." Alice Moqué encountered the Mor-lacchi women in the market at Zadar, squatting "in oriental fashion," be-dizened in "barbaric gorgeousness." She was reading Jackson closely enough to note "their embroidered leggings, which are worked in colored thread and adorned with many beads like the leggings and moccasins of an American Indian." By an indiscriminate combination of cultural asso-ciations these Morlacchi "made Zara's Piazza look like a stage-setting—reminding us of a scene in the 'Bohemian Girl.'" In Šibenik, however, the Morlacchi were "particularly fierce and savage looking," and "lacked the picturesqueness of those we had seen in Zara."[28] The formula of folkloric entertainment was sufficient to moderate troubling impres-sions so that primitive people appeared as theatrically, even operatically, picturesque.

Frances Hutchinson also admired "the barbaric costumes of the Mor-lacchi" in the market at Zadar ("Such bravery of color! Such gorgeous raiment! Such charming caps and kerchiefs!")—and she could not help regretting that "civilization is about to encroach upon picturesqueness." One member of her party exclaimed, "How monotonous a world en-tirely civilized would be!" Maude Holbach included a photograph of the Morlacchi women in the Zadar marketplace, and celebrated them as a highlight of the voyage:

Among the traveler's impressions there are always some that stand out vividly when others, even though more important, have grown dim. Among the first is my first sight of the market at Zara and of the Morlacchi, the peasants of Northern Dalmatia, who, seated on the ground in the fashion of the East, offered their eggs and vegetables for sale in the strangest tongue that ever assailed my ears. At the first glance they seemed to me more like North American Indians than any European race.[29]

By the associative logic of the traveler's impressions, the Morlacchi were both Oriental Easterners and American Indians at the same time. All three travelers had such a similar experience in the marketplace at Zadar that this "first sight" of the Morlacchi appears as almost a piece of packaged tourism, the requisite encounter with primitive people in Dalmatia evoking the appropriate response to their picturesque appeal. Indeed the name *Morlacchi* became the label under which these travelers could sum up their modern touristic impressions of folkloric phenomena and primitive customs.

Yet the term *Morlacchi* became increasingly irrelevant through the nineteenth century—Morlacchi (that means Serbo-Croatian)—and the population of Habsburg Dalmatia was counted by language in the census of 1910 as 96 percent *Serbisch-kroatisch* and 3 percent *Italienisch*, those formulated as the fundamental national categories. However, from a foreign perspective in England, the eleventh edition of the *Encyclopaedia Britannica* in 1910 seemed to invert the formula—Serbo-Croatian (that means Morlacchi)—and counted 96 percent of the Dalmatian population as Morlachs. The encyclopedia thus deployed "the name of Morlachs, Morlaks or Morlacks commonly bestowed by English writers on the Dalmatian Slavs."[30] While the name, or nickname, *Morlacchi* might be used less and less in Dalmatia, it maintained its meaning in international circulation and was used in the encyclopedia as an objectively ethnographic designation. A byword for barbarism, or perhaps semibarbarism, the term *Morlacchi* could be casually invoked to emphasize that aspect of Dalmatia as it appeared from abroad. Jackson in 1887 recognized "degrees among these Slavs," with the term *Morlacchi* denoting the lowest degree of civilization, "the wildest and rudest figures imaginable." He observed them, while they observed him: "They stare at you from under wild shocks of unkempt hair. . . . They wear long floating moustaches and ragged beards, and often cover their shoulders with a coat of goat's skin with the hair on."[31] Such was the mythology or anthropology of the Morlacchi, known as Morlacks to English writers.

Modern English and American travelers at the beginning of the twentieth century saw these Morlacks as relics of the primitive past, destined for extinction by the inevitable course of civilization, which would iron out the differences in customs and the "degrees" among the Slavs as the world advanced toward the monotony of modernity. It required the genius of science fiction for an English writer to imagine a different course of development, that of the distant future in *The Time Machine* by H. G. Wells, published in 1895. When the narrator sees a "queer little ape-like figure" disappear down a shaft into the subterranean world, he realizes that human evolution has not produced a uniformly civilized society: "The truth dawned on me: that Man had not remained one species, but had differentiated into two distinct animals: that my graceful children of the Upper World were not the sole descendants of our generation, but that this bleached, obscene, nocturnal Thing, which had flashed before me, was also heir to all the ages."[32] The graceful and refined beings of the Upper World were called the Eloi, and they were preyed upon by the sinister figures of the subterranean world, who only came out by night as nocturnal apparitions. These creepy creatures had regressively evolved away from civilization, and every science fiction aficionado knows that H. G. Wells named them the Morlocks.

In 1906 Wells met with Teddy Roosevelt in the White House, and they discussed, among other things, *The Time Machine.*

"Suppose, after all," said Roosevelt, crouching down and gesturing over the White House lawn as if over a battlefield, "that you should be right, and it ends with your butterflies and Morlocks. That doesn't matter now! The effort's real. It's worth going on with. It's worth it. It's worth it—even then."

Wells stood back and agreed with Roosevelt, and said that it was their challenge, and the twentieth century's, to make sure that whatever the fate of mankind, it would be achieved with dignity and fair-mindedness.

Roosevelt said, "Morlocks! Everywhere Morlocks!" And he pretended to shoot them as if with a hunting rifle, and then they both laughed.[33]

While American and English tourists were still admiring the picturesqueness of the Morlacchi in Dalmatia, Anglo-American culture had already endowed the name with a more menacing meaning in science fiction that was nevertheless closely related to its previous significance in Eastern Europe. In the civilized, progressive imagination it was already open season on Morlocks.

Conclusion: "Ex-Morlacchi"

Maria Todorova, in *Imagining the Balkans,* has described the emergence of "balkanism," a discourse of disparagement in which the name

Balkan "became a synonym for a reversion to the tribal, the backward, the primitive, the barbarian." Todorova's historical lexicography demonstrates the increasingly charged signification of that term at the beginning of the twentieth century: "What I define as balkanism was formed gradually in the course of two centuries and crystallized in a specific discourse around the Balkan wars and World War I."[34] The term *Morlacchi* in the eighteenth and nineteenth centuries similarly designated the tribal, the backward, the primitive, and the barbarian, and in a notable coincidence of chronology the Morlacchi vanished from history right around the time of the Balkan wars and World War I. The *Encyclopaedia Britannica* article of 1910, taken together with the three travel memoirs of 1908, 1910, and 1914, represent a last foreign effusion of interest in the Morlacchi under that name. Thereafter the meaning of Morlacchi, with its connotations of primitivism and backwardness in the mountains of Dalmatia, was absorbed into the more powerful concept of the Balkans and generalized over all of Southeastern Europe. The exceptional importance of the term *Balkans* in the twentieth century, as demonstrated by Todorova, suggests the earlier significance of the term Morlacchi, originating in the Enlightenment and inaugurating an imaginative evolution that related the issue of nationality among the South Slavs to the issue of civilization in Eastern Europe.

In an article published in Zagreb in 1929, in the journal *Hrvatsko Kolo*, Marijan Stojković noted that "today one does not speak any more, as one once did, about the Morlacchi," and he went on to make the Morlacchi "nation" parenthetically Croatian: "naroda 'Morlaka' (Hrvata)." The title of his article was "Morlakizam," an echo of the term *morlacchismo*, already coined by Bajamonti in 1797; by 1929 Stojković was already using the term in historiographical retrospect to designate the Enlightenment's fascination with the Morlacchi during the late eighteenth century.[35] When the Slovene-American immigrant Louis Adamic returned to visit Yugoslavia in 1932 and then published his account as *The Native's Return*, he included a description of the mountains of Dalmatia:

There were the several villages we visited in the Dalmatian highland—Dalmatinsko Zagoryé, as the mountain region immediately in back of Split, Trogir, and Shibenik is called in Slavic. Primitive in the extreme, both in comfort and socio-economic organization, they are vastly unlike the communities along the coast or on the islands. . . . On every stretch of level ground or some ridge above it is a huddle of stone houses, anywhere from ten to a hundred, most of them as unfit for human habitation as the musty wooden shanties of the "nigger towns" and white-trash communities in

Mississippi and Alabama. . . . The people are Croats. They have been living and dying there, under the heels of various foreign rules, for centuries.[36]

These were precisely the people who had been identified as Morlacchi ever since the eighteenth century, and even Cvijić at the beginning of the twentieth century still found—"in the course of my voyages in the Dalmatian Zagora"—that "the most primitive population" was the "Slavicized Vlachs or Morlachs." Yet Adamic, on the same terrain, seemed not to have heard the name of the Morlacchi; instead he denominated the inhabitants as Croats, and to do justice to their primitive way of life he resorted to American analogies. He had no doubt of their backwardness, and judged that "it will take decades, perhaps centuries, to raise the people from the level to which half a millennium of exploitation, disease, and neglect has pushed them."[37] Thus the philosophical meaning of *Morlacchi*, as established in the eighteenth century, still continued to be relevant to the mountains of Dalmatia, perceived as a domain of primitiveness and backwardness, but the term itself was no longer current; the Morlacchi were on the verge of lexicographical extinction.

During World War II, when fascist Italy occupied Dalmatia, the population of the province was perceived in modern national terms as divided between an Italian minority and a Slavic majority, with the Slavs divided between a Catholic Croatian majority and an Orthodox Serbian minority. Luigi Arduini, the Italian consul at Split, recalled that once "Venice had impressed the indelible mark of our superior civilization" upon Dalmatia, and the coastal Italians of Zadar prided themselves on their civilized superiority to the inland areas that were "permeated with balkanism (*balcanesimo*)." Yet the fascist imperial government also looked to the Serbs for possible support, since they generally preferred fascist Italian rule to the more deadly alternative of the Croatian Ustaša regime in Zagreb. Alessandro Dudàn of Split advised Mussolini to look to the Serbs of Dalmatia for some support and characterized them thus: "Orthodox Serbs (for the most part ex-Morlacchi)." In the 1890s the Morlacchi were being parenthetically redefined—Morlacchi (that means Serbo-Croatian)—and now, fifty years later in the 1940s, the category had been so successfully dissolved that they could only be parenthetically remembered, in reverse definition, as ex-Morlacchi. The Italian fascist occupation had reason to remember, since *morlacchismo* could still serve the imperial purposes for which it was ideologically created in the eighteenth century. When members of the Yugoslav resistance were condemned to death at Šibenik in 1941, the fascist prosecutor proclaimed the urgent need "to civilize and radically purge, so that this most Italian land need not be trampled by barbarians and Morlacchi."[38] His speech was cited in 1945, in the Titoist newspaper *Slobodna Dalmacija* (*Free Dalmatia*), making the point that the fascists were the true barbarians. Thus early modern *morlacchismo*, merging with the modern notion of *balcanesimo*, still played a part in articulating both adherence and resistance to imperial ambitions in Southeastern Europe.

4 An Island of Peace in a Turbulent World

*Old Ragusans' Statesmanship as a Paradigm
for the Modern Balkans*

BARIŠA KREKIĆ

In instructions of April 20, 1404, addressed to its ambassadors in Hungary, the Ragusan government ordered them to tell their protector, King Sigismund of Hungary and Croatia, that he can easily imagine "how much your city of Dubrovnik [Ragusa] is toiling to maintain the due fidelity [to him], because we are surrounded on all sides by enemies."[1] Years later, in August 1431 in a letter to Queen Joan II of Naples, the Ragusans were explaining that "this city of ours is situated on a steep cliff, almost completely surrounded by sea and, what is worse, surrounded by the Patarens, the most iniquitous enemies of those who worship the Catholic religion of Christ, and even worse than the Patarens, the infidel Turks are announcing their presence, and those just-mentioned neighbors of ours, by their innate double-faced, inhumane shrewdness, might by day and by night harm us in property and in person."[2]

The dramatic situation of Dubrovnik is equally vividly depicted in instructions that the Ragusan government sent on October 5, 1433, to its envoys in the court of the above-mentioned King Sigismund. The three patrician ambassadors were supposed to tell the king, among others, that "your most faithful city of Dubrovnik, which is the only one that has remained obedient to the Hungarians [*sic*] crown on that shore, is much envied and hated not only by schismatics and heretics, by whom it is surrounded, but also by other Christians in its vicinity, who do not obey your serenity."[3]

Finally, to give just one more illustration of the view that the old Ragusans had of their own position and of the skill with which they exploited that argument in dealings with foreign powers, let me quote from an instruction given on February 21, 1451 to the distinguished scholar, astronomer and bibliophile Johannes Gazulus,[4] who was going to visit Rome and the Pope Nicholas V as Ragusan envoy:

The city of Dubrovnik is located on the mainland and its jurisdiction is contiguous and surrounded on all sides by perfidious Patarens . . . without any separation, either by land or by sea, in such a way that [Dubrovnik] already from very ancient times has been and is in tribulation, because the place where the said city is located was a place of those infidels, and it was taken by Dubrovnik from the hands of the said infidels. And from then until now . . . [Dubrovnik] has been very much disturbed and harassed by those infidels.[5]

Indeed, Dubrovnik was squeezed between the Latin, Italian Roman Catholic West and the Slavic, Byzantine, Eastern Orthodox, partly heretical and later Islamic East. A Western, Roman Catholic city-republic, it had to be constantly on its toes to survive under such circumstances. To make the situation even more precarious, Dubrovnik could not feed itself, nor did it have sufficient resources on its small territory to survive on its own. Dubrovnik's predicament was clearly described in an instruction given to its ambassadors in the court of the King of Hungary and Croatia, Lajos I, written on April 26, 1375. The ambassadors were supposed to tell the king that "your city of Dubrovnik, as you might have been informed, does not sow any grains for its provision, nor does it have any land to sow it."[6] This is why it was of vital importance for Dubrovnik to be able to carry on trade, both on land and on sea. The Ragusans were very much aware of the necessity of trade for their survival and prosperity. This is obvious from many letters and other acts of the Ragusan government, and I shall quote here just a few. In April 1371, in a letter to King Lajos I, the Ragusans wrote that "we [Ragusans] cannot live, except by trading and we do the major portion of our trade in the Kingdom of Rassa [i.e., Serbia], and because of the poor state in which the Kingdom of Rassa is, because of the divisions of the barons, we cannot nor do we dare to carry on presently as much trade as we used to do in earlier times."[7]

The preoccupation with trade in the Balkans is evident also from a letter addressed to the Bosnian Duke Sandalj Hranić-Kosača in 1403, in which the Ragusan government stressed that "our merchants have always been free in Bosnia, in Sclauonia [i.e., Serbia] and in Bulgaria and have never been molested for anything."[8] Similar worries appear in a letter to King Sigismund in May 1463, in which the Ragusans were telling their protector that "this your Majesty's city is located in steep mountains, and it has been preserved and augmented not by income from estates, which is nil, but by frequent trade by merchants . . . without which it could not be and exist; [Dubrovnik's] merchants carry on their business mostly in Sclauonia, Bosnia and Zeta," areas which were then menaced by the Ottoman Turks.[9] Finally, in a letter to Janos Hunyadi, governor of Hungary, in August 1451, the Ragusan government pointed out that it had as neighbors the King of Bosnia and the Duke Stefan Vukčić-Kosača of Herzegovina, and therefore "it is most convenient with those neighbors of ours."[10]

The view of individual Ragusans on the importance of trade may be glanced from the will of ser Marinus Ni. De Gondola (Gundulić), of February 26, 1462, in which he stated: "I have been a Ragusan patrician and, having a big and onerous family, and wanting to avoid exposing myself to the misery of living from offices, I have toiled with commercial activity so that my sons also might take from me the example of some trade and follow the said commerce, through which they might ascend to some honor and prosperity."[11]

There were, however, difficulties for land trade. On the one hand, from the mid-fourteenth century, there was first the growing disintegration of Serbia, the Ottoman invasion of the Balkans, then the anarchy in Bosnia, and finally the disappearance of the Balkan Christian states by the mid-fifteenth century.

On the other hand, maritime trade was of great importance for Dubrovnik as well, and there the main problem was the Venetians, who did not want to have serious competition in the Adriatic basin. In this respect, the cessation of the Venetian domination in Dalmatia and in Dubrovnik, in 1358, and their passage under the protection of the Hungaro-Croatian rulers might have had grave consequences for Ragusan trade. Once again, partly through direct negotiations with Venice,[12] partly through diplomatic interventions of other powers, Dubrovnik managed, after some tribulations, not only to preserve but even to expand its naval trade in the late fourteenth and the first half of the fifteenth century at a critical time when trade with the Balkans was becoming increasingly insecure.

To be able to face all those problems and to survive and be successful, Dubrovnik needed in the first place to have capable and dedicated leadership and continuity of such leadership and its policies. It had to be a pragmatic, cautious, and far-sighted statesmanship with a sophisticated sense of reality and the "limits of the possible." It also had to have a developed capacity to calculate very carefully and meticulously its moves and their consequences. Dubrovnik was lucky to have such leaders in the patrician class, which was very much influenced by the Venetian model. Despite occasional internal dissent and various criticisms that could be directed at them, the patricians provided the kind of guidance that enabled Dubrovnik to survive and prosper for several centuries.[13]

The second element that greatly helped the Ragusans was the substantial wealth that the city had been able to accumulate and that the patricians knew how to use wisely. However, they were also very much aware that wealth can create corruption and all kinds of abuses. This is why, beginning with city statutes of 1272, through many later laws and decrees, the Ragusans fought against luxury and laziness.[14] Let me mention just one document that is indicative of the Ragusan attitude toward work and duty. On December 15, 1462, the Major Council decided that officials supervising the sewers "should not have from now on any salary from our commune, because they presently do not work, nor do they exercise their office, and it is not suitable that those who do not work eat, because salary is the reward for labor."[15]

The third important means of Dubrovnik's survival was an excellent system of information-gathering that the Ragusans had organized that allowed them not only to be well-informed themselves but also to serve as a valuable clearing house for the flow of news both eastward and westward. The information was collected through a well-developed courier service, through intelligence received from Ragusan merchants in various countries, and above all from letters of Ragusan ambassadors, which were full of interesting information and which the government very cleverly used.

To give just two examples: on May 18, 1430, in a letter sent to its ambassadors in the court of the Bosnian Duke Sandalj Hranić-Kosača, the Ragusan government wrote that "the Dauphin or King of France, having conquered Paris, has been advancing all the time and each day is prospering against the English, thanks to the guidance and leadership of a young virgin, who appeared to him miraculously and who governs and leads his army."[16] The second illustration is a whole group of letters full of information about preparations for the battle of Lepanto and in particular, a detailed description of the battle itself contained in a letter that the distinguished Ragusan government sent from Rome on October 24, 1571.[17] Incidentally, the Ragusan ambassadors were under strict orders not to keep for themselves but to surrender under oath to the Minor Council any gifts (except food) that they, their family members, and their servants might receive while pursuing their mission or that might be sent to their wives or other members of their households in Dubrovnik.[18]

The wisdom of the Ragusan statesmen is visible, among many other examples, in their letters to foreign rulers and, especially, in the instructions that they gave to their own envoys in various Balkan and European states and courts. Although those instructions are usually very detailed, the Ragusans relied also on their ambassadors' experience and common sense. Thus, for example, when writing to the patrician Pascus de Ragnina (Ranjina), their envoy in the city of Budva on the coast of Montenegro on October 15, 1362, after giving him instructions about what to say, when and to whom, the government added: "Because we cannot give you detailed instructions for everything that might occur . . . you, as [a person] knowing the intentions of the city, must answer as a wise [man] that you are in all things, always for the honor and safety of our city of Dubrovnik."[19]

However, the Ragusan government generally put precise limits on what an ambassador was allowed to say or do. To give just a few examples: the envoys in the court of the Bosnian Duke Sandalj Hranić-Kosača, in 1406, were told to give him the news on the negotiations between the Duke of Austria and the Hungarian king, "and do not expand further on news from those regions."[20] Even more interesting in this respect are the instructions for the patrician "Zanin de Gozze" (Gučetić), who was carrying the annual tribute to King Sigismund of Hungary and Croatia in November 1412. The government of Dubrovnik ordered the ambassador: "If, by chance, our lord [the king] asked you about any things concerning the situation in the land, tell him that you do not know and that you do not have commission for anything else, except to bring him the tribute. But if he asks about news, tell him those that are publicly known the best way you know how."[21] Not much different were the instructions given to Ragusan ambassadors going to the same king in November 1428: "If the king asks you about the situation concerning Venice or other topics, which are not in your commission, that is to say about war or peace, or alliance, and asked for your advice, you will answer that no commission has been given to you concerning those matters, and inform us by your letter. But as far as news and general matters are concerned, answer as you think best."[22]

One must keep in mind that those ambassadors were dealing with the protector of Dubrovnik and one might have expected more openness in such a situation, but the proverbially cautious and circumspect Ragusans did not want to risk any indiscretion even when it came to their overlord. In addition, the ambassadors were to be humble and show the greatest respect toward their hosts. Thus, the envoys to King Sigismund in November 1403 were instructed to say, should the king ask them about the situation in Bosnia: "Your majesty knows better, but nevertheless, we, small men, shall report the way we see things."[23]

However, despite their humility and circumspection, the Ragusans did not hesitate to take advantage of all occasions that might benefit their state. Among such occasions were contacts that the Ragusan ambassadors in various courts might establish with personalities and representatives of third countries, even spying on those individuals. These were widespread methods used in Ragusan diplomacy and required very careful calculation and precise determination on when and how such contacts should be established and maintained, and how much spying was permissible, so as not to offend both the host and the dignitaries from third countries. There are numerous examples that illustrate this point, but I shall mention here just two cases that seem to me to be particularly interesting.

In March 1405 when the Ragusan government had learned that envoys of the Serbian Despot Stevan Lazarević had arrived in the court of the Bosnian Duke Sandalj Hranić-Kosača, it instructed its ambassador in the same court "to write and inform us of all news that you might hear there. Also, start skillfully to pry about the embassy of the Despot which came to the said Duke, why did it come and with what did it leave, and inform us on everything you learn."[24] Years later, in November 1422, a courier of King Sigismund had arrived in Dubrovnik carrying a letter that the King was sending to Duke Sandalj. The Ragusans sent the letter to their ambassador at the Duke's court and instructed him to ask the Duke, "how does he want that you present him the letter, in secret or in public, and do as he says. And after giving him the letter, start spying on the contents of the same letter, and if the Duke tells you, fine; in case he does not, you then spy and best way you can, and whatever you obtain, you'll inform us."[25]

Here again it is necessary to keep in mind that the Ragusan diplomats were ordered to spy in the court of a friendly power (Duke Sandalj) on envoys of another friendly power (Despot Stevan of Serbia) and even on a letter from their own protector. But when it came to obtaining news that might be of use to them, the Ragusans did not consider such behavior reprehensible. The essential thing was to gather information and send it as rapidly as possible to the government in Dubrovnik, which knew very well how to make use of it in its diplomatic and other transactions.

The ambassadors, recruited mostly from the ranks of the Ragusan patricians but sometimes also from the ranks of commoners or of the clergy, were strictly controlled by the Senate, which issued instructions, received letters and information sent by ambassadors, and made all major decisions in the area of international policy, frequently in secret sessions. Still, as already mentioned, the patricians trusted their colleagues enough not only to leave them space to evaluate the situation on their own, but even to demand such independent evaluation of events.

In August 1494 the government wrote to its ambassadors in Venice: "As far as the news that you are reporting is concerned, you always refer to the public opinion. We would like you to tell us at times your own opinion on some matters, and not the public opinion, because you are wise and discreet."[26] This exhortation seems to have worked, because only two months later the government wrote to the same envoys: "We commend you very much for informing us of the news and we want you to stay very curious and to inform us daily about what you hear" concerning the movements of the King of France and other events.[27] But it was in December 1494 that the ambassadors in Venice received their highest praise:

You please us very much by writing extensively . . . the news, because, although that news is written and reported [to us] through other channels, we still have more faith in your writing, because we consider that, in view of the place in which you are [Venice] and in view of your prudence, all that you write you write with good reason and based on contacts that you must have with important men, and therefore persist as you have started.[28]

Of course, the government strictly controlled the dissemination of news thus gathered. This became a particularly sensitive matter after the Ottomans conquered the Balkans and became immediate neighbors of Dubrovnik in the mid-fifteenth century. Leaks of undesirable information on the Ottomans could be a mortal danger for the small republic. Aware of that, the government took at times severe measures to prevent such infractions, the most drastic case certainly being the ordinance adopted in a secret session of the Senate on October 11, 1566, after the death of the Sultan Suleyman the Magnificent.

In the first place, "for the sake of peace, welfare and preservation of this city, no nobleman of ours should dare or presume, either personally or through the medium of another person, to send news of any kind from the Levant to any prince or to his ministers, nor to any private individual in any shape or form." How serious this prohibition was can best be seen by the severity of sanctions that it imposed: patricians violating this ordinance would suffer "the penalty of the loss of nobility and a fine of 1000 golden ducats to be paid to our commune, and such [a nobleman] could never obtain pardon, except by all ballots in our councils," something that was practically impossible to achieve. In addition, patricians "receiving and delivering letters or persons of any prince or of his ministers, or [those who] in any way expedite and send the said letters and persons" would be punished in the same way, except "if they had previously informed the magnificent Lord Rector and his Minor Council of the matter."

The second clause of the same ordinance extended those prohibitions to all Ragusan citizens, with the difference that commoners were threatened "with the irremissible loss of life." Should a foreigner residing in Dubrovnik "dare and presume to send news from the Levant to any prince or to his ministers or other private individuals, or receive and deliver the said letters and persons," the Rector and the Minor Council would undertake an inquest and present to the Senate its outcome, after which they would together take the necessary measures. Finally, no Ragusan—whether patrician or commoner—was allowed to send ships of any kind "without the express knowledge and permission of the magnificent Lord Rector and his Minor Council." Officials in Ragusan territories outside the city were prohibited from allowing such departures without permission from the same authority.[29]

These measures were made even more severe in January 1567 when the Minor Council arrogated to itself the role of all official correspondence: "All letters to be sent outside our state, written from now on on behalf of the magnificent Lord Rector and [the Minor] Council by our notaries and chancellors, must be read in the Minor Council" in the presence of at least seven out of its eleven members.[30] The limitations and controls imposed on the circulation of news from the Levant—that is to say concerning the Ottoman Empire—were expanded in October 1567 to cover all regions, east and west.[31]

However, the Ragusans were aware of the importance of giving efficient and well-thought-through answers to the letters of foreign dignitaries. Each year, on January 1, they entrusted several patricians belonging to various committees with the task of "seeing to it that letters of princes and other illustrious persons get due answers in opportune time."[32] Even more interesting and instructive is the way the old Ragusans treated the problem of languages used in diplomatic correspondence. It was pretty easy to deal with letters directed toward the West, to the kings of Hungary and Croatia, to the Pope, to Venice and other Italian cities. Latin was the language commonly used in diplomatic contacts and letters, while the Ragusan instructions sent to their envoys were always written in Italian. As long as the Slavic states existed in the hinterland, letters written to Bosnian and Serbian rulers and potentates were written in the Slavic language ("*in lingua sclauonesca*") with Cyrillic letters.

Things were more complicated when it came to communications with the Ottoman Empire and its dignitaries. The Ottoman was a truly multinational empire, and among its leaders there were considerable numbers of officials of non-Ottoman origin, especially during the sixteenth century. The Ragusans knew very well that the influence of some such individuals was enormous and wanted not only to establish and to maintain contacts with them but also be in their good graces. Language was one tool to achieve such goals. Since many Ottoman high officials in the sixteenth century were of Slavic origin, the Ragusans used the Slavic language in their contacts with them, whether in the capital of Constantinople or in the provinces. For example, when writing in February 1529 to the Ottoman Sandjak of Herzegovina, Akhmed-beg Kusumbašić, the Ragusans decided that the letter should be written "in the Illyrian language" ("*in lingua illyrica*").[33]

Even more interesting is how language was used as a diplomatic tool when it came to writing to the Grand Vizier, Mehmed-Pasha Sokolović. In a secret session of the Senate, on December 3, 1568, the discussion took place about letters to be written to Ragusan ambassadors in Constantinople and to the Grand Vizier. The decision had to be made whether those letters would be written "in Italian or in Serbian language" ("*in sermone italico seu in seruiano*"). After a debate, a solomonic solution was found: the letter to Ragusan envoys would be written "in the Italian language and to the most illustrious Mehmed Pasha in the Serbian language" ("*oratoribus nostris in sermone italico et illustrissimo Mech. Bassae in sermone seruiano*").[34] Of course, the Ragusans knew very well that Sokolović was a Serb from Bosnia and to be able to communicate with him in his native language was certainly seen as an asset for Ragusan diplomacy, whereas the instructions to their ambassadors were to be written in Italian, as usual.

All of this is proof of the pragmatism and flexibility of the old Ragusans. The patricians, congregated in three councils (Minor, Senate, and Major), made all decisions collectively. In a letter to the Hungaro-Croatian King Lajos I of April 17, 1361, the Ragusans emphasized that "the decisions in your land [Dubrovnik] are not made by one citizen, but by many citizens organized in our councils."[35] When the Serbian Despot Stevan Lazarević demanded in 1421 that four Ragusans give an oath on behalf of the whole community, the government of Dubrovnik instructed its ambassadors in the Despot's court to tell him that "it can not be nor [can it be] reasonably feasible that four noblemen given an oath for the whole of Dubrovnik."[36]

Each and every letter, instruction, and major decision was first studied by a committee, usually consisting of three patricians, and was then proposed to the councils, which voted on them. Nevertheless, the role of outstanding individuals was not ignored. I believe that the old Ragusans understood very well that, even within a truly collective system of decision making, the wisdom and prestige of individuals of proven ability should be appreciated and made good use of. It is certainly not by chance that a number of distinguished patricians were repeatedly elected to the position of Rector, especially in critical situations, at times even breaking the rules that limited re-election.[37]

When speaking of the Ragusan system of government, it is necessary to emphasize the respect for the rule of law and for the institutions. This is visible already in the statutes of 1272, followed by the statutes of the customs house (1277) and several subsequent collections of laws and decrees.[38] All of these laws reflected, of course, their own time and must be judged from that point of view, not from the point of view of our time.

Let me illustrate with one example how high the awareness was of the importance of legality in the daily life of the city-republic. In June of 1556, a sharp conflict broke out in the Senate between two distinguished patricians, ser Paulus de Gradi (Gradić) and ser Bernardus de Çrieua (Crijević). They exchanged insults "in the presence of the exalted Senate" and Gradi—while defending a relative of his—stood up "within eyesight of the Lord Rector and the Council" and said to Çrieua: "If we were outside the Council, I would break your nose." Because of this ser Paulus de Gradi was sentenced to a fine of 30 ducats to be paid on the same day "for it is not good for the welfare of the city that anyone's relative rise against offenders, but courts and judges must be permitted to dispense justice." In addition, another member of the Gradi family was also fined 30 hyperpers (approximately 10 ducats) "because of insolent and offensive words that he has pronounced in the Minor Council in the presence of the Senate defending some of his relatives, because—for the sake of the salvation and welfare of the city—it is unseemly that any relative rise against offenders, but dispensation of justice must be left to city courts."[39]

Dubrovnik did indeed have a developed and complex structure of executive and judiciary institutions, all under the exclusive control of the patricians, whose rules and decisions, judicial or otherwise, were applied with a fair degree of even-handedness both to patricians and commoners.[40] All of this, of course, is very reminiscent of the situation in Venice—not surprisingly so, since the Ragusan institutions took shape mostly under Venetian influence—during the Venetian overlordship of the city between 1205 and 1358. However, it was the local patriciate, organized in its three councils, that implemented, improved, and added to those laws and made the institutions work successfully.[41]

Numerous deposits of money and other treasures by Balkan potentates over a long period are witness to this, but I would like to mention just two cases that illustrate how individuals inside and outside the city saw Dubrovnik at the beginning of the fifteenth century. During a fight between two groups of local people in October 1407, when one participant tried to convince the "Captain of the night," a patrician, to break the law, the captain responded: "We are not in Sclauonia, but in a land of laws and we must do what is lawful."[42] And in 1411, a man who had settled in Dubrovnik one year earlier stated that he had come to that city "to be in a safe place."[43]

It was principally in the Senate that the experience and wisdom, accumulated over the centuries, was concentrated. It was in the Senate that the most important decisions, especially in the area of foreign policy, were made, decisions on which the fate and the survival of the little city-republic frequently depended. But the sense of duty and responsibility was very actively cultivated within the patrician ranks in spite of many infractions of such principles.[44]

I shall give here only two illustrations of this point: when the plague struck Dubrovnik in 1439, in March of that year the Major Council enacted extraordinary measures to protect the city, with the following explanation: "Since it is a fact that in this present life there is no sweeter, dearer and to a free man more dignified thing than the well-being of his own fatherland, for which every good citizen must be vigilant at all times, now is the moment to preserve it, for the honor, benefit and glory and reputation which is derived from it, as well as for our immaculate freedom and unity."[45] Another clear example of the Ragusan notion of duty to the community is found in a decision of the Major Council of December 2, 1527: "Justice and good habits require that those who receive benefits and convenience from their fatherland should also feel some inconvenience and that they should help and support the fatherland with deed and word as much as they can and know how."[46]

The prudence and wisdom of the old Ragusan statesmen were, no doubt, the fruit of their personal experiences, but they were also influenced by their education. Many of the young patricians were educated in Dubrovnik itself, in elementary schools, and after 1430 also in the local high school. Quite a number of them were sent to study at Italian universities (Padua, Siena, Bologna) or in Paris.[47] Furthermore, young patricians entered very early into family business and were given low-echelon duties in the administration of the state. Thus, they gained experience in the business and political worlds by observing their elders at work.[48]

It is hard to overestimate the significance of the uninterrupted continuity of transmission of accumulated experience from generation to generation within the patrician families. This continuity of elites, in Dubrovnik as in Venice, was of greatest importance for the survival of the city until, beginning in the seventeenth century with the drastic decline in patrician numbers—accelerated by the catastrophic earthquake of April 6, 1667—the Ragusan patricians lost some of their famous political acumen and diplomatic skills.

If one takes a long look at the history of Dubrovnik and of its ruling classes, one observes several main characteristics of their statesmanship: political wisdom and its continuity; long-term thinking and the ability to compromise; careful study of each action and decision and meticulous calculation of its short- and long-term consequences; experience and caution; pragmatism and flexibility. The survival of Dubrovnik as an independent state in this precarious geopolitical situation depended very heavily on those qualities of its leaders. It depended also on Dubrovnik's wealth, which the government used wisely to bribe, cajole, and befriend its dangerous neighbors and its powerful protectors. Thus, it is appropriate to say that Dubrovnik indeed maintained for centuries its position as "an island of peace in a turbulent world" not by fighting wars but by using brains and money to its own best advantage.

How does all of this compare with the modern political situation in the Balkans and beyond its borders? Can old Dubrovnik really serve as a paradigm for that troubled part of the world? One thing that all epochs have in common is the desire of people to enjoy decent and normal lives and the hope that their leaders will do their best to meet those expectations. Old Ragusan statesmen tried to reach those goals in ways that reflected their own times. What about the present-day Balkan rulers?

When speaking of the subject, let me say first of all that in my opinion, none of the leaders of Balkan countries has near the sophistication and the qualities that I have enumerated above as characteristic of the old Ragusan statesmanship. Nor does the Western or American leadership fare much better. I am not advocating, of course, the revival of the patriciate or the return to a monopoly of power by the elites (although until recently a much worse monopoly of pseudo-elites dominated the area), but I do think that the lessons of Ragusan and Venetian patricians could be useful for the edification of today's politicians.

In the Balkans, and especially in the area of former Yugoslavia, we are witnessing an extremely short-sighted, narrow-minded, and intolerant policy inspired by nationalism and egoism, which leads to corruption and loss of human values. The selfishness and primitivism of political leaders, combined with the negative attitudes of intellectuals and destructive role of the media, have led the region into the tragic situation in which it is now, and it is hard to see how and when it is going to extricate itself from this predicament (this does not apply to Slovenia, and the other possible exception might be Croatia, but we must wait and see how things develop there).

As for the West and the United States, they have shown hardly more wisdom and statesmanship than did the Balkan politicians. The Western and American policy has been a reactive policy, short-sighted, without long-term planning and careful calculation. It shows enormous ignorance of the history and mentality of the Balkan peoples. The otherwise noble idea that every problem must have a quick solution and that what is good for America and the West must be good for everyone else in the world is too simplistic and unrealistic in situations like the Balkan one. This is why Western politicians and journalists are so surprised and dismayed when their "pet projects" such as "multiethnicism" and "multiculturalism" do not work in the Balkans. Anyone who knows something about the area could have told them so.

Whereas old Dubrovnik was, indeed, "an island of peace in a turbulent world," a truly cosmopolitan city open to the world and to its achievements, the wisdom and statesmanship of old Ragusans, which made it possible, seem to be far beyond the reach of modern Balkan, Western, and American politicians (none of whom I want to call a statesman).

The old Ragusans were guided by two principles, one engraved above the entrance to their strongest fort, the other above the entrance to the halls of governmental councils. The first one read: "NON BENE PRO TOTO LIBERTAS VENDITUR AURO" (Freedom is not sold for all the gold). The second read: "OBLITI PRIVATORUM, PUBLICA CURATE" (Forgetting private affairs, take care of public ones). In addition, they were certainly inspired by the old and wise Latin proverb "QUIDQUID AGIS, PRUDENTER AGAS ET RESPICE FINEM" (Whatever you do, do it prudently and mind the outcome).

If present-day Balkan leaders were inspired by those principles and if Western and American politicians made an effort to learn a little more about that part of the world, we might, maybe, see better days in that region, but I for one am not very optimistic in that respect.

5 Transhumance

WAYNE S. VUCINICH

Since medieval times the pastoral people in Bileća Rudine in eastern Herzegovina practiced transhumance[1] (see Map 1). They drove their animals from arid areas at lower elevations to higher ones where both water and grass were more plentiful. This pastoral practice was not unique to the Balkan region and could be found in other parts of the world. In Bileća Rudine, the summer transhumance customarily lasted from one to four days, and included herds of about 150 sheep and goats and a dozen or so of cattle.[2] The transfer of animals was managed by teams of three to four persons, occasionally aided by one or two others, when needed. Not all the animals were sent to the mountain pastures. Some were kept at home to provide food for those who had stayed behind.

The practice of transhumance has a long history in the Balkans. When the Slav tribes first arrived there in the sixth and seventh centuries, they found their Balkan predecessors organized into tribes that owned herds of animals, which they protected and cared for, just as the Slavs themselves had done in their Carpathian homeland.[3] Over time the Slavs mingled with and assimilated those whom they found in the Balkans, along with their culture.

Some Slavic tribes gradually descended to the lowlands, where they merged with the local inhabitants into the sedentary *župas* (parish-like communities). The establishment of *župas* and feudalization progressed more in some than in other regions. It did not reach Bosnia and Herzegovina until the arrival of the Turks in the fifteenth century.[4] Tribal organization was more enduring in Montenegro, where tribes did not constitute *župas*.

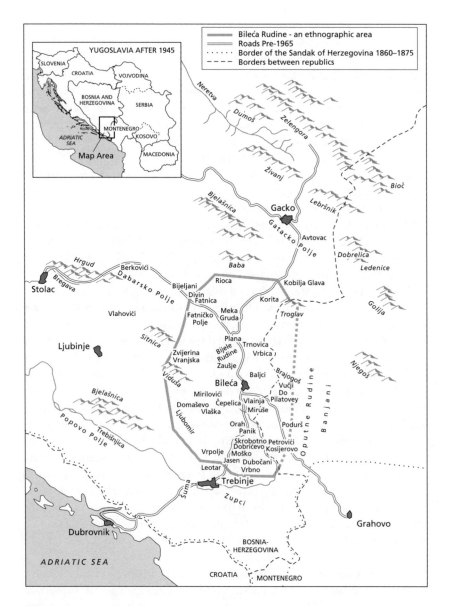

Map 1. BILEĆA RUDINE

SOURCE: Wayne S. Vucinich, *A Study in Social Survival: The Katun in Bileća Rudine* (Denver, Colo.: University of Denver, 1975). Redrawn by Bill Nelson after the original map by Ivo Banac.

Any discussion of *katun*—the mountain pastoral community—and transhumance provokes an excursion into the history of the Vlachs. Much has been written on them, but a complete history is not yet available. Vlachs could be found throughout the Balkans and mixed with other peoples to varying degrees. They engaged in animal breeding and a variety of other pursuits. This chapter is concerned primarily with those who were pastoral. They are especially important for understanding the problem of ethnogenesis in the Balkans.

In modern times some Croats and Muslims used the term *Vlach* pejoratively for Serbs and "outsiders." Further confusion is added by the fact that in some parts of coastal Dalmatia, both the Croats and the Serbs of the hinterland are called Vlachs. In recent times some Yugoslav writers have begun to make distinctions between the pastoral Vlachs and the ethnic Vlachs by writing the former in lower case and the latter with an initial capital. But whatever their origins, various Vlach subgroups were gradually assimilated into larger Balkan subcultures.

For understanding the Vlachs and their history, much has been achieved by the ongoing investigations of archival material in Dubrovnik, Venice, and Istanbul, among other important depositories. The regions of the Yugoslav Karst (limestone high country) once inhabited by Vlachs are being studied with increasing intensity, especially the political, social, and economic relations of the Vlachs with Dubrovnik. There were always important contacts between Dubrovnik and eastern Herzegovina in local and international trade and economic, cultural, political, and religious affairs. The city hired Vlachs as transporters, caravan drivers, craftsmen, farmers, and shepherds. It sent animals via Vlach intermediaries into the mountain pastures occupied by the Ottomans. These shepherds were hired to drive animals from Dubrovnik to the distant mountain pastures in Komarnica, Piva, and Durmitor, a journey that took several days.[5] Dubrovnik also purchased from its hinterland neighbors foodstuffs, cheese, fresh and smoked meats (*kaštradina*), and firewood. The coastal city benefited from regional transit trade and customs duties paid on salt.

In the Ottoman pastoral system, every family in Bileća Rudine knew where it had its mountain pasture and sometimes also its mountain cabin, for the use of which they paid a grass tax (*travarina*) and a cabin tax (*kolibarina*). Their right to annual transhumance was recognized by Ottoman, Austrian, and later Yugoslav authorities. Incidentally, Austria-Hungary was the first to record mountain pasture rights into the cadastral register, which was done to prevent disputes over conflicting claims.[6]

At times, however, transhumance was interrupted by social unrest, plagues, and drought. An example was the peasant upheaval against Turkish oppression from 1875 to 1878. This turbulence, coupled with wars between the Ottomans and the Serbs in Herzegovina and Montenegro, disrupted the regular transhumance and normal pastoral life of the people in Bileća Rudine. Neither my nor any other Christian family could escape this misfortune. My grandfather Jeremije participated in the war as a commander of the Rudine Battalion, made up largely of Montenegrin and Herzegovinian Serbs. Two of his children took part in the conflict as military auxiliaries. A crucial battle was fought at Vučji Do on August 28, 1876, and was won by the Serbs. They—and in particular the Herzegovinian fighters, who experienced the brunt of the fighting—attached considerable significance to this victory over the Ottomans.

The Treaty of Berlin (1878) marked the end of the war and recognized Montenegro and Serbia as independent states. Their borders and those of the Ottoman Empire and Austria-Hungary were fixed. Because my family's mountain pasture (*katun*) in Kručica was left in the Montenegrin Piva region, Austria-Hungary compensated for this loss by giving my family and others a pasture in the Zelengora Mountains in Austria-Hungary. Tranquillity was restored and the practice of transhumance recommenced, but not for long. Violence broke out again in 1881 when the Muslims and the Serbs rose against Austria-Hungary in defiance of the new military conscription law. Once the fighting ended, summer transhumance was restored in the peaceful years that preceded the First World War.

World War I and After

When World War I broke out and Austria-Hungary invaded Serbia in 1914, families in Bileća Rudine were faced with special hardships. At the beginning of the war, Austria-Hungary ordered frontier villagers to withdraw into the interior. My family found refuge with relatives, named Miljanović, who lived in the village of Borlovići, about three kilometers on the other side of the mountain Rogošina. The head of the family, Manojlo, was married to my aunt Jela.

The border region was inhabited mostly by Serbs. Only a few Muslims lived in Borlovići. As always, the Serbs in Herzegovina expressed sympathy for their co-nationals in Montenegro and Serbia and cooperated with them against their common Austro-Hungarian foe. In the first days of the war, the Montenegrins had themselves crossed over the border into

Herzegovina. Three of my cousins from Orah returned from America and volunteered to fight with the Montenegrin and Serbian armies. As it turned out, the Herzegovinian and Montenegrin Serbs were no match for Austria-Hungary. They were defeated in 1916 and placed under a harsh occupation regime. Individuals accused of collaborating with the enemy were seized, tried, and sentenced to prison terms. In many instances, they were hanged in public. To hunt down and arrest Serbs accused of collaboration with the enemy during the war, Austria-Hungary established a special paramilitary force called the *Schutzkorps*. Many Serbs from Bileća Rudine and Montenegro were sent to internment camps.

I remember when, in 1922, long after the war had ended, one of our neighbors, whose family name was Glogovac, at last returned home with his Russian wife. He quickly found out that his family was barely able to feed two additional members, and so found employment for his wife as a cook in the local gendarmerie station at Vraćevica. This helped the family to survive.

My cousin Tripo Petrov, after wandering from one place to another within the monarchy, also finally reached home. Whenever Cousin Tripo would see a group of relatives gathered, he would hasten to join them. He was six feet and three inches tall, handsome and loquacious, and in many ways typical of what some would call *Homo Adriaticus*, a man of the Karst region. Fresh from the Kaiser's army, he was always ready to tell us about his wartime experiences. I wanted him to say something in German so that I could hear how the language sounded. On request Tripo would rise, stand at attention, salute stiffly, and bark out his serial number and rank in German. He loved to impress us with his knowledge of a few German or pidgin German words. While standing at attention, he would say something like: "Melde gehorsamst, Herr Hauptmann! Infanterist Tripo Vucinich, 1. Kompanie, II. Bataillon, des bosnisch-herze-gowinischen Infanterieregiments Nr. 3, . . . nach Mostar." Vigorous applause would encourage Tripo to start another barrage of stories from his wartime experiences, inserting a German word now and then to impress his eager audience.

When the war ended in 1918, the conditions in Bileća Rudine were not stable enough to allow for an immediate return to normal pastoral existence and transhumance. Although people were slowly returning to traditional life, there was still shooting in the hills. This was not a continuation of the war but an insurrection in Montenegro inspired by ideological and political conflicts. The confrontation occurred between the "Whites" and the "Greens" over Montenegro's political future. Most of the Whites favored Montenegro's unconditional union with Serbia under the Karadjordjević dynasty. The Greens wanted either complete independence under the Petrović dynasty, or a South Slav federation of some kind in which the full individuality of Montenegro would be recognized. The Greens and King Nicholas, then in exile, charged that the Whites were installed in power illegally by the Serbs[7] and appealed for allied intervention to rectify the situation. The civil conflict spread beyond the Montenegrin borders into neighboring Herzegovina. I recall vividly when Majo Vujović, one of the last leaders of the predominantly Green insurgents called the Komiti, was killed in Baljci, a village near Bileća. His corpse was brought to Bileća for exhibit.[8] I can still hear Uncle Ivan saying to me one evening, "*Mali, čuvaj se da te Komiti ne ufate!*" ("Little one, be on watch lest the Komiti get you!"). I also remember the time when the local authorities distributed rifles to the men of Bileća to beef up the village gendarmerie if the Komiti attacked. Gradually, the conditions along the Montenegrin border settled down when the Komiti abandoned the fight and laid down their arms. It was once again safe to make the journey to the upland pastures.

Return to Transhumance

Just as we arrived from America in June 1920, ours and three other families decided to resume transhumance, which had been suspended during the war. In cooperation with the *smjes* (associates), the family planned to send what was left of our once large herd of animals to the mountains.[9]

It was not easy to organize transhumance and prepare the mountain cabin in Zelengora for summer occupancy after not having used it for three or more years. Our cabin and appurtenances in the mountains needed cleaning and repair, and the mountain pastures—which had remained unused for a number of years—were overgrown with undesirable grasses.[10] There were also the usual logistical decisions to be made. It took time and effort to prepare for transhumance.

Every year in late May, the interested families met to organize the summer pastoral association and to agree on the chores and responsibilities of the participating families. Those chosen to drive the animals to the mountain and care for them were called the mountaineers (*planinštaci*). The head (*domaćin*) of the mountain group was usually chosen from the family that owned the mountain cabin. In our case, Uncle Rade was a natural choice, having previously served in that capacity, and there was no argument over his selection. He had all the necessary qualifications: he had been in the mountains more than once as the head of a summer pastoral group, and his family owned the mountain cabin. Moreover, he was an amputee and would have been of limited value as a field worker during the summer harvest had he remained at home. His duties as head of the summer family were not difficult. Uncle Rade would manage the summer family, represent it in the *katun* community, and help pack the cheese into goat and sheep bags (sing. *mješina*). He also scrounged for firewood, supervised the milking, kept statistics on milk production, and watched over the health of the animals. Everyone in the village knew who was selected to make the summer mountain trip, what their assignments were, and which animals they would be in charge of during the summer. Each of the cooperating families contributed one or two shepherds. The group also agreed on the amount of food that each family should provide and on the choice of the cheese-maker (*planinka*) and the cheese-maker's assistant (*davijar*), should one be chosen. In some instances an ailing person might be brought along to the mountain for a short period of convalescence. The ailing guests were kept away from food and milk processing for health reasons.

The time I was sent to the mountains, our cheese-maker was Aunt Pava—Uncle Rade's wife. She, too, had previous mountain experience and was regarded as one of the best cheese-makers in the *katun* community. Apart from cheese-making, her other major function was to feed the family and receive visitors. In recognition of her important place in the family, on the eve of the departure for the mountains she was presented with a modest gift as a gesture of the family's gratitude for the hard work she would soon be undertaking. In planning for the transhumance, the participants had to estimate how much food they needed to bring with them to the mountains. Each family also contributed some salt, which was essential for occasional animal feeding, cooking purposes, and for the preservation of cheese. The food brought along consisted primarily of potatoes, maize and wheat flour, beans, pasta, sugar, coffee, and a bottle of brandy (Turkish, *raki*), either plum brandy (*šljivovica*; German, *slivovitz*) or *lozovača* (Italian, *grappa*), consumed exclusively by elders and visitors.

The utensils taken to the mountains included a large, two-liter container used for measuring milk and pouring it into wooden separating bowls, an elliptical water barrel (*burilo*), a pot for making buttermilk, wooden milking buckets, a coal-oil lamp, a couple of large cauldrons, and bedding. A few additional items needed in the cabin had been left behind by previous occupants.

I had to wait four years until I was eleven years of age before I had the opportunity to participate in the summer mountain venture. At the May meeting it was decided where and when the individual families of the summer pastoral group should deliver supplies, and the date of the departure for the mountains was set. When the cooperating parties delivered their animals, food, and freight, they also brought along with them their shares of the grazing tax (*pašarina*) and cabin tax (*kolibarina*), both of them reasonable. The government avoided levying exorbitant taxes on the impoverished peasantry.

Journey to the 'Katun'

It was the year 1924 when I was sent as one of the junior shepherds to help cousin Tripo, fifteen years my senior, drive about thirty head of scrawny cattle. Before the animals were sent off, the head of the *katun* family counted them in the presence of the owner of each herd. When the animals started to move, a few relatives escorted them for two or three miles.

The transhumance was initiated in mid-June and the animals were kept in the mountains until the final days of August. The time of day for the departure to the mountains depended on the distance of the village from the mountain pasture and the intensity of the summer heat. Some villages in Bileća Rudine were closer to the mountains than others. Thus the transhumance could start at dawn, late in the afternoon, or whenever it was most suitable. The time I went to the mountains was unusually hot, and our group departed after the heat subsided, covering only a short distance that first day. Each person carried over his shoulder a native-style bag (*torba*), which contained a lunch consisting of bread, cheese, and a bottle of water.

The shepherd in charge of a herd knew his animals by name and a distinguishing mark of some kind. All herds of our group were delivered to the area near the Mistijalj (*Mistihalj*) church, located near Orah, on the right bank of the Trebišnjica river. The animals quickly became accustomed to the road that would take them to the mountains. It appeared that the summer heat directed them by instinct toward higher elevations.

The shepherds shared the local people's preference for the neglected sections of an ancient Roman road over a better modern one, because they wished to avoid patrols of gendarmes and customs officers. Although in disrepair and more winding, the section of old road was less dusty than the modern state macadam, which was periodically covered with crushed limestone that quickly wore down into white powder. There were always some among the transhumants who from previous experience knew the location of the state-owned cisterns, traditional resting stops, and over-night camping places.

Having traveled the route so often, the peasants also knew which villages along the way were friendly and which were not. Two or three hours after the stock departed, the pack train followed them. Ours was one of very few families that owned a cart, which could be used to transport part of the freight over much of the road. Until the end of the road, cousin Miloš, who was Ivan's son and a man I admired, drove the cart loaded with supplies. The cart also carried our Uncle Rade and Aunt Pava. From the point at which the road abruptly ended on the periphery of the mountains, Uncle Rade and Aunt Pava rode horses. Throughout the journey the animals were driven slowly to allow them to graze along the way.

During the first day of transhumance, the peasants from our neighborhood in Bileća Rudine walked for about two to three hours and then stopped for a short rest (called *ljeljek*) in the vicinity of the villages of Trnovica and Bijele Rudine before resuming the journey. We watered our animals and continued. Although deserted, Trnovica was otherwise known for its busy medieval *karavanserai*, a place for people and animals to rest and store supplies. A sixteenth-century author reported an instance when a French traveler became ill in Trnovica and sought emergency medical assistance from Dubrovnik, two full days by foot or horse. Unfortunately, travel was difficult and the patient died before the medical aid arrived. Comparable tragedies occurred often along the itinerary.

According to the plan, the pack horses and the loaded carts normally reach the campsite before the shepherds and livestock. My family usually spent the first night somewhere between Planik and Kameno Brdo, about fifteen miles from Orah. One mountain group reached Planik in the early evening, and there we camped, near the village of Korita, not far from Kobilja Glava Mountain.

After reaching the camping ground, the senior members of the group unpacked and unharnessed the horses, started the fire, and prepared freshly ground coffee in Serbian and Turkish style, served in demitasses. Only the elders could partake of the coffee. When the animals arrived, they were milked, and the milk was boiled in large cauldrons. Some was consumed that very evening at dinnertime, and the rest was converted into cottage cheese. The whey (*surutka*) was fed to the dogs or thrown away. When we visited friends or relatives in nearby villages, we usually gave the left-over milk to them. Milk and maize porridge (*pura*, It.

polenta) was the staple diet during the trip and served for both breakfast and dinner. Porridge was easy to make and required little time to prepare.

We do not know when the camping areas along the road to the mountains were established. They usually covered an area of about one square kilometer of leveled ground, and were often situated in a slight hollow. They had easy access to the road and were far enough from the grain fields to prevent the animals from damaging them. In the past, on occasion, a friendly peasant family would invite the older travelers for an evening of conversation and refreshments, and put some of the more precious animals into the host's stables. The other animals were kept close to the campfire.

After dinner, Uncle Rade gave instructions for the second day of the journey. At night, a close watch was kept on the animals. There were no other children to play with, and I therefore mingled with the older members of the group, behaving and talking like one of them. Sometimes Rade and others would stay overnight at Svorcan's, telling stories about the past. Three of my aunts were married to Svorcan men. During World War II the fascists and their allies (*Ustaše*) murdered more than a hundred Serbs here and threw their bodies into a nearby cave. Today a monument with the names of those who perished stands there.

Early in the morning, after breakfast, every person received the daily ration of bread and cheese and a bottle of water. The light stock was sent off first and the packhorses (or cart, in our case) followed an hour or two later. The shepherds found driving the stock across the plain of Gacko particularly exasperating. The lush fields of grain and grass attracted the hungry animals, making it difficult to keep them from damaging the crops.

In some rare instances the Serbian peasants resented the intrusion of their co-nationals' animals, but on the whole the Orthodox Serbs were respectful of one another and reduced their bickering to harmless teasing and name-calling.[11]

Soon the heat subsided, drinking water became plentiful, and the walking easier. The road took us through Avtovac, a small fortified town at the head of the Gacko plain. It is often mentioned in epic poems as a onetime stronghold of Muslim feudal lords. This was the domain of the Avdić, Dizdarević, Tanović, and Čengić, feudal landlords who are said to have exacted a lamb from the transhumants on the way to the mountains, and a certain amount of cheese upon their return.

Of the local feudal families, the best known was that of Smail-aga Čengić (1788–1840), who held important positions in the Ottoman feudal system. He fought against the Serb insurgents led by Djordje Petrović ("Karageorge") (1804–1812), and was designated *muselem* (Tur. *müsellem*) of Gacko and put in charge of a large territory. During the rebellion against the Sultanic reforms (*Tanzimat*), Smail-aga stood by the Porte and opposed the Sultan's enemies, including the so-called "Dragon of Bosnia" (Husein-beg Gradaščević, 1802–1833). In 1833, the Sultan gave him the title of *Hadžibaša* (Tur.). Smail-aga (Suleiman) also distinguished himself in the conflict with the Montenegrins at Grahovo (1836), in which eight members of the ruling Petrović family were slaughtered. He fought frequently with the Montenegrin clan Drobnjaci. While collecting taxes in 1840, Smail-aga was killed fighting the Drobnjaci and Moračani tribesmen, who were aided by Bishop Peter II, the highly esteemed poet and ruler of Montenegro. These encounters involving Smail-aga are the subject of an epic poem entitled "Smrt Smail-age Čengića" ("The Death of Smail-age Čengića"), written in 1846 by Ivan Mažuranić, the prominent Croat politician and eminent literary figure.

After bypassing the city of Gacko, a few miles north, at Glavica, just before the first range of mountains, the road suddenly ended. From here onward all supplies had to be transported by horses. Many years after World War II, asphalt was laid in this region, making it possible to truck some of the animals to within two hours of our family's summer cabin in Stari Katun. In my childhood no one could have imagined this progress would be achieved, however modest it was. In 1924, the walk to Stari Katun from Glavica took us by way of a narrow mountain pass across the ravines, through forests, and along the slippery and precarious slopes of deep canyons. At several places we had to ford rapid streams and be on constant guard for sinkholes. The redeeming feature was that the fresh mountain air made the journey invigorating. I do remember one mishap, however. At some point, a small horse loaded with supplies began to sink into a quagmire. The men in the area rushed to save it from certain death. The rescuers put a rope around the horse in a variety of ways and succeeded in rescuing it from catastrophe.

On the second night, the mountaineers from Orah and other villages of Zavodje community usually camped at Lukavica or at Bukova Prodola on the Čemerno Mountain. We arrived there in the late afternoon. Other mountaineers moved into their cabins, which were scattered throughout the vicinity, and followed the standard procedures in unloading and unharnessing the horses, milking the animals, and preparing coffee for the older folks and dinner for all. After eating, we took up positions around the fire, and, as exhausted as we were, had no difficulty falling asleep. Suddenly, in the darkness, a wolf appeared. The animals became agitated and restless. The awakened campers grabbed brands from the fire and began waving them and shouting until the invader disappeared into the darkness of the forest. Early the next morning we started our third and final day, this time driving the animals to Stari Katun, where our cabin and animal stables were located.

Stari Katun was located on Zelengora Mountain, at the point where the borders of Bosnia, Herzegovina, and Montenegro converged. Administratively, it was a part of the Foča district in Bosnia. The summer pastures here drew pastoral people from as far as Stolac, Ljubinje and Popovo Polje in Western Herzegovina. Nearby was the source of the Neretva River (the Roman Narenta), which cuts through solid rock and winds a spectacular course to the Adriatic Sea. At Vita Bara we paused for a brief rest, and then continued for a few hours of slow movement to Stari Katun, arriving there late in the afternoon. After unloading the horses, we took supplies into the mildewed cabin, counted the animals, and milked them. We dusted the cabin superficially, checked and hastily repaired a few holes in the roof, set up the corrals, and drove posts into the ground to which some of the heavy stock would be fettered.

In the meantime, the small animals were allowed to graze near the cabin. After dinner, Uncle Rade assigned herding duties and explained at which place the animals should start grazing. On all sides there was knee-high grass. Uncle Rade reminded us again that the animals should start grazing away from the cabin in order to prevent them from trampling the grass around the cabin.

Zelengora abounds in rich pastures, numerous brooks and streams, and seven minuscule lakes; its forests consist mostly of beech, fir, pine, and maple, and of the local conifer called *omorica*.[12]

Daily Life in the 'Katun'

Each morning, the sheep, goats, and cows were separated from their yearlings. Experienced shepherds were put in charge of the sheep and goats, while the children, like me, were to watch over the lambs and calves. An older shepherd was put in charge of the cattle, which did not require much attention and largely took care of themselves. It did not take us long to adjust to our daily routine. After a couple of days of rest, the horses and their drivers returned to Orah, where they were needed for heavy seasonal work such as threshing grain and transporting it to storage.

Once the hay was cut and other major summer tasks completed, the horses would be sent back to the mountains to pick up what cheese had accumulated.

Although there was ample leisure time in the mountains, we did not forget that the main reason we were there was to take care of the animals and process the milk. During the first week or two in the mountains, the animals were milked twice a day. They were sent out to pasture early in the morning (*popas, popasak*) in close proximity to the cabin, and returned to the base at about nine o'clock in the morning to be milked (*jutrina*). Afterward, they were again dispatched to the pasture until the evening milking (*večerina*). When the grass near the cabin became depleted, the animals were driven further away in search of good pasture.

It was important to ascertain the volume of milk produced by the animals of each family member, because this would avert any later dispute over the division of the cheese. One day in July, the livestock was returned from the pasture earlier than usual to measure the amount of milk that each individual herd of the pastoral group produced. In my youth, the milk was measured by a 1.25-liter aluminum cup (*šalica*), while in the more distant past this was done by a large wooden dipper (*saplak*). The measured milk would indicate the quantity of cheese a particular herd could be expected to produce. Because the production of milk varied from time to time, the milk was measured once more later in the summer. By that time the quantity of milk produced by the animals had reached a plateau. While measuring milk was usually done twice during the summer, in some instances this was done three times. The herds of individual families were measured under the close supervision of a member of the family that owned the particular herd of animals. The head of the mountain family and the owner of the herd recorded the figures.

To make sure that none of the light stock had strayed away or had been lost to predators, the animals were counted each evening before they were sent into corrals and stables. They were counted either one by one (*pojedinačno*) or two at a time (*udvojeno*). While being counted, the animal was tapped by a crook, cane, stick, or by hand. Pointing at an animal with a finger was avoided, as it was believed that the animal may cease producing milk as a result.[13]

The animals were milked in a ritualized manner. A number of women, each with a wooden stool and a wooden milk bucket in hand, moved from one cow to another and milked them, while two or more shepherdesses sat at the entrance of the corral with buckets held between their feet, and milked sheep and goats as they entered the gate of the corral. The collected milk was called *jomuža*. When there was a need to produce a special kind of dairy product, the milk of the cows, sheep, and goats was kept separate. After the animals were milked, the yearlings were released from their closures and corrals to suckle from their mothers for a while.

The accumulated mixed milk had to be quickly processed, since there were no cooling facilities. After being strained through woolen cheesecloth to eliminate impurities, the milk was poured into cauldrons and boiled. The foam collected on the boiled milk was skimmed in order to obtain better-quality curd. Part of the boiled milk was put aside to be converted into sour milk and *kefir* (a fermented-milk beverage), while most of it was used for making cheese. The peasants in Orah did not drink raw milk. They made two kinds of cheese; one of these was *kajmak*, a native cream cheese, and the other *torotan*, a rock solid and heavily salted cheese. (The former did well at the market, but not the latter.) Furthermore, during the intermediate stages of cheese-making, a variety of other dairy products were concocted and consumed, adding variety to the peasants' diets and minimizing waste.

In making cheese, the boiled milk was poured out into two separating (skimming) bowls. During the two-day cooling period, curd (*kajmak* [*kaymak*, Tur.] or *skorup*) gathered on top of the milk. In cooler weather the milk was kept longer in the bowls, producing more curd and better *kajmak*. The curd was eaten fresh ("young" or *mladi kajmak*) or collected and put into a tall wooden vat (*kaca*), tapered toward the top, and salted to taste. In the bottom of the vat there was a hole through which the excess liquid drained. Every day fresh curd was put into the vat and salted. After the vat was filled and the curd matured into *kajmak*, the contents was taken out, drained, salted once more, if necessary, and put into a skin bag (from sheep or goats [Ser. *mješina*]). The bottom of the skin bag had to be left untied in order to drain the last drops of liquid whey, or *surutka*. After the whey was completely drained, the skin bag was tied and put aside in the *ćiler* to mature. The *kajmak* of better quality and taste was first placed into a cask and later stuffed into the skin bag. While the cheese-maker customarily put the *kajmak* into skin bags, the *domaćin* was the one who stuffed the cheese into the skin bag. To avoid spoilage, the cheese was packed in a way that would leave no air pockets inside the bag.

Finally, it should be noted that the people of Bileća Rudine rarely made butter because it could not be refrigerated or easily marketed. However, it was made occasionally for medicinal dietary purposes, that is, to aid ailing family members. One way of making it was to put sour milk (*kiselo [kisjelo] mlijeko*) in a churn (*stap*)—a one-meter-high rounded wooden container—and beat it with a wooden plunger until the butter was separated from the whey. After this, the butter was removed and washed in fresh water several times.

Another way of making butter was to put curd in a churn and beat it with a plunger until butter was produced. The whey that was left was boiled with rennet (*sirište, maja*; Lat. *abamasus*) to yield a product resembling cottage cheese (*provara, furda*; Tur. *hurda*; Per. *hurde*), sometimes called "fasting cheese" (*posni sir*) because it had low fat content. The product could be consumed fresh or allowed to harden into a granulated cheese. The natives called this latter, heavily-salted cheese *torotan*, a favorite of the people of Bileća Rudine. The remaining whey was normally thrown out, fed to the dogs, or taken as a laxative.

The peasants of Bileća Rudine also made what they called solid cheese. It was of low quality but locally cherished. After the curd was removed from the wooden bowls and placed into vats, the milk that was left was poured into a pot and warmed. After this, rennet was put into the pot and the mass was stirred, keeping it warm in order to hasten the process of conversion to cheese. In less than thirty minutes the milk began to harden and turn into cheese.

The cheese, which the peasants call "whole cheese," (*cijeli sir*) was made from fresh milk after the cream (*povlaka*) had been removed. The milk was strained, put on the fire and warmed; the rennet, also warmed, was then put into it. At first in lumps, the cheese was squeezed, and then drained through a cheesecloth (*cjedilo*). After this, it was cut up into small pieces, squeezed again, and drained, salted, and placed into wooden bowls to dry. In a few days, when about 20–30 kilograms of cheese was accumulated, it was packed into a skin bag. Sometimes the "whole cheese" was shaped into cakes (*prevlaka, preska, gruda*), or into something that was supposed to look like a bird (*tica*). The "birds" were passed on as gifts.

On occasion, in late summer, when the sheep milk became heavier, a special beverage called *gruševina* or *gruščevina* was made. The milk was strained, poured into a pot, a pinch of salt added, then put on a low fire and stirred until it boiled. After the water had evaporated and the contents thickened, it became *gruševina*.

Flora, Fauna, and 'Vila'

Of wild animals, the most common on Zelengora were deer, wild goats, wolves, bears, and boars. There were also such common animals as rabbits, fox, martens, hedgehogs, and weasels, and many species of birds, including ducks, which my uncle hunted. The most abundant and dreaded snakes were vipers (*šargan*).[14] Bears were few in number, and killing them was prohibited. One night a bear appeared in the *katun*, and the animals started to stampede. We went into battle. As on previous occasions, people grabbed firebrands, rushed out of their cabins, and waved and shouted at the top of their lungs until the animal ran back into the woods.

I enjoyed the mountain because there was always something new to see. Every day, for hours, I would stand at the foot of a high cliff watching the wild goats feed, jump over precipices, and dislodge loose boulders that rolled, bounced, and crashed to the ground with a thunderous noise. The banks of tiny brooks all around were carpeted with wild strawberries. Having been fed as a youngster on stories about nymphs (*vilas*), I thought that Zelengora's high peaks and deep canyons must be a perfect habitat for them. Always on guard, as a young shepherd I tried not to be caught alone in the woods lest a fairy or some other supernatural force confront me. My fears were strengthened by the strange noises emanating from the forest.

Vila, a supernatural being who figures prominently in Serbian epic poetry, is usually depicted as a beautiful young maiden in transparent robes. Her beauty, however, is sometimes detracted from by horse, donkey, or goat legs. Vila is born out of dew and herbs, and her habitats are the mountains, trees, plants, clouds, and lakes. She is a miraculous healer and is sometimes seen as a friend, mother, or blood sister of the great epic heroes, but she can also be mean and vindictive. She often figures in the epic poems about Marko Kraljević, the great Serbian medieval hero.[15]

Until World War II, the pastoral community in Stari Katun consisted of about ten cabins (sing. *koliba*), nearly all of them built around the turn of the century. Our community was located about a mile from the main pass in order to discourage visitors. The cabins were located near a spring (*česma*, from Turkish *çeşçme*) and were small, covering about fifteen by twenty feet. Their walls were built from unmortared stones (*sušica*), three to four feet high and about two feet thick. Our cabin was covered with a shingle roof. Cabins in some other *katuns* (such as that in nearby Poljana, and *katuns* at lower elevations) had roofs covered with rye straw. The end walls were pitched to about eight feet. Heavy beams were placed on the walls, usually two on each side, and were joined in the corners. The ridge-pole and the wooden plates on the two side walls supported the rafters connected by purlins. The Drinjaci, as the people who lived in the region were called (after the river Drina nearby), were the master-builders of the local-style cabins.

The thresholds of the cabins were high and the entrances low. When entering the cabins, adults had to crouch so as not to bang their foreheads on the doorframe. The entrance was closed with wooden shutters attached to beams on either side with iron clamps. To one side of the entrance into the cabin was a stone bench about a foot and a half high, two feet wide, and five feet long.

Life in the mountain cabin was not always pleasant. The fire in the open hearth kept the cabin full of smoke, and the inside of the cabin was stuffy from the powerful smell of dairy products. It was difficult to keep the cabin clean. Fortunately, the darkness inside kept the fly population down. Nonetheless, pesky flies regularly landed on unwashed utensils. The cheese-maker tried to keep the cabin clean, but was hampered by the cramped quarters and primitive utensils. On the outside, the cabin was surrounded by animal refuse. In the mountains, outhouses were nonexistent.

The light for the entire cabin was provided by two tiny windows. A hearth was usually located in the middle but could be closer to one end of the cabin. A fire was built upon occupancy and it burned until the end of the summer. On two sides of the hearth were foot-high wooden platforms, which served as beds. Our cabin had only one such platform and the cheese-maker slept on it. Most of the rest of the family slept in the attic of the calf stable (*telećar*). Along the wall at one end of the cabin, there were double-tier bunks with straw mattresses, a feature not common in traditional mountain cabins. In 1924, I was assigned the upper bunk, and Uncle Rade, the head of the family, whose one leg had been amputated at the knee, slept in the lower bunk.

Night after night, until overcome by sleep, I lay in horror, watching squealing rats playing games along the ledges a few inches away. It was a frightening experience for a youngster who had been told on many occasions tales about rats, which ate human ears, noses, and even gouged out eyes! The sole bedding consisted of heavy blankets of prickly goat hair. At one end of the room was a round table, one foot high and three feet in diameter (Tur. *sinija*; Per. *sini*), and at the other end bedding (*spremište*) was kept, consisting of straw mattresses and a few blankets. Some of the floor was pounded dirt. Pushed to one side of the cabin was a large flour box (*ambar* or *hambar*; Tur. *ambar*; Per. *anbar*). Either strips of dry, resinous pine (*luč*) or a coal oil lamp were sparingly used for lighting.[16]

There were also other problems. The animal shelters were neither adequate, nor kept in order. During protracted rainy weather, when the animals were kept in corrals and stables, the more fragile among them, especially the lambs, were kept from the pastures. The corrals were rarely cleaned, and the heavy stock, especially during the rains, stood deep in manure.

In the mountains one went to bed early and rose early. Occasionally during the week, in the evenings, and on Sundays and holidays, the people of the *katun* met in someone's cabin for a social get-together (*sijelo*). There they sang and told stories about the old days. There was frequently someone present who played the *gusle*, a one-stringed instrument and symbol of Serbian patriotic identity. At such gatherings, the mountaineers also played games, of which the most popular was the ring (*prsten*) game. This is a simple game in which the initiator surreptitiously deposits a small ring in the clenched fist of one of the other players. A contestant then must guess who has the ring. With a correct guess, the player becomes the new initiator; failures are rewarded with forceful belt lashes across the hand.

No one read in the evening because hardly anyone was literate and there was no light, except the meager illumination coming through the door and from the fire in the hearth.

In the mountains, a great deal of camaraderie was generated among the shepherds. But mountaineers also suffered hardships; they sometimes became ill and this created problems. As there was no doctor in the vicinity, seriously ill patients had to be taken over the mountains on horseback to a doctor in Foča, almost twenty miles away. Fortunately, no one was seriously ill during my tour of duty in the mountains.

The biggest daily event in the mountains was the evening dinner, which followed the milking of the animals and the boiling of the milk. A typical meal in the mornings and evenings consisted of *pura* and *tsitsvara*, the more elegant version of it, enriched with cheese and prepared for special occasions. From time to time we had heavy soup for dinner called *čorba* (Tur. *çorba*; Per. *šurba*), a type of unsalted *Gulaschsuppe* usually based on mutton. The cook put in *kajmak*, dry beans, pasta, maize, turnips, potatoes, and anything else she had at her disposal. From time to time, the *katun* family slaughtered a lamb or a sheep and shared it with the neighbors. The tastiest meal was roast meat with potatoes.

The shepherds' midday lunch consisted of a substantial piece of rye or maize bread (made of mixed flour), with a generous portion of fresh cheese, or *kajmak*. The shepherd took the lunch with him tucked into a small goat- or sheep-skin bag (*brzar*). Though the food in the mountains was monotonous, no different from that in the village, there was an abundance of it. The only difference between the diet in the village and that in the *katun* was that in the latter, more cheese and milk was consumed. Because of rich food, the mountaineers gained weight. Should a shepherd lose weight in the mountains, which was unusual, the cheese-maker was blamed (*"slaba ti je bila planinka-maja"*). Yet all participants in the summer transhumance were aware that the more dairy products they consumed, the less they would take home, so they avoided extravagance in food consumption.

In the mountains, the herdsmen had a great deal of leisure time. The principal holiday during the summer was St. Elijah's Day, which by the Orthodox calendar came on August 2. On that day, people from the neighboring villages and the *katuns* gathered on top of a prominent hill nearby to picnic, sing, dance, and tell stories. The young men competed in simple peasant contests, such as stone-throwing and jumping, both of them popular in the region. Peasants from the nearby Bosnian villages brought apples, pears, and plums, as well as other edibles for sale. A few persons came from the town of Foča about twenty miles away. These side attractions made the gathering all the more colorful.

Love that led to marriage between natives and summer visitors was not unusual. However, both sides tended to an old adage, "Pick your greens from around yourself" (*Beri zelje oko sebe*). The men of Bileća Rudine say sarcastically that when a woman from Bileća Rudine fails to find a husband in the vicinity of her home, she can always find one in Foča. There is also a local saying that "There is no place to which a female cannot adjust!" (*Nema mjesta gde se žensko ne može snaći*).

The peasants believed in the healing powers of mountain air, water, and good food. From time to time, ailing relatives visited the mountaineers to take advantage of abundant dairy products and fresh air and water.

While an occasional visitor from the village may break the monotony in the mountains, the visit also added to the daily social activity in the small and overcrowded mountain families. Besides caring for livestock and entertaining visitors, the mountaineers spent time carving wood and making wooden spoons and forks, spindles, distaffs, flutes, bowls, cigarette holders, tobacco boxes, tool handles, boxes, canes, smoking pipes, and other items. Some of the more talented men carved *gusle*, the one-stringed instrument. As a rule, however, year after year, the peasants carved the same kind of articles and in the same style. The standard ornamentation was usually patterned after patriotic and religious symbols. The women and girls knitted woolen sweaters and stockings.

Not everyone was preoccupied with crafts and art. Cousin Maksim, several years my senior, manifested a degree of business ingenuity. He organized a group of us youngsters to dig *čemerika* (*veratrum*), a medicinal herb, which grew in abundance in the mountains. The plant is tall and poisonous, and has a fibrous root (stock) and an erect stem with broad leaves. We gathered a large quantity of this plant during the summer while in the mountains, which Maksim transported by horses to Foča or Kalinovik several miles across the mountains, and from there it was forwarded to a pharmaceutical firm abroad.

In my spare time, I spent hours walking through the forest, searching for the initials preeminent men in Bileća Rudine had carved into the bark of beech and maple trees. I enjoyed reading and deciphering these engravings, some of which were of men who had long ago emigrated to America. An equally favored outdoor pastime of the younger members of the mountain family was an activity akin to sledding. For hours on end, my cousin Luka Radovanov and I would climb the grassy and unwooded Javorak hill, sit on broad, smooth pine planks, and slide down the slope at a speed just short of reckless.

At different times during the summer, some members of the families who had been left at home to harvest the crops were sent to the mountains to deliver fresh supplies and bring back some of the accumulated cheese and *kajmak*. Such visits often occurred during St. Elijah's Day on August 2, and Assumption Day (*Preobraženije*) on August 19. At this time, there was a lot to do in the mountains: caring for the animals, milking, preparing meals, building the fire, processing the milk, unloading and loading the freight, and finally driving the animals back home. Some items had to be returned to the village and others stored in the cabin for next year.

Transhumance During and After World War II

World War II profoundly affected the pastoral economy of Bileća Rudine. It discouraged livestock breeding and forced the suspension of transhumance. Native resistance to the Axis Powers swept Bileća Rudine and the Croatian *Ustaše* failed to hold the territory they had momentarily occupied. The civil war between Draža Mihailović's Četniks (Serbian nationalists) and Josip Broz Tito's Partisans (Communists) was fought there intermittently for control of Bileća Rudine. By the end of the war, the local economy was in a shambles, the rural population of Bileća Rudine was greatly reduced, and a great deal of their livestock had been decimated.[17]

Much of the wartime fighting between the Četnik and Partisan resistance forces, and between the Partisan and Axis forces, occurred in the same mountains to which the animals were sent for summer grazing. Some of the fiercest battles fought during the war took place on the river Sutjeska in the Zelengora mountains. The Communists celebrated the Battle of Sutjeska, which occurred at the end of May, 1943, as one of their greatest wartime victories.[18]

The conditions of war and civil strife caused a shortage of food and forced peasants to slaughter many of their animals. Italian and German occupation authorities requisitioned livestock to feed troops. The Italians also purchased and shipped home a large number of animals. The Četniks and Partisans requisitioned or confiscated livestock as a punitive measure meted out to ideological opponents. Thievery of animals during the war was widespread, and the mountain cabins owned by transhumants were occupied at times by guerrilla forces.

After the war, the Communist government discouraged transhumance, viewing it as an outdated and inefficient system of livestock breeding, ignoring the fact that in advanced countries such as Austria, Italy, Switzerland, France, and even the United States, animal breeders still engaged in transhumance of varying kinds.[19] The major agricultural policies of the Communist government were detrimental to private animal breeding. A particularly harmful measure was the 1945 Law on Agrarian Reform and Resettlement, which denied peasants the use and ownership of the mountain pastures.

The Land Reform and Resettlement Law of 1945 nationalized much of the private land and limited private land ownership to ten hectares. The Republican Executive Council made exceptions where families were large and owned land of marginal quality.[20] In Bileća Rudine, where the land was poor, families were permitted to own fifteen hectares of land and sometimes more. Land belonging to absentee landlords, "war criminals," and churches and monasteries were nationalized and transferred to collective and state farms. The Law of 1945 also provided for the migration and colonization of the Bileća Rudine peasantry to the fertile lands of the Vojvodina.

By reducing the peasant population and restricting landed property, especially forests and pastures, the Communist state undermined the pastoral economy. Traditional animal husbandry received an additional blow when, in 1947, the government assigned most of the mountain pastures to state-owned livestock-breeding farms. Nearly all the mountain pastures of Zelengora (except Vita Bara), Tovarnica, Kladovo Polje, Babin Do, and a part of Treskavica were turned over to the state animal farms.[21] The Communist planners expected the state pastoral farms to improve the pastures and to produce more and better-quality stock. The reduction of common pastures (*utrina*) in Bileća Rudine adversely affected the size and health of the herds of cattle and sheep.[22] Most of the grazing land had come under state and communal control with only a fraction of it remaining in private hands.[23] Although by 1951 the number of livestock had greatly declined, it still exceeded the size of the available pasture land.

The Communist planners tried a variety of innovations to promote livestock breeding and improve the dairy industry. The large "Miro Popara" State Farm, with its headquarters at Kalinovik, controlled a huge acreage of pasture land and much livestock. This ambitious plan offered considerable promise, but mismanagement and miscalculation impeded it. After the abandonment of forced collectivization of agriculture in 1953, various other measures were taken to stimulate private agriculture and animal breeding, and transhumance was neglected.[24]

For a number of years after 1945, the "old" regulation, dating from the Bogumil and Ottoman days, governed the use of the mountain pastures. Careless use of pastures caused heavy damages to them. In some places the wooded areas adjoining the pastures were devastated.[25] For a time after 1945, the pastures were entrusted to the forest and agricultural administrations. Direct responsibility for the pastures was passed on to republican, regional, and district authorities. In 1959, the management of pastures was entrusted to the agricultural cooperatives and eventually to the communal governments. These frequent changes in the administration were accompanied by neglect of the pastures.

The nationalization and collectivization of land radically changed the land tenure system in eastern Herzegovina. In 1952, some mountain pastures were turned over to the peasant worker cooperatives, and they took charge of land cultivation and livestock breeding. Under the peasant working cooperatives, the mountain pastures were allowed to deteriorate. Traditional grazing rights were ignored and the forests were cut indiscriminately. Once dense forests (such as Bukov Do and Visočica) were reduced to a few trees. The loss of trees caused ground erosion, and what had been once green and lush was turned into bare rock. The forests surrounding pastures, except those in Tovarnica, Zelengora, and Ulobić, were particularly damaged. The area covered by pasture land had rapidly shrunk because nothing was done to prevent overgrazing or to protect pastures from the growth of undesirable grasses. The shepherds grazed their animals on the choicest pastures, ignoring the condition of the pasture and the type of animal that grazed on it. After the

war, the peasants also paid little attention to the markers that set the
katuns apart. For a time, the families that engaged in transhumance under the sponsorship of the working cooperatives drove the stock not to
traditional *katuns* but to those assigned to them.

It soon became clear that animal breeding by the working cooperatives and the state animal farms was not yielding the anticipated results. Moreover, cooperative animal breeding proved too costly, and the
production of meat and dairy products continued to slacken. Therefore,
the government organized so-called "pasturing cooperatives" (*pašarinske
zadruge*) on the village and communal levels, and pasture lands were assigned to them.[26] Those who joined these cooperatives were promised
the use of mountain pastures, with the hope that in time the pasturing
cooperatives would win the peasants' support. Where there were no pasturing cooperatives, the peasant working cooperatives would provide
mountain pastures for their members.[27]

Pasturing cooperatives, established in 1952, accepted animals from
all owners, regardless of whether they had previously engaged in transhumance. Some peasants welcomed the new cooperatives because they
lacked both working hands and the financial means needed to send their
animals to summer pastures.[28] These newly distributed mountain pastures were assigned to villages and communes. Where there were no
pasturing cooperatives, the general agrarian cooperatives organized the
movement of stock to the mountains on their own. However, Article 30
of the Law on Pasture prevented the owners of livestock from entering
into animal pasturing arrangements with private persons.[29] Needless to
say, the state policies discouraged livestock breeding practices.

The Agrarian Reform Law of 1945 and the Law of 1952 on public
land ownership, while limiting the size of privately owned land, put no
limitation on the number of livestock that an individual or group could
own. However, by reducing the size of village and mountain pastures,
the scope of animal breeding was reduced. The government therefore
found it necessary to stimulate livestock breeding. In 1952–53, it permitted the breakup of the peasant working cooperatives and relaxed the
drive to collectivize livestock herds. Some mountain pasture lands
(Brekov Do, Treskavica) were returned to earlier users. The peasants who
engaged in transhumance were obliged to pay a grass tax for each animal and were prohibited from taking goats to the mountains.[30]

The uncertainty that accompanied the changing economic situation,
the exodus of the rural population to the towns, and the state's policy of
forced deliveries (*obavezni otkup*) of animals at dictated prices discouraged animal breeding.[31] Market and price controls and the government's

interference with the peasants' economic activity compelled many peasants to abandon animal husbandry.[32]

A Final Word

At the end of that summer in 1924, when my group returned to the village after a summer in the mountains, the trek back was much like the one to the mountain. When the animals were within two kilometers of home, they were met by a fresh team of herdsmen drawn from *smjesa* families to help drive them the rest of the way to the family corrals. As for me, I left the group at Podosoje for my home in Bileća, where my nuclear family had moved after our extended family had split up. Bileća was less than a mile away from the place where I had begun my mountain journey.

Before breaking up the herds, the animals were counted and claimed by their respective owners. The skin bags of collected hard and soft cheese were brought into the house and stables at Uncle Rade's house. He was the head of the *smjesa*. Soon, on a designated day (usually Sunday), the members of the *smjesa* would meet to divide the accrued cheese and celebrate the successful mission. Since it had already been established how much milk each participant's animals produced, there was no difficulty in dividing the cheese.

The skin bags of cheese were weighed on old Turkish scales, *kantar*, (from Ar. *quintar*; Lat. *centenarius*) in *okas* (Tur. *okka*) and divided, each member of the *smjes* receiving his share. If there was cheese and any other food left over, it was also divided among the cooperating families. Any expenses incurred by the family during the summer were paid by the *smjesa*, but each *smjesnik* assumed the loss for any of his animals. After the dairy products and provisions were divided and accounts settled, members of these families feasted on a dinner of *tsitsvara*, cooked in *kajmak* and cheese, brought from the mountains. The dinner marked the end of *smjesa*.

Some of the animals that had spent the summer in the mountains were sold, some slaughtered and smoked, and the rest of them were kept. The smoked meat (*kaštradina*; *suvo meso*) was consumed during the winter months, and those meats sent to market were often traded in Konavle in exchange for wine, brandy (*grappa*), *šljivovica*, and dry figs— items needed for the holiday season (especially Christmas and Patron Saint feast) and weddings, if any were planned. Autumn was the best time to market the animals, because it was then that they weighed the most and brought the best price. Each family was obliged to sell a number of its animals in order to obtain the cash needed to buy additional cereals and animal fodder, neither of which the peasant could produce in sufficient quantities on his limited and barren soil.

The reader should be reminded that I was taken to the mountains at a time when there were already ample signs of the weakening of the pastoral life and economy. The peasants had to do a great deal of improvising on traditional practices. The decline of the local pastoral economy, which had begun before World War I, was hastened during the war and in the inter-war period. World War II and the communist revolution that followed accelerated the dying out of the pastoral economy in Bileća Rudine. Communist land reforms led to the end of the traditional pastoral life as I have just described it.

Many years after my experience in 1924, during a 1970 visit to my relatives in Bileća, Danica, and Zora, I drove via automobile with them to meet the shepherds driving animals that were returning from their summer sojourn. Our assignment was to welcome cousin Jovana, who had married into the Tabaković family, who lived in Podosoje, near Bileća. Jovana had been chosen to be her family's cheese-maker summer after summer. From our vantage point atop a hill, we could see waves of animal herds approaching from a mile away, driven by shepherds toward their village homes. It was a dramatic moment—a closing chapter in the pastoral economy of Bileća Rudine.

PART II

Yugoslavia and After?

6 South Slav Education

Was There Yugoslavism?

CHARLES JELAVICH

The Emergence of Yugoslavism

In the decade before World War I, and even earlier, the nationalist aspirations of peoples of East Central Europe, especially those of the Habsburg Empire, were enthusiastically espoused by the Gladstonian-Wilsonian idealists. Give the people their freedom and the proverbial millennium will have been achieved. These opinions were often found in British, French, and American newspapers and periodicals. Perhaps the best expression of this sentiment with respect to the South Slavs was made in 1918 by Robert Joseph Kerner, an American authority on Yugoslavia, who, in an article entitled "The Jugo-Slav Movement" wrote:

If there are miracles in history, the Jugo-Slav movement is a miracle. . . . Religious differences, political rivalries, linguistic quibbles and the petty foibles of centuries appeared to be forgotten in the three short years which elapsed from Kumanovo to the destruction of Serbia in 1915. The Greater Serbia idea had really perished in 1915 as had the Greater Croatia idea in 1878. In their place emerged Jugo-Slavia. . . . Nationalism had proved stronger than opposing religions, more cohesive than political and economic interests. . . . The Jugo-Slav movement had ended in the formation of a nation which is neither a doctrine, nor a dream but a reality.[1]

Today Yugoslavia does not exist, nor, parenthetically, does Czechoslovakia. Although there were different issues and circumstances that contributed to the dismemberment of these states, they had one factor in common, namely, their education systems had not succeeded in creating a sense of identity within its citizenry given their multiethnic, multireligious, multicultural, and multilinguistic character.

In 1807 Fichte, in one of his addresses to the German nation, questioned the wisdom of spending "the largest part of the state's income . . . on the maintenance of standing armies," when, instead, he believed, "the state which introduced universally the national education proposed by us, from the moment that a new generation of youths had passed through it, would need no special army at all, but would have in them an army such as no age has yet seen,"[2] which others paraphrased as "a good education system is worth an army." Fichte's point was that if a people could identify with the nation's history, literature, culture, traditions, and so forth, the prospects for its success were almost guaranteed. It would be supported voluntarily in peace and war through the patriotism and loyalty of its citizenry. Bismarck was reported to have stated that the German nation was created by its schoolmasters.

My attention to the role of education within the South Slav kingdom was stimulated through discussions about Serbian and South Slav history I had in 1948–49 with Slobodan Jovanović, the most distinguished Serbian historian of the modern era. In discussing the brief fate of Yugoslavia, he stated that if one wanted to comprehend why South Slav unity had not developed in this period, one should carefully study the prewar and interwar education systems. He stressed that in order to understand why the interwar kingdom had been less than successful, one had to examine what the educated classes, that is, ministers, bureaucrats, legislators, mayors, councilmen, teachers, officers, clergy, and others, who assumed positions of leadership in the interwar decades, had been taught before 1914 and, more important, what the students in the interwar decades had learned about their own history and that of the other nations in the new state. Or to phrase it differently, did the Yugoslav concept supercede the Serbianism, Croatianism, and Slovenianism of the prewar decades? He was firm in his belief that one could not fully appreciate the historical development of the South Slavs without this background. Moreover, he reiterated a number of times that Yugoslav unity would require at least a century of peace and prosperity in which the citizenry through education would come to know, understand, appreciate, and respect the historical background and traditions of all its inhabitants. "We only had two decades in which to achieve this," he reiterated several times. The purpose of my paper is to examine his premise. It is based on a study of the prewar and interwar education systems and about 350 prewar and 200 interwar history, geography, literature, and religious textbooks and grammars.[3]

It is generally accepted that the South Slav state founded on December 1, 1918 was inspired by Yugoslavism, yet it was not called Yugosla-

via but the Kingdom of the Serbs, Croats, and Slovenes. There is no document that defines Yugoslavism. For some it meant the union of Serbia
and Montenegro with the South Slavs of the Dual Monarchy. For others
it represented only the unification of the South Slavs of the Habsburg
Empire, which it was hoped would lead to Trialism. Viktor Novak's *Antologija Jugoslavenske misli i narodnog jedinstva, 1390–1930* (Anthology of the Yugoslav Idea and National Unity, 1390–1930) records the
evolution of the idea of Yugoslav national unity, but also reveals differ-
ing views and approaches to it; it can be read as an exposé of the nebulous character of Yugoslavism.[4] Hence in this chapter Yugoslavism will
be considered information fostered by the education system and found
in the textbooks that prepared the students to accept the unification of
the Serbs, Croats, and Slovenes as one nation in a single state. Thus in
time *narodno jedinstvo* (national unity) would take precedence over national or tribal (*pleme*) identities and loyalties, that is, students would
proudly call themselves Yugoslavs and only then Serbs, Croats, and
Slovenes. The non-Slavs, the Albanians, Germans, Greeks, Hungarians,
Romanians, Turks, and others, were not a part of the equation.

The Yugoslav Idea in Serbian, Croatian, and Slovene Education

Notwithstanding the support that Yugoslavism enjoyed among
many intellectuals, students, and some politicians, as well as among
sympathizers in the Western states before Sarajevo, this sentiment was
not reflected in the prewar education systems and textbooks.[5] In Serbia,
from its independence in 1878 until 1914, the national goal was to liberate and unite all those lands in which Serbs lived and thus were considered part of the Serbian homeland. These lands included Croatia,
Slavonia, Dalmatia, Istria, Bosnia-Herzegovina, Old Serbia, Macedonia,
and Vojvodina. The only territory of the future Yugoslavia not included
was Slovenia, in which the štokavian dialect was not spoken. In all the
other lands a variant of štokavian was spoken, which was associated
with the linguistic contributions of Vuk Stefanović Karadžić, who was
identified in the textbooks as the greatest Serb of the modern period.
The issue of the Catholic Croats and Bosnian Muslims was met by identifying them as Serbs of the Catholic and Islamic faiths. In literature, the
Croatian authors and their works, which were rarely mentioned, were
described in the Serbian readers (*čitanke*) as the Serbian "Western" or
"Catholic" literature. The Latin alphabet was never taught in the Serbian
elementary schools before 1914, one of the goals advocated by supporters

of *narodno jedinstvo*. Consequently, 95 percent of the students whose education ended with the fourth grade were not prepared to read Croatian contributions. The extent to which the education system was focused exclusively on Serbian education is demonstrated by a political decision taken during the Balkan Wars.

Hoping to capitalize on the support for Serbia found in Croatia, in particular among intellectuals and students during the Bosnian crisis, 1908–1909, and the Balkan Wars, the minister of education, Ljubomir Stojanović, issued a directive in 1912 that "public, school and teachers' libraries and reading rooms" should purchase publications of the *Matica hrvatska* and *Društo hrvatskih književnika* in order to further Serbian "cultural unity" with the Croats.[6] In 1913 a committee to review elementary school readers, led by Jovan Skerlić, a strong advocate of South Slav cooperation and unity, recommended that "more space should be given to Croatian literature, at least as much space as there was in Croatian school readers for Serbian literature."[7] With the exception of this attempt and several geography and history textbooks published in 1912 and 1913 that sought to introduce some information about the Croats and Slovenes—without, however, having a tangible influence on Serbian education, which was disrupted by World War I—Serbian students were taught Serbianism, as their parents and grandparents had been. In the thirty-five years since gaining independence, Serbia had developed a good education system. Through their history, geography, literature, and religion textbooks, including grammars, students were well prepared to understand Serbia's historical development and to take pride in being Serbs. Fichte's dictum—"a good education system is worth an army"— had been realized.

In Croatia, Croatianism prevailed, notwithstanding the contents of textbooks, which could be construed as fostering South Slav unity and Yugoslavism. After gaining control of its education in 1868, in 1874 Croatia drafted its own education system, which was secularized over the strong objections of both the Catholic and Orthodox Church authorities. Since about one-fourth of the population in Croatia and Slavonia was Serbian, largely in the Vojna Krajina, the principal goal of the Croatian authorities was to gain the loyalty of the Serbian students, who were well aware of the call from Belgrade for the unification of all Serbs within the Serbian kingdom. Hoping to counteract this, 15–25 percent of the contents in Croatian readers was devoted to Serbian topics, printed in Cyrillic. Thus Croatian children learned about the Nemanja dynasty, Tsar Dušan's empire, the battle of Kosovo, Karadjordje, the Serbian revolution, and Vuk Karadžić, and they read extensively from selections of Serbian authors. The Croatian anti-Serbian Starčevićites and Frankovites never ceased criticizing the Croatian authorities and authors for being adherents of Karadžić's linguistic reforms, whose followers they derisively called the Vukovites. It must also be stressed that since 1861 the Cyrillic alphabet was taught in the second grade of the Croatian elementary schools, whereas, as noted earlier, Latin was never taught in the Serbian elementary schools before 1914. The language issue was sensitive and as late as 1909 attempts were made in the Croatian *sabor*, or assembly, to abolish the teaching of Cyrillic, precisely in the period when the Croatian-Serbian Coalition was most successful.

In contrast to the Serbian geography books, which identified all lands inhabited by štokavian speakers as Serbian, the Croatian textbooks did not advance claims to lands beyond the Habsburg Empire. They did, however, use the historic argument to defend their interests in Bosnia-Herzegovina even though the Orthodox and Muslims represented more than three-fourths of the population. No concessions were made to Serbian claims to Dalmatia, where the Serbs numbered less than 10 percent. The textbooks also provided very brief information on the history, customs, and literature of the Slovenes. Although some might contend that there was enough factual information on the Serbs and Slovenes to be the basis on which South Slav unity and even Yugoslavism could have been taught, the Croatian education system stressed Croatianism, not Yugoslavism. The goal was to instill in the students love for Croatia, its history, and traditions and to advance calls for the administrative unification of the lands of the Triune Kingdom of Croatia, Slavonia, and Dalmatia. The information on the Serbs in large measure was designed to preserve the integrity of the Croatian lands, not to foster Yugoslavism. Moreover, even if there had been an inclination to foster Yugoslavism, the Croatian authors and authorities would have opened themselves to charges of treason by Vienna and Budapest.

Unlike Serbia and Croatia, which established their own education laws, Slovenia, as a constituent part of the Austrian half of the Dual Monarchy, was subject to the imperial education law of 1869. Consequently, Slovenes abided by its terms. Yet paradoxically, the Austrian education system, in which the teaching of the cultural history of all the peoples of the empire was the norm, in effect made it possible to have information in the textbooks that was more favorable to the idea of Yugoslav unity. Thus, for example, a Slovenian student learned not only about the two dominant nations, the Austrians and Magyars, but also about the Czechs, Slovaks, Poles, and Romanians, as well as the Serbs and Croats. The latter two were presented as one people, who spoke the same language

called either Serbo-Croatian (*Srbohrvatije*) or Serbian or Croatian, written in two scripts. Even the Bosnian Muslims were presented as one
with the Serbs and Croats. Furthermore, Dalmatia was described as being inhabited by a single Serbo-Croatian nationality (*Srbsko-hrvatske
narodnosti*). The Serbs and Croats were only divided by religion. Serbian
and Croatian history was presented in the best romantic tradition, with
special attention given to the resistance to the Ottomans. The lessons
to be learned from the Battles of Kosovo and Siget (Szigetvár) were that
betrayal leads to national defeat and disgrace, whereas unity instills
pride and loyalty. The Montenegrins, who were regarded as Serbs, were
put forth as ones to be emulated by all who loved their nation.

Thus although it is possible to infer that information in support of
South Slav unity was presented, it had not permeated the Slovenian textbooks. The opposite was the case. The textbooks stressed undivided loyalty to the emperor, empire, and Catholicism. It was not South Slav unity
that the Slovenes sought, but the administrative unity of the Slovenes'
lands and control of their own schools.

In article 3 in its ultimatum to Serbia after the assassination, the
Habsburg government demanded that all textbooks containing information that advanced claims to lands within the empire be removed. Serbia
agreed to comply.[8] For the preceding decade Vienna had been increasingly convinced that its South Slav subjects had succumbed to the bugle-
call of Yugoslavism. Whereas individuals among the South Slavs espoused South Slav unity and there was much written about this in other
countries, the evidence found in the Serbian, Croatian, and Slovenian education systems does not confirm the existence of such unity. Instead
the dominant theme in each state was to further its own national interests, that is, Serbianism, Croatianism, or Slovenianism. In other words, the
evidence today is that 1914 cannot be construed as the dawn of South
Slav unity; rather it represents the benchmark to demonstrate the limited degree to which Yugoslavism had penetrated prewar education and
prepared the future leaders of the kingdom to rally behind it and lead the
new state. Hence the crucial test for Fichte's dictum would be the interwar years.

The Impact of Regional Differences and Political
Debates on Yugoslav Education

The immediate euphoria surrounding the formation of the kingdom on December 1, 1918, did not extend through the month. There
were many reasons, in part the legacy of the war. For example, the con-

stant friction between the Serbian government and the Yugoslav Committee over political leadership and the future structure of the new kingdom, disputes over Bosnia, and clashes of personalities all led to suspicion and mistrust in Belgrade, Zagreb, and Ljubljana. Coupled with these issues was the Italian threat to Dalmatia and the social unrest in the former Habsburg lands, which Serbian forces were called upon to suppress. The most serious problem was the formation of a new government and the adoption of a constitution, which affected all developments, including education, in the interwar years.[9]

In the thirty months between the creation of the kingdom and the adoption of the Vidovdan constitution, June 28, 1921, the debates over the principles on which the constitution should be based—centralism or federalism—became increasingly divisive and acrimonious.[10] By 53 percent, the assembly endorsed centralism, which was supported largely by the Serbs and modeled on their prewar constitution. In other words, 47 percent of the representatives, who opposed centralism, voted against the constitution, abstained, or, in the case of the Croats, walked out, hardly an expression of confidence in the future of the multinational, multicultural, multireligious, and multilinguistic state. It is important to stress that a swing vote of fourteen would have rejected the constitution.

The acrimony and bitterness of this period was never overcome and affected the remaining years of the kingdom. In the first decade, when political stability was most essential, the kingdom had seven prime ministers and twenty-four cabinet reorganizations, an average of one every five months. In 1928, after Stjepan Radić, the Croatian Peasant Party leader, was assassinated by a Montenegrin Serb in the skupština, King Alexander introduced his royal dictatorship. The state now became the Kingdom of Yugoslavia, whose motto was "one state, one nation, one king," which was a tacit admission that Yugoslavism as a concept had not been embraced by the citizenry. This point was reinforced when the new royalist constitution of 1931 reorganized the kingdom into provinces called *banovine*, in which the historical and national entities—Serbia, Croatia, Slovenia, and so on—were no longer identified on any contemporary maps, further confirmation of the strength of South Slav tribalism. In 1934 King Alexander was assassinated by Croatian Ustaše, with support from Macedonians, Hungarians, and Italians. In 1939 the *sporazum* (agreement) was reached with the Croats, and in April 1941 the kingdom was dismembered after the Nazi conquest. It was within this political, social, and economic context that the extent to which Yugoslavism had become an integral part of South Slav education must be examined.

The royalist government understood well that a major road to national unity led through education. Hence one of its first decisions was to call for uniform centralized education. However, the same issues that divided the skupština in its debates on the constitution, that is, centralism and federalism, surfaced in education. The two dominant Serbian political parties, Nikola Pašic's Radical Party and Svetozar Pribićević and Ljubomir Davidović's Democratic Party, supported centralism. Pribićević, a Serb from Croatia and wartime leader of the Croat-Serb Coalition, served as minister of interior in the first postwar regime and subsequently on three occasions as minister of education. He used both positions to further centralism. His supporters adamantly insisted that he was a committed Yugoslavist, whereas his critics charged that his Yugoslavism was a cover for Greater Serbianism. Pribićević repeatedly stressed that the Serbs, Croats, and Slovenes were one nation with three names (troimeni narod). He and his followers argued that historical differences in language, culture, and religion would vanish once the Yugoslavist unitarist view of South Slav history was accepted. From their point of view it was precisely because of their vast differences in educational development and historical experiences that nation-building mandated that the government impose a centralized education program. In simple terms they were determined through education to forge Yugoslavs out of Serbs, Croats, and Slovenes, thereby relegating their tribal identities to history. For their own political reasons the Agrarians, Yugoslav Muslims, and Slovene liberals also supported centralized education. The Croats and Slovenes rejected it. Having gained control of education from the Magyars in 1868, the Croats were not prepared to yield to Belgrade's centralism or what they perceived as a cover for Greater Serbianism. The Slovenes, in exchange for supporting Belgrade on some issues, were granted control over their education, including the foundation of the University of Ljubljana. They were not ready to surrender it on behalf of centralism or a nebulous Yugoslavism.[11]

The problems that the government would face surfaced with the report of the first committee appointed by the minister of education to examine the prewar education laws, practices, and curriculums in all the South Slav lands and to submit proposals for education. Acting hastily, the committee called for a single uniform education system and curriculum for the elementary schools.[12] Immediately the report was strongly criticized by teachers, education organizations, and even many politicians. They not only challenged the competence of the committee members but, more important, they charged that the committee had not taken into consideration the diverse educational experiences of the South Slavs.

In addition, since the committee was dominated by Serbs, suspicions grew that Belgrade's aim was to impose Serbia's prewar education system on the other lands.

The challenge had merit. The kingdom had inherited seven education systems. Serbia, Montenegro, and Croatia each had its own. Slovenia and Dalmatia were under the jurisdiction of Austria; Vojvodina was with the Kingdom of Hungary; and Bosnia-Herzegovina were administered jointly by the Dual Monarchy. Macedonia and Kosovo, which the Serbs acquired after the Balkan Wars, were never fully integrated into the Serbian system before World War I. The contrast in educational experiences was overwhelming. In parts of Slovenia eight grades of elementary schooling was the norm, whereas in regions of Macedonia and Kosovo schools were nonexistent. In Croatia and Serbia the norm was four years of elementary education, yet over half the eligible students did not attend school. In Slovenia literacy was above 85 percent, in Serbia and Croatia it was about 50 percent, and, of course, in some regions of Macedonia and Kosovo there was total illiteracy. Given these facts, the government's only alternative was to appoint a new committee whose members were better informed on the task before them.

Obviously it was not feasible to close all the schools until the new committee, comprising qualified representatives from all regions, submitted its recommendation. Hence, the committee proposed that until such time as a law was enacted the constituent parts of the kingdom should follow their respective prewar education laws, directives, regulations, and textbooks. There were thirty-seven regulations affecting education; the principal law in Serbia dated from 1904, in Croatia from 1888, and in Slovenia from 1869.[13] As for the textbooks, it was proposed that Serbian and Croatian readers should contain one another's selections, printed in both alphabets, as well as contributions in Slovenian; the Slovenian readers should present selections in Serbo-Croatian. The secondary school history books should include a brief history of the other two nations' pasts. With each new revision or edition, however, this material should be expanded until such time as an "ideal textbook" was produced in which the history of all peoples was presented in "equal proportions."[14] Thus, whereas the government's intent was to have a single, uniform, centralized education system in place, the committee advocated the continuation of the prewar "decentralized" system, which meant that Croatia, Slovenia, and Dalmatia, as well as the lands under Serbian control, would operate as separate entities in education. In fact, no education laws were enacted before 1929. As will be shown below, in effect the students in the 1920s were being educated in Serbianism,

Croatianism, and Slovenianism, as their parents had been. Or to phrase it differently, Yugoslavism had not emerged as the state concept. It must be stressed that this decision was made a year before the Vidovdan Constitution was adopted and in the period when passionate debates were held over the character and future of the kingdom.

In the lead article in the first postwar issue of *Učitelj* (Teacher), the prewar journal of the Serbian Teachers Society, which now served that function for the newly organized Yugoslav Teachers Society, Jovan P. Jovanović, its editor, precisely defined the problem the government would face in education. He wrote that the National Assembly would soon begin its deliberation on the constitution, which would end in the proclamation of "the unity of the Serbs, Croats, and Slovenes in one state, with one government and one law." However, he reminded all that it would only

be state and territorial unity not national. Three regions would be united in one state but not three tribes (*pleme*) in one nation. The Serbs, Croats, and Slovenes would remain citizens in one state, but they would not feel themselves members of one nation because the tribal difference, tribal feelings, and tribal patriotism created over the centuries could not instantly be eliminated by some laws and some proclamations. These tribal differences, tribal feelings and tribal patriotism could only be eliminated by the same means by which they had been created and that is by the education of future generations, who, in the future national schools, would be inspired with national feelings in place of tribal sentiments which had inspired the present generation of Serbian, Croatian and Slovenian tribes.[15]

Jovan Jovanović, in effect, had stated what Slobodan Jovanović would reiterate about three decades later. It would not be incorrect to conclude that the decision made in 1920 to carry on with the prewar education laws, which remained in effect until 1929, was the major factor determining why Yugoslavism had not developed within education.

Notwithstanding the vital role that the government assigned to education in unifying the nation, its actions belied its intent. There were thirteen changes at the head of the ministry of education, involving ten individuals, in the decade before the dictatorship—an average of one every nine months. With the possible exception of Milan Grol, 1927–28, none of the ministers had developed education plans, nor were they knowledgeable about education. Each minister appointed committees to study proposals for new laws, curriculums, and so forth. His successor disregarded the work of his predecessor and appointed other committees to study the same issues. In addition, in the parliamentary debates there is no convincing evidence that the ministers made concerted efforts to defend their budgets. Without strong leadership, it was inevitable that tribal politics would intrude into the education process, a concern addressed in numerous articles in the education journals.[16]

The first issue to raise suspicions and mistrust was the unilateral extension of Serbian education laws and practices into Vojvodina and Montenegro, which suggested to many Greater Serbianism. It was followed by the proposal that the birthday of Sveti Sava, the patron saint of the Serbs, and the anniversary of the Battle of Kosovo, June 28, be honored as national holidays. While acknowledging the significance of both events for the Serbian nation, the Croats, Slovenes, Bosnian Muslims, and others protested that they were not relevant to their respective histories. Perhaps the reactions would not have been so strong had the issues not come up during the divisive debates over the Vidovdan constitution. Subsequently, Croatian teachers charged that their nation's educational needs were being slighted in preference for those in Macedonia and Kosovo. Charges were also made that priority was given to Serbs for government stipends. The most frequently heard Serbian rebuttal to the anti-Serbian criticisms was that South Slav unity was being thwarted primarily because the Croats and Slovenes had not liberated themselves from the Catholic Austrian anti-Yugoslav influence that had permeated their prewar education. A few remarked that the University of Zagreb was a German university where courses were taught in Croatian. The purpose in pointing out these issues is to provide some indication of how sensitive the discussions had become.[17]

Not only did the government fail to provide effective leadership in education but also the teachers failed. The Belgrade based *Jugoslovensko učiteljsko društvo* (Yugoslav Teachers Society), the successor of the prewar *Srpsko učiteljsko društvo* (Serbian Teachers Society), became the strongest advocate of centralized education and was perceived by others as an organ of the government. Although Croatian teachers joined the *Jugoslovensko učiteljsko druuštvo*, the overwhelming majority retained their membership in the *Savez hrvatskih učitejskih društava* (Union of Croatian Teachers Societies). Its goal was to maintain Croatian control over education and to extend its influence into Dalmatia. Slovenian teachers also joined the Belgrade organization but, as in Croatia, the overwhelming majority supported their own Slovenian teachers' society. Their goal was to develop and strengthen Slovenian education and identity through their own schools and not have the nation absorbed into the amorphous Yugoslavism.[18]

Another criticism was that secondary education received higher priority than elementary education. About 90 percent of all students never advanced beyond the fourth grade, where Serbianism, Croatianism, and

Slovenianism were entrenched and were stimulated and exploited by tribal politicians, teachers, and clergy. In 1919, 1921, 1925, 1927, and 1928, draft laws for elementary education were prepared but never implemented. Even the repeated calls for eight years of compulsory schooling remained illusory. At the same time, however, secondary school reform became controversial. By placing greater emphasis on secondary education, the expectation was that its graduates would become the "apostles" of *narodno jedinstvo*. However, the criticism quickly centered on the merits of the three gymnasiums—classical, *realna*, and *realka*. Critics charged that the classical, with its emphasis on Greek and Latin, was elitist, whose sole function was to prepare students for the universities. In addition, its costs far outweighed the benefits to society. They preferred that resources be invested in the *realna* gymnasium and *realka* that trained students to serve the needs of modern society, for example, in business, commerce, trade, and teaching. Disputes also revolved around the "national" subjects, that is, geography, literature/grammar, religion, and history.[19]

To commemorate the creation of the kingdom on its tenth anniversary, in 1928 the government published the three-volume *Jubilarni zbornik*, whose purpose was to record its history and achievements. In his report on education, Milan Grol, the minister, discussed four subjects—elementary and secondary education, the role of teachers, and the government. He repeated the government's call for centralized elementary and secondary education, noting that there were thirty-seven "regional laws [regulations, directives] for public schools," inherited from the prewar years. He reemphasized the demand to have eight grades of compulsory education. He noted that secondary education suffered not only because of the diversity in curriculums but also because "deep traditions" and "mentalities" thwarted reforms in the gymnasiums. Yet a major obstacle in education was the shortage of teachers; only one-third had qualified teacher training. As a result, Russians, refugees from the revolution, became teachers who "without even knowing the language taught even national subjects," that is, geography, literature, grammar, and history.[20]

Grol's radical proposal concerned the government's role in education. Without rejecting centralized control of education, he foresaw the need to grant greater local autonomy to the schools. "By reducing the exclusive authority of the minister of education, decentralization would create a condition for the complete independence of teachers and thereby also the depoliticization of education." Henceforth all education officials would be "forbidden to be agitators or party candidates."[21] Grol, in effect, had admitted that no significant progress had been made in education and that local control of education demanded by the Croats and Slovenes could not be ignored. This point was best illustrated when Grol discussed the role of "national" subjects. "Teaching the mother tongue, especially Serbo-Croatian, and teaching history and literature, and in connection with them the question of textbooks, will for a long time present a most difficult task—very difficult in the clearly homogeneous regions of this or that tribe and especially complicated for the transitional zones [areas with mixed populations]."[22] This statement could be the epitaph for interwar education, because throughout these years the teaching of languages, history, geography, and literature remained steeped in their respective national identities, not in Yugoslavism or South Slav unity.

The Development of Education under Royal Dictatorship

The assassination of Stjepan Radić in 1928, following the constant parliamentary turmoil and political unrest in the country, ended whatever chance there had been for the greater local autonomy Grol was advocating. It also ended whatever hope there may have been to reconcile the differences that had emerged between the Serbs and Croats, because now the Croatian electorate turned against the very concept of the Yugoslav state. Thus on January 6, 1929, King Alexander introduced his dictatorship—"one state, one nation, one king"—in the newly proclaimed Kingdom of Yugoslavia. His goal was to create the Yugoslavs that had eluded the regime for a decade. Whereas hitherto no education laws had been enacted, six were enacted in the fall of 1929. They dealt with elementary, secondary, and teachers' schools; textbooks; religion; and the chief educational council. The government reaffirmed its call for centralized education, in which the minister of justice would review the laws, measures, and directives recommended by the minister of education, which would also require the approval of the ministerial council. These steps led to firmer political control over education. The government also decreed that education would reflect the ideology of the state, that is, *narodno jedinstvo* or Yugoslavism, which would be achieved through common textbooks. An oath would be required of teachers' loyalty to the Yugoslav idea and their adherence to the curriculum. Teachers also were expected to perform community service. In addition, all regional teachers' societies were disbanded except the Belgrade-based Yugoslav Teachers Society, which the government would use to convey its views on education.[23]

The task before the state was clearly stated by Voj. Petković, the editor of *Učitelj*, in the lead article addressing the opening of the first school year, 1930–31, after adoption of the education laws of 1929. Petković noted that there was considerable discussion regarding the merits of American, English, French, German, and Russian pedagogy, which had long traditions. Given the brief history of the kingdom a Yugoslav pedagogy had not developed: "Nor could any kind of Yugoslav pedagogy be created even if it had been intensively pursued. For such a task much time was necessary—decades and decades—because it must be based on deep understanding of traditions and the needs of our people with respect to education and for a deep understanding of the soul of our nation in all regions of our fatherland." Yet a Yugoslav pedagogy was required because "a great Yugoslav people exists, a strong Yugoslav state exists and our Yugoslav ideology exits."[24] In effect, what Petković wrote is what Grol had conceded in his report and what, in 1920, Jovan P. Jovanović, the postwar editor of *Učitelj*, had written would be the task confronting education, that is, making a Yugoslav nation out of three tribes.

In August 1931 the strongest case for Yugoslavism was made at the eleventh convention of the Yugoslav Teachers Society. Led by King Alexander, there were talks by Božidar Maksimović, the minister of education, Damnian Rasić, the president of the Yugoslav Teachers Society, Boško Bošković, a representative of the secondary school Yugoslav Professors Association, and Vladimir Ćorović, the historian.

In a letter, hand-written in the Latin script, King Alexander stated:

The Yugoslav teachers, imbued with love for their people and for their difficult but exalted calling, are the architects of the national soul, its national conscience and culture. In order that they respond completely to the wishes and hopes which their king and nation has entrusted to them, the Yugoslav Teachers Society, uniting all current and future Yugoslav teachers, must be the focus of education, the pillar of Yugoslav nationalism and stimulus for all the beautiful aspirations in the future of Yugoslavia.[25]

Maksimović called upon the teachers "to be the apostles of brotherly love for the young Yugoslav generations, the narrators of true unity, the teachers of a broad and healthy nationalism." Their task was to "unite into a single soul, one muscle, and one heart, which is the task of culture and education, whose development and success you serve."[26] Rasić reminded the teachers that because of the decade of partisanship "which nourished tribal, regional and religious differences that fragmented and jeopardized the existence of the state," the king had liquidated (*likvidacija*) "tribal and regional" organizations. Now all teachers should rally behind the Yugoslav idea.[27] Bošković stated that elementary school teachers instilled "basic national conscience and national feeling" in the students, while the secondary school teachers were responsible for developing "general culture, spirit, heart, and will-power." He stressed that "there is no well-being for our people without a pure unequivocal and deep conscience and that from Triglav to Kajmakčalan there is only one and the same people, one and the same idea, one sentiment and good will and there is no well-being for this nation without the deepest love for every region, for every corner of our vast land and its good people." Furthermore, a new student newspaper, *Jugoslovenče* (Little Yugoslav), would be published to foster understanding among the students.[28] It was left to Ćorović to put the Yugoslav idea in historical perspective. In the best tradition of romantic historic nationalism, he recounted the history of the South Slavs in the Balkans, taking note of their medieval states, their successes and failures, the hardships they endured under foreign domination, and finally the triumph they achieved in 1918. The key, however, was that when the Serbs fled northward to escape the Ottomans "a biological unity (*biološkog jedinstva*) [of the Serbs, Croats, and Slovenes] took place. In our blood no longer is there any difference. Thus the process of coming to know one another accelerated and progressed. . . . The task for all of us, and especially our national teachers, is that we create generations for whom cultural and political unity will surpass that of all others."[29] The basic theme of all these statements echoed Fichte's dictum: education would produce the Yugoslav citizen necessary for the success of the kingdom.

The teachers welcomed the challenge, believing that now education would receive the high priority it deserved. Since 1920 the Yugoslav Teachers Association had rejected tribal and regional division and was in the forefront of *narodno jedinstvo*. Whereas in the 1920s teachers regularly protested against the intrusion of politics into education, now they accepted it as necessary to rally the South Slavs behind Yugoslav unity. The teachers would indeed become "the pillar of Yugoslav nationalism." However, the enthusiasm generated at the convention was short-lived. In 1932 the minister of education informed the public and teachers that a single elementary school curriculum, one orthography, and uniform textbooks would be introduced and that the Yugoslav Teachers Association would be consulted on issues involving education. In May 1933 it was announced that a curriculum had been completed for elementary schools, that is, four years after the law was enacted. In fact, it was another four years, 1937, before a serious effort was made to implement it but without success.[30] The pronouncements on behalf of Yugoslavism in education had become little more than political rhetoric.

Whatever prospects there may have been for the success of King Alexander's goal of having teachers become the instruments of Yugoslav unity vanished with his assassination. It rallied the Serbs behind their nation as Radić's death had turned the Croats against the Yugoslav experiment. Furthermore, neither Prince Paul nor any of his prime ministers had the commitment or the prestige to carry on the king's plans. In addition, members of the Yugoslav Teachers Association had become disillusioned, not only because the goals they supported were not being realized, but also the Depression precluded any serious support for education. Schools were not being repaired, some even closed, fewer teachers were employed, and so on. By the mid-1930s morale in the ranks of the teachers began to decline. Thus, notwithstanding the abolition of all tribal and teachers' organizations, once again teachers in Croatia and Slovenia, and also Serbia and Bosnia, looked at education from their regional perspective. Furthermore, now the economic security and well-being of the teachers and their own tribal groups came to the forefront at the expense of Yugoslavism in education. Following the *sporazum* with Croatia in 1939, the separatist education interests that began to reemerge among all the nations after the king's assassination now were being openly espoused, especially in Croatia. Yugoslavism as an integral part of education had come to an end.[31]

Textbooks and Yugoslavism

The fate of Yugoslavism can also be studied through textbooks, in particular the four "national" subjects, geography, literature/grammar, religion, and history. However, one point must be made before discussing textbooks. Once the decision was made to permit each tribe to follow its own prewar education and textbooks until new laws were enacted, it was incumbent on the Serbs to introduce Yugoslavism into their textbooks, because it was not found in their prewar books. In contrast, the Croatian and Slovenian textbooks included information that could be interpreted as being in support of Yugoslavism. In other words, the Serbian textbooks had to have at least as much information on the Croats and Slovenes as theirs did on the Serbs or the Serbs would open themselves to the charges of perpetuating Greater Serbianism. Or to put it another way, the Croats and Slovenes did not immediately have to revise radically their prewar textbooks, whereas the Serbs did.

Of the four national subjects, the prewar textbooks on the history of the Orthodox and Catholic religions were not presented in an ecumenical spirit but in a way that stressed their religious differences. The Vidovdan constitution mandated religious toleration, and efforts were made to implement it. Nevertheless, at different times Muslims charged that both the Orthodox and Catholics exhibited a lack of tolerance and discriminated against Islam.[32]

The prewar teaching of geography had also been divisive, with both Serbs and Croats asserting rights to Bosnia, Herzegovina, and Dalmatia. Now, as citizens of one state in which *narodno jedinstvo* was the guiding principle, the prewar claims were foreclosed. Instead the geography books described the topography, beauty, and resources of formerly contested regions and, in addition, reminded the students where a tribal leader had been born, where a monastery or church was located, where battles had been won or lost, where statues of prominent individuals were located, and so forth, which, in the context of the textbook and the prompting of a teacher, would remind students of their historic domains. Thus, geography continued to be a divisive subject, but not as blatantly as before the war.

In one respect the readers were the most important textbooks. The elementary school children learned to read from them and came to know their hometown (*zavičaj*) and region. The secondary school students were exposed to the best of their own and some foreign literature. In the case of the Serbs and Croats a controversy arose regarding the number of selections from the other's literature. In other words, did the authors intentionally over-emphasize their own national literature to the extent that one could contend that South Slav unity was not reflected in the contents? The readers also became a part of the language controversy. Language, which many in the nineteenth century believed would be the bond that united the Serbs and Croats, divided them in the kingdom. Education journals regularly contained articles by Croatian teachers protesting the attempt to introduce ekavian (the Serbian dialect of Serbo-Croatian) readers in Croatian schools. Even before the death of King Alexander there was considerable resistance to ekavian; after his death there was open defiance in the Croatian schools. Thus, in 1938 Zagreb published the journal *Hrvatski jezik* (Croatian Language) to counter Belgrade's *Našjezik* (Our Language), which in effect consolidated the separation of Serbo-Croatian in education. Although the Slovenes agreed to have Serbian and Croatian readings and Cyrillic included in their curriculum, they were determined not to become "Serbo-Croatianized."[33]

The success of Yugoslavism, however, centered on the teaching of history. Its goal was to provide the identity and unity of the Serbs, Croats, and Slovenes, notwithstanding their respective religious, cultural, and political differences over a millennium. The task before the historian was defined by the directive in 1920 that authorized the use of the prewar secondary school textbooks that stipulated adding a chapter on each of the other two nations. With each new revision or edition the chapters would be expanded until an "ideal" history was produced. In effect, these were single volumes with brief separate chapters on the other two nations—or to put it differently, a single history with two appendices, or three histories bound in one volume. They did not present an integrated history of the South Slavs. That is what some historians attempted in the 1930s at the prompting of the dictatorship. Their aim was to allocate approximately proportional space to each nation during comparable historical periods, thus producing a symmetry of South Slav history. The authors who tried to write these "Yugoslav" histories inevitably were forced to omit those periods or events when Serbian and Croatian relations were strained. In other words, they produced romanticized histories that actually detracted from South Slav unity.

The points made above could be demonstrated by an analysis of numerous geography, history, and literature (čitanke) textbooks. Since the government believed that the success of Yugoslavism in the secondary schools was the key to the future of South Slav unity, two history books will be briefly described, one by Stanoje Stanojević, the other by Živko Jakić. Stanojević was a prominent Serbian historian who studied in Vienna, St. Petersburg, and Munich. An author of scores of monographs and articles, he also was the editor of the interwar *Narodna enciklopedia srpsko-hrvatsko-slovenačka* (National Encyclopedia Serbian-Croatian-Slovenian) and the twenty-volume *Srpski narod u XIX veku* (Serbian People in the Nineteenth Century), of which only fifteen volumes were published. His own prewar secondary school history textbook was not authorized by the government in large part because he rejected the romantic historical nationalist presentations that permeated so many other histories. However, as a strong advocate of South Slav unity from the prewar years, in the 1920s his two-volume textbook, now titled *Istorija srpskoga naroda (sa pregledom hrvatske i slovenačke istorije) za srednje i stručne škole* (History of the Serbian People [with a Review of Croatian and Slovenian History] for the Secondary and Vocational schools) was approved.[34]

As the title indicates, this was a history of Serbia with one chapter on the Croats and one on the Slovenes. Collectively the two volumes numbered 266 pages, with 205 on Serbian history, 36 on Croatian, and 13 on

Slovenian. A more revealing figure is that there were 53 pages on the nineteenth century, of which 35 dealt with Serbian affairs, 5 on Croatian, and one and one-half on Slovenian. The remaining pages discussed general themes. What is striking is that there were 12 pages on the Serbian revolution, 1804–15, or twice as many as for Croatia and Slovenia for the entire century. Thus Serbian students could take pride in learning about their history and nation, whereas the information on the Croats and Slovenes, which was factual but brief and dry, would not develop any curiosity. Moreover, as the last two chapters in the book, the history of the Croats and Slovenes appeared to be little more than appendices or afterthoughts, not to be considered seriously. Nothing in the presentation would lead one to believe this was a history of the South Slavs. Instead it was presented as the history of the Serbs, who, after the Serbian revolution, led the way to the unification of the Croats and Slovenes with Serbia. Their contribution could be interpreted as being insignificant in the creation of the kingdom. Even the number of illustrations could leave the same impression. In the 1926 edition there were thirty-five representations of Serbian leaders, monasteries, cities, and so forth, but only two from Croatia—Zagreb and Split—and two from Slovenia—Ljubljana and Maribor. The Serbian illustrations enabled the students to relate to their history; the Croatian and Slovenian could be discounted as not being relevant.

After the dictatorship Stanojević's textbook was now titled *Istorija Jugoslovena (Srba, Hrvata i Slovenaca) za srednje i stručne škole* (History of the Yugoslavs [Serbs, Croats, and Slovenes] for the Secondary and Vocational Schools).[35] Stanojević's revisions were both real and deceptive. First he took the basic information from the Croatian and Slovenian chapters and integrated it with Serbian history at the proper chronological place. It was done by writing transitions or even transposing paragraphs verbatim. More revealing is that throughout the new edition the subject of a sentence or paragraph became "Yugoslav" merely by substituting "Yugoslav" for "Serb" or using the pronoun "our" (*"naš"*). The paragraph remained the same. In other words what was previously presented as Serbian history now became Yugoslav. Thus the introduction of Yugoslavism was being cleverly disguised by the author. Students most likely did not realize what was transpiring, but the teachers surely did. Scores of examples indicating the shift from Serbianism to Yugoslavism could be cited; here only a few from the nineteenth century will be noted. For example: "At the end of the 18th and beginning of the 19th century a new period begins in the history of the Serbian [our] people";[36] "The principal program of Prince Michael was the political unification of the

Serbian [our] people";[37] "Belgrade became the cultural center of all the Serbian [our] people";[38] and "Serbs [Yugoslavs] at the beginning of the 20th century."[39] At the same time Stanojević identified the Croat-Serb Coalition as the "Serbo-Croatian Coalition" and the National Council of Slovenes, Croats, and Serbs as the "National Council of Serbs, Croats, and Slovenes."[40] Within the context of the book, students could rightfully assume that both organizations were inspired and led by Serbs, with the Croats and Slovenes playing a secondary role.

Stanojević's book posed the dilemma that confronted all authors. In his case, he was a strong prewar advocate of South Slav unity, but as the political events of the interwar years unfolded and Yugoslavism became more of an elusive concept, he and most of his Serbian, Croatian, and Slovenian colleagues gradually reverted to the defense of their respective national identities.

In contrast to Stanojević, who was a respected prewar historian, Živko Jakić came into prominence in the 1920s. He did not have the foreign training and scholarly achievements of Stanojević, yet his secondary school history textbook was very successful. Jakić was a professor in the *Državna muška učiteljska škola* (State Men's Teachers School) in Zagreb. Unlike Stanojević, in whose textbook Serbia was the focus, Jakić placed Croatian and South Slav history within a European context, which represented the way history textbooks were structured in the Habsburg Empire. Consequently, in his presentation Jakić pointed out developments unique in Croatian history and those experiences shared with the other South Slavs as a part of European history. It presented the students with a broader perspective of their own historical development.

As a postwar work, Jakić's two-volume *Povijest Srba, Hrvata i Slovenaca za niže razrede srednjih učilista* (History of the Serbs, Croats, and Slovenes for the Lower Grades of the Secondary Schools) sought to produce the government's "ideal" history.[41] For example, the divisions and chapters in Volume One were titled "Introduction to Our National History," "The Oldest Period of Our History," "The Dalmatian Croatian Princes," "The Serbian People," "The Croatian Kingdom," "What It Was Like in Croatia in the Oldest Times," "The Serbian Littoral," "Croatia and the House of Arpad," "Bosnia," "The Nemanjas Create Serbian National Unity," "Croatia and Bosnia during the Last Arpads," "Serbia the Leading State in the Balkans," "Bosnia as the Center of the Croatianserbian [Hrvatskosrpske] State," and "The Internal Conditions in the Croatian Kingdom." Serbian history was not slighted in Volume One or Two.

At the same time Jakić did not gloss over the issues that divided the South Slavs. For example, from the nineteenth century he pointed out that the Serbs and Slovenes did not embrace Gaj's Illyrian movement.[42] He stressed that Prince Michael's goal in the 1860s was the unification of the Serbs, not the Yugoslavs.[43] He described how the strong nationalist movement among the Serbs after 1878 and the strength of Starčević's Party of Right in Croatia, which was strongly anti-Serbian, precluded cooperation during the administration of Ban Khuen-Héderváry.[44] His account of the growth of Yugoslav sentiment from 1903 to 1914 followed the standard interpretations, but he did not discuss the issues that divided the Serbian government and Yugoslav Committee in the war.

Following the dictatorship, with its emphasis on Yugoslavism, in Jakić's new textbook, *Povijest Jugoslavije s općom historijom za IV razred srednjih i njima sličnih škola* (History of Yugoslavia including General History for the Fourth Grade of Secondary and Similar Schools), there were two notable omissions.[45] The differences between the Serbs and Croats at the end of the nineteenth century were deleted. More revealing was his account of the interwar period. It briefly described the unification of the South Slavs, the death of King Peter in 1921, Alexander's proclamation of the Kingdom of Yugoslavia in 1929, and his assassination in 1934. In the next paragraphs he discussed the Treaty of Versailles, the League of Nations, the establishment of the new East European states, the latest developments in electricity, railroads, telephones, x-rays, chemistry, physics, airplanes, and zeppelins. However, there was not one word about the major controversial issues in internal Yugoslav history from 1918 to 1935.[46] Notwithstanding these qualifications, in their totality Jakić's interwar textbooks provided some basis for a discussion of the growth of Yugoslavism with the students. However, the textbooks presented South Slav history as the Croats viewed it. By the mid-1930s, Yugoslavism as a unifying concept was dead for all practical purposes. This point can also be made by briefly examining the way in which Serbian and Croatian historians presented Slovenian history.

Although Stanojević and Jakić purported to write histories of the Serbs, Croats, and Slovenes, in fact they did not. Both gave scant attention to the Slovenes. In his two-volume history Stanojević collectively had thirteen pages on the Slovenes, Jakić only six. The illustrations tell the same story. In Jakić's two volumes (1926–29) there were thirty illustrations from Croatian history, eighteen Serbian, and two Slovenian, the same number of the latter as in Stanojević's textbook. Serbian and Croatian historians worked from the premise that the Slovenes did not have a national history after 843, when they came under Frankish and later German-Habsburg rule. They even slighted their achievements of the nineteenth century. Hence the Slovenes were not considered significant factors in South Slav history. The history books thus give us a good picture of the limited degree to which Yugoslavism was a part of the education system. The same conclusion could be drawn from an examination of the readers and geography books.

Conclusion

Notwithstanding the role that the government assigned to education in developing South Slav unity, support of education did not have high priority. The authorities seemed to believe that simply by issuing decrees, directives, and proclamations the Serbs, Croats, and Slovenes would respond to their call to embrace one another as Yugoslavs. Even the name of the state, the Kingdom of the Serbs, Croats, and Slovenes, not Yugoslavia, reminded its citizens that they were not Yugoslavs. The authorities did not fully appreciate the problem facing the kingdom, but the two editors of *Učitelj*, Jovanović and Petković, did. They stressed that just as each nation had developed traditions, customs, practices, beliefs, and prejudices through education over generations, so too would it take generations for them to develop new loyalties.

The decade of the 1920s sealed whatever chance there might have been for the success of Yugoslavism. By authorizing the use of prewar education laws, curriculums, and textbooks at the time of excessive political, economic, and social turmoil in the kingdom, the perpetuation of Serbianism, Croatianism, and Slovenianism seemed inevitable. It is understandable, therefore, that when problems arose that generated passion and touched on historical traditions, the leaders of each nation sought refuge and guidance in their respective prewar policies, which had served their nations well. Education was not immune to this pressure. Thus when the king sought to impose Yugoslavism through education, he was not only confronting the divisiveness of the 1920s but also the national, religious, cultural, and linguistic experiences of centuries. Fichte's dictum on the importance of education was prophetic— perversely, that is—because it was Serbia that had "a good education system," as did Croatia and Slovenia. Yugoslavia did not. Yugoslavism as a reflection of South Slav unity was not a dominant theme in the textbooks. The evidence in support of this conclusion is demonstrated in the textbooks for the national subjects. Thus, as Slobodan Jovanović noted, in order to succeed the South Slavs would need a century in which education would play a major role in educating the nation, coupled with understanding, prosperity, and peace. The interwar South Slavs did not have that luxury. Parenthetically it should be noted that Tito's claim that socialism would unite not only the South Slavs, but also the non-Slavs of Yugoslavia, was no more successful than the Yugoslavism of the interwar regime. Moreover, the textbooks published since Tito's death, especially those in the 1990s, demonstrate how much they continue to rely on historical Serbianism, Croatianism, and Slovenianism.[47]

7 Yugoslavism versus Serbian, Croatian, and Slovene Nationalism

Political, Ideological, and Cultural Causes
of the Rise and Fall of Yugoslavia

ARNOLD SUPPAN

November 1918

On November 8, 1918, during the Geneva meeting between Nikola Pašić, Ante Trumbić, and Anton Korošec, representatives of the Serbian government, the Yugoslav Committee, and the National Council of Slovenes, Croats, and Serbs, respectively, a Croat compatriot of Trumbić prepared an internal memorandum.

Although the author of the memorandum believed that the bonds between the South Slavs of the former Austria-Hungary and those at home in the kingdoms of Serbia and Montenegro were "the closest and most intimate that can exist among men of the same origin, tongue and blood," a further discussion about the relations between the Yugoslav Committee and Serbian Premier Pašić showed some of the tensions inherent in the Yugoslav unification process. The author was critical of what he called Pašić's "Balkan Prussianism," in that the Serbian leader seemed to be more interested in the creation of a Greater Serbia than a Yugoslavia: "It is the tragedy of history that in this most critical moment for the [Y]ugoslavs there stands at the head of the Serbian Government a man who is . . . the obstacle to a great future of a united [Y]ugoslav nation."

Some historians have argued that the National Council in Zagreb had no other choice but to join with the Serbian government. On October 29, 1918, the Croatian *Sabor* broke off all state links with Austria and Hungary and declared Dalmatia, Croatia, Slavonia, with Rijeka "as a completely independent state." After that the *Sabor* recognized the National Council (Narodno Vijeće) of Slovenes, Croats, and Serbs as the supreme power of the new "State of Slovenes, Croats and Serbs" including Slovenia, Croatia,

Dalmatia, Bosnia-Herzegovina, and Vojvodina—all the South Slav lands in the former Austria-Hungary. "In theory," Ivo Goldstein argues in his new history of Croatia,

the new state could opt for any possibility—to remain independent or to ally itself with other states—but in practice there was almost no choice. No allied government, including that of the United States, would recognize it. . . . During the thirty-odd days of its existence, there was an urgent need to re- solve all the dilemmas facing the state of Slovenes, Croats and Serbs: many matters that would remain important for decades to come had to be decided in that short time.[1]

Indeed, the circumstances of the Serb, Croat, and Slovene state were not promising—neither in foreign nor in internal affairs. But the situa- tion was also difficult in Austria, Hungary, Bulgaria, Poland, Ukraine, and the Baltic states. Already on October 31, 1918, the National Coun- cil in Zagreb "was ready to enter into a common state with Serbia and Montenegro," and as early as November 5, the National Council sent a delegation to the Serbian supreme command, pleading for the entrance of the Serbian army into Croatia-Slavonia. The main reason was not only the Italian occupation of Istrian and Dalmatian towns, but also the widespread turmoil in Northern Croatia and Bosnia-Herzegovina. In Slavonia, armed bands of so-called "green cadres" (mainly former Aus- tro-Hungarian soldiers) plundered and burned landed estates and estate manors, and looted stores. In Bosnia-Herzegovina, Serb peasants rebelled, burning the properties of Muslim feudatories and killing estate supervi- sors. At the same time, Muslim bands from Cazin fell upon Serb villages in neighboring Croatia. By the end of November 1918, the National Coun- cil was increasingly driven to seek Serbian intervention: "The people are in revolt. Total disorganisation prevails. Only the army, moreover only the Serbian army, can restore order."[2]

Svetozar Pribićević, the Serb vice-president of the National Council, became the power arbiter in Zagreb and urged in Belgrade that a com- mon government immediately supplant the "separate" ones. Stjepan Radić, the Prague- and Paris-educated head of the Croat Peasant Party, emerged as his strongest opponent. While fully accepting the dissolution of the Habsburg Monarchy, he now proposed a confederal state headed by three regents (the Serbian king, the Croatian *ban*, and the president of the Slovene National Council), with only three common ministers (for foreign affairs, food distribution, and defense) and six regions with their own parliaments and governments: Slovenia, Croatia-Slavonia, Serbia- Montenegro, Vojvodina, Bosnia-Herzegovina, and Dalmatia. The Central

Committee of the National Council rejected this proposal as an example of "extreme separatism."[3]

The most direct challenge to the Yugoslav unification process was Radić's famous speech to the Central Committee on November 24, 1918:

Gentlemen, . . . you think that it is enough to say that we Croats, Serbs, and Slovenes are one people because we speak one language, and that on account of this we must also have a unitary centralist state, moreover a kingdom. . . . [Y]ou evidently do not care a whit that our peasant in general, and especially our Croat peasant, does not wish to hear one more thing about kings and emperors, nor about a state which you are imposing on him by force . . . the whole Croat peasantry is equally against your centralism as against militarism, equally for a republic as for a popular agreement with the Serbs. . . . If the Serbs really want to have such a centralist state and government, may God bless them with it, but we Croats do not want any state organisation except a confederated federal republic.[4]

Neither the well-educated Stjepan Radić nor his peasant constituency feared the plundering, burning, and killing as did the Croat great landowners and richer burghers. Croatia-Slavonia, not to mention Dalmatia and Bosnia-Herzegovina, was still a predominantly rural area with 56 percent illiteracy in 1910, and only 1 percent of the population could be considered part of an intelligentsia (that is, graduates of a *gymnasium*). Only one-fifth of the population was employed in industry, crafts, trade, or rail, river and maritime traffic; 68 percent of all firms were engaged in crafts without hired workers; another 30 percent had between one and five workers. But the most important fact in explaining Radić's lack of influence was that only 2 percent of the men had the right to vote. Therefore, the political decision making in November 1918 was limited to the richer landowners, the upper middle class of bankers, industrialists, and merchants, the free professions, and the higher officials of the Croatian-Slavonian state administration. Especially in these influential groups, not only Croats but also many Serbs, Germans, Magyars, and Jews were represented. Political decisions were made by the Starčević Party of Right (Dr. Ante Pavelić) and the Serbian Independent Party (Svetozar Pribićević).[5]

In a tumultuous all-night session on November 24, 1918, the National Council decided on immediate unification with Serbia and Montenegro. The "Conclusions and Instructions of the Central Committee of the National Council about Unification with the Kingdom of Serbia" left the organization of the future state to the Constituent Assembly. Neither Radić nor Anton Korošec, the President of the National Council, took part in the delegation to Belgrade. Like Pašić and other Serbian leaders, Korošec was still abroad. Thus Ante Pavelić—the Croat vice-president of the National Council, not the Ustaša-leader—presented a rather general address to Prince-Regent Alexander of Serbia, who on December 1, 1918, formally proclaimed the new "Kingdom of Serbs, Croats, and Slovenes" (Kraljevstvo Srba, Hrvata i Slovenaca): " . . . I am convinced that by this act I am fulfilling my Royal duty and that I am thereby only finally realising what the best sons or our race—of all creeds and of all three names from both sides of the Danube, the Sava and the Drina—began to prepare already under the reign of my grand-father."[6]

Yugoslavism before 1918

Prior to November 1918, a number of differences existed in the national thinking of Serb, Croat, and Slovene political leaders and intellectuals. The French scholar Louis Leger predicted the disintegration of Austria-Hungary and the rise of Yugoslavia in his 1915 book *La Liquidation de l'Autriche-Hongrie*. Nevertheless, he believed that an "Illyrian Federation" would only be successful if it were organized as "some form of Slavic Switzerland," composed of autonomous cantons, which would be made up of "Slovene lands, Croatia, Dalmatia, central Serbia, and Bosnia and Herzegovina; Belgrade, as the seat of the central government, should have the same role as Bern in the 'Helvetian community.'" After the Niš Declaration of September 1914, in which the Serbian government proclaimed the founding of a strong "Serb-Croat-Slovene state" as its war aim, Leger warned the Serbs not to have overzealous Piedmontain or unitarist ambitions.[7]

The first Slovene national program was formulated in 1848 by a small group of educated Slovenes who demanded that their ethnic territory—hitherto split administratively in six Austrian provinces—be combined into a "unified Slovenia." Until the fall of the Dual Monarchy, this demand remained the primary goal of the Slovene national movement. They conceived of this unified Slovenia as an autonomous, self-governing unit within the framework of a federalized Habsburg Monarchy. One of the fundamental characteristics of this autonomy would be the free use of the Slovene language in offices, schools, and public life. The heightened Slovene-German national antagonism since the 1890s cemented the conviction of the Slovene political elite that it was necessary to seek a national solution through closer cooperation with the other South Slavs of the monarchy. As a result, in the years before World War I, all three

Slovene parties (the Catholic, Liberal, and Social Democrat) espoused the Yugoslav idea, but thoughts about the possible results of this Yugoslav cooperation varied greatly in practice. Common to all was the view that the Slovenes were pressed into a difficult position between the hostile German Austrians and Italians.[8]

The idea that an "association of the South Slavs of the monarchy in a separate political organism" under the Habsburg aegis would be the best solution was proposed in Ljubljana after the annexation of Bosnia-Herzegovina. In January 1909, the Carniola Provincial Diet announced: "The Provincial Diet welcomes the annexation of Bosnia and Herzegovina in the firm hope that, therewith, the first step has been made toward the unification of all the South Slavs of our monarchy into a constitutionally autonomous organism under the sceptre of the Habsburg Dynasty."[9] The Slovene youth organizations sponsored lectures in other South Slav tongues, traveled to the Balkans, and invited Serb, Croat, and Bulgar students to Carniola. Furthermore, Slovene students enrolled at Zagreb University and studied the Croat and Serb languages and cultures. During the Balkan Wars, Slovene youth organizations sent volunteers, along with military and medical equipment, to aid their fellow South Slavs.[10]

After the beginning of the First Balkan War in October 1912, the All-Slovene People's Party (Catholic) and the Croat Party of Right cooperated more closely, and the Slovene members of the Viennese Parliament (*Reichsrat*) declared their sympathies for the "Serb brothers." The chief ideologist of the Slovene Catholics, the priest Janez Krek, spoke to industrial workers in Jesenice in Carniola:

Wherever our rivers flow, there lives our race. We must only go farther East along the Sava and the Drava, everywhere we will meet with others of our kind who stand close to our heart in a particular way. Our rivers flow in the direction of Belgrade and the Black Sea, and not a single one of our rivers flows to Vienna. Along our Sava, from Triglav to the Black Sea, lives the same race that we are, one race, amongst whom we feel at home as nowhere else in the world.[11]

One could easily think these were the words of the Croat Illyrianists from the 1830s.

Nevertheless, the most important writer of the Slovene *Moderna*, Ivan Cankar, critically rejected the romantic attitudes of some Slovene intellectuals who were under the sway of advancing germanization, the aggravated national conflicts in the Habsburg Monarchy, and the awareness of Slovenia's small size. In a lecture entitled "Slovenes and Yugoslavs," which he gave on April 12, 1913, in Ljubljana's town hall, Cankar argued that:

[A]s the first shot fell on the Balkans, it echoed on our most far-flung village. People who had never in their lives taken an interest in politics looked on with sympathy, not merely intrigued by this great drama. And in all of us there awoke something much more significant and valuable: The sparks of that strength, the self-assurance and the will to live that had so powerfully unfolded in the South began to flare up on Slovene ground as well. The weakling saw that his brother was strong, and he began to believe in himself and his future.

Nevertheless, for Cankar the South Slav question was a purely political problem, and he decidedly denied a culturally and linguistically united South Slavdom.

[B]y blood we are brothers, by language cousins, by culture—which is the fruit of centuries of separate upbringing—we are less familiar with one another than the Upper Carniolan peasant is with the Tyrolean, or the Gorizian vintner with the Friulian.[12]

Although in July 1914 the Slovene population protested against the "Serbian murderers" of Sarajevo, many German-Austrian officials (and newspapers) mistrusted the influence of South Slavic propaganda among Slovene intellectuals and ordered investigations. This only strengthened the Yugoslav idea among the monarchy's South Slavs. On May 30, 1917, the South Slavic club in the Vienna *Reichsrat* (30 Slovene, Croat, and Serb delegates) promulgated a "May Declaration," calling for the union of the South Slavic lands of Austria-Hungary into an independent state with the Habsburg dynasty at its head. Within a year the declaration was signed by more than two hundred thousand Slovenes.[13]

The sudden dissolution of Austria-Hungary at the end of October 1918 was thus a genuine surprise for the Slovene political parties and their leaders. The appointment of the Slovene Catholic leader Anton Korošec to head the National Council in Zagreb seemed to the Slovene public an assurance that their interests would be honored in the negotiations regarding the internal disposition of the state. Against a small group of "Yugoslav" intellectuals, the great majority of the Slovenes thought about a Yugoslavia that would guarantee the Slovenes a degree of self-government, equality of national rights, and undisturbed future national development. But Korošec joined neither the meetings in Zagreb nor the discussions in Belgrade—he went on a journey to Geneva, trying to ascertain the international position of the Yugoslav cause. Together with Trumbić he talked Pašić into creating a twelve-member common ministry, and on November 9, 1918, a united state of the Serbs, Croats, and Slovenes was agreed upon. But the main decisions were made in Zagreb and Belgrade. Nevertheless,

the Kingdom of Serbia had been an internationally recognized ally of the victors in the war; its sacrifices and heroism in the struggle against Austria-Hungary were fresh in everyone's memory, and the Serbian political elite in Belgrade promised an agreeable arrangement on the future of a common state. Despite political decisions and measures, . . . people in Ljubljana continued for some time to look optimistically to Belgrade.[14]

Despite the "Yugoslavism" of Bishop Josip Juraj Strossmayer and his Catholic priests and fear of many Croatian intellectuals that the Croat nation could not survive as an independent entity between such large nations as the Germans, the Italians, and the Magyars, Croatian-Serbian political relations were disturbed both by the question of Bosnia-Herzegovina and by the many social and cultural tensions in the Croatian-Slavonian villages. Furthermore, the Hungarian Ban Khuen-Héderváry was skilled at playing the Croatian and Serbian middle classes against each other, thereby improving the position of the Serbian Independent Party. But the student generation of 1895 (with Stjepan Radić) burned the Hungarian flag when Emperor Francis Joseph came to Zagreb to open the new Croatian national theater. The engagement of some Dalmatian politicians such as Fran Supilo and Ante Trumbić, who saw the German *Drang nach Osten* as a danger for the development of all the small nations in the region, was crucial. The new generation formed a new "Croat-Serb Coalition" demanding democratic freedoms, labor legislation, and the protection of peasant holdings.[15]

Budapest and Vienna tried to break the "New Course" in 1908, preparing a trial for high treason against fifty-three Serbs from Croatia-Slavonia, most of them members of the Serbian Independent Party. They were accused of promoting the "Greater Serbian" national program in Croatia-Slavonia, Dalmatia, and Bosnia-Herzegovina and of engaging in subversive antigovernment activities for the annexation of those lands to Serbia. Although all the accused were sentenced in 1910, the trial and the convictions were annulled. Still, the art historian Izidor Kršnjavić argued to Robert William Seton-Watson, an observer of the trial:

As Director of the education administration [in Zagreb] I so favored the Serbs that [even] my fellow party members—the Serbophile members of the National Party—warned me. It took many, many bitter experiences before I became convinced that it is impossible to get along with the Serbs. One must either be a hammer or an anvil.[16]

Since the First Balkan War, the infusion of Serbophilia and belief in Serb superiority influenced some parts of the educated Croat youth. Belgrade became a Mecca of both young Croat artists and visionaries such as the journalist Milan Marjanović, the famous sculptor Ivan Meštrović, and the poet Augustin Ujević. Meštrović, the son of a poor Croatian farmer from the Dalmatian uplands, was accepted as a student at the academy in Vienna. Beginning in 1902, his work had been exhibited together with other artists of the Viennese "secession." In 1907, he moved to Paris, where his exhibition drew praise from Auguste Rodin. But at the Rome Exposition of 1911, Meštrović refused to show his work at the pavilion of the Habsburg Empire and presented his wooden scale model of a so-called Kosovo temple at the Serbian pavilion: "I tried to give a single synthesis of the popular folk ideals and their development, to express in stone and architecture how deeply rooted in all of us are the memories of the greatest moments and most significant events of our history."[17]

When the mentor of the Young Croatians, the leading modernist writer-critic Anton Gustav Matoš, died in April 1914, the Višegrad-born Catholic Serb Ivo Andrić[18] wrote an article in memoriam:

The fiery glow of the Battle of Kumanovo [the Serbian victory over the Ottomans] filled the whole country, from Carinthia and Ljubljana to Dubrovnik and Varaždin and to Szent Endre near Budapest, to the walls of Thessaloniki, Split, and Istria. Our people perceived the Balkan War of 1912 as the flame of a historical torch. . . . It can be stated with historical objectivity that, in millions of South Slav minds, one could feel how a massive, dark stone wall had crumbled in one festive moment, and how the chapter of six centuries of suffering and need had come to an end.[19]

In his letter from July 21, 1914, to Friedrich Funder, the editor-in-chief of the Catholic Vienna *Reichspost*, a British expert on the South Slavic question, Robert William Seton-Watson, explained some of the internal causes for the "disgraceful deed of Sarajevo": "Unfortunately, one need not go to Belgrade to find explanation for this crime. . . . The idea of unity is so strong in the youth—even among the clergy—that it can no longer be contained, most certainly not by repressive means." Then Seton-Watson warned against a "punitive expedition" against Serbia: "It seems to me that such a step could very easily lead to a European war."[20]

Many Croats, Slovenes, and Bosnian Muslims, even Serbs, fought in the Austro-Hungarian army against Russia, Italy, and Serbia. Many South Slavic civilians were evacuated from Bosnia-Herzegovina, Gorizia-Gradisca, Carniola, Istria, and Dalmatia into camps in Hungary, Austria, Bohemia, and Moravia. There was famine in some parts of Croatia and Bosnia-Herzegovina at the end of the war, and about seventeen thousand children from Herzegovina were relocated to more prosperous Croatian families in Slavonia and Syrmia. Starting in the spring of 1918, some hundred thousand South-Slavic deserters appeared in Croatia-Slavonia and began to attack landowners, merchants, and money-lenders. Morale was low everywhere, as Croatian author Miroslav Krleža observed. Some Slovene and Bosnian Muslim regiments in the Habsburg army suffered the highest casualties. Hence the successful attack of the Entente army (with some Serbian divisions) in Macedonia did not threaten the Croats and Slovenes as did the Italian attack against Slovenia, Istria, and Dalmatia.[21]

The most common approach to the question of the new "ethnonationalism" in Serbia identifies the roots of political authoritarianism in the existence of a rigid, traditional, and pre-modern culture that had already taken shape in the nineteenth century. Svetozar Marković, the founder of Serbian socialism, argued in 1872 that the Serbian political system was a mixture of oriental despotism and the European conservative police state. The leader of the Serbian Radicals, Nikola Pašić, followed to a great extent Ilija Garašanin's design in *Načertanije* (1844), creating a "Serbian state" with "all the Serb peoples." A common thread in *Načertanije* was also a strong anti-German sentiment and hatred of Austria, which were perceived as the key impediments to the fulfillment of Serbian national ambitions. However, Garašanin looked to France and Britain for help in achieving his grand political design.[22]

After the turn of the century, Jovan Skerlić became the literary mentor for the newly educated youth of Belgrade. Attracted to French literature and belligerently enthusiastic ethnic nationalists, Skerlić warned: "Religious divisions and political life have made their mark, and the Slavic South is today divided into four national groups and three religions. Religious and national proselytising are not possible, nor are cultural or political hegemony." On the other hand, the ethnographer Jovan Cvijić, who studied in the 1890s at the University of Vienna, argued that most Serbs and Croats belonged to a "Dinaric" type. He believed a Yugoslav nation could and would be created as an amalgamation of this Dinaric type with other closely related South Slavic racial types. At the end of World War I, the Serbian government supported the publication of Cvijić's famous book *La péninsule balkanique. Géographie humaine* in Paris as part of its campaign to convince the allies of the wisdom of a postwar Yugoslav state.[23]

Prime Minister Nikola Pašić began contemplating common action with the monarchy's South Slavs only after Serbia's victories in the Balkan wars, but even then his intentions did not go much beyond the idea of Serbia's expansion. The Black Hand—a secret officers' group—felt that the "Serb provinces" of Bosnia-Herzegovina, Montenegro, Croatia, Slavonia and Syrmia, Vojvodina, and Dalmatia should be joined to Serbia. In the aftermath of the Sarajevo assassination, Serbian politics were thrown into a state of confusion. As early as September 4, 1914, the Serbian government informed its Allies that, should victory be achieved, it expected "to create out of Serbia a powerful south-western Slavic state; all the Serbs, all the Croats, and all the Slovenes would enter its composition." But Pašić—the legendary *Baja*, as the Serbian masses affectionately called him—distinguished between the Serbian claims to the territories inhabited by Serbs, defined linguistically (along the frontiers of Vuk Karadžić), and his government's demands for purely Croat and Slovene territories.[24]

Pašić's main fear was that the Allies might decide to give their support to an independent Croatia, embracing most of the Habsburg South Slavic possessions. Therefore, he requested several studies by eminent Serbian scholars (among them Jovan Cvijić and Stanoje Stanojević) to prove that the Serbs and Croats were one people by virtue of colonization and linguistic assimilation of the Croat lands. After the Treaty of London, the Allies offered Serbia compensation in the form of control over Bosnia-Herzegovina, Slavonia, the Bačka, southern Dalmatia, and northern Albania. Following the major defeat of the Serbian army in fall 1915 and their retreat to the Albanian coast and Corfu, the power of the Serbian government seemed to be broken. The revolution in Russia meant the collapse of Serbia's most important ally of 1914. But even in the Corfu Declaration of July 20, 1917, Pašić promised only a united and independent state of Serbs, Croats, and Slovenes in a "constitutional, democratic, and parliamentary monarchy headed by the Karadjordjević dynasty." It is significant that the declaration recognized the equality of the three "tribal" names, the three flags and religions, and the two alphabets but made no mention of any historical territories or autonomies.[25]

In January 1918, when President Wilson promised autonomy, but not independence, to the peoples of Austria-Hungary, Pašić instructed his envoy in Washington "to see if the Americans could be persuaded to support the voiding of Austria-Hungary's annexation of Bosnia-Herzegovina," keeping secret these inquiries from the Yugoslav Committee. Then, on October 5, 1918, after the Entente troops—with the Serbian divisions in the center, which stormed in the direction of Belgrade—had crushed the resistance of the Central Powers on the Saloniki front, Pašić categorically opposed Trumbić's demand that the Allies acknowledge the Yugoslav Committee as the legitimate representative of the monarchy's South Slavs:

Serbia wants to liberate and unite the Yugoslavs and does not want to drown in the sea of some kind of Yugoslavia. Serbia does not want to drown in Yugoslavia, but to have Yugoslavia drown in her.[26]

Yugoslavism in the Interwar Period

The creation of the first Yugoslavia was understood by leading Serbian politicians primarily as the extension of Serbia and Montenegro. As a result, the Serbs responded to the permanent crisis of the first Yugoslavia with the question: Why did we go to war? But the Croats and Slovenes had another question: Why should we have less within a new Yugoslav state framework than we had within Austria-Hungary?[27]

Already in 1921, the famous thinker Albin Prepeluh formulated the Slovene view of the constitutional question in Yugoslavia by noting that it was by no means a juridical and political issue, but above all a matter of sociology. The constitution, which is supposed to be effective and not cause conflicts, has to reflect the realities of the area of governance and respect the diversity of life there. "The 'tribes' which have been united into the Yugoslav state developed for centuries severed from each other, and they took on their cultural-historical, religious, and socio-economic forms in milieus that were completely different, even mutually contradictory." The centralist Vidovdan constitution, which was ratified in Belgrade on June 28, 1921, with a majority of votes from the eastern part of the monarchy and which divided the Yugoslav state into thirty-three provinces with no regard for ethnic composition, thus signified a great disappointment to both Slovenes and Croats.[28]

Many negative stereotypes, prejudices, and reproaches that one or the other national group was secessionist, nationalist, and hegemonistic emerged during the first years the Yugoslav peoples lived together in a common state. These things combined to cement the conviction among the Slovenes that Yugoslavia was exploiting them economically. In 1927, the Catholic party leader Korošec summed this up in a saying, which remained popular among the Slovenes until the fall of Yugoslavia: "In Yugoslavia it is thus: the Serbs rule, the Croats debate, and the Slovenes work."[29]

On December 8, 1920, Stjepan Radić, who had won 14.3 percent of all Yugoslav votes in the first Yugoslav parliamentary election, proclaimed the "Independent and Neutral Croatian Peasant Republic"—but without serious consequences. In February 1922, sixty-three Croat deputies from Croatia, Slavonia, Dalmatia, and Bosnia-Herzegovina sent a memorandum to the Conference of Genoa protesting against the Vidovdan constitution of 1921. Three days before the next parliamentary election on March 18, 1923, which brought the Croatian Republican Peasant Party 21.8 percent of all Yugoslav votes, Stjepan Radić spoke at an election meeting in Zagreb at which Robert William Seton-Watson was also present. Seton-Watson said of Radić's speech:

He called both, Pašić and Ljuba Jovanović, the 2 chiefs with whom he had been negotiating 2 days before, *magarac* [i.e. "asses"], was very rude to the King, very tactless to the Serbs, and plunged into foreign policy with a hymn to Germany! Altogether the fat was in fire, and when I reached Belgrade, I found what I had expected, namely that everyone was furious and saying, what can one do with such a man? It is indeed difficult to know, for he is a real weathercock. Entre nous, I suspect him of having drunk too much before his meeting, or else of having got intoxicated with his own eloquence.[30]

In the same year, Stjepan Radić published a booklet in London: "A general view of the present situation in Central Europe and in the Balkans." He pointed out that the existing Yugoslav kingdom must become "a federation of its free peoples. If this does not happen, then a means must be found of giving to Croatia the right of self-determination, so that pacifist Croatia, as an independent state, may form an economic union with the Austrian Republic, as the first step towards an economic Commonwealth of all the Danubian and Balkan peoples." Radić, who was a political emigrant in 1923–24, ignored the fact that no Danubian or Balkan nation wanted such a confederation. On the other hand, he criticized Balkan politics:

In Belgrade the secret military societies, the Black and White Hand, and in Bucharest the groups of the most influential Boyars (landlords) have concentrated all power in their hands, and are entirely dominating the nation, the state and dynasty. Budapest and Sofia waver between these two policies, between Western Humanism and Eastern Despotism. Athens is quite apart, and sinks every day nearer to Levantine chaos. Prague is also in a class by itself, in spite of its alliance with Belgrade and Bucharest, because it feels that the Balkans can again easily become an open abyss which might swallow up its newly-won freedom.[31]

After the assassination of Stjepan Radić in the Belgrade Parliament on June 20, 1928, and the introduction of King Alexander's dictatorship on

January 6, 1929, the newly appointed British ambassador in Belgrade, Sir Neville Henderson, gave an even more drastic judgment of the situation:

The Serbs don't have any tradition, apart from warfare, no experience in administration, no concern for compromise. If they are in power, their chauvinism and despotism appears; corrupt, conceited, suspicious, they obey the advice that force is the best and most certain method to realize their goals. . . . Chauvinism is flourishing, the minorities are oppressed, the representatives of the police are barbarians, corruption is flourishing not only on the level of the lower civil servants, but also in the higher ranks.[32]

Even the Yugoslavia-friendly Seton-Watson changed his opinion:

The Decree of October 3, 1929, has not diminished by an iota the power of the central Belgrade authorities: so far from being an act of devolution or decentralisation, it has even accentuated centralistic tendencies, and nothing of any real importance can happen in the provinces without reference to a Ministry and generally to the Prime Minister and the King. The suppression of the names of the old historical provinces is entirely contrary to nature and not likely to be permanent. The actual boundaries drawn are in almost every case artificial and intensely unpopular, alike for reasons of sentiment and convenience. That Šabac and Užice should be placed under Sarajevo; Travnik and Mostar under Split; Kragujevac and Smederevo under Novi Sad; Dubrovnik, Korčula, Novipazar and Mitrovica all under Cetinje, is so grotesque as to require no refutation. . . . [Nevertheless] the conflict between Serbs and Croats still remains the fundamental problem, because the [Y]ugoslav state was not in the first instance established on sound lines, and every change attempted during these eleven years has merely been a variation of the original attempt to enforce a rigid centralism, controlled by a small clique in Belgrade.[33]

In a new memorandum of November 10, 1936, Seton-Watson demanded for the Slovenes, Croats, and even the Serbs in Vojvodina "a minimum of autonomy, equality of status with the Serbs of Serbia and equal opportunities of advancement in the state service." The British expert proposed to the Foreign Office, the Prince-Regent Paul of Yugoslavia, the former Czechoslovak President Thomas G. Masaryk, and his Foreign Minister Edvard Beneš the formation of five federal units—Slovenia, Croatia-Dalmatia, Bosnia-Herzegovina, Vojvodina, and Serbia with Montenegro and Macedonia (autonomous). Furthermore, all parties that were in existence on January 1, 1929, would be admitted to new constitutional elections. Finally, the British expert proposed a principal accord among Prime Minister Milan Stojadinović (a Serb), the Croat peasant leader Vladko Maček, the Slovene Catholic leader Anton Korošec, and the leader of the Bosnian Muslims, Mehmed Spaho. Stojadinović headed a coalition government with Korošec and Spaho starting in June 1935, but failed to reach a compromise with Maček.[34]

The permanent conflict between the French centralized model of a nation-state (demanded by the Serbs) and the federalized model of a nationalities-state (demanded by the Croats, Slovenes, and Bosnian Muslims) ended temporarily in August 1939, when the government of Dragiša Cvetković accepted Croatian demands to create a separate unit, the *Banovina* of Croatia. The new province covered not only all Croatian districts, the Slavonian districts up to Ilok in Syrmia, and the Dalmatian districts down to the Bay of Kotor, but also the Bosnian-Herzegovinian districts of Brčko, Gradašac, Derventa, Livno, Bugojno, Fojnica, Konjic, Mostar, and Stolac. The agreement (*sporazum*) between the rulers and the Serbian and Croatian political elite included a common government—with Maček as vice president—and a *ban* responsible to the King and the *Sabor* in Zagreb. Although no final arrangement was reached in financial affairs, as late as 1941 Maček still did not want an independent Croatia that would depend on the Axis Powers.[35]

Yugoslavism under Communist Rule

After the destruction of the Yugoslav kingdom within two weeks in April 1941, Hitler and Mussolini divided the country among Germany, Italy, Hungary, and Bulgaria. In the center they established the so-called "Independent State of Croatia" (NDH), which was ruled by about six hundred Ustaša leaders from Italy, Germany, and other countries. These extremist Croat nationalists mirrored Italian Fascism and German National Socialism. They considered the Muslims of Bosnia-Herzegovina a part of the Croatian nation, but planned to expel and destroy the Serbs, Jews, and Roma. Of almost 40,000 Jews in the NDH territory, only about 9,000 survived the war; almost all of the Roma, some 15,000, were killed. The mass murders against the Serbs began in late April 1941; in the concentration camp Jasenovac alone between 80,000 and 100,000 people—Serbs, Jews, Roma, and others—were killed. Up to the end of World War II, about 330,000 Serbs died in the NDH state, about 200,000 murdered by the Ustaše. More than 100,000 fell while fighting German and Italian units, as well as in the civil wars between the Domobranci, Četniks, Muslims, and Partisans. In May and June 1945, the Partisans killed about 45,000–55,000 former Domobranci and Ustaše around Bleiburg in Southeast Carinthia and on the "Way of the Cross" through Yugoslavia. The total war losses in Yugoslavia are estimated now at 1,027,000 persons: 530,000 Serbs, 192,000 Croats, 103,000

Bosnian-Herzegovinian Muslims, 80,000 Danube Swabians, 57,000 Jews, 25,000 Slovenes, and 18,000 Roma.[36]

In the mortal conflict between the Ustaše and the Četniks from the spring of 1941, the ideologies of Garašanin and Starčević clashed once again. The crimes of Muslim Ustaše against Serbs in eastern Herzegovina and the revenge of Četniks against Muslims in eastern Bosnia—in the valley of the Drina—were similarly terrible. On the other hand, the Partisans defended Serbian villages from Ustaša terror much more efficiently than the Četniks did, and enjoyed much stronger support among the Serbs in the NDH. Aware of the widespread dissatisfaction that had existed in pre-war Yugoslavia, the Communists argued theirs was a struggle for a better postwar order in the country, with a fairer inter-ethnic balance. The Federal People's Republic of Yugoslavia was proclaimed to be a community of equal peoples, organized in six republics and two autonomous provinces. But the struggle for the independence of nations/republics continued, and many people fled or had to leave Yugoslavia, among them 400,000 ethnic Germans (Danube Swabians, Lower Styrians, and Gottscheer) and 200,000 Italians (from Istria and Dalmatia).[37]

Communist Yugoslavia was founded by the Declaration of Jajce in central Bosnia on November 29, 1943. Although the former *ban* of the Croatian *banovina*, Ivan Šubašić, became the new head of the government in exile and signed an agreement with the communist leader Josip Broz Tito in November 1944 in Belgrade, the whole power in the new state was concentrated in the hands of the Communist Party of Yugoslavia (CPY) and its notorious secret service, the OZNA. At the end of 1945, the Constituent Assembly proclaimed the Federal People's Republic of Yugoslavia, and Tito began to rule on the Stalinist Soviet model. Enemies were killed or persecuted without trial, and their property was confiscated. After some revisions of the borders of the new republics—Slovenia got northern Istria and Gorica, Croatia the main part of Istria, the Baranja, and western Syrmia, Serbia the two provinces of Vojvodina and Kosovo, while Macedonia was established as a new republic—the CPY kept national antagonisms hidden below the surface.

So why did the communist politics of inter-ethnic balance fail? While direct contacts between members of Slovene, Croat, and Serb middle-class parties after the occupation in 1941 were for the most part broken off, the communists organized a common resistance against the German and Italian occupiers. As a result, even during World War II, the Slovenes did not opt against Yugoslavia, but rather for it. After 1945, the communist political leaders and ideologues maintained that the national question was solved once and for all.[38]

Still, even Edvard Kardelj, the leading Yugoslav Communist theoretician, had to admit in 1957—in the introduction to the second edition of his book *On the Development of the Slovene National Question*—to the tenacity of intra-Yugoslav national tension after 1945. He attributed it to "remnants of bourgeois nationalism," to the differences in development of different parts of Yugoslavia, and to bureaucratic-centralistic tendencies in the top Yugoslav leadership. Some years later, Dobrica Ćosić—who was then Yugoslav and centralist-oriented—proclaimed Yugoslavism to be an "internationalist practice" and a component part of "the historically unavoidable integration of the world and the inception of socialist civilisation on the planet." But the Slovene literary historian Dušan Pirjevec responded that "nationality is a constituent element of human personality, the basis of human existence."[39]

At the Sixth Congress of the League of Communists of Slovenia in 1968, speakers criticized the postwar national policy and spoke of the republic's sovereignty and of Slovene statehood, and even engaged in polemics with the organization of the Yugoslav army. Hence the Kavčič government supported the formation of Slovenian military units. The reform movement in Slovenia, however, unlike that of Croatia, did not have broad support.

In the mid-1960s political and economic changes created a new atmosphere in which people began to raise matters that had been previously taboo. One of them was the question of inter-ethnic relations, which could be discussed most freely in the context of the language problem. At the beginning of 1967, a Zagreb literary weekly published a document called the "Declaration concerning the Name and Position of Croatian Standard Language," signed by 180 scholars and cultural institutions in Croatia, who wanted to establish the equality in status and use of Slovenian, Croatian, Serbian, and Macedonian in federal institutions. The government in Belgrade branded the "Declaration" tendentious and politically damaging, and some signatories were removed from public life. In 1968, Zagreb students demonstrated: "Down with the red bourgeoisie!" In 1969, for the first time there emerged differences between the republics and federal bodies, when Slovenia demanded priority for the construction of highways to Austria and Italy. In the same year units of territorial defense were introduced in each republic. These became the embryo of the national armies of Slovenia, Croatia, and Macedonia.[40]

In solidarity with the "Prague Spring" came the "Croatian Spring" as a national and liberal-democratic movement. Even the leadership of the Croatian League of Communists, headed by Savka Dabčević-Kučar, demanded a say in the way the state's financial resources were distributed and in the foreign currency system. In spring 1971, a new nationally in-clined student leadership was elected at Zagreb University, and the *Matica hrvatska* began to publish a weekly, voicing the platform of non-communist intellectuals. As the national protagonists demanded the in-divisible sovereignty of the Croatian nation in Croatia (mentioning the Serbs as a minority), a complete change in the political and economic system, and a reorientation of foreign policy, Tito decided to crack down on the Croatian movement. The leaders of the Croatian communists were removed for not resisting the "growth of nationalism, chauvinism and the class enemy," over four hundred people were forced to resign their positions, several thousand people were detained, and prominent cultural figures, editors, and student leaders were sentenced. A large number of people fled the country. "Croatia descended into political ap-athy from which it did not emerge for almost two decades."[41]

The Serbian national question was opened with the political defeat of the so-called "Serbian Liberals" in 1972. This group of reform-minded communists, headed by Marko Nikezić, followed Svetozar Marković's perceptions of Serbian identity and focused their national policy on the modernization of Serbia. Their vision of modern Serbia was "an attempt to build a non-national republican (Serbian) identity." They advocated the replacement of Titoist politics of socialist self-management with market-oriented economic reforms. After his intervention in Croatia, not surprisingly, Tito also disposed of the Serbian party leadership in a brutal fashion. The Serbian reform elite of some six thousand people lost their jobs overnight; the option of a democratic Serbia was closed.[42]

The ethnicization of the Serbian national movement was undertaken by writers such as Dobrica Ćosić and Vuk Drašković, as well as histori-ans such as Milorad Ekmečić and Vasilije Krestić. The movement was then accelerated by the Albanian nationalist demonstrations in Kosovo in 1981. The claims of Albanian students for a "Kosovo Republic" and an "ethnically pure Kosovo" threatened Serbia's territorial integrity and thus reawakened Serbian nationalist sentiments. Representatives of the Kosovo Serbs came to the Federal Assembly in Belgrade to present griev-ances arising from the increasingly tense interethnic situation in Kosovo, and they claimed there existed an organized campaign of "ethnic cleans-ing." The *Memorandum* of the Serbian Academy of Sciences and Arts in 1986 portrayed the Serbs as the only nation in Yugoslavia without its own state, traced Serbia's lack of economic development compared to that of Slovenia and Croatia, and claimed that there was an "anti-Ser-bian coalition" led by Slovenia, Croatia, and the Vojvodina based on the premise "weak Serbia, strong Yugoslavia."[43]

Those clichés eventually became the essence of Slobodan Milošević's populist policy. Already in 1987, Milošević posed as a "national savior" by protecting a group of Kosovo Serbs from a beating by the Kosovo police: "No one should dare to beat you. . . . You should stay here. This is your land. These are your houses. Your meadows and gardens. Your memories. You should not abandon your land just because it is difficult to live, because you are pressured by injustice and degradation. It was never part of the Serbian and Montenegrin character to give up in the face of obstacles, to demobilize when it is time to fight. . . . You should stay here for the sake of your ancestors and descendants." Belgrade Television, which went down to Kosovo Polje for this special event, showed Milošević's speech over and over again on the TV.[44]

In 1988–89, Milošević's campaign of orchestrated mass marches of Kosovo Serbs was directed toward gaining full control over the Serbian autonomous provinces of Kosovo and the Vojvodina. The slogans were brilliant in their simple appeal: "Kosovo is Serbia, the Vojvodina is Serbia, together we are stronger." The peak of these marches was reached with the one-million-person rallies in Belgrade (in the autumn of 1988) and on the Kosovo Polje (on June 28, 1989). Milošević descended from the heavens by helicopter and announced: "Six centuries later [after the battle on Kosovo Polje against the Ottomans], again we are in battles and quarrels. They are not armed battles, though such things should not be excluded yet." Milošević's use of mass politics fascinated and attracted the national intelligentsia, and was calculated to show Yugoslavia that the new Serbian leadership stood for a united and strong Serbia. Popular enthusiasm for Milošević's approach to the national question blocked any possibility of a democratic solution to Yugoslavia's crisis. In the name of the glories of the Serbian past, the Serbian public was to forget the realities of their common life in a multinational state.[45]

"At first glance it might seem paradoxical that the first to leave Yugoslavia were the Slovenes, who had no independent state legal tradition."[46] Since the early 1980s, the federal economic policy was just one of the causes of Slovenia's increasingly critical attitude toward Yugoslavia. Belgrade's calls for repressive measures against opposition intellectuals and for centralization in the fields of education, science, and culture did more to mobilize public opinion than did economic problems. In Ljubljana, *Neue Slowenische Kunst* (New Slovenian Art), the musical group *Laibach* (Ljubljana), and *Mladina*, the weekly magazine of the socialist youth organization, appeared to challenge parochial Slovenia, and were tolerated. Slovene youth caused a scandal over state-sanctioned holidays—such as Youth Day and Tito's birthday—by proposing the use of a Hitler youth poster to promote Yugoslavia's annual relay race coinciding with the celebrations.[47]

In the mid-1980s, Yugoslavia was for the most part already divided into an eastern centralist camp and a western autonomist camp. Simultaneously, strained polemics regarding "Yugoslavism," "nationalism, unitarism, and federalism," and "unity" and "the right to diversity" completely crippled the Yugoslav writers' organization. In this atmosphere, the Slovene educated strata, surrounding the writers' society and the journal *Nova revija*, formulated a national program—in some senses an answer to the Serbian *Memorandum*. In their national program the Slovene intellectuals pushed for "realization of the Slovene right to self-determination" and to an independent state with a democracy following the Western model.[48]

Admiral Branko Mamula, the Yugoslav Defense Minister, condemned the Slovene National Program but did unintentionally more for Slovene independence than anyone else. When, in the spring of 1988, *Mladina* attacked him for selling weapons to Ethiopia and building a private "castle" in Opatija—a famous Adriatic resort popular with Viennese and Budapest high society before World War I—the Yugoslav National Army (JNA) and the military counter-intelligence (KOS) struck back. After publishing secret documents from the Army, one JNA sergeant and three journalists of *Mladina* were arrested. The trial in Ljubljana was conducted in Serbo-Croatian instead of Slovene and became a catalyst for the creation of a Committee for the Defense of Human Rights, which collected a hundred thousand signatures and brought even the Slovene communist leaders closer to the dissidents.[49]

Surprisingly, it was not Franjo Tudjman's Croatian Democratic Union (HDZ) but the Croatian Social Liberal Party (HSLS) that took the initiative in October 1989 for the return of Ban Josip Jelačić's statue to Zagreb's main square (from which the communist authorities had removed it in 1945). On a rainy morning, about seventy thousand citizens signed the Liberals' petition—the clearest indication up to that time as to what people were thinking before the 1990 elections. The Serbian media called the introduction of a multiparty system the "awakening of retrograde ideas": "The Ustaša spirit is stirring." Meanwhile the Četnik spirit threatened the Croats and Slovenes when Serb militants from Kosovo, in collusion with Serbian authorities, announced that they would organize a "rally of truth" in Ljubljana on December 1, and on their way there would stop in Zagreb, where they also wanted to stir up disorder. The Slovene authorities denied them entry, and the Croatian authorities announced that they would use police force against the demonstrators.

Milošević's pressure on Croatia helped Tudjman's HDZ win the first free parliamentary elections since 1927 in April-May 1990. Already in March 1990, tens of thousands of Serbs from Croatia, Bosnia-Herzegovina, and even from Serbia attended a mass meeting in Kordun and shouted, "This is Serbia!" The nationalistic Serbian Democratic Party, established in Knin and backed by Milošević and the JNA (General Kadijević), initiated an open confrontation with the nationalistic Croatian government. On August 17, 1990, the mayor of Knin, Milan Babić, proclaimed a state of war, and on December 22, 1990, the Serbs of Knin responded to the new constitution of the Republic of Croatia by proclaiming the Statute of the Serb Autonomous District of Krajina. At the end of March 1991, rebel Serb units occupied the area of the famous Plitvice Lakes national park, and in the fighting that ensued between the Serbs and the Croatian police, one of the latter and a Serbian fighter were killed. These were "the first war victims in Croatia."[50]

Milošević's rise to the top of the Serbian Communist Party quickly shattered any remaining illusions in Slovenia that an agreement among the various peoples would be possible at some time in the future. The Serbian media staged a genuine propaganda war against opponents of Belgrade's positions, particularly against those who criticized the Serbian use of force in Kosovo in 1989, when more than 100 Albanians were killed. Finally, Serbia broke off economic relations with Slovenia in December 1989. In January 1990, the Slovene (and Croat) communists walked out of the Fourteenth Congress of the League of Communists of Yugoslavia. The multiparty elections in Slovenia and Croatia in April and May 1990 disrupted all further political relations. At the same time, when the republic's new governments were established, the JNA began to disarm the Slovene and Croatian Territorial Defense forces. Milošević's access to the federal financial system in fall 1990 led to the further deterioration of relations. Yugoslavia had disintegrated even before Slovenia and Croatia formally declared their independence. The one powerful organization that still functioned, the Yugoslav National Army, could only prolong the dissolution process.[51]

Conclusions and Suggestions

The nineteenth-century dream of unity for the South Slav peoples, which had been nurtured by many intellectuals and politicians of all South Slav nations—even in the Habsburg Monarchy—was realized in November 1918 as a result of external and internal threats following World War I. But the Yugoslav-centralistic Serbian monarchy became a dictatorship against which the political elite of the other Yugoslav nations often protested and sometimes revolted. After the invasion of the Axis Powers in 1941 and the partition of Yugoslavia, the Croatian Ustaša regime initiated a civil war between the Croats, Serbs, and Muslims that claimed around 600,000 victims. Although suppressed in Tito's Yugoslavia, the memories of the bitter internecine fighting were perpetuated in families and passed down from generation to generation.

Marshal Tito tried to prevent his communist state from falling under the hegemony of its most powerful component nation, the Serbs, as did its predecessor. In his incessant battle to keep the Yugoslav nations on an equal footing, Tito ruthlessly suppressed any expression of resurgent nationalism. Enforcing his doctrine of "Brotherhood and Unity," he carried out purges of Serbs, Croats, and Muslims, Slovenes, Macedonians, and Albanians, balancing the repression of any one nation against that of the others and using the Yugoslav People's Army as well as the secret police forces. Nationalists were forced into exile or they were jailed. When Tito died in May 1980, nobody knew—although some supposed— that they were also burying Yugoslavia. The chance to change the communist system and to establish a modern democratic confederation existed only for a few years. Already in 1987, with the nationalistic mass mobilization of Milošević and the critical reaction of the Slovenes, positive trends were reversed. Neither the state chancelleries nor the intellectuals in the West and East understood the clear signals. After the collapse of the Iron Curtain, Yugoslavia lost its strategic importance to Washington and Moscow. For the first time in history, no external threat forced Yugoslavia to remain whole, and none of the component nations had a need for it any longer.

The breakup of communist-ruled Yugoslavia was not the fault of the international community. Neither the United States, the Soviet Union, NATO, nor the European Community were engaged in the dissolution process; quite the reverse. The civil wars as well as the successor wars in Yugoslavia were planned and waged by Yugoslavs, mainly by the Serbian leadership around Slobodan Milošević and the Yugoslav National Army. Milošević's policy tried to win control first over Serbia, then over Yugoslavia. His politics of ethnic oppression against the Albanians and the nationalization of Serbian society provoked the newly elected leadership in Slovenia and Croatia. President Milan Kučan, as well as President Franjo Tudjman, jumped to take the challenge. Serb-Slovene relations had been disrupted earlier, as well, especially following the trial in spring 1988. Furthermore, Croat-Serb relations had been troubled since the mobilization of the Serb minority in the Krajina. Only the Bosnian

Muslims were unprepared for the conflict and subsequently became its most common victims.[52]

For analytical purposes, Vesna Pešić tried to separate the breakup of Yugoslavia and the war, but she had to admit that "the two processes are indisputably linked." She attributed the cause of the war

to the creation of new national states in which the leadership of the individual republics brought them into conflict over the distribution of Yugoslav territory, borders and ethnic boundaries. The national heterogeneity of all the republics, with the exception of Slovenia, led not only to the problem of integrating the existing states, but also to the conflicts between them. . . . The war was initiated because of boundary changes and the alteration of ethno-demographic structures (the movement of the ethnic population). When conflicts are defined as being about border changes and the creation of ethnic homogeneity in future national states, these ends are naturally served by the leadership of individual states through unilateral decisions, *fait accompli* strategies, military force, and even genocide. A war for border changes between the republics, and the expulsion of other ethnic groups was initiated by the political leadership in Serbia as a means of creating a Serbian state. The Croatian leadership chose a similar strategy . . . as seen in the discrimination and open intolerance towards the Serbs in Croatia, and territorial pretensions towards Bosnia-Herzegovina. By agreement this republic should have been shared between Serbia and Croatia.[53]

Nevertheless, one should emphasize that in June 1991, only Milošević and the JNA had sufficient weapons at their disposal to start the war.

In a recent article in *Foreign Affairs*, David Rohde illustrated the depth of animosity between Albanians and Serbs in Kosovo and the unbounded obsession with revenge.[54] He warned against a partition of Kosovo, because it could set a precedent. Furthermore, Rohde still sees the former Yugoslavia as an economic unit, although the Slovenian and parts of the Croatian economy found their way (back) to Central European markets. In the same issue Ivo Banac points out that most observers ignore "that the reconstruction of Bosnia holds the key for overall regional recovery."[55] The press overlooks "the daily battles against the ruling ethnic cleansers who continue to frustrate refugee return. . . . Last year's Stability Pact has been nothing but a photo opportunity, without any teeth or credibility, despite its promises of security and economic aid." Therefore, according to Banac,

the whole area desperately needs a new vision after Western intervention. Such a vision would require the independence of all the former federal units of Yugoslavia—but it would also require cohesion within a larger regional scheme that includes a customs union, a multilateral security system, and freedom of travel and information. This is impossible as long as Milošević is in power. His regime caps two centuries of ethnic forest fires that have destroyed the Balkans' complex multiethnicity. Indeed, this task is impossible as long as the general Balkan national-revolutionary model, which seeks to establish nationally homogeneous states, remains credible.

Banac's argument needs to take into account the fact that the process of ethnic homogenization within the Yugoslav nations ran along the Western and Central European model that dates back to the independence of Bulgaria and Greece in 1830. After 1945, the Serbs carried out assimilation policies in the Vojvodina, the Sanžak of Novipazar, and Kosovo, the Croats in Istria and Baranja, the Slovenes in Gorica, Koper, and Lower Styria, and the Albanians in Kosovo. During the dissolution process of Yugoslavia, the Serbs tried to force such processes in Bosnia-Herzegovina, the Croats in the Krajina (between Sisak and Knin), the Montenegrins in Ulcinj, and the Albanians in Kosovo and Macedonia. Not just nationalists in Belgrade demanded the creation of a "Greater Serbia," including larger parts of Bosnia-Herzegovina, Croatia proper, and Dalmatia. Hence, early on, the Croats and Bosnian Muslims tried to defend the boundaries of their republics, which were not always ethnic boundaries. The wars in Croatia, Bosnia-Herzegovina, and Kosovo, with the expulsion of some hundreds of thousands of Bosnian Muslims, Croats, Serbs, and Albanians, created new ethnic realities in many regions. The Dayton Agreement demanded the return of the refugees, so far without much success. It is therefore advisable that the international community not accept the new ethnic "realities" without demanding the return of former multiethnic entities.

The dissolution of Yugoslavia also fits the model of national self-determination in Europe as it has developed in the twentieth century. In 1905 Norway separated from Sweden, in 1913 Albania from the Ottoman Empire, in 1917 Finland from Russia, in 1918 the Baltic states, Poland, and Ukraine from Soviet Russia, in 1918 Austria, Czechoslovakia, Hungary, and Yugoslavia from Austria-Hungary, in 1922 Ireland from the United Kingdom, in 1939 Slovakia from Czechoslovakia, in 1941 Croatia from Yugoslavia, in 1944 Iceland from Denmark, and so on through the breakup of the Soviet Union and Czechoslovakia. Thus, during the twentieth century smaller and more ethnically homogenous countries have continually been created—and no one spoke of a "balkanization" of Northern or East Central Europe. The international community should accept this process of the building of new nation-states. Even the smallest nations wish to have sovereignty and their own governments and administrations.

Historical experience from former multinational states such as the Habsburg Monarchy and Yugoslavia points to the fact that in many cases of political, economic, social, or cultural troubles, there was always a search for a scapegoat—national or religious. In ethnically homogenized countries such as Poland, the Czech Republic, Austria, or Slovenia, the nation-state bears the sole responsibility for its participation within the European state system. During the whole process of reconstruction in Bosnia-Herzegovina, Kosovo, and other Balkan regions, the local populations need more political, economic, and social control over their own destiny. The international community should encourage this process by establishing new sovereign entities: for the Albanians, for the Bosnian Muslims, for the Croats, for the Macedonians, and for the Serbs. But political criteria, "historical rights," strategic reasons, economic demands (for example, mines), and cultural heritages (for instance, monasteries) should be secondary to the political will of the clear ethnic majority in a region, district, or community, thus conforming to the Declaration of Human Rights.

In November 1918, threatened and endangered small nations entered the "Kingdom of the Serbs, Croats, and Slovenes," and in 1945—once again threatened and endangered—the Federal People's Republic of Yugoslavia. Three generations later, in 1991, the realism of the small nations prevailed once more. In the words of Slovene historian, Rado Lenček:

[H]uman beings are mortal and are inevitably replaced by new individuals and new generations. And it is these generations who in the long run decide how much of what they have received from their predecessors will be preserved or changed, abandoned or destroyed.[56]

8 The Macedonian Question and Instability in the Balkans

ANDREW ROSSOS

Since the aftermath of the Crimean War, the Macedonian question has been the central issue dividing the Balkan peoples as well as their respective patrons from among the Great Powers. It involved most Balkan peoples, especially Macedonia's neighbors, the Bulgarians, Greeks, and Serbs, and, at one time or another, all the Great Powers in the European state system.[1]

The literature on the Macedonian question is vast, both in the major European languages and even more in the Balkan languages. Indeed the Bulgarians have probably published more on the "Makedonskiat vŭpros," the Greeks on the "Makedoniko zitima," and the Serbs on the "Makedonsko pitanje" than on themes that one might rightly consider more significant in their modern histories or integral to their national development. And, of course, there was always the Macedonian preoccupation with the "Makedonsko prašanje." For the most part these writings tend to be polemical, partisan, and of uneven scholarly quality. However, the great volume, the sheer vastness of this literature is a clear indication of the great significance that all of them, Great Powers as well as Balkan states, ascribed to the Macedonian question.[2]

In this chapter, it is not my intention to analyze critically the irreconcilably contradictory writings on the Macedonian question or to try to provide a detailed survey of the history of the Macedonian question since its inception. Either of these tasks would require more time and space than I have at my disposal. Instead, I will focus in rather general terms on the Macedonian question as a critical factor in Balkan politics, on its impact on inter-Balkan relations, or, more precisely, on instability in the Balkan peninsula.

First, I will define briefly the Macedonian question. Second, I will examine the Macedonian question as a Balkan problem; that is, as the central issue dividing Macedonia's neighbors, and their attempts to settle it to their own advantage. Third, I will deal with the Macedonian question as a Macedonian problem and with the various Macedonian notions and attempts to resolve the Macedonian question on a Macedonian basis. In fact, I will argue that from its very inception, but particularly after the emergence of Macedonianism (*Makedonizm*) in the 1860s, the Macedonian question was primarily a Macedonian problem; that is, a problem concerning first and foremost the Macedonians, the Slavic-speaking majority of its inhabitants, to be resolved by the Macedonians and for the Macedonians.[3] Finally, I will touch briefly on the state of the Macedonian question today; that is, since the bloody dissolution of the Yugoslav federation and the declaration of Macedonian independence.

I. What Is the Macedonian Question?

There is no simple way to define what had become known already in the second half of the nineteenth century as "the thorny" or "the perennial" Macedonian question. Perhaps the best way to define it would be to state that it concerned the future, the fate of Macedonia, which was and remained an integral part of the Ottoman Empire until 1913, and of the Macedonians, or, more precisely, the Macedonian Slavs, its Slavic-speaking majority, who beginning in the 1860s gradually adapted the name of their land Macedonia as a national name and symbol. Or to put it in the form of a question, who would obtain control of Macedonia and the Macedonians once the expected, indeed imminent, collapse of the Ottoman Empire, "the Sick Man of Europe," took place?[4]

Although it is sometimes claimed even in scholarly writings that the Macedonian problem was created by the 1878 Congress of Berlin,[5] its roots and origins are to be found in the first Slavic and thus anti-Patriarchist, anti-Greek, and anti-Turkish cultural strivings in Macedonia in the second quarter of the nineteenth century. However, it assumed a much more acute, political form in the aftermath of the Crimean War (1854–56). By that time the small Kingdom of Greece had been in existence for nearly three decades and the small Principality of Serbia had acquired real autonomy.[6] The Bulgarian national movement was gaining strength and with the help of Russia would soon score its most significant victory, the establishment of a Bulgarian national church, the Exarchate, in 1870. After that there was no doubt that sooner rather than later a Bulgarian state would come into existence.

And it did in 1878, after the Russo-Turkish war and the Congress of Berlin.[7]

In the meantime the Ottoman Empire was proving convincingly to all concerned, the Great Powers as well as the small Balkan states, that it was incapable of reforming itself. The *Tanzimat* reforms added a certain modern, Western veneer to the Ottoman legal and administrative facade but did hardly anything substantial to slow down, let alone stop, the decline of the empire or improve the position of its shrinking Orthodox Christian population.[8] The ruling elites of the Balkan national movements, as well as the chanceries of the Great Powers, were becoming convinced that the demise of "the Sick Man of Europe," if not imminent, was certainly unavoidable. Hence, they all focused their attention on the remaining Ottoman possessions in Europe—on the post-Ottoman inheritance. The most important of these lands from a geopolitical, strategic, and economic point of view was, of course, Macedonia, the heart of the peninsula.[9]

It was this overall importance of Macedonia that sparked the vicious struggle for its possession on the part of the neighboring Balkan nationalisms supported by their patrons from among the Great Powers: a struggle that represented the essence of the Macedonian problem. As I have already stressed, this struggle became and has remained to the present day the critical issue dividing the Balkan peoples. It transformed Macedonia into an "apple of discord," "a stumbling block" to any semblance of cooperation among the Balkan peoples and states. This leads me to the second topic that I wish to examine: the Macedonian question as a Balkan problem.

II. The Macedonian Question as a Balkan Problem

All three nationalisms, the Bulgarian, Greek, and Serbian, denied the existence of a separate Macedonian identity and claimed Macedonia and the Macedonians as their own for their national states. All three developed complex justifications and rationalizations of their respective claims, which were based on a confusing array of irreconcilably contradictory historic, linguistic, cultural, ethnographic, and other arguments with accompanying statistics.[10] In order to prove their respective claims they became directly involved in every sphere of life in Macedonia. Each sought to establish or control the local churches, schools, communal organizations, reading rooms, guilds, and so on. Until the 1890s they carried on the struggle mainly through extremely well-financed propaganda institutions and campaigns and relied on pressure tactics and intimidation.

After that, and particularly after the unsuccessful Macedonian Ilinden uprising of 1903, they increasingly resorted to armed struggle. Armed bands of *komitas* from Bulgaria, *andartes* from Greece, and *četniks* from Serbia crossed into Macedonia to fight each other, Macedonian bands (*četas*), and the Turks. Macedonia became a battleground of the competing neighboring Balkan nationalisms. The aim of the three was the same throughout the struggle: to win the hearts and minds of the Macedonians or to force them into submission in order to justify their respective territorial aspirations.[11]

At the outset, each of the three put forward claims to the whole of Macedonia for its own national state. By the late 1890s, however, partly as a result of the rapid spread of Bulgarian influence in Macedonia but mainly due to the realization that they could not acquire it in its entirety, Athens and Belgrade began to consider seriously its partition.[12] Sofia did not move in that direction until much later, after the suppression of the Ilinden uprising in Macedonia, and with far greater hesitation. In fact, it did not accept partition officially until the negotiation of the alliance with Serbia in the aftermath of the Annexation Crisis of 1908–1909. It appears that in the end Bulgaria embraced partition, at least in principle, partly as a result of the growth of authentic Macedonian patriotic and autonomist sentiment but also because Sofia, it would seem, had come to the conclusion that Greece and Serbia and their supporters from among the Great Powers would not permit a Bulgarian annexation of the whole of Macedonia.[13]

However, embracing the principle of partitioning Macedonia was one thing and the easy part; reaching agreement on the actual terms of the partition was much more difficult, and proved, as it turned out, an impossible task. During the protracted and difficult negotiations leading to the creation of the Balkan system of alliances against the Turks in 1912, the terms of the partition of Macedonia was the issue that divided them the most. The Bulgarians and the Serbs reached an agreement of sorts, but they had to relegate important territorial differences and disagreements over Macedonia to the arbitration of the Russian czar.[14] The Bulgarians and the Greeks could not reach an agreement on the division of Macedonia at all and side-tracked the issue; it was to be resolved somehow after a victorious war against the Turks.[15]

Consequently, even while the so-called allies were engaged in the war against the Turks or the First Balkan War of 1912–13 and long before it came to a final conclusion with the Treaty of London of May 30, 1913, the differences over Macedonia were undermining the Balkan system of alliances. The Greeks and the Serbs engaged the Turks primarily in Macedonia, occupied most of its territory, and claimed most, if not all, the areas under their military control. The Bulgarians, who carried the brunt of the fighting in the East, in Thrace, near the center of Ottoman power, occupied only a small part of Macedonia but claimed most if not all of it on the basis of their Treaty of Alliance with Serbia. A deadlock ensued, the lines became rigidly drawn, and a negotiated resolution of their irreconcilably contradictory claims in Macedonia was impossible.[16] Greece and Serbia drew closer together and on June 1, 1913 signed a defensive treaty of alliance directed against Bulgaria, which undermined the original Balkan system of alliances.[17] Moreover, it set the stage for another war over Macedonia, the Inter-Allied or Second Balkan War of 1913, which destroyed the Balkan system of alliances of 1912. This war between Bulgaria, on the one hand, and Greece and Serbia, on the other, when Romania and Turkey also jumped into the fray and attacked Bulgaria, resulted in the humiliating defeat of Bulgaria and the partition of Macedonia, by force of arms, largely on the basis of the terms dictated by victorious Greece and Serbia.[18]

The Treaty of Bucharest of August 10, 1913, which ended the war and sanctioned this partition of Macedonia, in fact, did not resolve the Macedonian question. It only set the stage for yet another war over Macedonia. Bulgaria was determined to overturn this settlement, and there is no doubt that for Sofia World War I represented mainly a continuation of the Second Balkan War. Bulgaria moved into the sphere of influence of the Central Powers and in 1915 intervened on their side in the Great War by attacking Serbia primarily because of its frustrated territorial ambitions in Macedonia.[19]

The peace conferences and treaties ending the Great War confirmed the partition of Macedonia and the Macedonians based on the Treaty of Bucharest (August 10, 1913), with some minor modifications at the expense of the once again defeated Bulgaria. Greece acquired Aegean Macedonia, the largest Macedonian territory; Serbia got Vardar Macedonia, with the largest Macedonian (Slavic Macedonian) population. Bulgaria, whose influence in Macedonia had grown steadily since 1870 and who was obsessed with the idea of annexing all Macedonia and thus creating a great San Stefano Bulgaria, ended up with the smallest part, Pirin Macedonia.[20]

For the Kingdom of Greece and the former Kingdom of Serbia—now the dominant factor in the newly created Kingdom of the Serbs, Croats, and Slovenes, or Yugoslavia—and their patrons from among the victorious allies, especially Great Britain and France, this meant putting the Macedonian problem to rest. Even though the territorial acquisitions in Macedonia did not necessarily satisfy their fondest hopes, official

Athens and Belgrade pretended that Macedonia and the Macedonian problem had ceased to exist. Belgrade proclaimed Vardar Macedonia to be Old Serbia and the Macedonians Old Serbs; for Athens, Aegean Macedonia became simply northern Greece and its Slavic-speaking Macedonians were considered Greeks or at best "Slavophone" Greeks.[21]

Once the new rulers had consolidated their controls over the respective parts of Macedonia, they initiated policies the aim of which was the destruction of all signs of Macedonian nationalism, patriotism, or particularism. This was to be accomplished through forced deportation and so-called voluntary exchanges of populations, forced transfers of the Macedonian population internally, colonization, social and economic discrimination, and forced denationalization and assimilation through the total control of the educational systems and cultural and intellectual life as a whole.[22]

Needless to say, the claims of official Athens and Belgrade that the partition and their policies solved or put an end to the Macedonian problem turned out to be no more than wishful thinking and self-deception. Macedonians rejected the partition of their land and the settlement based upon it. And there is no doubt that the policies of repression had failed. In April 1926, after a tour of Yugoslav (Vardar) Macedonia, R. A. Gallop, the third secretary of the British Legation at Belgrade, reported:

The most striking thing to one familiar with North Serbia [Serbia proper], who has been accustomed to hear Macedonia described as Southern Serbia and its inhabitants as Serbs, was the complete difference of atmosphere which was noticeable almost as soon as we had crossed the pre-1913 frontier some miles south of Vranje. One felt as though one had entered a foreign country. Officials and officers from North Serbia seemed to feel this too, and I noticed especially in the cafes and hotels of Skoplje that they formed groups by themselves and mixed little with the Macedo-Slavs. Those of the latter that I met were equally insistent on calling themselves neither Serbs nor Bulgars, but Macedonians. . . . There seemed to be no love lost for the Bulgars in most places. Their brutality during the war had lost them the affection even of those who before the Balkan War had been their friends. . . . [23]

Almost two decades later, in December 1944, Captain P. H. Evans, an agent of the Special Operations Executive (SOE) who spent eight months in Western Greek (Aegean) Macedonia as a British Liaison Officer (BLO) and station commander, reported to the Foreign Office:

It is a predominantly a SLAV region not a GREEK one. The language of the home, and usually also of the fields, the village street and the market is MACEDONIAN, a SLAV language. . . . The place names as given on the map are GREEK . . . , but the names which are mostly used . . . are SLAV

names. The GREEK ones are merely a bit of varnish put on by Metaxas. . . .
GREEK is regarded as almost a foreign language and the GREEKS are dis-
trusted as something alien, even if not in the full sense of the word, as foreigners. The obvious fact, almost too obvious to be stated, that the region is
SLAV by nature and not GREEK, cannot be overemphasized.[24]

Throughout the interwar period, Macedonians supported the terrorist activities of the Internal Macedonian Revolutionary Organization (VMRO)
and the underground work of the communist parties, and contributed to
the internal instability of both countries.[25] More on this later.

What was more significant from the point of view of inter-Balkan relations and stability in the peninsula, however, was the decisive rejection of the terms of the partition by the third partitioning power, Bulgaria. Unlike official Athens and Belgrade, the ruling elite in Sofia did
not consider this settlement permanent or final. But without sympathy
among the victorious Great Powers and threatened by revolutionary turmoil at home, they had to swallow the bitter pill and accept it for the
time being. After the overthrow of the Stamboliski regime in June 1921,
however, revisionist Bulgaria assumed a more ambiguous stance: Sofia
chose to continue its traditional patronizing attitude toward all Macedonians and to claim them as Bulgarians. It allowed for a more tolerant
milieu for Macedonian activism. Sofia encouraged and sought to use
Macedonian discontent and patriotism and Macedonian movements to
further its own nationalist and revisionist aims.[26] By the mid-1920s, the
VMRO had regrouped and clearly emerged as a terrorist organization, a
virtual ruler in Pirin Macedonia and a state within a state in Bulgaria. It
conducted armed raids into Yugoslav (Vardar) and Greek (Aegean) Macedonia, relied on Bulgarian revisionism and Italian fascism, and allowed
itself to be used by both.[27]

No matter how much Greece and Yugoslavia and their patrons from
among the Great Powers pretended officially that the Macedonian question had been resolved and now ceased to exist, Bulgarian revisionist
policies split the ranks of the partitioning states and continued to keep
it alive internationally. It remained the chief stumbling bloc to all attempts at inter-Balkan cooperation, "the apple of discord," the most important bone of contention dividing the Balkan states, and thus the major factor of instability in the Balkans throughout the interwar years.[28]

Indeed, there is no doubt that the Balkan Conferences of the early
1930s, which aimed to establish Balkan inter-state cooperation, failed because of Bulgarian revisionist aims. The Commission on Political Relations prepared a Balkan pact of nonaggression but it was never adopted.

The Bulgarian delegates rejected any and all proposals that suggested formal acceptance of the existing borders, and they also demanded minority rights for the "Bulgarian-speaking" population of Greece and Yugoslavia.[29]

Bulgaria's revisionist policies exacerbated the already tense relations with her neighbors not so much because isolated Bulgaria threatened them, but rather because behind Bulgarian revisionism stood revisionist Italy and after 1933 the rising influence and power of Hitler's Germany. It was this fear and apprehension that Bulgaria would become a base for revisionist Great Powers, such as Italy and Nazi Germany, which were intent on destroying the Versailles territorial settlement, that drove Bulgaria's neighbors to seek greater cooperation and the formation of a Balkan security system. The negotiations were carried out in Geneva and Belgrade and resulted in the formation of a four-power Balkan pact including Greece, Yugoslavia, Romania, and Turkey. The agreement was signed at Athens in early February 1934. The aim of this Balkan Entente was to safeguard the security of the existing frontiers. Unlike the Balkan Conferences, which sought to unite all Balkan states, the Balkan Entente was formed to maintain the territorial status quo and was thus directed primarily against revisionist Bulgaria.[30]

The fundamental weakness of the Balkan Entente was apparent from the very beginning. Its member states could not agree on a common approach to the challenges posed by the growing power of Germany.[31] This became even more obvious in 1938 as a result of the German annexation of Austria and the Sudeten regions of Czechoslovakia. Members of the Balkan Entente embarked on a policy of appeasement toward Bulgaria. Already on January 24, 1937, Premier Milan Stojadinović of Yugoslavia signed a pact with Bulgaria providing for peace and friendship between the two countries.[32] On July 31, 1938, the Balkan Entente concluded a Treaty of Friendship and Nonaggression with Bulgaria.[33] It is important to note, however, that neither agreement represented a real accommodation of the differences that divided them over Macedonia. They avoided any specific mention of the two critical issues: the permanence of the territorial status quo and Bulgarian membership in the Balkan Entente.[34]

In any event, by the time World War II began, the Balkan Entente was for all practical purposes dead and buried. As was the case during World War I, it was mainly due to their irreconcilable differences over Macedonia that the partitioning powers found themselves again at war against each other—with Bulgaria in the camp of the Axis Powers and Yugoslavia and Greece on the side of the Allies. Already before Hitler invaded Yugoslavia and Greece in April 1941, Bulgaria was an active participant in the German war effort. In January the Bulgarian government allowed the stationing of German troops on its territory, and in March formally joined the Tripartite Pact.[35]

The Third Reich rewarded its Balkan ally generously. After their defeat Yugoslavia and Greece were partitioned and Vardar and Aegean Macedonia were once again repartitioned. Bulgaria was allowed to occupy and annex most of Yugoslav (Vardar) Macedonia, eastern Greek (Aegean) Macedonia, except for the Salonika area, which remained under German control, and a small part of western Greek (Aegean) Macedonia. The northwest district of Yugoslav (Vardar) Macedonia, Tetovo, and so forth, was attached to Italian-occupied Albania, and the rest of Greek (Aegean) Macedonia came under Italian occupation until Italy's collapse in 1943.[36]

World War II, the fourth war fought for control of Macedonia by its claimants, the neighboring Balkan states, did not bring the "perennial" Macedonia problem any closer to a settlement acceptable to all of them. It only proved that their divisions over Macedonia were so deep-rooted and fundamental that they defied resolution even by the most radical changes of political systems and ideologies. The dramatic events of this war only transformed the Macedonian problem from "an apple of discord" dividing the Balkan bourgeois states into one dividing the Balkan communist parties and, after the Stalin-Tito conflict and the Greek Civil War, into one dividing three divergent political systems and ideologies— pro-Western capitalist Greece, pro-Soviet communist Bulgaria, and Titoist federal Yugoslavia.

During the interwar years, the communist parties of Bulgaria (KPB), Greece (KKE), and Yugoslavia (KPJ) were the only parties in the three partitioning powers to recognize the existence of a Macedonian identity and ethnic nation. And as Marxist-Leninists, they accepted, at least officially, the Leninist principle of national self-determination and hence of Macedonian national liberation and unification: the right of the Macedonians to have their own state.[37] However, this did not mean—and events during the war and its revolutionary aftermath in the Balkans proved that it did not mean—that they were in complete agreement on the final resolution of the Macedonian question or that they were willing to give up or give up unconditionally their countries' respective Macedonian possessions. The truth was far from it. The KPJ and the KPB each hoped that Macedonian unification would be achieved under its own auspices, or within its own country, or within the context of a South Slav or Balkan federation that it hoped to dominate.[38] The KKE, which would obviously not be a member of a South Slav federation and could hardly expect to dominate a Balkan federation, may therefore have wished that Greek (Aegean) Macedonia would be left out of these plans for a united Macedonian state. In any case, the leadership of the KKE emphasized equality for and the protection of the national rights of the Macedonian minority in Greece rather than Macedonian statehood.[39]

Indeed, with the outbreak of World War I, the collapse of the old order, and the rise of powerful communist-led resistance movements in Yugoslavia and Greece, all these differences came into the open. The three communist parties became entangled in a struggle for the hearts and minds of the Macedonians, which continued as long as communism survived in the Balkans. Throughout the struggle, they "betrayed a chauvinism regarding Macedonia not unlike that of their respective [bourgeois] governments."[40] By 1943 it became clear that the Yugoslav communists, and here I am including the Macedonian leadership in Yugoslavia, had won the competition among the Balkan communist parties. Josip B. Tito, the leader of the KPJ, who was neither Bulgarian, Greek, nor Serb and was able to consider the Macedonian question more objectively, realized that the Macedonians would be satisfied with nothing less than "a free Macedonia," Macedonian statehood. Under his leadership, the KPJ developed a winning strategy that overshadowed the Macedonian policies of the other two fraternal parties, exercised great influence even on the Macedonians in Aegean and Pirin Macedonia through the 1940s, and assured Yugoslavia of a dominant say in Macedonian affairs until the collapse of the Yugoslav federation in 1991. Whereas the KKE could only make vague promises of equality in a future and uncertain communist Greece, and the weakened KPB could promise a united Macedonia in an even more uncertain Balkan communist federation, the KPJ guaranteed Macedonian statehood and equality with the five other units in a new federal Yugoslavia and promised Macedonian unification within Yugoslavia or in a Yugoslav-dominated South Slav or Balkan federation.[41]

With the proclamation of the Macedonian state in Yugoslavia on August 2, 1944, Tito's triumphant regime consolidated its dominant role in Macedonian affairs. It had won the support of leading Macedonian activists, communist and noncommunist, not only in Vardar but also in Aegean and Pirin Macedonia.[42] And even before the Second World War had officially ended the confident leaders of victorious Yugoslavia began to assert their solution of the Macedonian question vis-à-vis the weak and uncertain communist-dominated Fatherland Front Government of the once again defeated Bulgaria. Throughout the negotiations for a Yugoslav-Bulgarian federation (which began in November–December 1944 and reached a climax with the Tito-Dimitrov meetings at Bled, Slovenia, in August, and at Evksinograd, near Varna, in November 1947), the Macedonian question was the focal point. The Yugoslavs sought to impose on the hesitant Bulgarians the unification of Pirin Macedonia with the Peoples' Republic of Macedonia (NRM) in Yugoslavia or in a Yugoslav-dominated South Slav federation, and this was one of the major obstacles to an agreement.[43] At the same time, Tito became the principal patron of the Greek communists in their struggle for power. Yugoslavia provided moral support and helped rally the Macedonians in Greece and their organizations behind the National Liberation Front–Greek Popular or Liberation Army (EAM-ELAS) in the war, and then to the communist side in the Civil War (1947–49). During the latter, the Yugoslavs provided food, transport facilities, the use of camps, arms, artillery and ammunitions, and so forth. They hoped that with the communists in power in Greece, the Yugoslav solution of the Macedonian question would be completed. Aegean Macedonia, or its Macedonian-populated areas, would be united with the Peoples' Republic in Yugoslavia or in a Yugoslav-dominated Balkan communist federation that would include Greece.[44]

In the end, Tito's attempt to solve the Macedonian question by establishing a united Macedonia or a greater Macedonia under Yugoslav auspices failed. Stalin saw in Tito's plan and growing power and prestige a real or potential challenge to Soviet hegemony not only in the Balkans, but in the entire Soviet sphere of influence in Eastern Europe and, indeed, in the international communist movement.[45] He vetoed the plans already before 1948 and, after the historic break with Tito, turned the Macedonian issue into an instrument of the Cominform anti-Yugoslav campaign. The Bulgarian and Greek communist parties, who resented Tito's overbearing tactics as well as his solution of the Macedonian question, were only too glad and eager to side with Stalin. They were convinced, as was Stalin, that Tito would be toppled from power and, with Yugoslavia humbled and under Soviet control, they would enjoy a free hand in their respective parts of Macedonia—or, in the case of Bulgaria, settle the Macedonian question under its own auspices.[46] In any event, Tito was not overthrown and the "perennial" Macedonian problem again remained unresolved, the "apple of discord" dividing the Balkan states and communist parties.

In the aftermath of the Soviet-Yugoslav conflict and the Civil War of Greece, in both of which the future of Macedonia was a critical issue, the Macedonian question, potentially at least, posed a greater danger to stability in the Balkans then ever before. As I already pointed out, until World War II, the partitioning bourgeois states claimed the Macedonians as their own and justified their claims to Macedonia on irreconcilably contradictory ethnic, linguistic, or cultural grounds. However, they were officially in agreement on one thing: all three denied the existence of a Macedonian people, identity, or nation. The establishment of the Macedonian Republic as an equal partner in the Yugoslav federation in 1944, the recognition of the Macedonians in Várdar Macedonia as one of the state nations of Yugoslavia, and the acceptance of the Macedonian language as one of the four official languages of the federation, deepened even more the gulf dividing the partitioning states. Federal Yugoslavia assumed the role of the champion of all Macedonians and placed Bulgaria and Greece on the defensive.[47] After the defeat of the communist side in the Civil War in Greece, the pro-western Royalist Government in Athens equated expressions of Macedonianism with communism, which became illegal in Greece. It denied even more vociferously than before World War I the existence of a Macedonian identity, of a Macedonian national minority within its own part of Macedonia, and continued to call the Macedonians in the republic to the north Serbs or at best "Skopians."[48] Communist Bulgaria found itself in an even more awkward situation. As I have already pointed out, like the other two fraternal parties, the KKE and the KPJ, the KPB had recognized the existence of a separate Macedonian nation, and the Fatherland Front Government had endorsed Macedonian unification at least in principle. After the expulsion of Yugoslavia from the Cominform, communist Bulgaria gradually moved from recognition to the earlier position of Royalist Bulgaria, negating the existence of Macedonians in the Yugoslav republic and of a Macedonian national minority in Bulgaria and claiming all Macedonians as Bulgarians.[49]

However, in spite of the deep differences that divided Yugoslavia, Bulgaria, and Greece on the Macedonian question, they recognized that in the context of the Cold War, of a Europe divided in two opposing camps, and two military blocs armed with nuclear weapons, they could do nothing to alter the territorial or national status quo in Macedonia. As if by mutual consent and agreement, they decided that it was in their best interests to put the Macedonian question "on ice." With the exception of some broadsides fired periodically by academics or journalists in Skopje, Sofia, and Salonika, the most responsible political leaders, generally speaking, acted as though the Macedonian question had indeed been settled and now ceased to exist. As a Serbian official of the Yugoslav Ministry of Foreign Affairs told me in 1980: "It was more important for Belgrade to sell 'Fićos' [Yugoslav FIATS] in Greece than to concern itself with the human or national dimensions of the Macedonian problem." Sentiments of this kind were undoubtedly shared by his counterparts in Athens and Sofia.[50] The collapse of communism in Europe, the bloody disintegration of Yugoslavia, and the declaration of independence by the Republic of Macedonia exposed these attitudes and pushed the Macedonian question once again into the forefront of Balkan politics as the central issue dividing the Balkan states.[51]

To conclude this part of the discussion, I would like to emphasize the following points. First, in a struggle that continued for well over a century, the three claimants to Macedonia could not impose or agree on a lasting and viable solution of the Macedonian question, because their aims were and remained irreconcilably contradictory. Second, even if they had been able to agree on the terms of a mutually acceptable partition of Macedonia, it would not have represented a lasting and viable resolution of the Macedonian question, because partition and foreign rule based on national denial or nonrecognition was being rejected by Macedonians. And third, and most important, on the basis of the latest research on the Macedonian question, it seems obvious now that after the appearance of the *Makedonists* and *Makedonizm* in the 1860s and particularly of organized Macedonian activity in the 1880s and 1890s, there could have been no viable or lasting solution of the Macedonian problem without the consent and the support of the Macedonians. And this leads me to the next part of my discussion, namely, the Macedonian question as a Macedonian problem.

III. The Macedonian Question
as a Macedonian Problem

For the small Macedonian intelligentsia and, as time went on, for the Macedonians in general, the Macedonian question was not a Greek, Bulgarian, or Serbian problem but exclusively their own. It concerned the future of their own land, Macedonia; and from the 1860s, when they first adopted the name of their land as a national name and symbol, it involved their own self-definition, identity, interests, and future as Macedonians. Virtually all members of the small Macedonian intelligentsia were educated in schools operated by the neighboring Balkan nationalist institutions in Macedonia or, with their financial support, in Athens, Belgrade, or Sofia. With the exception of those of them who were for all practical purposes assimilated into what appeared as a superior culture and embraced the nationalist ideology and aims of the host-benefactor state, they repudiated assimilation and the outside nationalist ideologies and assumed leadership positions in both the Macedonian national and revolutionary movements. They rejected all schemes for the annexation or partition of their land and instead put forward the idea of Macedonian statehood.[52] This idea became and remained an integral component of Macedonian national development. A "free Macedonia" (*slobodna Makedonija*) comprised the central plank in the program of virtually all Macedonian patriotic, revolutionary, and national organizations and movements since the 1878 Congress of Berlin.[53] This was true of the Internal Macedonian Revolutionary Organization (VMRO) of the Ilinden period,[54] as well as the *Makedonisti* of the generation of Krste P. Misirkov, the leading ideologist of Macedonian nationalism after the turn of the century.[55] It was also equally true of both the Macedonian political right[56] and left,[57] which in the much more difficult circumstances of post-Ottoman, post-partition, divided Macedonia, at least up to the end of the Civil War in Greece in 1949, called for a united Macedonian state.

Although they all sought the establishment of a Macedonian state—a "free Macedonia," to use the most frequently employed term—statehood did not necessarily or always denote total independence. Many Macedonian spokesmen, conscious of the relative weakness of Macedonian nationalism and the comparative combined strength of its opposition, assumed a more pragmatic stance. They sought a place for a free or autonomous Macedonian state in a larger unit or supranational association: a Balkan federation, a Balkan socialist federation, a reorganized Ottoman Empire in the period before 1912,[58] and a Balkan communist federation, a South Slav federation, a Yugoslav federation, and so forth in the years after the partition of Macedonia.[59]

On the eve of World War II the two dominant conceptions of Macedonian statehood were represented by the political right and left. The right, grouped around the weakened VMRO led by Ivan Mihailov, called for the establishment of a united independent Macedonian state.[60] The left, organized in the three Balkan communist parties (the KPB, KKE, and KPJ) and the Internal Macedonian Revolutionary Organization (United) (VMRO [0b]), endorsed the Comintern policy of 1923, which advocated the establishment of a united Macedonia in a future Balkan communist federation.[61] Another version of the left's conception of Macedonian statehood began to crystallize in the late 1930s in Yugoslav (Vardar) Macedonia, which comprised the largest Macedonian population, after the KPJ under Tito's leadership began to move in a decidedly federalist direction. It envisaged the establishment of a Macedonian state in a Yugoslav federation, which, further down the road, would play the role of a Piedmont for Macedonian unification within Yugoslavia or in a wider South Slav or Balkan communist federation.[62]

The "free Macedonian" idea was deeply rooted among the Macedo-nians in the divided land. This was the prime reason for the support that Macedonians gave during the interwar years to the terrorist VMRO[63] and to the communist parties—the only parties on the political spec-trum in Bulgaria, Greece, and Yugoslavia to have recognized their na-tional identity and their right to self-determination.[64] Early in 1941, the British vice consul at Skopje, Thomas, estimated "that 90 percent of all Slav Macedonians are autonomists in one sense or another." He also pointed out that the VMRO of Mihailov had lost ground since it was banned in Bulgaria and its leaders exiled in 1934. While acknowledging the close relationship between autonomism and communism in Mace-donia, he argued that since virtually every Macedonian was an autono-mist it was almost certain "that Communists and autonomists are the same people." "My own opinion," wrote Thomas, "is that they are au-tonomists in the first place and Communists only in the second."[65] Or as Captain P. H. Evans, the previously quoted agent of the Special Operations Executive (SOE) who spent eight months in western Greek (Aegean) Mace-donia, emphasized a few years later, in 1944, if "a plebiscite were freely and fairly held, it is more likely than not that a free MACEDONIA would result."[66]

Inspired by such aims—national liberation and unification, a free Macedonia—conscious Macedonians, both communists and bourgeois nationalists, responded to the calls of the communist-led resistance movements in Bulgaria and particularly in occupied Yugoslavia and Greece. In Yugoslavia large numbers of Macedonians joined Tito's par-tisan movement.[67] Even before the Second Session of the Anti-Fascist Council for the National Liberation of Yugoslavia (AVNOJ) (November 29–30, 1943) proclaimed the establishment of the new federal Yugosla-via in which Macedonia obtained equal status with the five other fed-eral units,[68] the partisan units were formed into the National Liberation Army and Partisan Detachments of Macedonia.[69] Eight months later, on Ilinden (St. Elijah's Day), August 2, 1944, the anniversary of the Mace-donian uprising of 1903, the Anti-Fascist Assembly of the National Lib-eration of Macedonia (ASNOM) met for the first time and proclaimed the formation of a Macedonian Peoples' Republic in federal Yugosla-via.[70] From a Macedonian national perspective, the establishment of Macedonian statehood, of a free Macedonia, within the confines of the communist Yugoslav federation represented at least a partial Macedon-ian solution of the Macedonian question.

In Greece, as in Yugoslavia, large numbers of Macedonians joined and fought with the communist-led National Liberation Front–Greek

Popular Liberation Army (EAM-ELAS) during World War II[71] and then on the communist side with the so-called Democratic Army of Greece (DSA) during the Civil War (1947–49).[72] However, the KKE did not at any point recognize sincerely the right of the Macedonians to self-determination.[73] In any case, and as already pointed out, the Soviet-Yugoslav conflict and the defeat of the left in the Greek Civil War represented a crushing blow for the national aspirations of the Macedonians not only in Greek (Aegean) Macedonia but also in Bulgarian (Pirin) Macedonia.

Consequently, viewed from a Macedonian national perspective the dramatic events of the Second World War and its revolutionary aftermath in the Balkans resulted at least in a partial Macedonian resolution of the Macedonian problem. The Macedonian question had been transformed. To be sure, they failed to achieve national unification, and the Macedonians in Greek (Aegean) and Bulgarian (Pirin) Macedonia did not even win national recognition; they remained unrecognized and even repressed national minorities. However, the Macedonians of Yugoslav (Vardar) Macedonia, the largest Macedonian population, won not only national recognition but also legal equality with the other nations of the new, communist-led, federal Yugoslavia.

Within the confines and the legal limitations of the one-party Yugoslav federation, Macedonia and the Macedonians made remarkable progress during its nearly half-century-long existence. Even though by the end of this period Macedonia was still one of the least developed regions of Yugoslavia compared to its situation in pre–World War I royalist Yugoslavia, the federal republic of Macedonia had undergone a veritable economic transformation and revolution. The achievements were even more striking in the cultural sphere, in the area of Macedonian national culture. The standardized Macedonian language became the official language in the republic, one of the four official languages of the federation, and the foundation for the growth and development of a vibrant and dynamic Macedonian national culture.[74] It was in the context of this growing national confidence that the denial of the existence of Macedonian national minorities and their national rights in the neighboring Balkan states, Bulgaria and Greece, became so glaringly unjust. This in turn gave rise, especially within the ranks of the intelligentsia and the large community of Aegean Macedonians, to dissatisfaction with what they perceived as unwillingness on the part of the federal government to work on their behalf. Although rarely expressed publicly, there was a widespread feeling that as far as Belgrade was concerned it was not worth risking the friendly relations with Greece and stable relations with Bulgaria by raising the question of the Macedonian national minorities there.[75] On balance, however, most Macedonians realized and valued the benefits of membership in the federation. It provided them with a sense of security, a sense of security both against unfriendly, even antagonistic states—Bulgaria, Greece, and to a certain extent Albania—and against a condescending and patronizing partner and neighbor inside Yugoslavia, namely, Serbia.

IV. The State of the Macedonian Question Today

It is, therefore, easy to understand why Macedonia and the Macedonians did not play a decisive or even a major role in the disintegration of Yugoslavia. Indeed, until the very end, the Macedonian leaders on the federal and republican levels sought to bridge the differences between the main players in the Yugoslav drama, the Serbs on the one hand, and the Croats and Slovenes on the other, and preserve a reformed and decentralized democratic federation or confederation.[76] The attacks of the Yugoslav National Army (JNA) and the spilling of blood in Slovenia and Croatia, however, forced the Macedonian leadership to face reality and accept the fact that the federal Yugoslavia, which, as I have already pointed out, provided the Macedonians with a balance of sorts between external security and a limited but clearly defined autonomy, had ceased to exist. They had to seek and consider alternative solutions to the question of national survival.

In the summer of 1991 two options were available to them. One called for the incorporation of Macedonia into a third, or, what was referred to at the time, reduced Yugoslavia. This was the preferred solution of Belgrade and Athens. Without Croatia and Slovenia to counterbalance the predominance of the Serbs, however, the Macedonians would have found themselves in an extremely weak and unfavorable position in the new federation. Consequently, this option was entirely unacceptable to the Macedonians and they rejected it from the outset. The other option, the one that was considered more seriously inside the republic, was the declaration of complete sovereignty and independence. It was the only option acceptable to the Macedonian majority of the population, as well as to the overwhelming majority of the total population of the republic, including the Albanians of Macedonia, who, as a result of domestic disagreements, chose to boycott the actual referendum on independence on September 8, 1991.[77]

By the establishment of an independent Republic of Macedonia (RM)—today still the only viable, realistic, and practical solution of the Macedonian problem—for the first time in the long history of the "perennial"

Macedonian question at least the people of one major part of Macedonia—both ethnic Macedonians and those belonging to the other nationalities—were free to decide democratically their own fate and future. This was and remains an indispensable precondition to any lasting settlement of the Macedonian problem, which in turn is indispensable for stability in the Balkan peninsula.

The Republic of Macedonia is a small landlocked country in the heart of the Balkans, with a population of about 2.3 million. From its inception as an independent state, it has struggled to govern itself democratically.[78] Already in the autumn of 1991, Macedonia met all the conditions for recognition imposed by the European Community, now the European Union, including the policies toward its national minorities.[79] This was not the case with the other former Yugoslav republics; and, more important, Macedonia's minority policies contrasted with the denials of the very existence of Macedonian minorities in neighboring Bulgaria and Greece. Macedonia accepts the existing borders and it has no territorial claims against any of its neighbors. Even though some extreme Macedonian nationalists may dream about or continue to voice the dream of Great Macedonia, the state does not possess the means to threaten any of its neighbors, let alone challenge the existing territorial status quo. It does not have the material means, manpower, and so on.[80]

Nevertheless, the declaration of independence by the Republic of Macedonia in September 1991 provoked a dangerous political and diplomatic crisis. Potentially, it posed a far greater threat to Balkan and European stability than the war in the north, in Slovenia, Croatia, and Bosnia-Herzegovina. A war over Macedonia would have been, from the very outset, a much wider conflict, an international war. It would have involved not only former republics of Yugoslavia, but all of Macedonia's neighbors and possibly Turkey. And since Greece and Turkey were certain to be on opposite sides, it would have become the first armed conflict between two member countries of the NATO alliance.

The crisis was the result of the determined opposition, in some cases direct and open and in others indirect and concealed, of the neighboring Balkan states to the establishment of an independent Macedonian state. The reasons are obvious. As I have stressed repeatedly, all of Macedonia's neighbors either consistently or at one time or another chose to deny the existence of a Macedonian people, and hence its right to possess its own state, and claimed Macedonia and the Macedonians as their own. All of them viewed the establishment of the small, independent republic as a threat to their past gains or future aspirations in Macedonia, and rejected the new state as an artificial creation.[81]

During the last few years Macedonia's position in the Balkans and internationally appears to have improved. The conclusion of the interim accord with Greece in New York in September 1995 and the establishment of diplomatic relations with Yugoslavia in early 1996 after the signing of the Dayton Accords completed the formal recognition of the new state by its neighbors. This had undoubtedly contributed to the easing of tensions in the republic and in the region as a whole.[82]

As I have sought to emphasize, however, stability in Macedonia and consequently peace in the region can only be attained through the acceptance—not just the formal recognition, but the genuine acceptance—of the existence of a Macedonian nation, Macedonian national minorities, and the new independent state by its neighbors. A grudging, conditional recognition of the country, especially when achieved mainly as a result of strong international pressure, as was the case of both the Serbian and Greek recognition, is not enough. It is not the same as the acceptance of the Macedonian nation, the Macedonian identity. It is unfortunate that thus far none of its neighbors has accepted Macedonia genuinely and unconditionally as a nation and state.

Bulgaria was among the first to recognize Macedonia as a state but continues to deny the existence of a Macedonian identity, a Macedonian nation, and hence a Macedonian minority in Bulgaria, and claims all Macedonians are Bulgarians. Greece now recognizes the existence of a country to the north but denies it the right to use its constitutional name, Macedonia or rather Republic of Macedonia, and thus denies also the existence of a Macedonian identity, nation, and national minority in Greek (Aegean) Macedonia. Having recognized the Macedonians officially for more than half a century, it would be awkward and difficult for Yugoslavia, or, more precisely, Serbia, to deny their national identity and existence now. However, it is not entirely clear how seriously Belgrade accepts the sovereignty and territorial integrity of the new state. It is also worth noting that influential or at least some influential Serbian politicians refer to Macedonia as South Serbia and to the Macedonians as Southern Serbs, as their counterparts did in pre–World War I royalist Yugoslavia. Finally, the Albanian position is a little more ambiguous. It has fluctuated between recognition and questioning the existence of both the nation and the state, reflecting Tirana's ambivalent and changing perception of the treatment of the substantial Albanian minority in the Republic of Macedonia. What is needed is the genuine acceptance by Macedonia's neighbors of the existence of a Macedonian identity, nation, state, and external minorities. This will in turn contribute to internal stability and security in the Republic of Macedonia, which is a necessary precondition for its transition to democracy and a market economy, and for enlightened interethnic relations. As long as Macedonia's neighbors, the traditional claimants to the territory and its inhabitants, do not do so, Macedonia will remain a potential "tinder box" of the Balkans and of Europe.

Throughout this chapter, I have stressed that beginning with the rise of Macedonianism in the 1860s there was no other and no better solution of the Macedonian problem than some form of Macedonian self-rule, autonomy, or statehood, "a free Macedonia." It seems to me that the time has come for a historic accommodation between the Macedonians and their neighbors; and the precondition for that is the genuine acceptance by the latter of a Macedonian identity, nation, state, and external national minorities. Indeed, by now this has become a Balkan necessity. There is no other acceptable solution of the Macedonian question.

Historians will continue to debate and argue questions relating to the formation of the Macedonian identity. However, there can no longer be any doubt that a Macedonian nation exists. Denying the existence of Macedonians in all parts of Macedonia did not help solve the Macedonian problem and did not contribute to Balkan stability in the past, and it will not do so in the future. Only a settlement that recognizes the Macedonians and respects their national rights will be of lasting value and contribute to stability and tranquillity in Southeastern Europe.

9 A Crisis of Identity

Serbia at the End of the Century

THOMAS A. EMMERT

During the NATO bombing of Yugoslavia in 1999 one could easily find numerous examples in the Western media of a clear bias against Serbia and the Serbs. Because of the wars in Slovenia, Croatia, and Bosnia earlier in the decade the Serbs were already branded as an outcast nation in Europe; but the conflict in Kosovo enabled Serbia to emerge more clearly as a challenger to Iraq for the position of the Western world's most demonic nation. One could even argue that Serbia held an unfair advantage over Iraq in this unenviable contest, since the Iraqis themselves were not blamed for Saddam Hussein's policies but were portrayed as victims of a terrible dictator. The Serbian people, on the other hand, were brazenly described as "Europe's outsiders, seasoned haters raised on self-pity."[1]

Some were quick to draw less than careful comparisons between the fascist era in Europe and contemporary Serbia. NATO justified its bombing by comparing Nazi Germany and Hitler to Yugoslavia and Milošević. On Memorial Day in 1999 the president of the United States remarked in an address that Milošević's government, like that of Nazi Germany, rose to power in part by getting people to look down on people of a given race and ethnicity and to believe that they had no right to live. Harvard Professor Daniel Goldhagen in the *New Republic* compared Serbia to Nazi Germany as well, and considered the Serbs "Milošević's willing executioners." He argued that since the beginning of the 1990s Serbia, like Germany and Japan in an earlier age, had been waging a brutal imperial war, seeking to conquer area after area, expelling unwanted populations and perpetrating mass murder. Since he found the "vast majority of Serbs . . . animated by a particularly virulent variant of nationalism," the only remedy in his estimation was to "conquer Serbia, de-Nazify her and reeducate the population."[2]

In a modern world that demands quick answers to complex problems, all of the Serbs were painted as pariahs with the same broad brush. They and their leaders were characterized as the aggressors in a conflict that destroyed Yugoslavia, devastated the lives of millions, and threatened the stability of all of Southeastern Europe. The Serbian people seemed to perpetrate and tolerate a level of violence that Europe had not seen since the Holocaust. Their opponents and some Western observers were certain that explanations for the violence were readily apparent in Serbian history and culture, and yet by the end of the war few had done much to advance a broader understanding of Serbia and Serbian history. Nevertheless, without much of an intellectual and historical framework, many journalists and others concluded that Serbia seemed to lie just outside the limits of Western civilization. Metternich said the same thing about the broader region in an earlier century; and although we are amused by his observation, it is a view that is not completely rejected in some analysis. Fortunately, Maria Todorova in her masterful *Imagining the Balkans* has helped us understand this persistent doubt about Southeastern Europe.

Understandably, this attitude toward Serbia and the questioning of its place in Europe have fueled an effort by some Serbs to defend their rightful place in European civilization. In a rather transparent effort to address its tarnished image, the Serbian Academy of Sciences and Arts organized a major conference on the subject of "Europe and the Serbs" in December of 1995.[3] In an introduction to the published proceedings, Aleksandar Despić, president of the Academy at that time, contrasted two aspects of Europe that had both influenced Serbia: the Europe of enlightenment of which Serbia had become an inseparable part, and the Europe of arrogant aggression with a bloody history of conquest and slaughter that threatened Serbia at the end of the twentieth century. Accepting no responsibility for Serbia for the tragedy that befell Yugoslavia in the 1990s, Despić expressed incomprehension at the harsh response of many European states to Serbia and the Serbian people. While he hoped that the conference papers would shed some light on the possible historical reasons for "such a course of events," he also wanted to make one thing absolutely clear from the start: "We were Europe, we are Europe today and we will be Europe."[4] Unfortunately, this somewhat meaningless proclamation masked a fundamental and persistent insecurity concerning Serbia's historical character, contemporary political reality, and its place in modern Europe.

It has been argued that the struggle for identity in Serbia as regards its relationship to Western Europe began already near the dawn of the Nemanjić era. As Milorad Ekmečić has suggested, the recent wars have resurrected the old argument of two distinct cultures in the former Yugoslavia, roughly following the supposed line between Eastern and Roman Empires. NATO officials and popular journalists alike have pontificated over the long-lasting effects of "Byzantine influence" in the eastern part of the Balkans.[5] At the heart of the argument seems to be a gnawing sense that the long centuries of Byzantine and Ottoman influence made Serbia's integration into the mainstream of modern European culture difficult if not unsuccessful. Ekmečić, of course, interpreted all of this as a revival of an argument made often during the 1930s that the critical difference between Serbs and Croats was the influence each experienced from rather unequal civilizations.

No one expressed that observation more blatantly, of course, than Rebecca West in *Black Lamb and Grey Falcon*. Before she left Zagreb at the end of her self-declared epic journey, she says that she spoke to a number of people who expressed a "loathing" for the "inferior Oriental civilization of the Serb."[6] On the border between East and West, Croats defended themselves and in turn defended Western civilization itself, or so the canon concludes. Very recently the Croatian essayist Dubravka Ugrešić made a similar observation about some contemporary Croatian perspectives on Serbia:

For the Croatian media, political leaders and ordinary people Europe was a territory, from which the Balkans, Serbia, were erased. (The Serbs do not belong in Europe). That is why the Croatian political scene keeps doggedly sending love signals to its Europe: we are anti-communists, Catholics, we are a democratic country, we are defending Europe from Serbo-bolshevism, communism, Byzantinism, barbarism, balkanisation, we are a civilisational, European, Christian shield which will prevent that terrible *East* from reaching Vienna.[7]

Of course, in her frequent conversations with Serbs, Rebecca West identified reciprocal attitudes toward the Croats. Unlike much of the analysis today, of course, West in her rejection of the politics of capitulation admired the Serbs and celebrated their decision to stand up to Hitler whatever the consequences. Hers, indeed, was a one-woman crusade to introduce the South Slavs and particularly the Serbs to the Western public. Before her baptismal journey to the Balkans, she admitted no knowledge about the South Slavs nor any acquaintance with anyone who did know them. The only word that she associated with the region and its people was "violence."

It is incontestable that the long centuries of Ottoman control essentially removed the Serbs from the mainstream of European development and largely from the consciousness of Europeans. Isolated travelers left sparse accounts of their experiences in Ottoman Serbia, while a few histories and encyclopedias revealed their authors' essential ignorance about the region. By the eighteenth century Serbia was summarily dismissed in a French encyclopedia as a land "depopulated, without culture or money."[8] Only as Serbia began to emerge from its Ottoman isolation in the nineteenth century after the uprisings against the Turks did the curtain of ignorance about them in Europe began to rise as well.

Modern interest in Serbia was first stimulated by those Serbian uprisings during the Napoleonic era and by the dissemination of Serbian epic poetry in translation later in the century. Eventually one could not follow the Eastern question without some familiarity with the perspectives, objectives, and fortunes of the Serbs. In the half century or so before World War I and especially after 1878 when Serbia was recognized as an independent state by the Great Powers, it enjoyed a much wider reputation. This was the period when Serbia experimented with parliamentary democracy, expanded its territories to encompass regions it considered its historical core, and struggled to articulate its responsibility to other Serbs and other south Slavs under Ottoman or Habsburg rule.

Travelers to the region were still often shocked by the relatively primitive conditions of life outside of the capital and a few large towns; and Serbian territory that had not been liberated from the Ottomans remained terra incognita (with brief exceptions due to the remarkable courage and curiosity of those indomitable English Victorian women, Miss Irby and Miss Mackenzie, who traveled from one end of the old Serbian lands under Ottoman control to the other in the 1860s in an effort to enlighten their compatriots at home). Nevertheless, progress continued in Serbia. On the eve of World War I, William Morgan, a rather naive American journalist from the Midwest, returned from a trip to the Balkans to write that Serbia was "doubtless on its way to civilization. . . . Belgrade is marching on. The Serbians have licked the Turks and the Bulgarians. Next they will have bathtubs and then they will be redeemed but still uninteresting."[9] But he was also optimistic about the future:

Of course, the Serbians say they are the best of the Balkan people. They may be. At any rate, they are getting up to date. Their pride is aroused to make Serbia one of the modern states of Europe and they are doing it rapidly. The school teacher is abroad in the land, and that means good-bye to superstition, brutality, and dirt. This is a democratic country. . . . The people come closer to running their own affairs in Serbia than they do in New York.[10]

Morgan, like others in his own time and like many others much later in the century, was not particularly informed or sophisticated in his analysis. He does remind us, however, that by the beginning of the twentieth century the West could hardly ignore Serbia. During the last third of the nineteenth century Serbia had shaped its own parliamentary democracy with a constitution, an independent judicial system, and modern political parties. There is no doubt that the more developed West was the model for this rapid transformation of the young state, and in many ways Serbian political life by the end of the century was as modern as it was in many places in Western Europe. Of course, as Gale Stokes has described so well, the Serbs took a very different path from that of their Western mentors. Serbia managed to develop a working democracy by the end of the century without social and economic transformation.[11] In fact, even the Radicals who supposedly championed the cause of the peasantry were, in the end, not a peasant party. They, too, succumbed to the reality that political power was all that mattered. To be sure the peasants were eventually integrated into the system, which was increasingly defined by national interests and controlled by political and military elites. Stokes' conclusion concerning nineteenth-century Serbian politics has an element truth for Serbia at the end of the twentieth century as well: "Political struggle took place in the competition over control of the rhetoric of legitimacy, which the participants correctly perceived as being directly related to power in a system that was static socially but fluid politically."[12]

It was Serbia's potential as a Balkan Piedmont that stimulated most of the interest in the fledgling state, especially by Austria and Russia. As they carefully constructed their modern society, Serbia's leaders never lost sight of their historic obligation to help liberate their brethren from the control of foreign powers. Landlocked and otherwise confined by the imprecise conspiracy of the Great Powers to maintain their control in the Balkans, Serbia walked a delicate tightrope between national dreams and practical possibilities. While Serbian political leaders sought to bring European civilization to the banks of the lower Danube, there was still room for argument about just where Serbia belonged. The two parties that dominated the politics of the new state were sharply divided. The Progressive Party was drawn to Austria and the West, convinced that Serbia's future lay in its integration into Western culture. The Radicals, on the other hand, while not anti-Western in any way, looked to Russia as the protector of the Slavic world, especially in that world's perceived struggle with its traditional enemies, the Germans and the Turks. Until 1889 Serbia's course was clearly pro-Austrian, and indeed

Serbia's economy was almost completely dependent on the Habsburg Empire. Moreover, Prince Milan (king after 1882) accepted Austria's political demands on Serbia, which undermined its flexibility internationally and which were clearly designed to eliminate the possibility that Serbia would indeed serve as a kind of Balkan Piedmont. This subservience, the success of the rival Radical Party in Parliament, and a defeat by Bulgaria in an 1885 war all led eventually to the increasing unpopularity of Milan and to his abdication in 1889.

The new king, Alexander Obrenović, eventually unpopular because of his choice of queen, vacillated between Russia and Austria for support and turned increasingly to repressive measures in an attempt to frustrate the popular Radical Party. In early June 1903, the world awakened to the news of the bloody murder of Alexander and his queen by a conspiracy of Serbian military officers. Not only were they riddled with bullets as they hid in the Royal Palace but their bodies were then stabbed and tossed from the second floor to the garden below. Before the night had ended the conspirators also murdered the prime minister, the minister of the interior, several officers who had remained with Alexander, and the queen's two brothers. Europe was horrified. After all that Serbia had achieved in the last half of the nineteenth century, these murders seemed to confirm a persistent image many had of this backward region and to perpetuate the myth of those unshakable "Byzantine" qualities of its political culture.

Nevertheless, Serbia recovered under the restoration of the Karadjordjević dynasty, enjoyed the restoration of civil liberties and democratic freedoms, and attempted to free itself from some of its dependence on the Habsburg Empire. In spite of the infamous Pig War that followed, Serbia did manage to diminish its economic subservience to Austria and enjoy the beginnings of a much healthier national economy. The reality at the beginning of the twentieth century was that Serbia for all its backwardness had made credible progress in the direction of Western-style political development and clearly set its course to rejoin Europe after its centuries of Ottoman control—all in time, of course, for the crisis over Bosnia in 1908, the Balkan Wars, and the assassination in Sarajevo in 1914.

It was the brutality of the Balkan Wars that most blame for the extremely pejorative connotation associated with the term "Balkan" and with many of the peoples who inhabited the region. The Carnegie Foundation, which investigated the wars and issued a report in 1914, suggested among other things that the Balkans were clearly on the outer edge of civilization. Eighty years later when George Kennan was asked to offer his perspectives in an essay appended to a reissue of the original 1914 report, the octogenarian spoke from Olympus with an astonishing ahistorical analysis. He saw little difference in the worlds of 1913 and 1993:

... the strongest motivating factor was aggressive nationalism. But that nationalism ... drew on deeper traits of character inherited from a distant tribal past. ... And so it remains today. ... What we are up against is the sad fact that developments of those earlier ages ... had the effect of thrusting into the Southeast reaches of the European continent a salient of European civilization which continues to this day to preserve many of its non-European characteristics.[13]

By the beginning of World War I, therefore, one could argue that Serbia's efforts to achieve new respect and understanding in the West were threatened by the images of the Balkan Wars and by persistent doubts about its success in making the transition from Ottoman subject to modern European state.

But things changed with the Great War. The terrible tragedy in Serbia generated great sympathy for the Serbs in the West. Serbia, the "darling" of the Allied forces, paid an enormous price for its efforts to preserve its sovereignty. Hundreds of thousands met their death in the army or in the deportations and concentration camps of the enemy. Those who remained behind were decimated by the privations of war and the occupation and by disease. "Is it possible for the Serbs ever to recover from the desolation that has swept over them?" asked R. G. D. Laffan, a British historian who gave a series of lectures on the Serbs to British forces in Salonika and then collected these lectures in a book entitled *The Serbs*.[14] While Laffan argued that it would be very difficult "to build up once more the national life," he never doubted the ability of the Serbs to overcome their misery and "resume the almost forgotten arts of peace." It was, he believed, the defining part of their spirit: "If ever a nation bought its union and its liberty with blood and tears, the Serbs have paid that price. For five hundred years they have never been content to submit to slavery, but have unceasingly struggled towards the light."[15] This was the characterization of the Serbs that mirrored the Serbs' own self-image and that would dominate Western views of the Serbs for decades.

Laffan observed the world's woeful ignorance about anything that had to do with the Balkans. "Nine out of ten [Englishmen]," he remarked, "have said that all the Balkan nations were as bad as each other ... that all were savages and cut-throats and past praying for. The tenth man has usually been a philanthropic crank, who would only see good points in his own pet Balkan nation."[16] Having discovered, however, that the Serb soldiers in his midst were "the best of fellows,"[17] he hoped that some discourse about their history would contribute to a broader appreciation for them and for their sacrifices in the Great War. He was clearly partisan in all this. He wanted his own work to play a part in preparing for the day when the Serbs "will again take their place among the mighty nations of the earth."[18]

The tragedy of Serbia in World War I indeed seemed to erase the memory of some of the negative characterization of the Balkans—at least as far as Serbia was concerned. During the war Serbia was the subject of great affection not only among the English and French publics but also in the United States. In a celebration of Serbia at the Waldorf-Astoria Hotel in New York City on June 17, 1918, James Beck, former U.S. Assistant Attorney General, remarked: "If Serbia is temporarily defeated, she has triumphed at the great bar of public opinion and she stands in the eye of the nations as justified in her quarrel. Serbia was not only the innocent, precipitating cause of this world war, but it is the greatest martyr, and I am inclined to think in many respects its greatest hero."[19]

Even some of the other South Slavs who would eventually join the Serbs in a common state were eager to praise Serbia's sacrifice during the war. In April 1916 the Yugoslav Committee in London proclaimed in a message to the Prince Regent of Serbia:

Serbia of today is no longer isolated as was the Serbia of the past. The heroism and superhuman sacrifices of her sons have earned Serbia universal moral prestige and today it is supported by powerful allies. . . . The country which will arise from the terrible ordeal of which we are the spectators will not be merely a restored, or even an aggrandized Serbia, but one that includes the entire Yugoslav nation, and the whole of its national territory, united in one single State under the illustrious dynasty of your revered father. The state will be the rock against which the waves of Germanism will dash themselves in vain.[20]

This heroic, martyrological image of Serbia clearly impressed many in the Balkans and in the West, which they inevitably traced to its source in the mythical cult of Kosovo. This cult, which evolved after the conquest of Serbia by the Ottoman Turks in the fourteenth and fifteenth centuries, celebrated martyrdom on the one hand but also demanded of all generations of Serbs that they avenge the loss of Serbian freedom at Kosovo and liberate all Serbs from oppression. It was this element in Serbian historical consciousness and political life that inspired the nineteenth-century wars of liberation, ultimately shaped the nascent democratic tradition in Serbia's nineteenth-century history, and challenged the multinational state that emerged in the aftermath of the Great War.

None of Serbia's history after the end of the fourteenth century can be understood without taking this martyrological image and the ethos of Kosovo into consideration. Serbia's identity is tied to both the physical territory of the region and its mythology. Tragically, at the beginning of the twenty-first century, Serbia's identity and future still appear hopelessly compromised by a dependence on Kosovo and its historical ethos for the Serbian people.

Today it is perhaps almost a cliche to suggest that the Serbs have been imprisoned by the mythology of Kosovo. In the conclusion to his new history of Kosovo, Noel Malcolm suggests that the future stability of the region depends "to a large extent on the ability of ordinary Serbs to challenge the fixed pattern of thought which has held them in its grip for long . . . when ordinary Serbs learn to think more rationally and humanely about Kosovo, and more critically about some of their national myths, all the people of Kosovo and Serbia will benefit—not least the Serbs themselves."[21] He poses an important question although it is arguable whether one can separate the responsibility of "ordinary Serbs" from that of their intellectual, political, and spiritual leaders who have nurtured and manipulated the Kosovo ethos over time.

Scholars speak about the tradition of Kosovo as a centuries-long inspiration for freedom among Serbs that evolved because of the loss of their medieval state, because of sacrifices against the Ottoman Turks, and because their intellectuals and bards encouraged such ideas. Just how this tradition emerged and was nurtured over the centuries is not altogether clear. As Dimitrije Djordjević has observed in particular, "We do not know how deep the historical heritage rested in peasant memory."[22] Whatever the process of development, however, few deny the existence of the heritage and its importance in preserving historical memory and some kind of collective identity among the Serbs.

The Kosovo ethos was imposed upon the society by its religious leaders and nourished by them over the centuries. The twin elements of heroism and betrayal became permanent symbols of the Kosovo ethos and shaped much of the Serbian historical experience. In the poetry of the Montenegrin Prince Njegoš:

> Those who escaped the Turkish sword
> Who did not blaspheme against their faith
> Those who refused to be chained
> All of us have gathered high in these mountains
> To give our lives, to spill our blood
> To preserve our heroic heritage—
> Our glorious name and sacred liberty.[23]

In this world defeat was only possible when Serbs were not united. Therefore, it was necessary to be vigilant against those who betray the nation and remove them from the body. Njegoš breathed new life into the Kosovo ethic and colored it with an intolerance of those who did "blaspheme against the faith." A recent book by Michael Sells, an American theologian of Serbian descent, discusses the phenomenon of Christoslavism—a Serbian premise that Slavs are by essence Christian and that conversion to another religion is thus a betrayal of the people or race.[24] Sells argues that this idea is central to the Serbs' attitude toward Muslim Slavs, that it was enshrined in Njegoš's poetry, and that this influence encouraged generations of Serbs to see the cleansing of these traitors as a kind of religious duty. Sells is not the first scholar to suggest that Njegoš gave fresh impetus to new generations of revenge and to that peculiar "Dinaric" character of some mountain Serbs and other South Slavs that was identified early in the twentieth century by Jovan Cvijić. The Dinaric personality saw his life's goal as the liberation of his brothers "with a constant heroism, a never-ending sacrifice, and with blood."[25]

This ethos was essential to Serbian ethnic consciousness where, in the words of Miloš Blagojević, "the heroic deed of the warriors and death of the Christian martyrs are interwoven into an inseparable whole."[26] Blagojević argues that it is a collective responsibility where, in the clash between two civilizations, Serbs accept the sacrificial ideal mandated to them by the medieval prince who sacrificed himself on Kosovo: "We shall die in order to live forever. We shall be the living sacrifice to God." "To ignore this message," Blagojević observes, "would have been to destroy the Serbian national being."[27] But the Serb people could not survive and maintain their vigilance and ethnic consciousness without leaders who maintained and embellished the legend; and Blagojević concurs: "In order to survive as a whole, the Serbian nation had to return to its oldest roots, re-creating wherever possible its military, political and spiritual elites."[28]

Radovan Samardžić explains this dependence on the elite as an essential characteristic of Serbian society. Throughout history whenever the aristocracy was eliminated, Serbs would regroup around a new elite who would preserve their history and articulate the tradition of the Nemanjić dynasty and the glory of the military class on Kosovo. "Finding support in their new leaders," Samardžić argues, "they found support in themselves."[29] It is suggested that it was in recognition of this close relationship between people and leaders in Serbia that foreign powers constantly tried to "keep the population beheaded." Offering this analysis in 1993 as the war raged in Bosnia, Samardžić clearly had his sights on his own contemporary Serbia; but, nevertheless, his deeper interpretation reveals a troubling ambiguity about Serbia's history, character, and relationship to the Western European tradition. While the system that emerged in Serbia in the last part of the nineteenth century has often been described as patriarchal democracy, Samardžić suggests:

If one were to penetrate deeper into the internal relations that were the expression of a society's unwritten law, one might establish instead, the existence of a certain patriarchal aristocratism with the Serbs. . . . Since the equality of the members of a community could not presume any personal self-will, the public interest had complete predominance over self-interest and individually excessive desires . . . the advice of those who had acquired the highest reputation was followed without fail. . . . Thus in its beliefs, morale, customs and understanding of life, this nation remained united, having identical spirit and customs, free from the division characteristic of western peoples, where, with time, every social class built its own mentality.[30]

Seemingly unaware of the essential contradiction, Samardžić attempts to conclude that this unique characteristic of Serbian society was not incompatible with more progressive ideas that emanated from the West. In his words, the Serbian middle class "accepted the western style and ideas, yet maintained its medieval cults, its traditional comprehension of history and patriarchal norms of behavior, close to those of the common folk . . . it accepted without exaggerated boldness, ideas of the European Enlightenment as [these] posed no hindrance to the preservation of its religious and historical orientations."[31]

But there clearly is a conflict between the essential ideas that inspired the Enlightenment and eventually led to European parliamentary democracy and the heroic, martyrological, warrior mentality of the Serbian experience that colored much of modern Serbian history and that found new expression in the Serbia of Slobodan Milošević. There is an essential antimodern phenomenon in the recurring warrior tradition in Serbian society. As a result, as Aleksa Djilas has noted, "parliamentarism in Serbia was not deeply rooted, nor did it enjoy the mass support necessary to contain the ever-increasing power of the [monarchy] and the military."[32]

No one disputes the historical glorification of war and respect for violence that is central to the Kosovo ethos and that found its voice throughout much of Serbian history. A number of recent critics, however, suggest that it is this very mentality that still dominates Serbian society, imprisons the Serbs, and explains their action in the wars of the

1990s. Branimir Anžulović in a recent highly biased study of the myth of Kosovo argues that the evolving myth led to centuries of "endemic violence" that was nurtured in the "patriarchal-heroic" culture of the Dinaric mountains, particularly in Montenegro. Thus he revives some of the old arguments concerning the "social character" of the Dinaric population that were popularized first by Cvijić and later by Dinko Tomašić. Anžulović, like Sells, is especially critical of Njegoš and suggests that Njegoš's epic poem together with the continuing myth of Kosovo encouraged a tradition of genocide among the Serbs that he believes is clearly reflected again in the wars of the 1990s. According to Anžulović this "pagan-heroic" culture in Serbia together with the symbiotic relationship between the Serbian Orthodox Church and the Serbian state and nation completely undermined the more progressive influences of the Enlightenment so that Serbs have been always "torn between the model of Western civil society and ethnic tribalism."[33] In his analysis this mentality led to a destructive fear of being dominated by others or even eliminated as a people and to the obsession Serbs had in Yugoslavia with trying to maintain their dominant position. In the end he believes that Serbia fell victim to the perceived fears of its artists, intellectuals, church and political leaders, and generals who then used ordinary citizens as tools in the destruction of Yugoslavia.

It is not difficult to accept Anžulović's latter conclusion. As with so much analysis in recent years, however, much of his effort to trace contemporary atrocities to a centuries-old Serbian pathology rests on a disturbingly simplistic determinism. In spite of the author's admonition to avoid the trap of seeing nations only in black and white, as good and evil, and as heavenly and demonic, that is exactly the narrow framework in which he structures his argument. Few would disagree that the Kosovo myth and a certain preoccupation with the past have played a significant role in Serbia's particular responses to the challenges of the 1970s and 1980s in the former Yugoslavia, but such myth must be analyzed in a much broader framework of the Serbian national question and of the economic, political, and social tensions that shaped much of the discourse of the era.

In a much more balanced analysis Olivera Milosavljević argues that the continuing presence of this warrior mentality in contemporary Serbia is tragically anachronistic. It encourages an integral nationalism and the dangerous view that only the national group can guarantee freedom.[34] This fascination with war and conflict allowed Serbs to ignore or perhaps even support a strong independent military, which necessarily compromised any movement toward a meaningful parliamentary democracy.

Milošević insisted on meeting Europe on Serbia's own terms and with its own unique socialist system, but the character of much of what was evolving in Serbia during the era of Milošević brought much of its European orientation into question. As Latinka Perović observes:

Serbia was removed from Western European civilization even before the outbreak of the war. The war only made the process faster, and its end made the distance drastically visible. In addition, it was the victory of a cultural model the mainstay of which was a semi-intellectual, a man whom Slobodan Jovanović described as having a diploma from school but no cultural and moral education. During the anti-bureaucratic revolution he spread hatred and laid the grounds for the policy of war from the pages of *Politika*. For the first time he broke off the Western European orientation that, while never dominant, had always been present in Serbia's political culture, and proclaimed Serbia's self-sufficiency.[35]

Perović argues that the Serbian Church had a long tradition of rejecting the values of Western Europe, but in the climate of Milošević's Serbia that rejection spread to intellectual and political elites. Of course this was not a new development. In spite of the relative success of parliamentary democracy at the end of the nineteenth century, Serbian society experienced neither true social and economic transformation nor viable and meaningful democratic institutions. Perović and others argue that this is still the dilemma and trauma for those who choose to lead the Serbian people.

It appears that all of the Serbian elites and their institutions have conspired in the last two decades to turn their backs on Western traditions and rally the wagons around their historic myths. Miodrag Popović foresaw the danger in this attitude twenty-five years ago, long before the revival of the Kosovo ethos was evident. In his words:

The cult of St. Vitus' Day, which combines historical reality with myth, a real fight for freedom with pagan tendencies . . . potentially has all the characteristics of a milieu with untamed mythical impulses. As a phase in the development of national thought, it was historically indispensable. However, as a permanent state of mind, the St. Vitus cult can be fatal for those who are not able to free themselves from its pseudo-mythical and pseudo-historical snares. Caught in these snares, contemporary thought and the human spirit can experience another Kosovo, an intellectual and ethical defeat.[36]

By the time Serbia entered the post-Tito era, this admonition was long forgotten. Led first by a cautiously aggressive Serbian Orthodox Church and then by its intellectuals, Serbs were encouraged to follow their own path away from the "Western-Roman tradition" and along the well-traveled road of the Kosovo ethic.

In a growing number of provocative articles beginning in the early 1980s the Church admonished the faithful that as children of the Byzantine world, there was no meaningful place for them in the West. Using the evolving crisis in Kosovo as a theme for its own revival as an effective force in Serbian society, the Church presented itself as the defender of the Serbs of Kosovo, revisited the "martyrdom" of Serbs in World War II, and finally supported the dissolution of Yugoslavia and the creation of a greater Serbia. As Sabrina Ramet has observed, this encouraged a kind of traumatic nationalism in Serbia, "drawing its energy, by habit and by nature from a reinterpretation of Serbia's history in terms of suffering, exploitation, pain, and justice."[37] While one may argue that this is the very character of the Kosovo ethos, Ramet suggests that this traumatic character is not a constant and has only become so as a result of a conscious and careful manipulation by Serbia's elites, particularly the Church.

Not surprisingly, the Church resurrected the writings and personal example of Bishop Nikolaj Velimirović to serve as a guide for the present times. Velimirović was a kind of twentieth-century Pius IX who ranted against the modern "isms" of progressive Europe, seeing them all as a kind of poison from which Serbs must protect themselves. In an introduction to a recent edition of some of Velimirović's sermons and essays, Nebojša Krstić sees a particular relevance for the bishop's admonitions at the end of the twentieth century: "Velimirović's warning is especially meant for Serbia's intelligentsia who have rejected their Orthodox roots, for those who spin around in a witch's brew of ecumenism, and for those who insolently lie that it does not matter if Serbs live in a God-centered monarchy or in some kind of democratic republic."[38] Krstić certainly did not have to worry about the majority of Serbia's intellectuals. As the Church became more and more aggressive, resurrecting images of victimhood and justifying the idea of revenge for past sufferings, Serbian intellectuals joined the march and demonstrated their willingness to push forward an aggressive, integralist nationalist agenda.

Much has been made, of course, of the role of prominent writers like Dobrica Ćosić whose concerns for the unity of Serbian culture and nation certainly well predate the post-Tito era. Nicholas Miller points out in a recent article in *Slavic Review* that we have not clearly understood postwar Serbian nationalism, which, he argues, began as a "legitimate and humane movement."[39] At least a small number of leading Serb writers as early as the late 1950s encouraged a reorganization of the League of Writers of Yugoslavia that would move toward more "substantive Yugoslavism."[40] By the mid-1960s, however, this effort was essentially defeated by those who viewed it as another manifestation of thinly veiled Serbian centralism. Miller argues that Ćosić was particularly disappointed that there was no support for this Yugoslav supranationalism from the regime. This eventually convinced him "that the failure of his attempts to keep integration on track implied the continued division and perhaps eventual destruction of the *Serbian* nation."[41] Finally concluding that the regime was anti-Serbian, Ćosić turned his emphasis to unifying Serbian culture and the Serbian nation. In other words if Yugoslavism had to fail, it did not have to take the possibility of a revived and integrated Serbian culture down with it.

The story of Dobrica Ćosić is the story of an intellectual who publicly voiced his concern about new expressions of nationalism among the nations of Yugoslavia while he struggled to encourage a renewal and recognition of the spiritual unity of the Serbian people wherever they may live. Eventually Ćosić and others became integral Serbian nationalists convinced, in Miller's words, "that Titoism had failed in its basic universalist and humanitarian promise."[42] Miller seeks to argue that it is helpful to realize that this new nationalism as expressed at least by people like Ćosić was not simply some retro nationalism from an earlier authoritarian era, but a movement "conditioned by the failure of communism."[43] While people like Ćosić were not necessarily activists in the revival of nationalism in the 1980s, Miller believes that they provided much of the context or images for that eventual movement. That said, he concludes at the same time that once these new nationalists offered a new vision of Serb unity and revival, it was taken in new directions that did not necessarily bode well for the future of Serbia and the whole of Yugoslavia. He observes that this new nationalism bears a resemblance to that of fascist movements of the 1920s and 1930s, although he is very careful to point out that none of the intellectuals he studied in this analysis were ever political fascists.

Clearly by the middle of the 1980s Ćosić and many other leading Serbian intellectuals took upon themselves the responsibility of defending the interests of the Serbian nation and giving rather unqualified support to those political authorities who were willing to take on that mantle. The now-famous Memorandum of the Serbian Academy of Sciences and Arts reflects best perhaps the transition of someone like Ćosić from a much earlier concern for the integrative and humane possibilities of Yugoslav communism to the integralist and more narrow perspectives of a Serbian nationalist. Thus the Academy's provocative Memorandum pretended to offer a critical analysis of the problems facing Yugoslavia and could express its concern with the lack of progress in building a multiethnic society, but it couched that analysis and its solutions in the very narrow context of Serbian national interests. Horrified by what they believed was happening in Kosovo and in other places in Yugoslavia where Serbs were a minority population, they resurrected the myth of Kosovo and its warrior culture and turned away from Western European political values to embrace mass culture and an anachronistic view of the nation-state. They gave credibility to incendiary issues of historical revisionism which had at first shocked the establishment when they were initially presented in the late 1970s and early 1980s. They seemed unafraid of isolating themselves from the rest of Europe and certainly found a ready ally in the Church, which had already made its voice clear about what it thought of Western European values. Brave souls in the Academy, such as the esteemed historian Sima Ćirković, warned their peers that they were moving in a very dangerous direction; but by the end of the 1980s such admonitions were not only unheeded but often perceived as traitorous. To the myth of Kosovo was added the myth that Yugoslavia had only been a disaster for the Serbian people and the myth that the Serbs had suffered throughout the century from exploitation by other Yugoslavs. All of them contained the common symbol of victimhood, which sadly and increasingly defined the Serbian national experience.

Vesna Pešić characterizes this national consciousness as a resentful nationalism that "presumes some kind of 'neurotic' national identity."[44] She suggests that much of this was historical given the centuries of subjugation, the trauma of World War II, and the failure to achieve a meaningful process of national reconciliation after that war. Part of it was also a feeling of inferiority toward Western Europe, which then contributed an anti-modern, anti-European, and anti-democratic complexion to Serbia's new nationalism. Since politics in this new Serbia was reduced to a struggle for the very survival of the nation, it had to be treason to oppose those politics.

To be sure there have been opposition voices that offer a very different perspective and critique. A number of smaller groups including the Association for a Yugoslav Democratic Initiative, the Republican Club, the Civil Alliance of Serbia, and a smattering of feminist and antiwar organizations attempted to voice antiwar, parliamentary, and democratic principles and to support human rights and the rights of national minorities while they struggled against the tradition of integral nationalism. Unfortunately, like the mainstream opposition groups, they failed to work closely together and were easily marginalized in the process.

Some have argued that Serbia both at the beginning of the twentieth century and at its end simply did not enjoy the social conditions that would have allowed it to develop a real political pluralism. In spite of some movement toward parliamentary democracy Serbia remained politically unstable with a constant undercurrent of terrorism, assassination, election fraud, and dirty tricks. The end result was that a strong, bureaucratic centralized state, often repressive and always authoritarian, enjoyed a long tradition in Serbia.[45] According to the analysis of Dubravka Stojanović, collective, national interests took precedence over individual interests. New parties emerged, but not from the evolving consciousness of the interests of a certain part of the population but rather from the ideas of the new parties' leaders. Charismatic leaders were, therefore, more important than anything else. Stojanović suggests that it was not a difficult move from totalitarianism in the name of class to totalitarianism in the name of nation.[46]

In his recent study of Serbia during the reign of Milošević, Robert Thomas strives to explain why Serbia was unable to make the transition from totalitarianism to pluralism. In his meticulously detailed account of the fractured political life in Serbia, Thomas describes a land in "a classificatory limbo where stunted *democratic* institutions mix uneasily with *authoritarian* structures and both of these elements are overshadowed by the *sultanist* influence of the leader of the ruling party, Slobodan Milošević."[47] He argues that the many divisions within Serbia (ethnic, ideological, social-developmental) not only defined the political language but served as easy targets for manipulation by the many political factions in the country. Most tragic for Serbia was the fact that Slobodan Milošević, addicted to his own personal rule, was most successful in this manipulation. He won and maintained throughout most of the 1990s the loyalty of an important sector of the electorate, while the opposition fragmented hopelessly in intense and acrimonious arguments over egos and issues. Divided between what Thomas labels the "rationalist/modernists" and the "national romantics/neo-traditionalists" the opposition never succeeded in creating the coalition so desperately needed to move Serbia in a new direction.

All of this suggests, of course, that it is much too simplistic to blame Milošević and his ruling party for everything that happened. Most political, intellectual, and religious voices appeared to express a common message by the end of the 1980s. Eventually the media joined the national crusade as well and contributed its own unique dimension to the hysteria. The print and electronic media fell hostage to the authoritarian government but also to the national mythology. Ultimately, the Serbian media played its own willing part in hyping the Serbian myths, demonizing non-Serb populations, and supporting the nondemocratic processes that undermined Serbian society.

It will not be easy for Serbia to find its way along the contemporary European road. The traffic on that road moves much too quickly and has little patience for those it willingly leaves behind. More than a century ago Nikola Pašić knew that Serbia's future depended on its political and economic modernization and its successful integration into the modern arena of Western Europe. To fail in those efforts, he admonished, would condemn Serbia to a life on the periphery. Unfortunately, that admonition is still appropriate today. Looking at the early years of Serbian democracy begs us to seek parallels with the murky world of today's Serbian political jungle. In both eras one finds politicos with insensitive egos, paternalistic concerns for the Serbian masses, insecurity about Serbia's place in the civilization of Europe, misguided myths about the indomitable Serbian peasant-warrior, and opportunistic dreams about a Greater Serbia. In a multinational state, democracy depends on a commitment to safeguard the equality and rights of all the constituent nations. It is totally incompatible with the kind of integralist nationalism that John Stuart Mill condemned for making people insensitive or indifferent to the rights of anyone outside of their own nation.

One would like to hope that a unified opposition would find its true voice and offer a legitimate democratic alternative to the authoritarian nationalism that has characterized the last fifteen years in Serbia. Unfortunately, such unity is still elusive. It is a terrible truth that the old Serbian adage, "only unity will save Serbia," has never accomplished its implicit goal. The crisis that faces Serbian identity today is acute and reflects a long history of conflict and ambiguity about its place in Europe. In one of his last published works celebrating some of Serbian literature's most important contributions in the last quarter of the twentieth century, Predrag Palavestra ends with a query concerning the character of Serbia's "spiritual and civilizational drama" at the end of the century:

To designate it two ways—politically, considering that we now stand at the bottom of Europe's civilizational scale, as our fate lies in the hands of those who are incapable of governing people's destinies; then, spiritually and creatively, as our tragedy may be alleviated by the fact that the Serbian creative intelligentsia stands in the forefront of European spirituality and culture. It stands there not only with its literary achievements, which have reached much farther than our politics, but [also] with the many breakthroughs made in film, art and theatre. Therefore, I cannot but pose this question in the end: what is the internal discrepancy of our culture and our being, where the internal damnation of our destiny?[48]

The answer to that question may hold the key to Serbia's most uncertain future. Unfortunately, we will most probably wait a very long time for that answer.

10 Heretical Thoughts about the Postcommunist Transition in the Once and Future Yugoslavia[1]

JOHN V. A. FINE

Thoughts about Recent Depictions and the Reality of Yugoslav Communism

Academic and, in particular, journalistic labeling and generalizing have blurred all sorts of distinctions that need to be made and have obscured past conditions in the various East European states and produced a monolithic depiction of former communism in all these states. Communist East Germany, Romania, and Albania, for example, were horrors; but Yugoslavia's communist state was very different.

Yet it has proved useful for the mini-nationalists in the former Yugoslavia, in order to justify their moves for secession, to depict Yugoslav communism as if it had been the same as that of the harshest of the Warsaw Pact states.[2] This ploy, condemning Tito and his state, won sympathy for the Croats and Slovenes, for it allowed them to play on alleged past suffering under "repressive" communism and, by depicting their opponent, Slobodan Milošević of Serbia, as a continuing communist, to make foreign leaders and the public believe that these two republics deserved an escape from Yugoslavia. Milošević had risen through the communist system, as had Croatia's Franjo Tudjman, but Milošević had far more recently than Tudjman dropped the communist label to call his party socialist. The two leaders were equally dictatorial, however. And Milošević was certainly not a Titoist communist, but instead was a brutal authoritarian who was playing the nationalist card, not because he even believed in that, but because it seemed the way (and events proved him right) to gain power in Serbia. In any case, this line enabled the Croats and Slovenes, in their independence campaign and prior to the outbreak of fighting, to

present to the world a misleading image of being a victim, and thus re-
acting to victimization, rather than a picture of what they were in fact
doing, namely initiating an activist policy for independence that was
soon to result in the Croats oppressing their own Serb minority and un-
leashing a brutal war that was to produce enormous numbers of victims, including thousands of Croats.[3]

These so-called needs of Croatia's chauvinist regime, to achieve secession and to gain and maintain international sympathy, required a
major rewriting of the previous fifty years of Croatia's (and Yugoslavia's)
history to demonstrate the alleged victim status of the Croat people.
And the communist years were duly depicted as years of tyranny, whose
chief purpose seems to have been to suppress the Croats' attempts to express themselves as a nation. And as far as one can tell, in these claims,
the only things Croats have ever wanted to express was national feelings. That many Croats had other interests, including a genuine support
for socialism, is forgotten. Indeed, most Croat communists, such as Tito
and Vladimir Bakarić, have been depicted as traitors to the Croat nation.
So in order to capitalize on all the anticommunism being expressed across
Eastern Europe after the collapse of communism in the various Soviet-
bloc states, nationalists in Yugoslavia, and especially in Croatia, have
chosen more and more to depict the Tito regime as a typically oppres-
sive communist one.

That regime's first decade (1945–55) was, indeed, rather rough as it put
down the chauvinist forces (and their perceived sympathizers), which
during the war had carried out genocide and whose forces still remained
active within Yugoslavia at war's end, in some places into the 1950s.
And these chauvinists had organizations with support abroad that were
in fact bent on the new communist regime's destruction. Then followed
Stalin's expulsion of Yugoslavia from the Communist International in
1948, leading to difficulties with the Cominformisti. But in time the
regime gradually liberalized and in the 1960s produced a fairly free society (in terms of civil liberties, but not in terms of democratic multiparty
elections) that was actually very pleasant to live in, unless one was a political activist with an agenda that threatened either the delicate balance
of nationality relations or self-management socialism. The Croats were
perfectly free to live as Croats—in fact they had their own autonomous
republic. The federal party's foolish policy of discouraging a Yugoslav
(ethnic) identity even reinforced their right to be Croats and guaranteed
that a second broader identity could not take precedence over the narrow
Croat one. It was only when some extremists advanced positions that
seemed to endanger other nationalities in Croatia or what remained of

the fragile unity of Yugoslavia that Tito cracked down, as he did when the so-called "Croatian Spring" got out of hand. But critics of Tito's 1971–72 actions must pause before condemning him. What Tito feared was the breakup of Yugoslavia and the violence likely to result: events of the 1990s show his fears to have been real ones.[4] The few expulsions from the party and short jail terms for a small number of ultranationalists that were carried out in the early 1970s certainly seem to be a petty blemish (if a blemish at all) on his record compared to the massive death and destruction unleashed by the chauvinism that blots Tudjman's record.[5]

Moreover, if communism is depicted as out-and-out evil, then anyone who opposed it cannot be all that bad; thus the local fascist opponents of Tito's Partisans during World War II should be regarded not as fascists but as nationalists. And both Croat and Serb nationalists have been pressing this idea in recent years. Thus while the Serbs have been rehabilitating Draža Mihailović's Četniks, the Croats have done the same with the Nazi collaborators who led the so-called "Independent" State of Croatia, the fascist Ustaše, who massacred several hundred thousand Serbs, in carrying out the most massive example of ethnic cleansing in the Balkans ever. The viciousness of the Ustaše has been downplayed recently in Croatia, and these war criminals are being depicted as respectable fighters for Croat nationalism, thus as strugglers for a worthy cause. People like Mile Budak, who called for a third of Croatia's Serbs to be killed, a third to be expelled, and a third to be converted to Catholicism, are now fit figures to name schools and streets after. And Alojzije Stepinac, the Archbishop of Zagreb during World War II, who was a chauvinist and either a conscious Ustaša collaborator or a coward afraid to stand up to the regime, has been pushed for sainthood by the Croatian HDZ leadership and the Vatican. But if Budak and Stepinac are honored so today, can Ante Pavelić, Slavko Kvaternik, and Andrija Artuković be that far behind?[6]

This process has not only been rehabilitating the World War II collaborators but has also led to a rewriting of the war's history to debunk the Partisans and their achievements. It may not be strange that current chauvinists from Yugoslavia do this, but foreign scholars and journalists have allowed themselves to be sucked into the enterprise as well. As capable a student of Balkan nationalism as Michael Ignatieff is able to write: "He [Tito] portrayed himself as the leader of a national uprising against the German and Italian invaders. In reality, he won power in a vicious civil war against Ante Pavelić's Croatian Ustaše and Draža Mihailović's Serbian Četniks." But why the either/or? In fact, Tito fought both the Germans and Italians as well as a civil war against the occupiers' local

surrogates.[7] And Tito's activities, regardless of the opponent—foreign occupiers or local collaborators—were part of a broad antifascist campaign. That current nationalist Croats and Serbs may not like the defeat
of their chauvinistic predecessors is understandable, but there is no reason for objective foreigners to follow in their footsteps or to join, as
many have, in the across-the-board uncritical Tito-bashing that is now
going on in today's Once and Future Yugoslavia.[8]

*Thoughts about the Circumstances Surrounding and the Responsibility
for the Tragic and Unnecessary Breakup of Yugoslavia*

Yugoslav communism, in fact, became very different from that of
its neighbors; moreover, its policies from the mid-1960s particularly favored Croatia and Slovenia at the expense of the other four republics in
the federation. Croatia and Slovenia were the most advanced republics
economically and objected to the initial postwar system of central planning, under which their earnings were quite heavily taxed by the central
government to subsidize industry (and especially employment) in the
other less-developed republics. These two relatively wealthy republics ignored the fact that a good proportion (about 60 percent, varying from year
to year) of their exports, and hence profits, resulted from tariff-protected
sales to the rest of Yugoslavia. In any case, in the 1960s, after heated debate, the Slovene and Croatian view won out, and Yugoslavia began a
rapid process of decentralization (eventually enshrined in the 1974 constitution) that gave huge autonomy to the individual republics (which basically ran themselves and concluded foreign trade deals more or less
without consultation with central authorities); the party was decentralized into a loose alliance of republic parties, joined together in the League
of Communists of Yugoslavia. In this arrangement the individual republic parties, before going off to the federal plenum, held congresses to
work out their agendas and positions. For all practical purposes the Communist Party of Yugoslavia had broken up into eight local-interest parties (one for each of the six republics and two autonomous regions). The
only authority to hold them together was that of an aging Tito, who finally died in 1980.

After that the executive (the presidency) of Yugoslavia was an un-
wieldy arrangement with an eight-person committee (one representative from each of these eight entities) with a chair rotating on a one-year
term. Each entity basically also had a veto, so solutions on major issues
for all practical purposes required unanimity. The economic problems
through the 1980s became more and more serious, but owing to differ-

ences in economic conditions among the various republics, what was good for one was bad for another. No solutions were reached, and Yugoslavia found itself in gridlock. We should pause here, for the monolithic model for (Soviet and East European) communism stresses centralization on a state (or federal) level and ease in reaching and carrying out decisions. Clearly, considering Yugoslavia in terms of the Soviet-bloc model is misleading and unfair. Moreover, a state as decentralized as Yugoslavia should not be, as it often is, labeled "totalitarian," a term which, it should be noted, had been fitting for its first ten or fifteen years.

In any case, Yugoslavia was unable to resolve any of its major difficulties; obviously some sort of constitutional reform or restructuring of the state was necessary. Two contrary models were advanced: one to decentralize even further and more or less make Yugoslavia into six independent states (allied and presumably having a customs union); the other to create a more centralized state, with a central government able to make decisions for the whole state. The Croats and Slovenes, needless to say, were advocates of the former, and Serbia was the strongest advocate of the latter. Milošević had, by this time, risen to the top in Serbia and would presumably, should the Serb plan carry, find himself leader of Yugoslavia. This was clearly something none of the other republics wanted. The result was the usual deadlock, with the Slovenes and Croats free to continue their autonomous existences; their nationalist leaders, elected in 1990 in the first multiparty elections, however, wanted independence and decided the deadlock was a "crisis" that justified it. Yet there was no "crisis," there was merely gridlock; and with things deadlocked at 4–4 in the presidency neither group could impose its plan on the other. Slovenia and Croatia thus faced no danger from Milošević under these conditions.[9] It was only with the actual breakup on June 25, 1991 that the Yugoslav army (JNA) took action; the JNA officers had been unwilling to take action as long as Yugoslavia remained a single state and its presidency did not give it an order to act that was agreed upon by all the republics. The JNA's restraint before June 25, 1991, was remarkable, for the activities of the would-be separatists (in particular, the stockpiling of weapons by the Territorial Defense forces in Slovenia and Croatia) were treason by the laws of any state. Imagine what the FBI and U.S. Army's response would be if the Idaho militia were collecting weapons with a goal to secede from the United States.[10]

So, the various republics could have continued to discuss matters indefinitely. It certainly was a frustrating situation, but sooner or later, if Milošević failed to realize his policy goals and had no crisis to take action over, he would most likely have fallen from power. Therefore, since the stakes and risks were so high, it made sense not to give up when Milošević refused to negotiate but to wait him out. After all, although a resolution to difficulties would have been preferable, a decision of this magnitude should not have been rushed into, particularly since the existing confederate system left Croatia in the hands of Croats.

Indeed, the main political objection to the state over the years had been the monopoly of political power by the Communist Party. However, that had disappeared in 1990, and all the republics had carried out multiparty elections. The economic problems, of course, were serious, but the new federal Prime Minister Ante Marković, a Croat, was moving toward improving matters, bringing the horrendous inflation down below 10 percent. However, instead of seeing this as providing improved conditions to allow for more drawn-out negotiations, the nationalist leaders saw economic improvement as threatening their nationalist agendas and went out of their way to sabotage the reforms, so that economic difficulties, instead of being lessened, would continue and contribute to the sense of crisis.

Clearly, to launch impetuous actions that were going to affect some twenty-three million people was foolish, if not criminal. But Tudjman and Milan Kučan, the Slovene president, wanted independence and instant gratification, so even though their republics faced no actual danger, they declared independence. They did so completely irresponsibly, since a host of major matters that involved the whole federation—shares of the international debt, multirepublic enterprises, property owned by citizens of one republic in another republic, rights of minorities (for example, Serbs in Croatia), and so forth—were unresolved. Making matters worse, Tudjman declared Croatia to be a state of Croats, leaving Croatia's Serb population of about 15 percent as an unwanted second-class nuisance. Not surprisingly, the Serbs in Croatia, having suffered the World War II horrors from the Ustaše, whose symbols were now being resurrected rapidly by the Tudjman regime, and with Milošević playing upon these and stirring up their fears, demanded autonomy. Determined not to weaken the Croatness of their new state, the Croats refused any concessions. War soon followed. Regardless of the right of Slovenia and Croatia to eventual independence, the hasty, irresponsible way these two republics effected that independence brings upon them the lion's share of the responsibility for the war that followed.[11] After all, Milošević, usually depicted as the main villain in Yugoslavia's destruction, had hoped Yugoslavia would not break up. His switch to a policy of trying to create a greater Serbia emerged only early in 1991 in response to the threat of Croatia's secession (which would place many

Serbs outside of Yugoslavia/Serbia) and was then acted upon only after Croatia's actual secession. Without Croatia's declaration of independence, the war that followed in Croatia would not have occurred, at least not at that time.

A peaceful resolution of the many issues facing the republics might have taken several years and a great deal of frustrating discussion, but independence could still have eventually come about, if a majority of citizens in the given republics continued to want it. And such a delayed, negotiated settlement would have spared hundreds of thousands of lives lost—not to speak of over a million refugees—and who knows how many billions of dollars in destroyed property and lost trade, as well as the destruction of the multiethnic culture of Bosnia and Herzegovina (a republic that opposed in vain the breakup of Yugoslavia) and devastating damage to the relations among these people who will need to have good relations in the future if any of these ministates expect to survive as independent entities.

Thoughts on the Bosnian and Kosovo Wars and International Involvement

Other wars followed in Bosnia and Kosovo, most of the details of which the reader knows. Salient in these conflicts was the failure of the West and the United Nations to diagnose what was going on and intervene, particularly when the war spread in April 1992 to Bosnia, which truly supported a multiethnic state—something that Croatia never claimed to be, a fact that gave the Serbs of Croatia a legitimate reason to rebel. The West and the UN encouraged Bosnian independence, recognized it, and then allowed it to be overwhelmed by the Milošević version of the JNA and Serbian paramilitaries, acting on behalf of the Bosnian Serbs. A series of peace plans were advanced by the international community during this warfare, and all adopted the ethnic terms of the aggressors and provided partition schemes completely undercutting the multiethnic Bosnian government's insistence on multiethnicity, a position that represented the values of the UN, United States, and the European Union. The earliest of these wartime partition plans, Vance–Owen, created a series of cantons dominated by particular ethnicities. The Bosnian Croats, Bosnia's untrustworthy allies, did unusually well by the plan and decided to implement it at once, even though the plan had not been adopted. This led them to stab the Bosnians in the back and to start ethnically cleansing, exactly as the Serbs had been doing, their claimed territory. The United States finally brought about a truce, establishing in July 1994 a federation between the Bosnians and the local Croats to oppose the Serb separatists. This "federation" never went into effect, for the local Croats of Herceg-Bosna (the territory they had seized) would not allow anyone to interfere in it. Tudjman sabotaged the agreement as well, supporting his local surrogates in the lands he wanted Croatia to annex.

Eventually, after three and a half years of horror, the West intervened militarily in the fall of 1995 and coerced Milošević, Tudjman, and Bosnia's Alija Izetbegović to come to Dayton in November to negotiate a treaty. At the start, as has now become normal, we gave the negotiators a very brief deadline (in this case, by our Thanksgiving).[12] A series of major issues had to be settled, and they could not be settled in so short a time and thus serious negotiations (not that the Balkan negotiators were necessarily seriously committed) were impossible; so the result was browbeating and coercing the parties into the acceptance of an agreement totally unsatisfactory to the Bosnians, for whom the West allegedly had sympathy. The United States knew it was a poor agreement and I would say a fraud, but Clinton's reelection campaign was fast upon him, and he had to have the Bosnian nuisance resolved. We, as usual following the ethnic categories of the aggressors, set up two entities, an All-Bosnia in which existed two *sovereign* entities, a Serb Republic of Bosnia, Republika Srpska (thereby rewarding the most outrageous aggressor) and a Bosnian-Croat federation. And the insertion of the "federation" is what made the accords a fraud. The federation established on paper fifteen months earlier was a total fiction; it had not been realized at all, and its complete failure was described in the report of the EU administrator Hans Koschnick in July 1995 to the EU. Thus the United States, with full knowledge that the federation did not exist (and that the Croat-occupied territory was as ethnically cleansed and uni-ethnically run as Republika Srpska), saddled the Bosnians with an albatross of Croatian chauvinists, who hated the Bosnians as much as the local Serbs did. This meant that in theory the Croats had a say in what went on in every part of the alleged federation. To pay lip-service to Bosnia, we created the all-Bosnian entity but gave it a very limited sphere of activity and saddled it with two *sovereign* entities, to each of which belonged a very broad sphere of activities.[13] This was a blueprint for failure, since each ethnicity could prevent anything from being accomplished. All-Bosnia, as created, was going to fall into gridlock; thus it laid a foundation for the partition, which separatist Serbs and Croats, as well as Serbia and Croatia, wanted, but we insisted we did not want. It was a dreadful treaty, but as various American diplomats argued, it was the best that we could get under the circumstances, that is, if we were not willing to seriously intervene militarily.

For the treaty to work at all, its guarantors (NATO) would have to play an active role in bringing about massive refugee return and arresting the war criminals. Neither has yet happened.[14] The only hope that Bosnia now has (which it did not have before) lies in the new Croatian government, whose leaders have promised (and in office are working) to recognize Bosnia with its 1991 borders, stop financing the Croat separatists in former Herceg-Bosna (which is "former" only on paper), and eliminate the dual citizenship of Bosnia's Croats, which allows them to vote (and thus support chauvinists) in Croatia's elections. We can only hope that the new leaders are able to carry these proposals out and have enough support behind them, for they will face much opposition in both Herceg-Bosna and Croatia. The death of Tudjman and the rapid decline of his HDZ party are the most positive things that have happened in the Balkans since June 1991.

Meanwhile the violence that erupted in 1998 in Kosovo (staved off for over a decade by a vicious Serbian martial-law regime combined with a Kosovar policy of disciplined nonviolent resistance) was in great part brought about by the United States and its allies, which at Dayton showed that violence pays, by awarding the Bosnian Serb aggressors with a minirepublic in Bosnia while ignoring the nonviolent Kosovars entirely. Impatient Albanians turned to armed resistance, which, naturally, gave the Serbs an excuse to brutally crack down on the Albanians. Moreover, when Serbia started its campaign against the Kosovars, the United States from the start, though condemning Serb violence, insisted that Kosovo should remain within Serbia. This told Milošević that he was free to do whatever he wanted, for no matter what he did, the United States saw Kosovo as Serbian. We never should have given him this green light; we should have said that we did not care where Kosovo ended up, whether as a part of Serbia or as an independent state, and our (and probably including the EU, NATO, UN) decision would be based on the behavior of the two sides; thus Serb violence could well result in Serbia forfeiting its claims to Kosovo.

Our response to the war that ensued in Kosovo over the next two years ended up showing the same sort of ambiguity that our policy in Bosnia does. After the usual delay—though this time one of only slightly more than a year—the U.S. and EU came to support Albanian rights against the vicious Serb repression. But in our military intervention against this repression in March 1999, we continued to support an autonomous Kosovo within Serbia while naively or unthinkingly accepting and utilizing the support of the Albanian Kosovo Liberation Army (KLA), a very decentralized organization, with many strands, from idealists to drug merchants, about whom we knew little; but since it was so clearly stated by all KLA spokesmen, we ought at least to have seen that all the factions were zealously for an independent Kosovo. So, we linked ourselves to both a constitutional plan and a group opposed to that plan.

It was not surprising, and also apparent from the start, that the KLA was strongly chauvinistic and sought a Kosovo ethnically cleansed of Serbs. Thus, when Milošević decided to make peace to end the bombing and NATO (plus Russia) entered Kosovo, if we were to have any hope of peace there, we needed to disarm and demobilize the KLA, as we had stated as an objective earlier and as the KLA had agreed in the Rambouillet meetings. If the KLA wanted to convert itself into one or more political parties, great; but the provincial and local police and militia should have been created from scratch and volunteers accepted individually, though not excluding those who had been in the KLA (one would hope after a background check). Instead we capitulated to the KLA, which now dominates local institutions and Albanian opinion in Kosovo, sabotages efforts to preserve a Serb population there, and even turns irredentist eyes toward those parts of Serbia with large Albanian populations that lie to the east of Kosovo. Thus, once again in Kosovo we find ourselves for multiethnicity merely on paper, tied up with a variety of programs that will sabotage it, and on a path (with Serb population concentrations in Mitrovica and to its north) that could lead to partition; and since the area in question is the richest mining area in Kosovo (though some analysts think the mines are near exhaustion), an attempt at partition could lead to a resumption of war. Needless to say, Milošević is provoking the Serbs in their part of Mitrovica and his agents are active in that whole area.

Moreover, as during our military intervention, U.S. policy toward its peace-keeping troops remains "no American casualties." In Bosnia, this means do not try to arrest war criminals, they might resist. When things recently got ugly in Kosovska Mitrovica, the NATO command summoned some Americans to beef up the French units there. When these soldiers became the targets of some stone throwing, U.S. commanders ordered them out.[15] If we will not face violence and take risks, what sort of armed forces does the United States have? Clearly, we are only a superpower in the air, but a nation that will not risk casualties among its troops will be pushed around by any little militia or paramilitary band that wants to assert itself. If the KLA can browbeat us into allowing it to continue to function, despite initial agreements to the contrary, we clearly are no superpower.

Lessons from the Yugoslav Tragedy

The message in all this must be unity of the Balkan peoples. Tito briefly succeeded in standing up to dependence on one or another of the various foreign actors. But independence from foreign actors (allowing the Balkanites to determine their own fate) can occur only if the Balkan peoples awaken to obvious facts and realize that together (if they cooperate politically and economically) they can prosper, whereas as individual peoples they cannot. The leadership of the rest of Europe does not care a hoot about any of them (except as sources of profit or in terms of some strategic interest). The sooner the Balkanites realize the common interests they have among themselves and that their common interests are on major issues while their feuds are on trivia, the better off they will be. At such time they could start making agreements and alliances among themselves, and maybe eventually a Balkan equivalent of the EU, if not a more integrated federation.

But with all the suffering resulting from the secession of Croatia (and Slovenia) and the horrible wars that followed, one cannot help but wonder, and many Croats must surely wonder too, if it was really worth it.[16] For, after all, they were in 1991 perfectly free to be as Croat as they wished in their autonomous republic—assuming that being Croat did not mean being free to repress Croatia's Serbian minority—within a very decentralized federation of fellow South Slavs. Instead, in the independent ministate that emerged no checks stood over Tudjman, who, using the war that he initiated as an excuse, was free to set up a new party-state and ride roughshod over basic civil liberties and create an establishment even more corrupt and more based on cronyism than anything the communists had ever produced. Not only that, these little Balkan nations, for centuries too small to command respect in their own right, had finally in the creation of Yugoslavia—and particularly under Tito who, through his genius, was able to make Yugoslavia a respected country and a fairly major player on the world scene—risen above being playthings of the Great Powers. Now as mini-statelets, the South Slavs have returned to their pre–World War I condition of major dependence on the indifferent Great Powers, courting the Powers and begging them for loans and political or military support against their neighbors, to be let in or kept out by the whims of international bodies (like NATO, which no Balkan state should but most want to be part of) that make the important decisions and, always vulnerable, available to be sacrificed by these Powers, whose priorities always put their own mutual relations above the needs of a mini-statelet. Thus the West's Bosnia policy during the war in that unfortunate country took the needs of Bosnia into consideration only after relations among the Western allies (and NATO's interests) and then relations with Russia (and keeping the disreputable, but thankfully now retired, Yeltsin in power) were all accommodated first. Needless to say years went by before anything serious was done about Bosnia. As a result, Bosnia and now Kosovo may well find themselves partitioned in the interests of the balance of power, be it the Powers' vision of a Balkan one or that among the Powers themselves. Faced with Croatia's present international position, it should be evident, even to a die-hard Croat nationalist, that to be part of a Yugoslav federation, as long as it is decentralized and leaves an autonomous Croatia, is far more in the Croat national interest than the present independent state of Croatia.

✺

Yugoslavia's was a beautiful society. Under Tito's tolerant guidance Yugoslavs, by the 1960s, appeared to have overcome the ethnic hatred that had overwhelmed them during World War II and had come to live together as harmoniously as people can, where regionalism and economic differences may set them at odds. But eventually after Tito's death major economic difficulties and unscrupulous politicians, playing the nationalist card for their own ambitions with the help of politically controlled media and taking advantage of real difficulties (which, though soluble, were depicted otherwise), were able to stir up fears and turn one South Slav nation against another, even though such hostile feelings were completely contrary to the interests of any of these peoples.

Yugoslavia was anything but an artificial country. It was created voluntarily by the South Slavs themselves (at least by the Serbs, Croats, and Slovenes); the Powers at Paris merely adjudicated its borders. The new state, in theory, met the needs of all these peoples, who had been the playthings of the Great Powers for centuries. The ideas behind it were those of a broad South Slav movement, the brain child of Ljudevit Gaj (and the Illyrians) and the great Bishop Josip Strossmayer, Croats both. In the 1840s, the Illyrians generously, in seeking a standard language, rejected their own Zagreb dialect in favor of the Štokavian dialect, the one used most widely by the South Slav peoples, by the Bosnians, Serbs, and some of the Croats. They encouraged broadness of vocabulary, consciously including synonyms from different dialects, lest they exclude speakers of any dialect from their Illyrian vision. They even began to call the language Croato-Serbian.[17] How selfless, generous, and intelligent was the vision of these nineteenth-century Croats when compared to those advocating a narrow Croatian language today, who seek to ban from speech any word that might be of Serbian origin.[18]

Despite much idealism behind it, the Yugoslav state did not develop between the two World Wars as it might have. It is often said by nationalists and foreign journalists that this failure was owing to ancient ethnic (and/or religious) hatreds. However, this was not the case. In the medieval history of this area, there had been many wars between dynastic states and many civil wars among nobles or between king and nobles; but all the civil wars were fought over land or hegemony. There were no religious wars (if we exclude wars of conquest launched by Hungary and the Ottomans) or ethnic ones in the whole Middle Ages. And in the years of the Ottoman (and where relevant, Habsburg) Empire, there were no civil wars among the ancestors of the future Yugoslavs either. Ethnicity became a feature of Balkan society only in the course of the nineteenth century, and became important only late in that century when it was pushed by the ambitious and irredentist states of Serbia, Bulgaria, and Greece. And even as ethnic feelings rose, most of it was directed against the Ottomans, Habsburgs, or within the latter empire the Hungarians, who ran Croatia for the Habsburgs. Though in Croatia anti-Serb publications and speeches appeared in the late nineteenth century and there was even a major riot in 1902, throughout the years just preceding World War I there still were many more examples of cooperation than hostility among the Habsburg South Slavs, and one should note that the alleged bearers of the greatest enmity (the Serbs of Serbia and the Croats) had had no relationship (and certainly never a war) until they put themselves for the first time in a state together—Yugoslavia—at the end of World War I. Thus one might have expected the new state to be a success. After all, 70 percent of the people of the new Yugoslavia had a common first language (Serbo-Croatian), a great deal of goodwill, and little or no history of antagonism.[19]

However, despite the variety of factors favoring the creation of Yugoslavia, owing to the greed, ambition, and nationalism of politicians—particularly Serbs (who turned the state into a greater Serbia)—resentment (growing into hatreds) that had not previously existed among the nationalities emerged in the course of the 1920s and 1930s. Serious ethnic (and religious) animosity among the Yugoslav peoples is thus a feature of the twentieth century.

The Germans invaded in April 1941 and dismembered Yugoslavia, and another great Croat, Josip Broz Tito, led the movement to put it back together again in an ethnically just state that gave, to the degree it was humanly possible, equal rights to all the nationalities. Ambitious and unscrupulous Serb, Croat, and Slovene politicians after Tito's death brought it all crashing down. But one cannot believe that something so much in the interests of all South Slavs (and so important in allowing them to be significant actors on the European stage rather than mere playthings again of their Germanic and Russian neighbors) can have disappeared forever or, indeed, even for a long time.[20]

But a restoration, unfortunately, is not just around the corner; so the Balkans can expect much more turmoil in the years to come. Thus, I fear that the Balkan peoples will be faced with a decade or more of continued economic suffering, exploitation by international finance, short-sighted and selfish leadership, local corruption, and probably a great deal more ethnically and criminally based violence. But counter-forces must sooner or later emerge, and then, under new generations, we should see before the twenty-first century comes to an end (assuming that states are still important in the Europe of that time) what is so greatly in all these peoples' interests, the reestablishment of the Once and Future Yugoslavia.

11 | Solving the Wars of Yugoslav Succession

GALE STOKES

Warren Christopher, former secretary of state, once described the wars of Yugoslav succession as "the foreign policy problem from hell." Despite increasingly committed efforts by the United States and Europe to bring stability to the portions of the former Yugoslavia occupied by Serbs, Croats, Bosnians, and Albanians, the best the Western powers have been able to do is stop the massive killing and ethnic cleansing by imposing military force under the auspices of NATO and the United Nations. The present policy goal is to create multiethnic democracies in Bosnia and Kosovo through the assistance of outside advisers backed by force. But this policy is not working. Bosnia remains split in all but the most formal ways and although the UN maintains the fiction that Kosovo remains part of Serbia and Yugoslavia, there is no likelihood that Kosovo will return to Serbian administration. Slobodan Milošević, the key stumbling block to creating Balkan stability, remains in power and economically the situation in Bosnia, Kosovo, and Serbia is dire.

Is there no solution to these problems? Some have suggested there is not. The hatreds are too powerful, the principles involved are too conflicting, and the outside powers are too divided. I do not agree. I believe there is a solution. It is to redraw the state borders in the Balkans along ethnic lines. To state the position this baldly raises immediate questions—does not such a policy reward the worst fanatics among the antidemocratic nationalists? Does such a policy violate the Helsinki accords? What would happen to the Bosnian Muslims, or to Vojvodina? Wouldn't such a policy require more forcible population exchanges? Could Macedonia survive? Isn't this against our policy of multiculturalism and tolerance? Granted, these and other issues are difficult and require thought. But our current policy of imposing multiculturalism and tolerance on Bosnia and Kosovo cannot work. Democracy and the attributes that go with it cannot be imposed—they must be chosen. The Balkan peoples will be able to develop the confidence needed to chose to enter into the multifaceted system of buffering mechanisms and negotiating nodes that constitutes today's security system in Europe only when each of them has their own, self-contained country.

I have come to this conclusion by placing the Yugoslav disaster in its largest European context. Once we do that it becomes clear that the events of the past decade are not some aberrant outburst of primitive behavior (although there have been many such outbursts) but rather a late stage of a long-standing and fundamental European process. The argument has three parts:

1. Nationalism in Europe can best be understood as a set of powerful mobilizing ideas generated by the French Revolution. The ethnic homogenization of European states was in part the result of nationalistic political figures pursuing their own interpretation of the ideas of popular sovereignty, equity, and freedom within an already existing state system. The wars in Yugoslavia are a continuation of that process.

2. The redrawing of state borders onto ethnic lines has always been brutal. The violence of the wars of Yugoslav succession is fully in keeping with the vicious nature of a long-standing European process.

3. Despite the strains that recent events have placed on the European security system, buffering mechanisms are in a permanent process of construction that will greatly lessen the chances of future outbursts of massive self-destruction in Europe.

The intrusive, omnicompetent state came into being in Europe independently of both capitalism and nationalism, two elements often closely linked to it. As Hendrik Spruyt puts it, "States preceded the development of a capitalist world economy, rather than the reverse."[1] The late medieval Italian model of interacting city-states, the so-called "new monarchies" of the sixteenth century, the consolidation of Muscovy under Ivan III and Ivan IV, the re-formation of Europe through the wars of religion that culminated in the Thirty Years' War, the success of Frederick William the Great Elector in taming his Junkers, and the need for revenue called forth by changes in warfare all contributed to the emergence of strongly organized state apparatuses on the continent by the mid-seventeenth century. Jean Bodin and Hugo Grotius introduced the secular ideas of sovereignty and international law, and the Treaty of Westphalia (1648) formalized a structure within which states that had just come to understand themselves as sovereign could interact. A neat developmental line for this system can be drawn from Westphalia through the Treaty of Utrecht (1713), the Congress of Vienna (1815), the League of Nations (1919), and the United Nations (1945). In our day, the international system of well-defined states has become the fundamental worldwide structure within which large-scale political interaction takes place.

The lineage of this system is clearly Central European, but this fact is less clear than it might be because the powers that pushed European norms and practices into the rest of the world were primarily the Atlantic-facing communities or Spain, Portugal, France, England, and the Netherlands. The latter two, in particular, were the societies in which market principles took hold earliest and most fully, so that when world-system theorists or the subaltern studies group, to take two examples, consider the impact of colonialism on Latin America or South Asia, the rationalizing state they analyze is often also a capitalist state.

But rationalizing states are not necessarily capitalist. Making this distinction will go a long way toward clarifying the ideological and institutional nature of nationalism and sustaining the point that nationalism is not based primarily on social or economic determinants. The Central European states that created the original European state system that later encompassed the world were not capitalist at the time they were creating that system. The characteristic political philosophy of states such as Austria, Prussia, Sweden, and Russia was cameralism, or the science of state administration, not laissez-faire. Cameralist theory held that society consisted of well-defined social strata, each of which had its characteristic needs. By implementing proper fiscal and economic policies, state administrators hoped to produce economic growth that would enable each stratum to exceed its customary wants. Then the state could appropriate the surplus for its purposes. Cameralists pursued economic growth, but through rationally structured taxation, fiscal policies, and industry, not through market mechanisms.

The rationale for public policy of the well-organized state, the *Polizeistaat*, that emerged in Central Europe was significantly at odds with liberal economic theories of capitalism. Instead of stressing the individual, cameralists stressed community. Instead of depending on public initiative to set or at least affect public policy, they left all initiative in the hands of the prince and his bureaucracy. Instead of seeing law primarily as a device to protect property, they understood law as an administrative mechanism. And instead of (eventually) setting limits on state power, they saw power as a tool to be used by the state for its purposes.

These pre–French Revolutionary states were not capitalist, but they were nevertheless modern. The tendency of some historians to interpret state development in social or class terms has obscured this point. Perry Anderson observes that "the Absolute monarchies introduced standing armies, a permanent bureaucracy, national taxation, a codified law, and the beginnings of a unified market." But Anderson associates the modernity of states with their class, not their institutional, structure. Therefore, the Central European states cannot be modern, or capitalist as he would put it, because groups he classifies as feudal remained in power. "Absolutism was essentially just this: *a redeployed and recharged apparatus of feudal domination*, designed to clamp the peasant masses back into their traditional social position."[2] If one drops the a priori necessity for class deployment, however, the data that Anderson presents make it clear that the Central European polities had what Charles Tilly calls "stateness" well before they had the qualities of capitalism.[3]

This helps illuminate the problems with Benedict Anderson's often cited term *print-capitalism*.[4] There is no question that the introduction of movable type was of the utmost importance in shifting the modal cognitive style of Europeans over time. Print made widespread literacy possible, promoted schooling, encouraged linear thinking, allowed for accurate maps, made novels possible, and changed concepts of time. Moreover, publishing was the first widespread industry to use mass means of production systematically and to develop a body of specialized workers who sought and gained benefits for themselves. Printers also distributed goods by means of far-flung and complex markets, and its successful practitioners gained large profits. Nevertheless, these events took place in an atmosphere of regulated enterprise that had little to do with the norms of laissez-faire, supply and demand, and protection of property rights that characterize capitalism. In the nineteenth century, of course, this changed, but the process was difficult and the cost high.

The point here is that modern nationalism emerged only *after* an effective international structure of rationalizing continental states had already formed. This structure had little to do with modern forms of economic behavior, but a lot to do with an orientation toward community rather than toward the individual. In other words, nationalism as an ideology emerged within an already mature system of sovereign states whose basis was neither laissez-faire nor individualistic.

The ideology of nationalism itself grew out of a particular interpretation that some nationalists placed on three emotionally powerful ideas put onto the public agenda by the French Revolution. The first of these was the notion of popular sovereignty. In a sense the modern idea of nation was simply one of the answers to the question implicit in this idea, namely, who are the people? The French Revolution irrevocably put this question into play but provided very little guidance on how to answer it. Women were not included in the concept, for example, nor were slaves. During the nineteenth century, the idea slowly expanded. At first, liberals proposed that only property owners, those with a stake in society, should constitute civil society. But during the second half of the century socialists insisted that those who created wealth through their labor, the workers, should also be included. Later, suffragists demanded that their half of the human race also be included, and in the second half of the twentieth century, African-Americans in the United States demanded that they, too, be able to take part freely in public life. Today, as a result of two hundred years of struggle, "the people" comprises all competent adults.

At the same time that this final stage in the migration of the locus of sovereignty from God to the people was unfolding, a second revolutionary idea was maturing as well, the idea of equity or fairness. Until the French Revolution, all human societies had been organized on the basis of the obvious fact that human beings differ in terms of their strength, intelligence, social position, and gender, among other things. Strong, intelligent, prominent, or rich males ran societies on what seemed, to them at least, to be the God-given or natural principle of hierarchy. But in the eighteenth century, rationalist philosophers postulated that the differences that justified social hierarchy were superficial, perhaps even the result, said Rousseau, of social conventions such as those associated with private property. According to the new idea, all human beings were in some sense equal.

What that sense is, of course, has been a contested matter ever since. As the process of trying to work out its meaning matured, the term *equality* was transmuted into the more general concept of equity. We agree that the state is not obliged to treat its citizens with exact equality. No one argues that federal judges and army privates should be paid the same for their services. But we do insist that the state conduct its affairs fairly. Justice, as John Rawls has argued, can proceed only from an initial assumption of fairness.[5] The demand for equity, voiced today in so-called "rights" talk, is the justification used by every group that seeks to achieve recognition of its position in society or pursues its access to some public good. We accept that equality is impossible in almost every real-world situation, but we consider ourselves grievously wronged if we perceive that our right to be treated fairly has been infringed.

Nationalists began to appear in the nineteenth century. They combined these two eighteenth-century notions—the ideal of popular sovereignty and the demand for equity—into a political ideology that differed markedly from liberalism, socialism, and other political doctrines. The nationalists had a straightforward answer to the question "Who are the people." Who are the people? We are! We who recognize one another for some reason of culture, history, or religion. At first glance, this position seems to be a restatement of the ideal of equity. The nation is the all-inclusive "we" in which all are equal in their "we-ness." But the nationalist form of equality is not an equity statement. Everyone may be equal as a member of the nation, but in order to be able to recognize those who are co-cultural there must be an Other. If nationalism is to exist at all, it must draw distinctions between those who may enjoy equality as members of the nation and those who may not.[6] This primary community-defining mechanism of nationalism cancels out the "multiplicity of individual and private interests" and re-aggregates them by postulating "the existence of a historical contract harking back to the nation's origins" that constitutes the common interest of the entire community.[7]

When nationalists consider the question of equity, therefore, they do not think of individual rights, as persons operating in the Anglo-American tradition often do. They focus on the rights their people as a whole need and deserve. To the rabid nationalist, rights are not individual—they are communal, and they do not extend to those outside the national community. This is why nationalists have been able to routinely trample on the rights of people they define as Other who by chance happen to live in "their" nation-state. Indeed, the homogeneous nation is indifferent to social or political philosophy. The nation can conduct its affairs as a dictatorship, a centrally planned socialist economy, or a liberal democracy. The specific characteristics of political structures are irrelevant to membership in the "we." Thus, inherent in the nationalist interpretation of equality in "we-ness" is a rejection of the individualistic principle of equity that lies behind the concept of human rights in the contemporary world. Slobodan Milošević may seek what he thinks of as equity for Serbs, but as a Serbian nationalist he has no commitment to equity for Kosovars or Bosnians, who are not among the "we."

The elaboration of the nationalist version of popular sovereignty and equity took place in relationship to a third innovation of the French Revolution, an explicit desire for freedom. In early modern Europe, freedom, often called liberty, effectively meant privilege, the right to exclude others from a public good or to be exempt from some public obligation. Guilds had the freedom to produce their products exclusively in the areas where they were active. The Holy Roman Emperor's duty was to protect the liberties (that is, privileges) of the knights of his realm. By the time of the French Revolution, however, liberty "was no longer deemed a possession to be preserved, but was regarded as the continuing condition necessary for action, . . . the socializing faculty that gave every individual will an equal share in the general will to act."[8] In the Anglo-American redaction of this change in the notion of liberty, an individual was free to act in any way that did not infringe on the freedom of others to act. Law, rather than being primarily an administrative mechanism as it was in Central Europe, maintained social order by drawing the lines between acceptable and unacceptable acts. In the nationalist version of popular sovereignty, however, it is not the individual who is free to act as much as it is the allegedly homogenous people. For the nationalist, therefore, the important social issue was not so much defining individual rights as it was asserting the autonomy of the whole.

The key structuring element of these ideological developments was the already highly elaborated state system of nineteenth-century Europe. The highest level of autonomy in the state system is the sovereign state. The only nations fully acknowledged as free to act in their own interests are those that participate in the state system as sovereign entities. This is why nationalists in the nineteenth century were led inexorably from their initial demands for cultural autonomy to the view that if their nation was to be fully competent to conduct public affairs it had to have its own state. Freedom for the nationalist, therefore, especially in the continental context, is not individual autonomy but the autonomy of the community as a whole within a system of states. This is exactly what Kosovars in Serbia (along with Kurds in Turkey and many others) have been seeking—membership in the state system, because only that will certify their acceptance into the modern world as an authentically free people.

Much of the political history of nineteenth- and twentieth-century Europe can be read as a working out of a homogenizing style of autonomy within the state system, a redrawing of state borders onto ethnic lines. In 1850, most of Europe was governed by four great multiethnic empires—Russian, Austrian, Ottoman, and German (in the last case, by the German Confederation, the heir to the Holy Roman Empire). Today Europe consists of dozens of independent, self-governing entities, most of which are more or less ethnically homogeneous. These bland sentences do not hint at the frightful cost of this enormous change. For millions of people, redrawing boundaries meant brutal uprooting, economic catastrophe, or death. The unification of Italy and Germany, the creation of the Balkan states in Southeastern Europe, the construction of new states in Central Europe in 1918, and the redrawing of East European borders in 1945 all were instances of mapping state borders onto a homogenizing definition of the people—the nation. One of the best examples of the process is Poland, which did not exist in 1850. When Poland was restored after World War I only about two-thirds of the people living within its boundaries were Polish. Today about 96 percent of the persons living in Poland are Polish, thus creating a situation of stability that makes Poland today politically workable and an ally of its ancient enemy Germany. Because of this relatively benign outcome, which was duplicated in much of Europe, the savage violence that was an integral part of this cartography of homogenization tends to be forgotten. A continentwide thirty-year war replete with massacres and ethnic cleansings of the most horrible kinds killed perhaps fifty million people. The Holocaust, along with the killing of several million Poles, the forcible eviction of about eight million Germans, and the moving of Polish borders about 150 kilometers to the west, is what made Polish homogenization possible. Massive population exchanges among Bulgaria, Greece, and Turkey at the beginning of this century, the expulsion of millions of Germans from Eastern Europe after World War II, and, in our own time, the wars of Yugoslav succession are other notable instances.

In this context, the Yugoslav wars of the 1990s are not an anomaly but rather a late phase of a deep transformation that is only tangentially related to industrialization or the development of capitalism but is fundamentally related to specific attempts to put into effect certain inspiring notions from the eighteenth century.[9] This is not to deny that many other changes took place in the same period—technological, economic, social, and cognitive. Doubtless industrialization created new social classes that participated in this process in their particular ways. But social change and class relations were not the primary ingredients in the formulation of the principles and actualities of the nation-state. Nationalism is a specific way of trying to effectuate the ideas of popular sovereignty, equity, and freedom within an already existing state system. Separating out these ideological and structural determinants from the socioeconomic factors that also are part and parcel of European history after the French Revolution makes it possible to think clearly about the wars of Yugoslav succession.[10]

Before we turn to a proposal for achieving stability in the former Yugoslavia, it is useful first to establish how the rest of Europe managed to become stable after the catastrophes of the first half of the twentieth century. The process began at least as far back as the Congress of Vienna in 1815, at a time when no European state was organized explicitly on the national principle. Contrary to the view put forward by Henry Kissinger, it was not the Congress of Vienna's re-establishment of a balance of power that brought stability, but just the opposite—the abandonment of the balance of power rules.[11] As Paul Schroeder has convincingly argued, balance of power politics as practiced in the eighteenth century actually promoted conflict rather than fostering stability.[12] Eighteenth-century conflicts were not couched in nationalist terms, but they were functionally similar to some nationalist conflicts in that many states, especially small ones, had to worry about their neighbors' territorial demands. Frederick the Great seized Silesia from Austria, for example, and by the end of the century Poland's three neighbors had swallowed it up. Alliances were instruments for accruing power and capability or for enhancing the honor and prestige of the monarch, not for creating stability. This meant that as soon as reasons of state required it, agreements were broken. Allies sought indemnities for services or losses, and even if they were not involved in a conflict they sought compensation if one of their rivals seemed to gain. Every vicious practice under these rules was justified in terms of balance of power, because it condoned all efforts and explained all outcomes. Invocation of the balance of power was like the invocation of "national interest" today. It simply referred to actions the leadership of a state wanted to undertake for one reason or another.

At the Congress of Vienna, negotiators from Europe's five most powerful states, fresh from twenty-five years of warfare, consciously confronted Europe's structural problems and conflicts. They sought not mere victory but stability. Their innovation was to put aside the balance of power rules and to create in their place, as Schroeder puts it, "an international system of political equilibrium based on benign shared hegemony and the mutual recognition of rights underpinned by law."[13] The powers agreed to respect one another's integrity and at the same time to take on joint responsibility for maintaining the status quo in what they called the Concert of Europe. They did not rely entirely on one another's goodwill, however. For one thing, they implicitly agreed to leave the flanking powers—Great Britain and Russia—to their extra-European adventures. By tacitly accepting Britain's control of the seas and Russia's likely expansion into Central Asia, the powers made certain that extra-European controversies would no longer be part of continental conflicts as they had been in the eighteenth century. On the continent itself they created intermediate bodies that provided buffering zones. The most important of these were Belgium, Switzerland, and the German Confederation. In these areas the powers could compete but without threatening a major war. The smaller states accepted the hegemony of the five Great Powers that devised these principles because under them their existence was guaranteed. Until Bismarck unified Germany in 1871 and removed the main Central European buffer zone, the German Confederation, these agreements kept Europe relatively stable. Bismarck's actions began a process that divided the continent into two competing camps. Buffeted by nationalism, social Darwinism, and racism, as well as many other factors, the two camps went at each other's throats in 1914.

After the ensuing decades of war and depression ended in 1945, West Europeans invented an elaborate new system of "benign shared hegemony" that has striking similarities to the Vienna schemes but obvious differences as well. Once again the continental powers left the flanking powers (now the Soviet Union and the United States) to their worldwide spheres. Ironically, Soviet domination of Eastern Europe enabled West Europeans to ignore many difficult problems of ethnicity and nationalism that might have disrupted the postwar innovations. More important, Europeans, with the United States, constructed a far more sophisticated buffering system than existed after 1815. This system consisted of a wide variety of international agencies to which countries could repair for negotiation in case of conflict. The Bretton Woods agreements (the formation of the International Monetary Fund and the World Bank) maintained monetary balance for twenty-five years, and the Marshall Plan fostered the ideal of cooperative competition rather than the beggar-thy-neighbor economic policies common during the interwar period. The success of the European Coal and Steel Community led directly to the Treaty of Rome in 1957, the growth of the Common Market, and eventually the European Union. The General Agreement on Tariffs and Trade (GATT), which grew into the World Trade Organization (WTO), was another important link in the network.

These, and an alphabet soup of institutions—WEU (Western European Union), IMF (International Monetary Fund), OSCE (Organization for Security and Cooperation in Europe), UN (United Nations), NATO (North Atlantic Treaty Organization), OECD (Organization for Economic Cooperation and Development)—each of which was constructed for its own purposes, actually constitute a single huge buffering mechanism. Taken together, the vast array of venues at which issues are discussed under agreed-upon rules and assumptions make up a coherent, if stupefyingly complex, network of mutually related constraints. It is no longer possible to "wave a red cloth in front of the Gallic bull" and provoke a war, as Bismarck did in 1870. Today, when European countries disagree, governments tell their negotiators to pack their notebook computers and cell phones and repair to the appropriate negotiation node in Brussels, Strasbourg, Geneva, or elsewhere. These interlinked nodes constitute Europe's new social contract, a decision consciously agreed upon to create a mutually beneficial politics of accommodation. The constraining force of the diverse web of interdependencies gives all the European states far more resources for resisting domination than they had when they were single states or when they were attached to relatively limited alliances.[14] Linking together an increasing number of their own and their neighbors' interests in one interrelated system frees all participants from fears about the crudest forms of aggression and pressure.

This new social contract has more staying power than did the old Concert of Europe because it has been created and sustained through democratic procedures. Membership in each of the numerous organizations that constitute the buffering network is voluntary in the sense that pluralist states approved the conditions of creating and sustaining them via democratic mechanisms. That is, the interacting security framework is considered legitimate because it was chosen, not imposed. The underlying assumption is that each nation or people has the right to make decisions regarding their own interests, as long as these decisions are made by using the general principles of pluralism, democracy, and human rights. Thus, in the European "pluralistic security community," as it has been called, the most important element is not military might but common democratic values.[15]

The chaos in the former Yugoslavia has temporarily obscured the fact that in Central Europe the process of integration into the new social contract is already well advanced. For the first time since the creation of the new states in Central Europe following World War I, Poles, Czechs, Slovaks, and Hungarians, among others, have recognized the security value of voluntary and interlocking negotiating mechanisms. Most of the former communist states are members of the World Trade Organization, the Council of Europe (which concerns itself with human and minority rights), the International Monetary Fund, and the Organization for Security and Cooperation in Europe. Many indigenous economic and political negotiating nodes are in various advanced stages of formation. The members of the Central European Free Trade Association have agreed to coordinate their commercial law to that of the European Union and to drop all tariffs among themselves. The Central European Initiative meets regularly to discuss cultural projects and other infrastructure items, such as joint highway construction. The Black Sea Economic Cooperation Group, consisting of states bordering on the Black Sea, plus one or two others, such as Greece, has established a development bank. The Southeast European Cooperative Initiative is beginning to coordinate various development plans in the Balkans. Many bilateral agreements exist as well, such as the successful Hungary-Ukraine cultural exchanges, the Carpathian Eurogroup, the Brandenburg-Gorzów cooperation, the Polish-German University at Frankfurt am Oder, and the friendship agreement between Romania and Hungary. At this stage, it is impossible to tell which of these initiatives will prove healthy and which will fail. The point is not their current viability but the indication they provide that East Europeans understand the functionality of buffering mechanisms in creating stability and are busily trying to construct them.

What are the implications of this way of looking at nationalism for policymakers, especially those concerned with the former Yugoslavia? First, nationalists are imbued with an intrinsically powerful idea that does not relate significantly to economic factors. An excellent demonstration of this was the unwillingness of the Yugoslav republics to bury the hatchet in 1991, despite the large number of contracts with foreign firms that had been signed under Ante Marković's regime and despite the significant financing that the international community was prepared to offer a stable Yugoslav state. The eagerness of nationalists throughout the former Yugoslavia to destroy economic assets in the name of their nation, not to mention to kill neighbors and burn villages, should make it clear that nationalists in their crudest form are motivated primarily by an idea, not by any cost-benefit calculus.[16] In dealing with nationalists, therefore, an economic stick, such as sanctions, will not work. Continued Serbian resistance to European pressure despite the debilitating effects of economic sanctions and even bombing amply demonstrates this point.

Second, by forgetting the enormous costs that Europe sustained through the past 150 years of remapping state borders onto ethnic lines, analysts have misunderstood the wars of Yugoslav succession. They are not an aberrant Balkan phenomenon or the striking out of backward peoples involved in tribal warfare. They are the final working out of a long European tradition of violent ethnic homogenization. In other words, analysts need to think of Balkan events in terms of how Europeans have solved or not solved questions of remapping and not in terms of how to suppress a strange and foreign phenomenon or how to introduce North American notions of multiculturalism.

Once one starts to think in this way, the ultimate solution in the Balkans becomes obvious: stability will come only when state borders there are redrawn on ethnic lines, as they have been in the rest of Europe. Acute observers such as Lord Owen and Timothy Garton Ash have begun to suggest that adjustments along these lines will be needed, but most analysts are still wedded to imposing some form of multiculturalism or minority protection in places like Bosnia and Kosovo.[17] Warren Zimmerman, the former U.S. ambassador to Yugoslavia, hopes to uphold the multiethnic character of Bosnia, for example. He rightfully deplores the spectacle of genocide, ethnic cleansing, and wanton destruction that has characterized the wars of Yugoslav succession. He is absolutely correct that "ethnic crises are better solved through tolerance and civility than through nationalism and separation."[18] But the historical fact is that the homogenization of national entities has proceeded in Europe not through tolerance and civility but through rampant violence and copious bloodshed. Only after the violence created more or less ethnically homogeneous entities did the Europeans develop a method of interacting with a significant level of tolerance. If Europe's experience is any guide, a genuine, voluntary, multiethnic solution can arise in the Balkans only when the remapping process is complete there. Only when the peoples of the region feel that they are included in the state system as authentic, autonomous units enclosing most of their own peoples and excluding most others will they be able to develop the confidence necessary to reach accommodation with their neighbors. Only then will they be able to chose to enter into the buffering mechanisms that have brought stability to the rest of Europe. This is not so much a matter of "joining Europe" as it is of creating a baseline of ethnically homogeneous entities that can begin a process of conciliation.

"Ethnically homogeneous," of course, does not have to mean that every single person in these new states is of the same ethnic group. That is not the case in any country in Europe, or probably in the world. National groups are in a continuous state of construction and contain all sorts of fissures, marginal groups, and power sources. The Roma also present a special case. But several countries of Eastern Europe, notably Poland, Hungary, Slovenia, and Bulgaria, have found ways to treat ethnic minorities fairly and within the parameters of well-developed European standards. Those standards of human and minority rights can become meaningful in the former Yugoslav states, however, only if the majority population adopts them voluntarily, and that will happen only when they feel themselves autonomously able to do so. Multiculturalism cannot be imposed.

Redrawing state boundaries will create enormous problems. These include creating a large Albanian Muslim state in the middle of the Balkans (or possibly as many as three of them) and having to endure what would

almost certainly be a political cauldron of disagreement among the Albanians themselves; rewarding the aggressor Serbs with portions of Bosnia
and perhaps Kosovo; exchanging populations (a euphemism for violent,
involuntary uprooting); finding a way to deal with the Vojvodina (some
have recently suggested creating a federal Serbia, for example); creating a
small Bosnian Muslim state; possibly, although not necessarily, reducing
the size of Macedonia, a country whose leaders have made heroic efforts
to survive and create a modicum of ethnic tolerance; negating some important elements of the Helsinki accords; and going against the stated
policy of most of the Great Powers. In addition, it is likely that redrawing borders will not mean just readjusting maps. It will almost certainly
mean significant violence, not to mention wrenching personal pain for
tens of thousands of people who will have to give up either their current
homes or the hope of returning to their former homes. It is highly unlikely that any democratic government, from the United States to its
smallest European ally, would be able to take the aggressive steps that
would make the various realignments possible, even if Russia and China
permit it.

Bad as these options are, what is the alternative? Indefinite occupation? Constant squabbling in the Security Council and with our European
allies as to who will pay for what, when? There is no light at the end of
either the Bosnian or the Kosovo tunnel. To the best of my knowledge, no
one has put forward a viable long-range vision or plan specifying what a
stable outcome might look like or when and how the current occupying
forces (or peacekeepers if you prefer) will depart. This is not to say that
there are no people of good will trying to make the multicultural solution work. The Balkan stabilization plan is a large-scale effort to create
infrastructure, and many NGOs are working hard under difficult conditions. One hopes that their efforts will bring about the desired result.
The historical experience outlined in this chapter, however, makes it unlikely, especially given what will almost certainly be a lack of patience
by important members of the shaky international coalition that now
supports the stabilization efforts.

The proposal suggested here does not specify how to get from our
current situation to a stable one, but it does at least tell us what stability eventually would look like. Adoption of this understanding of the
situation would permit policymakers to adjust their day-to-day decisions in such a way as to move toward that stability. It is not likely that
a negotiated solution will be possible as long as Slobodan Milošević is
in power in Serbia, but the recent governmental change in Croatia hints
that a day will come, sooner or later, when that impediment to rational

decision making will no longer be in place.[19] We need to take a realistic, fresh look at the only long-term solution to the endemic unrest of the past decade in the former Yugoslavia—creating compact, ethnically homogeneous states for the majority Balkan peoples. If the analysis suggested here is correct, the question is not *whether* a remapping in the Balkans will happen, but *how*. If we can lessen the human cost of these difficult but necessary adjustments, we will have served the situation well.

Reference Matter

Notes

PREFACE

1. E. H. Carr, *What is History?* (Basingstoke: Palgrave, 2001).

2. Robert Kaplan, *Balkan Ghosts: A Journey Through History* (New York: Vintage, 1994).

3. Among the sources that discuss the influence of *Balkan Ghosts* on President Clinton, see David Halberstam, *War in the Time of Peace: Bush, Clinton, and the Generals* (New York: Scribner, 2001), 228.

4. For histories written by policymakers, see Richard Holbrooke, *To End a War* (New York: Modern Library, 1999); Warren Zimmermann, *Origins of a Catastrophe: Yugoslavia and its Destroyers* (New York: Times Books, 1996); and David Owen, *Balkan Odyssey* (Harcourt, Brace, & Co., 1995).

5. See, among others, Tim Judah, *The Serbs: History, Myth and the Destruction of Yugoslavia* (New Haven: Yale University Press, 1997); Marcus Tanner, *Croatia: A Nation Forged In War* (New Haven: Yale University Press, 1997); and Laura Silber and Alan Little, *Yugoslavia: Death of a Nation* (New York: TV Books, 1995).

6. For interesting insights into the role of the media in the making of policy in the wars in the Balkans, see Samantha Power, *"A Problem From Hell": America and the Age of Genocide* (New York: Basic Books, 2002), 406–73.

7. Roy Gutman, *A Witness to Genocide* (New York: Macmillan, 1993).

8. See David Rohde, *Endgame: The Betrayal and Fall of Srebrenica, Europe's Worst Massacre since World War II* (New York: Farrar Straus and Giroux, 1997).

9. See, especially, Chuck Sudetic's moving *Blood and Vengeance: One Family's Story of the War in Bosnia* (New York: W. W. Norton, 1998).

10. See Noel Malcolm, *Bosnia: A Short History* (New York: New York University Press, 1994) and his *Kosovo: A Short History* (New York: New York University Press, 1998).

11. For a review of the initial historical literature that appeared in the wake of the conflicts, see Gale Stokes, John Lampe, and Dennison Rusinow with Julie Mostov, "Instant History: Understanding the Wars of Yugoslav Succession," *Slavic Review*, 55, no. 1 (Spring 1996): 136–60. See also John Lampe, *Yugoslavia as History: Twice There Was a Country* (Cambridge: Cambridge University Press, 1996).

CHAPTER I

1. For discussions of this trend, see Eric H. Monkkonen, ed., *Engaging the Past: The Uses of History across the Social Sciences* (Durham, N.C.: Duke University Press, 1994), and Terrence J. McDonald, ed., *The Historic Turn in the Human Sciences* (Ann Arbor: University of Michigan Press, 1996). Of course, not everyone was inclined to take this turn. Philippe C. Schmitter and Terry Lynn Karl, for instance, advocated treating transition from communism as part of a much larger phenomenon of regime change, decrying "the usual protestations by area specialists that 'political culture,' 'historical legacy,' or 'national character' renders their case or cases incomparable." ("The Conceptual Travels of Transitologists and Consolidologists: How Far to the East Should They Attempt to Go?" *Slavic Review* 53 [1994], 173–85; quotation on p. 181, n. 15. See also their subsequent exchanges with Valerie Bunce: *Slavic Review* 54 [1995], 111–27, 965–87).

2. A remarkable manifestation of these debates was the Clinton administration's shift from Robert Kaplan to Noel Malcolm as its preferred Balkan expert. See Lenard J. Cohen, chapter 9, "Unraveling the Balkan Conundrum: The History-Policy Nexus," in *Serpent in the Bosom: The Rise and Fall of Slobodan Milošević* (Boulder, Colo.: Westview Press, 2001), 377–405.

3. Mark Wheeler, "Preludes to a Crisis," *Times Literary Supplement*, June 16, 1989, 65. See also Horace G. Lunt, "Notes on Nationalist Attitudes in Slavic Studies," *Canadian Slavonic Papers* 34 (1992), 445–70. For a frank and thoughtful discussion of the polarization in Yugoslav studies, see Joel M. Halpern and David A. Kideckel, "Introduction: The End of Yugoslavia Observed," in Halpern and Kideckel, eds., *Neighbors at War: Anthropological Perspectives on Yugoslav Ethnicity, Culture, and History* (University Park: Pennsylvania State University Press, 2000), 3–18.

4. A striking example of the which-side-are-you-on approach is a review essay by noted political scientist and Yugoslav specialist Sabrina P. Ramet. She states that the basic divide in Yugoslav studies was once between those who were sympathetic to Tito and optimistic about Yugoslavia's survival, and those who were not. Today, on

> one side are those who have taken a moral universalist perspective, holding that there are universal norms in international politics. . . . On the other side are authors who . . . embrace one or another version of moral relativism. . . . Authors in this second school tend to be more sympathetic to Milošević, Karadžić, and their collaborators and to express Germanophobic (and, in [Susan] Woodward's case, also Slovenophobic) views.

Ramet, "Revisiting the Horrors of Bosnia: New Books about the War," *East European Politics and Societies* 14 (2000), 475.

5. A number of newer works published through 1995, on both historical and current events, are discussed in Gale Stokes, John Lampe, and Dennison Rusinow with Julie Mostov, "Instant History: Understanding the Wars of Yugoslav Succession," *Slavic Review* 55 (1996), 136–60. See also James Gow, "After the Flood: Literature on the Context, Causes and Course of the

Yugoslav War—Reflections and Refractions," *Slavonic and East European Review* 75 (1997), 446–84. For a more comprehensive list, see Rusko Matulić, *Bibliography of Sources on the Region of Former Yugoslavia* (Boulder, Colo.: East European Monographs, 1998). Cathie Carmichael has compiled bibliographies of *Slovenia* (1996) and *Croatia* (1999) for the World Bibliographical Series of Clio Press (Santa Barbara, Calif.). On Bosnia-Herzegovina, there is Quintin Hoare and Noel Malcolm, eds., *Books on Bosnia: A Critical Bibliography of Works Relating to Bosnia-Herzegovina Published since 1990 in West European Languages* (London: Bosnian Institute, 1999).

6. Sylvia Poggioli, "Scouts without Compasses," *Nieman Reports* 47, no. 3 (Fall 1993).

7. Ivo Banac, "Misreading the Balkans," *Foreign Policy* 93 (1993–94), 174; Pavlowitch, from the preface to his survey, *Yugoslavia* (New York: Praeger, 1971). Useful bibliographies of the antediluvian literature include Mary Beth Norton, ed., *American Historical Association Guide to Historical Literature*, 3rd ed., vol. 1 (New York: Oxford University Press, 1995), 1025–32, 1062–69; Francine Friedman, ed., *Yugoslavia: A Comprehensive English-Language Bibliography* (Wilmington, Del.: Scholarly Resources, 1993); John J. Horton, ed., *Yugoslavia*, 2nd ed. (Santa Barbara, Calif.: Clio Press, 1990); Gale Stokes, ed., *Nationalism in the Balkans: An Annotated Bibliography* (New York: Garland, 1984); Michael Boro Petrovich, *Yugoslavia: A Bibliographic Guide* (Washington, D.C.: Library of Congress, 1974).

8. John Lampe, *Yugoslavia as History: Twice There Was a Country*, 2nd ed. (Cambridge: Cambridge University Press, 2000), 4.

9. Mark von Hagen, "Does Ukraine Have a History?" *Slavic Review* 54 (1995), 662.

10. April 18, 1993. At least readers had the benefit of John Ackerman's letter in reply (May 16). Pointing out that Kaplan's list comprises "works that illustrate his thesis that the peninsula is a 'caldron' of intractable cultures that are distinguished, it seems, only by the ferocity of their hatreds," Ackerman suggested, on the former Yugoslavia,

> books by Ivo Banac, C. Wendy Bracewell, Charles Jelavich and Barbara Jelavich, Ivo J. Lederer, Michael Boro Petrovich, Peter Sugar, Jozo Tomasevich and Wayne S. Vucinich. None of these books is as easy to read as those on Mr. Kaplan's list, in part because they're written by professional historians who recognize that lazy invocations of "historical destiny" serve only to perpetuate the status quo. What they supply is tough critical analysis and the potentially liberating recognition that history (and with it, national culture) is an ever-shifting dialectic of possibility.

11. Maria Todorova has stated: "As a specialist in Balkan history, I have refrained from making brief pronouncements about the present affairs in the Balkans (2 or 10 minutes long depending on the news program; 600–800 words, depending on the paper or journal). After all, my profession is about arguing complex issues and avoiding simplified recipes, and I happen to believe in this professional ethos." Todorova, "The Balkans: From Invention to Intervention," in William J. Buckley, ed., *Kosovo: Contending Voices on*

Balkan Interventions (Grand Rapids, Mich.: William B. Eerdmans Pub., 2000), 159. Another reflection on the role of academics during the Kosovo conflict: Stephanie Schwandner-Sievers, "Help to Wage War on the 'Simplifiers' of Kosovo," *Times Higher Education Supplement*, April 2, 1999.

12. Robert Baldock, "Looking Beyond Academe for the Best Scholarly Books," *The Chronicle of Higher Education* (July 3, 1997), B6; Anatol Lieven, *The Baltic Revolution: Estonia, Latvia, Lithuania and the Path to Independence*, 2nd ed. (New Haven, Conn.: Yale University Press, 1994), xxxvi.

13. Tim Judah, *The Serbs: History, Myth and the Destruction of Yugoslavia* and Marcus Tanner, *Croatia: A Nation Forged in War* (both from Yale, 1997). I discuss these two books at some length in "Croats and Serbs: Two Popular Histories," *H-Net Reviews* (November 1997): http://hnet2.msu.edu/reviews/showrev.cgi?path=5848881962016. The articles appeared in *Daedalus* 126, no. 3 (Summer 1997), an issue on "A New Europe for the Old?": Tim Judah, "The Serbs: The Sweet and Rotten Smell of History," 23–46, and Marcus Tanner, "Illyrianism and the Croatian Quest for Statehood," 47–62.

14. K. E. Fleming, "Orientalism, the Balkans, and Balkan Historiography," *American Historical Review* 105 (2000), 1218–33.

15. Larry Wolff, *Inventing Eastern Europe: The Map of Civilization on the Mind of the Enlightenment* (Stanford, Calif.: Stanford University Press, 1994); Ivo Banac and Katherine Verdery, eds., *National Character and National Ideology in Interwar Eastern Europe* (New Haven, Conn.: Yale University Press, 1995); André Gerrits and Nanci Adler, eds., *Vampires Unstaked: National Images, Stereotypes and Myths in East Central Europe* (New York: Royal Netherlands Academy of Arts and Sciences, 1995).

16. Maria Todorova, *Imagining the Balkans* (New York: Oxford University Press, 1997). An insightful piece predating Todorova's essential book and the current boom is John B. Allcock, "Constructing the Balkans," in Allcock and Antonia Young, eds., *Black Lambs and Grey Falcons: Women Travellers in the Balkans* (Bradford, U.K.: Bradford University Press, 1991), 170–91. Valuable guides to the literature are K. E. Fleming, "Orientalism," and the special issue of *Balkanologie* [Paris] 3 (1999), "South-Eastern Europe: History, Concepts, Boundaries," especially the introductory essay by Wendy Bracewell and Alex Drace-Francis, 47–66.

17. Todorova, *Imagining*, 173.

18. Gale Stokes, review of Todorova, *Imagining*, on H-Net, September 1997 (http://hnet2.msu.edu/reviews/); Tony Judt, "Freedom and Freedonia," *The New Republic*, September 7, 1998, 29. Stokes' generally favorable review was followed by an exchange with Todorova and comments by other scholars in a valuable forum organized by the electronic history list "HABSBURG": http://www2.h-net.msu.edu/habsweb/.

19. "The Balkans: Realia—Qu'est-ce qu'il y a de hors-texte?" *Imagining*, 161–83. An earlier version appeared as "The Ottoman Legacy in the Balkans," in L. Carl Brown, ed., *Imperial Legacy: The Ottoman Imprint in the Balkans and the Middle East* (New York: Columbia University Press, 1995), 45–77.

20. Paschalis Kitromilides, "'Balkan Mentality': History, Legend, Imagination," *Nations and Nationalism* 2 (1996), 163–92.

21. Michael Radu, "The Burden of Eastern Orthodoxy," *Orbis* 42 (1998), 285.

22. George Schöpflin, "Defining South-Eastern Europe," *Balkanologie* 3 (1999), 71. See also his article "Central Europe: Definitions Old and New," in Schöpflin and Nancy Woods, eds., *In Search of Central Europe* (Cambridge: Polity Press, 1989).

23. Andrew C. Janos, *East Central Europe in the Modern World: The Politics of the Borderlands from Pre- to Postcommunism* (Stanford, Calif.: Stanford University Press, 2000), 1, 326. The relevant historical differences between the lands of Eastern and Western Christianity are introduced on pages 38–48.

24. Alexandru Duțu, *Political Models and National Identities in "Orthodox Europe"* (Bucharest: Babel, 1998), 164. There is a large body of work on the issue of Islam's supposed incompatibility with modernization, often referring back to the influence of Max Weber. For a brief critical discussion as it concerns the Balkans and Yugoslavia, see John B. Allcock, *Explaining Yugoslavia* (London: Hurst & Co., 2000), 29–31. For contrasting approaches to the role of Western Christianity, from an equally extensive literature about the identity of Central Europe, see Piotr S. Wandycz, *The Price of Freedom: A History of East Central Europe from the Middle Ages to the Present* (New York: Routledge, 1992), especially "Introduction: What's in a Name?" (pp. 1–11), and the rejoinders of Hans-Heinrich Nolte, who sees "the image of Latinity and Catholicism as distinct qualities of East Central Europe" as essentially "a Slavophile thesis turned upside down," in "The Alleged Influence of Cultural Boundaries on Political Thinking: Images of Central Europe," in Gerrits and Adler, *Vampires Unstaked*, 41–54 (quotation on p. 48).

25. Some recent work on religious culture and politics: Sabrina Ramet, "Nation and Religion in Yugoslavia," in *Nihil Obstat: Religion, Politics, and Social Change in East-Central Europe and Russia* (Durham, N.C.: Duke University Press, 1998), and *Balkan Babel: The Disintegration of Yugoslavia from the Death of Tito to Ethnic War*, 2nd ed. (Boulder, Colo.: Westview, 1996), 135–94; Paul Mojzes, *Yugoslavian Inferno: Ethnoreligious Warfare in the Balkans* (New York: Continuum, 1994); Mojzes, ed., *Religion and the War in Bosnia* (Atlanta, Ga.: Scholars Press, 1998); Peter F. Sugar, "Nationalism and Religion in the Balkans since the Nineteenth Century," and "Religion, Nationalism, and Politics in East-Central Europe," in *East European Nationalism, Politics and Religion* (Brookfield: Ashgate, Varorium, 1999); Robin Okey, "State, Church, and Nation in the Serbo-Croat Speaking Lands of the Habsburg Monarchy, 1850–1914," in Donal A. Kerr, ed., *Religion, State, and Ethnic Groups* (New York: New York University Press, 1992), and "Austro-Hungarian Diplomacy and the Campaign for a Slavonic Liturgy in the Catholic Church, 1881–1914," *Slavonic and East European Review* 70 (1992), 258–83; Peter T. Alter, "Nineteenth-Century Serbian Popular Religion: The *Millet* System and Syncretism," *Serbian Studies* 9 (1995), 88–103; Sergej Flere,

"Denominational Affiliation in Yugoslavia 1931–1987," *East European Quarterly* 25 (1991), 145–65; Ger Duijzings, *Religion and the Politics of Identity in Kosovo* (New York: Columbia University Press, 2000).

26. Against Kitromilides's notion of a common identity, for example, one might pose Peter Sugar's argument: "What emerged in the seventeenth and eighteenth centuries was not the disintegration of the Orthodox millet opening the door to new foci of loyalty. What emerged were old differences and antagonisms that could not be expressed openly so long as the millet leadership was protected by the power of a strong state and could not be challenged." Peter F. Sugar, *Southeastern Europe under Ottoman Rule, 1354–1804* (Seattle: University of Washington, 1977), 232. In notes at the end of his volume of collected essays, Kitromilides recognizes his overreliance on the Greek case in generalizing about the Balkans: *Enlightenment, Nationalism, Orthodoxy: Studies in the Culture and Political Thought of South-Eastern Europe* (Aldershot, U.K.: Varorium, 1994).

27. See for instance these recent surveys: Mark Mazower, *The Balkans: A Short History* (New York: Modern Library, 2000); Stevan K. Pavlowitch, *A History of the Balkans, 1804–1945* (London: Longman, 1999); Misha Glenny, *The Balkans: Nationalism, War and the Great Powers, 1804–1999* (London: Granta, 1999); A. L. Macfie, *The Eastern Question, 1774–1923*, rev. ed. (New York: Longman, 1996).

28. Stokes, "Introduction: In Defense of Balkan Nationalism," in Stokes, *Nationalism in the Balkans*, viii.

29. "The Sociocultural Bases of National Dependency in Peasant Countries," in Kenneth Jowitt, ed., *Social Change in Romania, 1860–1940* (Berkeley: University of California Press, 1978), 20.

30. Gale Stokes, "Dependency and the Rise of Nationalism in Southeast Europe," in *Three Eras of Political Change in Eastern Europe* (New York: Oxford University Press, 1997), 34; reprinted from *International Journal of Turkish Studies* 1 (1980), 54–67.

31. Janos, *East Central Europe*, 132.

32. Eugen Weber is often cited on this point: *Peasants into Frenchmen: The Modernization of Rural France, 1870–1914* (Stanford, Calif.: Stanford University Press, 1976).

33. Diana Mishkova, "Modernization and Political Elites in the Balkans Before the First World War," *East European Politics and Society* 9 (1995), 63–89.

34. Gary B. Cohen, "Neither Absolutism nor Anarchy: New Narratives on Society and Government in Late Imperial Austria," *Austrian History Yearbook* 29, no. 1 (1998), 39, 37. In this same issue, in an extended discussion of modern political culture in both halves of the Empire, George Barany offers a more mixed assessment: "Political Culture in the Lands of the Former Habsburg Empire: Authoritarian and Parliamentary Traditions," 195–248.

35. See the issue on "Multiple Modernities," *Daedalus* 129, no. 1 (Winter 2000), especially S. N. Eisenstadt, "Multiple Modernities," 1–30.

36. Vicente L. Rafael, "Regionalism, Area Studies, and the Accidents of Agency," *American Historical Review* 104 (1999), 1208–20.

37. Schöpflin, "Defining South-Eastern Europe," 70.

38. Martin Malia, "A New Europe for the Old?" *Daedalus* 126, no. 3 (Summer 1997), 19. He adds: "This division, however, does not coincide with the divide between Latin Christendom and the Orthodox East (p. 9), insisting on Russia's inclusion in Europe.

39. Gale Stokes, *Politics as Development: The Emergence of Political Parties in Nineteenth-Century Serbia* (Durham, N.C.: Duke University Press, 1990); "Nineteenth-Century Serbia: So What?" in *Three Eras*, 73–82.

40. Stokes, "The Social Origins of East European Politics," in Daniel Chirot, ed., *The Origins of Backwardness in Eastern Europe* (Berkeley: University of California Press, 1989), 210–51. Another comparative piece is Victor Roudometof, "Invented Traditions, Symbolic Boundaries, and National Identity in Southeastern Europe: Greece and Serbia in Comparative Historical Perspective (1830–1880)," *East European Quarterly* 32 (1999). A few other articles of note on political and ideological modernity: Wolfgang Höpken's brief but useful look at "Political Culture in the Balkan States during the Interwar Period," offering a gloomy assessment of the degree to which Western ideas and institutions took root (in Günay Göksu Özdoğan and Kemâlî Saybaşili, eds., *Balkans: A Mirror of the International Order* [Istanbul: EREN, 1995], 85–100); Roumen Daskalov, "Ideas about, and Reactions to Modernization in the Balkans," *East European Quarterly* 31 (1997), 141–80, which includes an excellent bibliography of the relevant literature; and Dimitrije Djordjević's interesting observations in "Ottoman Heritage versus Modernization: Symbiosis in Serbia during the Nineteenth Century," *Serbian Studies* 13 (1999), 29–58.

41. Max-Stephen Schulze, "Review Article: Economic Development in the Nineteenth-Century Habsburg Empire," *Austrian History Yearbook* 28 (1997), 293–307. Bosnia-Herzegovina is something of an exception: since the appearance of Peter F. Sugar's seminal study nearly forty years ago, Habsburg economic policy in the province has continued to receive some attention as a distinctive case study: Sugar, *The Industrialization of Bosnia-Hercegovina, 1878–1914* (Seattle: University of Washington Press, 1963); Priscilla T. Gonsalves, "Study of the Habsburg Agricultural Programmes in Bosanska Krajina, 1878–1914," *Slavonic and East European Review* 63 (1985), 349–71; Michael Palairet, "The Habsburg Industrial Achievement in Bosnia-Hercegovina, 1878–1914: An Economic Spurt That Succeeded?" *Austrian History Yearbook* 24 (1993), 133–52.

42. See for example David F. Good, "The Economic Lag of Central and Eastern Europe: Income Estimates for the Habsburg Successor States, 1870–1910," *Journal of Economic History* 54 (1994), 869–91, and his subsequent exchange with Michael Pammer in volume 57 (1997), 448–63.

43. John R. Lampe and Marvin R. Jackson, *Balkan Economic History, 1550–1920: From Imperial Borderlands to Developing Nations* (Bloomington: Indiana University Press, 1982); John R. Lampe, "Imperial Borderlands

or Capitalist Periphery? Redefining Balkan Backwardness, 1520–1914," in Chirot, *Origins of Backwardness*, 177–209. See also his and other essays in Gerasimos Augustinos, ed., *Diverse Paths towards Modernity in South-eastern Europe: Essays in National Development* (New York: Greenwood Press, 1991).

44. Michael Palairet, *The Balkan Economies c. 1800–1914: Evolution without Development* (Cambridge: Cambridge University Press, 1997).

45. Traian Stoianovich, *Balkan Worlds: The First and Last Europe* (Armonk, N.Y.: M. E. Sharpe, 1994); Allcock, *Explaining Yugoslavia* (New York: Columbia University Press).

46. Jozo Tomasevich, *Peasants, Politics, and Economic Change in Yugoslavia* (Stanford, Calif.: Stanford University Press, 1955).

47. Charles Tilly, "Retrieving European Lives," in Olivier Zunz, ed., *Reliving the Past: The Worlds of Social History* (Chapel Hill: University of North Carolina Press, 1985), 11.

48. See the special issue of *History of the Family* 1 (1996); Maria Todorova, *Balkan Family Structure and the European Pattern: Demographic Developments in Ottoman Bulgaria* (Washington, D.C.: American University Press, 1993); Miroslav Jovanović, Karl Kaser, and Slobodan Naumović, eds., *Between the Archives and the Field: A Dialogue on Historical Anthropology of the Balkans* (Graz, Austria: Zur Kunde Südosteuropas; Belgrade: Institut za društvenu istoriju, 1999); Kaser, "The Balkan Joint Family Household: Seeking Its Origins," *Continuity and Change* 9 (1994), 45–68; Kaser, "The Balkan Joint Family: Redefining a Problem," *Social Science History* 18 (1994), 243–69; Michael Palairet, "Rural Serbia in the Light of the Census of 1863," *Journal of European Economic History* 24 (1995), 41–107; Richard A. Wagner, *Children and Change in Orašac, 1870–1975: A Serbian Perspective on Fertility Decline* (Amherst: University of Massachusetts, 1992: Program in Soviet and East European Studies, Occasional Papers, 22).

49. What little there is has tended to concentrate on World War II, e.g., Barbara Jancar-Webster, *Women and Revolution in Yugoslavia, 1941–1945* (Denver, Colo.: Arden Press, 1989); Yeshayahu A. Jelinek, "On the Condition of Women in Wartime Slovakia and Croatia," in Richard Frucht, ed., *Labyrinth of Nationalism, Complexities of Diplomacy: Essays in Honor of Charles and Barbara Jelavich* (Columbus, Ohio: Slavica Publishers, 1992), 190–211.

50. Jeffrey Brooks, *When Russia Learned to Read: Literacy and Popular Literature, 1861–1917* (Princeton, N.J.: Princeton University Press, 1985).

51. The bibliographies in Allcock's, Stoianovich's, and Lampe's recent surveys and in the Halpern-Kideckel volume offer an indication of this work.

52. Justin McCarthy, *Death and Exile: The Ethnic Cleansing of Ottoman Muslims, 1821–1922* (Princeton, N.J.: Darwin Press, 1995); Rogers Brubaker, "Aftermaths of Empire and the Unmixing of Peoples: Historical and Comparative Perspectives," *Ethnic and Racial Studies* 18 (1995), 189–218, and reprinted in Brubaker, *Nationalism Reframed: Nationhood and the National Question in the New Europe* (Cambridge: Cambridge University Press, 1996);

Daniel Chirot, "Nationalist Liberations and Nationalist Nightmares: The Consequences of the End of Empires in the Twentieth Century," in Beverly Crawford, ed., *Markets, States, and Democracy: The Political Economy of Post-Communist Transformation* (Boulder, Colo.: Westview Press, 1995); Dimitrije Djordjević, "Migrations during the 1912–1913 Balkan Wars and World War One," in Ivan Ninić, ed., *Migrations in Balkan History* (Belgrade: Serbian Academy of Sciences and Arts, 1989), 115–30.

53. Several works of note: George Schöpflin, "Why Do Empires Fail?" in *Nations, Identity, Power* (New York: New York University Press, 2000); Dominic Lieven, *Empire: The Russian Empire and Its Rivals* (London: J. Murray, 2000); Lieven, "Dilemmas of Empire, 1850–1918: Power, Territory, Identity," *Journal of Contemporary History* 34 (1999), 163–200; Karen Barkey and Mark von Hagen, eds., *After Empire: Multiethnic Societies and Nation-Building: The Soviet Union and the Russian, Ottoman, and Habsburg Empires* (Boulder, Colo.: Westview Press, 1997); Raymond Pearson, "Empire, War and the Nation-State in East Central Europe," in Paul Latawski, ed., *Contemporary Nationalism in East Central Europe* (New York: St. Martin's Press, 1995); Geir Lundestad, ed., *The Fall of Great Powers: Peace, Stability and Legitimacy* (New York: Oxford University Press, 1994); Richard J. Rudolph and David F. Good, eds., *Nationalism and Empire: The Habsburg Empire and the Soviet Union* (New York: St. Martin's Press, 1992); Uri Ra'anan, Maria Mesner, Keith Armes, and Kate Martin, eds., *State and Nation in Multi-ethnic Societies: The Breakup of Multinational States* (New York: Manchester University Press, 1991).

54. Celia Applegate, "A Europe of Regions: Reflections on the Historiography of Sub-National Places in Modern Times," *American Historical Review* 104 (1999), 1164.

55. An exception are some of the studies on borderland identities, especially of Slovenes and Macedonians, cited in notes below.

56. Recent studies of Jews in former Yugoslav lands: Esther Benbassa and Aron Rodrigue, *The Jews of the Balkans: The Judeo-Spanish Community, 15th to 20th Centuries* (Cambridge, Mass.: Blackwell, 1995); Paul Benjamin Gordiejew, *Voices of Yugoslav Jewry* (Albany: State University of New York Press, 1999); Zvi Loker, "Patrimony and Ethnic Identity: Ethnicity among Sephardim in Yugoslavia between the Two World Wars," in I. K. Hassiotis, ed., *The Jewish Communities of Southeastern Europe: From the Fifteenth Century to the End of World War II* (Thessaloniki: Institute for Balkan Studies, 1997), 295–301. Of Roma: David M. Crowe, "Historical Evolution of the Gypsies in the Contemporary South Slavic State," *Macedonian Studies* 11, no. 1–2 (1994), 3–46; Dennis Reinhartz, "Damnation of the Outsider: The Gypsies of Croatia and Serbia in the Balkan Holocaust, 1941–1945," in David Crowe and John Kolsti, eds., *The Gypsies of Eastern Europe* (Armonk, N.Y.: M. E. Sharpe, 1991). Of Vlachs: Tom Winnifrith, *The Vlachs: History of a Balkan People*, 2nd ed. (London: Duckworth, 1995), and *Shattered Eagles, Balkan Fragments* (London: Duckworth, 1995); Noel Malcolm, *Bosnia: A Short History* (New York: New York University Press, 1994). Of Muslims:

Edward Allworth, ed., *Muslim Communities Reemerge: Historical Perspectives on Nationality, Politics, and Opposition in the Former Soviet Union and Yugoslavia* (Durham, N.C.: Duke University Press, 1994); H. T. Norris, *Islam in the Balkans: Religion and Society between Europe and the Arab World* (Columbia, S.C.: University of South Carolina Press, 1993); Hugh Poulton and Suha Taji-Farouki, eds., *Muslim Identity and the Balkan State* (New York: New York University Press, 1997). There are a number of works on Muslims that focus on current affairs in both Eastern and Western Europe.

57. Çaglar Keyder, "The Ottoman Empire," in Barkey and von Hagen, *After Empire*, 30.

58. See for example Robert Bideleux and Ian Jeffries, *A History of Eastern Europe: Crisis and Change* (New York: Routledge, 1998), and Brown, *Imperial Legacy*. For divergent views from a generation ago, see the discussion of Ottoman rule and its legacies among three leading postwar historians of the Balkans—Wayne S. Vucinich, Stanford J. Shaw, and Traian Stoianovich—in *Slavic Review* 21 (1962), 597–638. On the long history of the "two opposing myths on the question of Muslim tolerance and intolerance" in the Ottoman Empire, see the editors' introduction in Benjamin Braude and Bernard Lewis, eds., *Christians and Jews in the Ottoman Empire: The Functioning of a Plural Society*, vol. 1 (New York: Holmes & Meier, 1982).

59. Geoff Eley, "Remapping the Nation: War, Revolutionary Upheaval and State Formation in Eastern Europe, 1914–1923," in Peter J. Potichnyj and Howard Aster, eds., *Ukrainian-Jewish Relations in Historical Perspective* (Edmonton: Canadian Institute of Ukrainian Studies, 1988), 222. For interesting reflections on this phenomenon with regard to another new European state, see von Hagen, "Does Ukraine Have a History?"

60. Noel Malcolm, *Bosnia*, and Robert J. Donia and John V. A. Fine, Jr., *Bosnia and Hercegovina: A Tradition Betrayed* (New York: Columbia University Press, 1994); quotation from pp. 8–9. A useful review essay is Nicholas Miller, "Coming to Terms with Bosnia's History," *Nationalities Papers* 25 (1997), 317–20.

61. Mark Pinson, ed., *The Muslims of Bosnia-Herzegovina: Their Historic Development from the Middle Ages to the Dissolution of Yugoslavia*, 2nd ed. (Cambridge, Mass.: Distributed for the Center for Middle Eastern Studies of Harvard University by Harvard University Press, 1996); Francine Friedman, *The Bosnian Muslims: Denial of a Nation* (Boulder, Colo.: Westview Press, 1996); Aydin Babuna, "The Emergence of the First Muslim Party in Bosnia-Hercegovina," *East European Quarterly* 30 (1996), 131–51; "Nationalism and the Bosnian Muslims," *East European Quarterly* 33 (1999), 195–218; Anita Lekić, "'Gajret' and the Bosnian Muslim Intelligentsia," *Serbian Studies* 10 (1996), 188–97; Sabrina Petra Ramet, "Primordial Ethnicity or Modern Nationalism: The Case of Yugoslavia's Muslims, Reconsidered"; Georg Brunner, "Status of Muslims in the Federative Systems of the Soviet Union and Yugoslavia"; Wolfgang Höpken, "Yugoslavia's Communists and the Bosnian Muslims"; and Alexandre Popović, "Islamic Movements in Yugoslavia," all in Allworth, *Muslim Communities Reemerge*.

62. Useful articles include Robin Okey, "State, Church, and Nation," and "Education and Modernization in a Multi-Ethnic State: Bosnia, 1850–1914," in Janusz Tomiak, ed., *Schooling, Educational Policy, and Ethnic Identity* (New York: New York State University Press, European Science Foundation, 1991), 319–41; Jelena Milojković-Djurić, "Culture in an Occupied Territory: Bosnia-Hercegovina in the Aftermath of the Berlin Congress," *Balkanistica* 13 (2000), and "The Eastern Question and the Voices of Reason: Panslav Aspirations in Russia and in the Balkans, 1875–1878," *Balkanistica* 11 (1998); Wayne S. Vucinich, "Introduction: Ivo Andrić and His Times," in Vucinich, ed., *Ivo Andrić Revisited: The Bridge Still Stands* (Berkeley: International and Area Studies, University of California at Berkeley, 1995), 1–46; Yeshayahu A. Jelinek, "Bosnia-Herzegovina at War: Relations Between Moslems and Non-Moslems," *Holocaust and Genocide Studies* 5 (1990), 275–92.

63. Jill Benderly and Evan Kraft, eds., *Independent Slovenia: Origins, Movements, Prospects* (New York: St. Martin's Press, 1996), especially the articles by Carole Rogel, Peter Vodopivec, Žarko Lazarević, and Ervin Dolenc. The quote is from Wendy Bracewell's review essay, "The End of Yugoslavia and New National Histories," *European History Quarterly* 29 (1999), 149–56.

Although I know of no historical survey, Slovenia has received that other stamp of legitimacy, the historical dictionary: Leopoldina Plut-Pregelj and Carole Rogel, *Historical Dictionary of Slovenia* (Lanham, Md.: Scarecrow Press, 1998). This series includes all five (so far) successor states: Robert Stallaerts and Jeannine Laurens, *Historical Dictionary of the Republic of Croatia* (1995), Ante Čuvalo, *Historical Dictionary of Bosnia and Herzegovina* (1997), Valentina Georgieva and Sasha Konechnim, *Historical Dictionary of the Republic of Macedonia* (1998), and Željan Šuster, *Historical Dictionary of the Federal Republic of Yugoslavia* (1999). A sense of their strengths and weaknesses can be gleaned from Nicholas Miller's review of the volumes on Slovenia and Croatia: [www.h-net2.msu.edu/habsweb/] (May 1997).

64. Robert Gary Minnich, *Homesteaders and Citizens: Collective Identity Formation on the Austro-Italian-Slovene Frontier* (Bergen: Norse Publications, 1998); Andreas Moritsch and G. Baumgartner, "The Process of National Differentiation within Rural Communities in Southern Carinthia and Southern Burgenland, 1850–1940," *Comparative Studies on Governments and Non-Dominant Ethnic Groups, 1850–1940* 8 (1992), 99–143; Christian Promitzer, "Ecotype—Mentality—Nationality: Dominant Agricultural System and the Process of National Differentiation at the German-Slovene Linguistic Border," in Jovanović, et al., *Between the Archives*, 141–58; Tom Gullberg, "The Primacy of the Nation and Regional Identity: Carinthia, Burgenland, and State-Formation after the Dissolution of the Dynastic System," in Sven Tägil, ed., *Regions in Central Europe: The Legacy of History* (London: Hurst & Co., 1999), 147–77; Vladimir Klemenčič and Milan Bufon, "Cultural Elements of Integration and Transformation of Border Regions: The Case of Slovenia," *Political Geography* 13 (1994), 73–83.

65. Hannes Grandits and Christian Promitzer, "'Former Comrades' at War: Historical Perspectives on 'Ethnic Cleansing' in Croatia," in Halpern and Kideckel, *Neighbors at War*, 125–42; Grandits, "'From Reliable Bordermen to Good Taxpayers'—Problems of Economic and Social Integration of the Former Habsburg Military Borderland into Croatia," in Jovanović et al., *Between the Archives*, 115–24.

66. Ivo Goldstein, *Croatia: A History* (Montreal: McGill-Queen's University Press, 1999); Mark Biondich, *Stjepan Radić, the Croat Peasant Party, and the Politics of Mass Mobilization, 1904–1928* (Buffalo: University of Toronto Press, 2000). Also notable: Mirjana Gross, "The Union of Dalmatia with Northern Croatia: A Crucial Question of the Croatian National Integration in the Nineteenth Century," in Mikuláš Teich and Roy Porter, eds., *The National Question in Europe in Historical Context* (Cambridge: Cambridge University Press, 1993); Okey, "Austro-Hungarian Diplomacy"; Ivo Banac, "'Emperor Karl has Become a Comitadji': The Croatian Disturbances of Autumn 1918," *Slavonic and East European Review* 70 (1992), and "Zarathustra in Red Croatia: Milan Šufflay and His Theory of Nationhood," in Banac and Verdery, *National Character*; Jill A. Irvine, *The Croat Question: Partisan Politics in the Formation of the Yugoslav Socialist State* (Boulder, Colo.: Westview Press, 1993); Nicholas Miller, *Between Nation and State: Serbian Politics in Croatia before the First World War* (Pittsburgh, Pa.: University of Pittsburgh Press, 1997).

67. To take just a few clear examples, relatively prominent books by respectable publishers: Defensive nationalist agendas detract considerably from Alex N. Dragnich, *Serbs and Croats: The Struggle in Yugoslavia* (New York: Harcourt Brace Jovanovich, 1992), and most of the essays in Peter Radan and Aleksandar Pavković, eds., *The Serbs and Their Leaders in the Twentieth Century* (Aldershot, U.K.: Ashgate, 1997). Two studies that explore important topics, but in which censorious zeal trumps balanced scholarship, are Branimir Anzulović, *Heavenly Serbia: From Myth to Genocide* (New York: New York University Press, 1999) and Philip J. Cohen, *Serbia's Secret War: Propaganda and the Deceit of History* (College Station: Texas A&M University Press, 1996).

68. In two volumes (New York: Harcourt Brace Jovanovich, 1976).

69. Roudometof, "Invented Traditions"; Mile Bjelajac, "King Petar I Karadjordjević," in Radan and Pavković, *The Serbs and Their Leaders*; Alex Dragnich, "Populism in Serbia," in Joseph Held, ed., *Populism in Eastern Europe: Racism, Nationalism, and Society* (Boulder, Colo.: East European Monographs, 1996), 219–44; David MacKenzie, "Serbia as Piedmont and the Yugoslav Idea, 1804–1914," *East European Quarterly* 28 (1994), 153–82; Stokes, *Politics as Development*. MacKenzie has completed his trilogy on the "Black Hand" leader, Apis, and his controversial trial and execution in 1917: *Apis: The Congenial Conspirator: The Life of Colonel Dragutin T. Dimitrijević; The 'Black Hand' on Trial: Salonika, 1917; The Exoneration of the 'Black Hand,' 1917–1953* (Boulder, Colo.: East European Monographs, 1989, 1995, and 1998, respectively).

70. Most notably, Wayne S. Vucinich and Thomas A. Emmert, eds., *Kosovo: Legacy of a Medieval Battle* (Minneapolis: University of Minnesota, 1991). See also Emmert, *Serbian Golgotha: Kosovo, 1389* (Boulder, Colo.: East European Monographs, 1990), and "Miloš Obilić and the Hero Myth," *Serbian Studies* 10 (1996), 149–63; John B. Allcock, "Kosovo: The Heavenly and the Earthly Crown," in Ian Reader and Tony Walter, eds., *Pilgrimage in Popular Culture* (Basingstoke: Macmillan, 1993), 157–78; Judah, *The Serbs*; Anzulović, *Heavenly Serbia*; Ivo Žanić, "New Myths for Old," *Index on Censorship* 28, no. 4 (July-August 1999), 157–65; Olga Zirojević, "Kosovo within Collective Memory," in Drinka Gojković (English version) and Nebojša Popov, eds., *The Road to War in Serbia: Trauma and Catharsis* (New York: Central European University Press, 2000).

71. Traditional national interpretations of the Serbian uprisings were challenged by several American historians in the 1970s (these articles are cited and placed in broader context in Daniel Chirot and Karen Barkey, "States in Search of Legitimacy: Was There Nationalism in the Balkans in the Early Nineteenth Century?" *International Journal of Comparative Sociology* 24 [1983], 30–45). But these were historiographical debates rather than studies of the uprisings in public memory, popular culture, or political discourse. See however David MacKenzie, "The Serbian Warrior Myth and Serbia's Liberation, 1804–1815," *Serbian Studies* 10 (1996), 133–48, and Dimitrije Djordjević, "Vuk Karadžić: The Historian of the Serbian Uprising," in Robert Conquest and Dušan Djordjevich, eds., *Political and Ideological Confrontations in Twentieth-Century Europe* (New York: St. Martin's Press, 1996).

Historiography of World War I has paid insufficient attention to Southeastern Europe, and the same is true of the recent boom in studies of the war's remembrance. For a useful review of the "history and memory" literature on Western Europe, see Catherine Moriarty, "The Material Culture of Great War Remembrance," *Journal of Contemporary History* 34 (1999), 653–62.

72. Noel Malcolm, *Kosovo: A Short History* (New York University Press, 1998); Miranda Vickers, *Between Serb and Albanian: A History of Kosovo* (New York: Columbia University Press, 1998). Anthropologist Ger Duijzings is well versed in the historical literature and offers insightful observations on the past in his aforementioned collection of case studies dealing primarily with contemporary (pre-1999) Kosovo, *Religion and the Politics of Identity in Kosovo*.

73. Mark Mazower, "Introduction to the Study of Macedonia," *Journal of Modern Greek Studies* 14 (1996), 229.

74. Basil C. Gounaris, "Reassessing Ninety Years of Greek Historiography on the 'Struggle for Macedonia' (1904–1908)," *Journal of Modern Greek Studies* 14 (1996), 237–51; Victor Roudometof, "Nationalism and Identity Politics in the Balkans: Greece and the Macedonian Question," *Journal of Modern Greek Studies* 14 (1996), 253–301; Iakovos D. Michailidis, "The War of Statistics: Traditional Recipes for the Preparation of the Macedonian

Salad," *East European Quarterly* 32 (1998), 9–21; Martin Rady, "Austrian Maps of the Bulgarians in the Nineteenth Century," *National Identities* 1 (1999), 73–79.

75. Two collections with a number of useful essays on various aspects, domestic and international, of the history of the Macedonian Question: Victor Roudometof, ed., *The Macedonian Question: Culture, Historiography, Politics* (Boulder, Colo.: East European Monographs, 2000), and James Pettifer, ed., *The New Macedonian Question* (London: Macmillan, 1999). On the turn-of-the-century diplomatic crises, see Nadine Lange-Akhund, *The Macedonian Question, 1893–1908, from Western Sources* (Boulder, Colo.: East European Monographs, 1998), and Angelos A. Chotzidis, Basil C. Gounaris, and Anna A. Panayotopoulou, eds., *The Events of 1903 in Macedonia as Presented in European Diplomatic Correspondence* (Thessaloniki: Museum of the Macedonian Struggle, 1993). Several authors have written on the Macedonian Question during the Greek Civil War, including Andrew Rossos, "Incompatible Allies: Greek Communism and Macedonian Nationalism in the Civil War in Greece, 1943–1949," *Journal of Modern History* 69 (1997), 42–76; Rossos, "Great Britain and Macedonian Statehood and Unification 1940–49," *East European Politics and Societies* 14 (2000); Anastasia Karakasidou, "Fellow Travelers, Separate Roads: The KKE and the Macedonian Question," *East European Quarterly* 27 (1993), 453–77; David C. Van Meter, "The Macedonian Question and the Guerrilla War in Northern Greece on the Eve of the Truman Doctrine," *Journal of the Hellenic Diaspora* 21 (1995), 71–90.

76. There are several important anthropological studies on the historical formation of Macedonian identity: Anastasia N. Karakasidou, *Fields of Wheat, Hills of Blood: Passages to Nationhood in Greek Macedonia, 1870–1990* (Chicago: University of Chicago Press, 1997); Loring M. Danforth, *The Macedonian Conflict: Ethnic Nationalism in a Transnational World* (Princeton, N.J.: Princeton University Press, 1995); and Peter Mackridge and Eleni Yannakakis, eds., *Ourselves and Others: The Development of a Greek Macedonian Cultural Identity since 1912* (Oxford: Berg, 1997). Works by historians include Michael Seraphinoff, *The 19th-Century Macedonian Awakening: A Study of the Life and Works of Kiril Pejchinovich* (Lanham, Md.: University Press of America, 1996); Basil C. Gounaris, "Social Cleavages and National 'Awakening' in Ottoman Macedonia," *East European Quarterly* 29 (1996), 409–26.

On interwar Yugoslav Macedonia, see two articles by Andrew Rossos: "The British Foreign Office and Macedonian National Identity, 1918–1941," *Slavic Review* 53 (1994), 369–94, and "Macedonianism and Macedonian Nationalism on the Left," in Banac and Verdery, *National Character and National Ideology*, 219–54. On early postwar Yugoslavia, see Stefan Troebst, "Yugoslav Macedonia, 1944–53: Building the Party, the State and the Nation," in Melissa K. Bokovoy, Jill A. Irvine, and Carol S. Lilly, eds., *State-Society Relations in Yugoslavia, 1945–1992* (New York: St. Martin's Press, 1997), 243–66. See also Hugh Poulton, *Who Are the Macedonians?* (Bloomington: Indiana University Press, 1995).

77. Andrew Wachtel, *Making a Nation, Breaking a Nation: Literature and Cultural Politics in Yugoslavia* (Stanford, Calif.: Stanford University Press, 1998); Aleksandar Pavković, *Slobodan Jovanović: An Unsentimental Approach to Politics* (Boulder, Colo.: East European Monographs, 1993); Ralph Bogert, *The Writer as Naysayer: Miroslav Krleža and the Aesthetic of Interwar Central Europe* (Columbus, Ohio: Slavic Publishers, 1991); Vucinich, *Ivo Andrić Revisited*; Thomas Butler, "Ivo Andrić, a 'Yugoslav Writer,'" *Cross Currents* 10 (1991), 117–21; Ivo Ćurćin, "The Yugoslav *Nova Evropa* and Its British Model: A Case of Cross-Cultural Influence," *Slavonic and East European Review* 68 (1990), 461–75; Banac, "Zarathustra in Red Croatia"; Daskalov, "Ideas about, and Reactions to Modernization"; Biondich, *Stjepan Radić, the Croat Peasant Party, and the Politics of Mass Mobilization, 1904–1928*.

78. J. B. Hoptner, *Yugoslavia in Crisis, 1934–41* (New York: Columbia University Press, 1962). Srdjan Trifković ("Yugoslavia in Crisis: Europe and the Croat Question, 1939–41," *European History Quarterly* 23 [1993], 529–62), and James J. Sadkovich (*Italian Support for Croatian Separatism, 1927–1937* [New York: Garland, 1987]) have updated an important aspect of Hoptner's work. Most of the new studies on Yugoslavia's economic and political relations with individual countries have been published by East European Monographs (Boulder, Colo.): Frank C. Littlefield, *Germany and Yugoslavia, 1933–1941: The German Conquest of Yugoslavia* (1988); Eugene Boia, *Romania's Diplomatic Relations with Yugoslavia in the Interwar Period, 1919–1941* (1993); Linda Killen, *Testing the Peripheries: U.S.-Yugoslav Economic Relations in the Interwar Years* (1994); Nicolas J. Costa, *Shattered Illusions: Albania, Greece and Yugoslavia* (1998). See also Peter C. Kent, "The 'Proffered Gift': The Vatican and the Abortive Yugoslav Concordat of 1935–37," in Dick Richardson and Glyn Stone, eds., *Decisions and Diplomacy: Essays in Twentieth-Century International History* (London: Routledge, 1995), 108–28; Rossos, "British Foreign Office."

79. The best attempt so far remains Jozo Tomasevich's chapter in Wayne S. Vucinich, ed., *Contemporary Yugoslavia: Twenty Years of Socialist Experiment* (Berkeley: University of California, 1969). This collection also contains probably the best single text on interwar Yugoslavia, by Vucinich.

80. A worthy model would be Mark Mazower, *Inside Hitler's Greece: The Experience of Occupation, 1941–1944* (New Haven, Conn.: Yale University Press, 1993).

81. Simon Trew, *Britain, Mihailović and the Chetniks, 1941–42* (New York: St. Martin's Press, in Association with King's College, London, 1998). Also Ann Lane, *Britain, The Cold War and Yugoslav Unity, 1941–1949* (Portland, Oregon: Sussex Academic Press, 1996); Thomas M. Barker, *Social Revolutionaries and Secret Agents: The Carinthian Slovene Partisans and Britain's Special Operations Executive* (Boulder, Colo.: East European Monographs, 1990). On American relations with the rival resistance movements, there is Kirk Ford, *OSS and the Yugoslav Resistance, 1943–1945* (College Station: Texas A&M University Press, 1992), and what is probably one of the last as

well as one of the best of the many memoirs by Allied operatives in Yugoslavia: Franklin Lindsay, *Beacons in the Night: With the OSS and Tito's Partisans in Wartime Yugoslavia* (Stanford, Calif.: Stanford University Press, 1993).

82. Whereas emphasis was once placed on the Partisans' successful championing of Yugoslav patriotism, attention is turning to their different appeals to various groups. See for instance Ivo Banac, *With Stalin against Tito: Cominformist Splits in Yugoslav Communism* (Ithaca, N.Y.: Cornell University Press, 1988); Irvine, *The Croat Question;* and Attila Hoare, "The People's Liberation Movement in Bosnia and Hercegovina, 1941–1945: What Did It Mean to Fight for a Multi-National State?" *Nationalism and Ethnic Politics* 2 (1996), 415–45.

83. Recent studies include Jonathan Steinberg, *All or Nothing: The Axis and the Holocaust, 1941–1943* (London: Routledge, 1990), and "The Roman Catholic Church and Genocide in Croatia, 1941–1945," in Diana Wood, ed., *Christianity and Judaism* (Cambridge, Mass.: Blackwell, 1992); Jelinek, "Bosnia-Herzegovina at War," and "On the Condition of Women"; Reinhartz, "Damnation of the Outsider"; Aleksa Djilas, *The Contested Country: Yugoslav Unity and Communist Revolution, 1919–1953* (Cambridge, Mass.: Harvard University Press, 1991), 103–27; Jonathan Gumz, "German Counterinsurgency Policy in Independent Croatia, 1941–1944," *Historian* 61 (1998), 33–50; Srdja Trifković, *Ustaša: Croatian Separatism and European Politics, 1929–1945* (Aiken, S.C.: Lord Byron Foundation for Balkan Studies, 1998).

84. An important article that situates the Yugoslav case within this literature: Wolfgang Hoepken, "War, Memory, and Education in a Fragmented Society: The Case of Yugoslavia," *East European Politics and Societies* 13 (1999), 190–227. Hoepken's specific topic is the official Titoist view of World War II as portrayed in textbooks; the volatile rise of competing unofficial memories in the 1980s; and their co-optation and promotion by the new nationalist regimes. On the emotionally and politically charged memories and controversies regarding wartime killings, see also Ljubo Boban, "Jasenovac and the Manipulation of History," *East European Politics and Societies* 4 (1990), 580–92, and his subsequent exchange with Robert M. Hayden, *East European Politics and Societies* 6 (1992), 207–17; Vladimir Žerjavić, *Population Losses and Manipulations with the Number of Second World War Victims* (Zagreb: Zagreb Information Centre, 1993); Robert Hayden, "Recounting the Dead: the Rediscovery of Wartime Massacres in Late- and Post-Communist Yugoslavia," in Rubie Watson, ed., *Memory, History and Opposition under State Socialism* (Santa Fe, N.M.: School of American Research Press, 1994); Bette Denich, "Dismembering Yugoslavia: Nationalist Ideologies and the Symbolic Revival of Genocide," *American Ethnologist* 21 (1994), 367–90; Antun Miletić, "Establishing the Number of Persons Killed in Jasenovac Concentration Camp, 1941–1945," *Serbian Studies* 12 (1998), 18–26; Srdjan Bogosavljević, "Unelucidated Genocide," in Drinković and Popov, *Road to War*. For a look at commemorations of resistance, see Drago Roksandić, "Shifting References: Celebrations of Uprisings in Croatia, 1945–1991," *East European Politics and Societies* 9 (1995), 256–71.

85. On communists' views and internal debates on the national question: Djilas, *The Contested Country*, and Irvine, *The Croat Question*. See also Banac, *With Stalin against Tito*. The latest biographies of Tito are Stevan K. Pavlowitch, *Tito—Yugoslavia's Great Dictator: A Reassessment* (Columbus: Ohio State University Press, 1992)—brief, learned, and critical—and Jasper Ridley, *Tito* (London: Constable, 1994), and Richard West, *Tito: And the Rise and Fall of Yugoslavia* (New York: Carroll & Graf, 1995)—popular and sympathetic.

86. Jill A. Irvine, "Introduction: State-Society Relations in Yugoslavia, 1945–1992," in Bokovoy, Irvine, and Lilly, *State-Society Relations*, 5.

87. In addition to the essays in the collection noted above, see Melissa Bokovoy, *Peasants and Communists: Politics and Ideology in the Yugoslav Countryside, 1941–1953* (Pittsburgh, Pa.: University of Pittsburgh Press, 1998), and Carol Lilly, *Power and Persuasion: Ideology and Rhetoric in Communist Yugoslavia, 1944–1953* (Boulder, Colo.: Westview Press, 2001). Smaller studies of note on early postwar society include Mirjana Prosić-Dvornić, "The Reurbanization of Belgrade after the Second World War," in Klaus Roth, ed., *Das Volkskultur Südosteuropas in der Moderne* (Munich: Südosteuropa Gesellschaft, 1992), 75–100, and Dijana Alić and Maryam Gushesh, "Reconciling National Narratives in Socialist Bosnia and Herzegovina: The Baščaršija Project, 1948–1953," *Journal of the Society of Architectural Historians* 58 (1999), 6–25 (on the regime's efforts to reconcile modernization with Ottoman cultural heritage). On Yugoslavia's place in the wider historiography of state-society relations and the early years of communist rule, see Irvine, "Introduction: State-Society Relations," and Norman Naimark and Leonid Gibianskii, eds., *The Establishment of Communist Regimes in Eastern Europe, 1944–1949* (Boulder, Colo.: Westview Press, 1997).

88. Complaints about the ghettoization (from within and without) of Russian and East European studies are of long standing; see for instance Robert F. Byrnes, ed., *Bibliography of American Publications on East Central Europe* (Bloomington: Indiana University Press, 1958), xv–xxx, reprinted in his collection, *A History of Russian and East European Studies in the United States: Selected Essays* (Lanham. Md.: University Press of America, 1994), 35–51. More recently, on Balkan history in particular, see Thomas W. Gallant, "Greek Exceptionalism and Contemporary Historiography: New Pitfalls and Old Debates," *Journal of Modern Greek Studies* 15 (1997), 209–16, and Fleming, "Orientalism." Parochial tendencies among historians of the Balkans, and other historians' ignorance of the region, are somewhat curious and certainly unfortunate in light of the fact that "Greek and Balkan history have long offered routes to world history. . . . One thinks of Arnold Toynbee, William H. McNeill, and L. S. Stavrianos. The Balkans are a microcosm of the world." Kevin Reilly, "Foreword" to Stoianovich, *Balkan Worlds*, xv.

89. Jonathan Schell, "The Unfinished Twentieth Century," *Harper's Magazine*, January 2000.

90. Ingrao, "Handling Milošević: Three Scenarios," *Central Europe Review* 2, no. 29 (September 4, 2000): [http://www.ce-review.org/00/29/ingrao29.html]; Allcock, *Explaining Yugoslavia*, 439; Latinka Perović, "Flight from Modernization," in Drinković and Popov, *Road to War*.

91. Barkey and von Hagen, *After Empire*.

CHAPTER 2

1. In his classic study, *Bandits* (London: Weidenfeld and Nicolson, 1969), which has in turn spawned a vast literature, though, oddly, there has been little written on Balkan banditry in general beyond the separate national historiographies.

2. For Enlightenment anthropology, see especially Larry Wolff, *Inventing Eastern Europe: The Map of Civilization on the Mind of the Enlightenment* (Stanford, Calif.: Stanford University Press, 1994), and also in this volume; for popular fiction (largely British), see Vesna Goldsworthy, *Inventing Ruritania* (New Haven, Conn.: Yale University Press, 1998); for travelers and popular journalism, Maria Todorova, *Imagining the Balkans* (Oxford: Oxford University Press, 1997).

3. See "Ivan Lovrić i njegovo doba," *Zbornik Cetinske krajine* (Sinj) 1 (1979); Andrei Pippidi, "Naissance, renaissances et mort du 'Bon Sauvage': à propos des Morlaques et des Valacques," *Hommes et idées du Sud-Est européen à l'aube de l'âge moderne* (Paris: Editions du C.N.R.S., 1980).

4. For recent studies, see especially the excellent analyses by Ivo Žanić, *Prevarena povijest: guslarska estrada, kult hajduka i rat u Hrvatskoj i Bosni i Hercegovini 1990–1995. godine* (Zagreb: Durieux, 1998); and by Ivan Čolović, *Bordel ratnika: folklor, politika i rat* (Belgrade: XX vek, 1993).

5. Characteristic examples of the way that national ideologues made bandits into national symbols can be found in G. S. Rakovski's "Poiaviavane na haidushki cheti prez robstvoto," in *Bulgarijo, maiko mila* (Sofia: Bulgarski pisatel, 1967), 218–22; or Vuk Stefanović Karadžić's definition of "hajduk" in *Srpski rječnik (1852)* (Belgrade: Prosveta, 1986), 1085–87. The Greek case is discussed in some detail in Michael Herzfeld, *Ours Once More: Folkore, Ideology and the Making of Modern Greece* (Austin: University of Texas Press, 1982).

6. Dušan Popović, *O hajducima*, vol. 2 (Belgrade: Narodna štamparija, 1931), 155.

7. Popović, *O hajducima*, vol. 1 (Belgrade: Narodna štamparija, 1930), 10; vol. 2, 156–57.

8. A. Mladenović, *Pedagogija naših narodnih pesama* (Belgrade: Štamparija M. Sibinkića, 1937), 28.

9. Vuk Stefanović Karadžić, *Prvi i drugi srpski ustanak* (Belgrade: Prosveta, 1947), 37.

10. *Srpski rječnik* (1818), 1085.

11. See Slobodan Jovanović, *Iz naše istorije i književnosti* (Belgrade: SKZ, 1931), 12–17; J. Koliopoulos, *Brigands with a Cause: Brigandage and Irreden-*

tism in Modern Greece, 1821–1912 (Oxford: Clarendon Press, 1987); Duncan Perry, *Stefan Stambulov and the Emergence of Modern Bulgaria, 1870–1895* (Durham, N.C.: Duke University Press, 1993), 141–45.

12. Pera Todorović, *Listovi iz "Hajdučije"* (Prosveta: Belgrade, 1985), 127–28.

13. Herzfeld, *Ours Once More*, 66–68; Romilly Jenkins, *The Dilessi Murders* (London: Longmans, 1961). Here too explicit semantic distinctions were made: between (demotic, patriotic, pre-indendence) *kleftouria* and (neo-Classical, venal, post-revolutionary) *listia* or banditry.

14. Karen Barkey, *Bandits and Bureaucrats: The Ottoman Route to State Centralization* (Ithaca, N.Y.: Cornell University Press, 1994); cf. Anton Blok, *The Mafia of a Sicilian Village, 1860–1960* (New York: Harper & Row, 1974).

15. John Koliopoulous treats the Greek case in depth in *Brigands with a Cause*; for Serbian četnik actions in Macedonia after 1904, see Jovan M. Jovanović, *Južna Srbija od kraja XVIII veka do oslobodjenja* (*Srpski narod u XIX veku*, vol. 16) (Belgrade: G. Kon, 1941), 141–84; for terrorist organizations in Macedonia, Duncan Perry, *The Politics of Terror* (Durham, N.C.: Duke University Press, 1988).

16. See, for example, R. Samardžić, ed., *Starina Novak i njegovo doba* (Posebna izdanja Balkanološkog instituta, vol. 35) (Belgrade: SANU, 1988).

17. See the discussion in John K. Vasdravellis, *Klephts, Armatoles and Pirates in Macedonia During the Rule of the Turks (1627–1821)* (Thessaloniki, 1975), 161–62.

18. Vassilis Colocotrones, "L'Âme bulgare et l'âme grecque d'après la poésie populaire," *Revue de Grèce* 1, no. 1 (1918), 129–43, quoted in M. Herzfeld, *Ours Once More*, 66. Jovan Cvijić made similar distinctions between Serbs and Bulgarians, also using bandit traditions to support his case: *Balkansko poluostrvo i južnoslovenske zemlje* (trans. of *La Péninsule balkanique*, 1918), vol. 1 (Belgrade: Državna šamparija, 1922), 378; vol. 2 (Belgrade: Izdavačka knjižarica Gece Kona, 1931), 213, 219, 223.

19. Jovan Cvijić, "Jedinstvo i psihički tipovi južnih slovena," *Autobigrafija i drugi spisi* (Belgrade: Srpska književna zadruga, 1965), 140–41. These passages are a revision of sections of *La Péninsule balkanique*, published in 1921 as a separate essay.

20. Vladimir Dvorniković, *Karakterologija Jugoslovena* (Belgrade: Kosmos, 1939), 548–53.

21. L. von Südland, *Južnoslavensko pitanje* (trans. of *Die südslawische Frage* [Vienna, 1918]) (Zagreb: Matica hrvatska, 1943), 184, 185.

22. Dinko Tomašić, "Plemenska kultura i njeni današnji ostaci" (1936), reprinted in *Društvena istraživanja* 2, no. 6 (1992), 889–906; *Personality and Culture in Eastern European Politics* (New York: G. W. Stewart, 1948).

23. Nikola Andrić, "O hrvatskoj duhovnoj individualnosti (na osnovu narodnih pjesama o hajduku Mijatu Tomiću)," *Hrvatske narodne pjesme* (vol. 8, *Junačke pjesme*) (Zagreb: Matica hrvatska, 1939), 13, 20. For a similar idealization of the quintessentially Croatian qualities of the Senj uskoks, see Bare Poparić, *Povijest senjskih uskoka* (Zagreb: Matica hrvatska, 1936).

24. Michael Herzfeld, *The Poetics of Manhood: Contest and Identity in a Cretan Mountain Village* (Princeton. N.J.: Princeton University Press, 1985), 19–33.

25. Carol Silverman, "The Politics of Folklore in Bulgaria," *Anthopological Quarterly* 56, no. 2 (1983), 55–61.

26. See for example, A. Pavelić, *Doživljaji* (Madrid, 1968); D. Ljotić, *Odabrana dela*, vol. 2 (Munich, 1990), 209.

27. For anti-European polemics among interwar Serbian intellectuals, see Branka Prpa-Jovanović, "Izmedju istoka i zapada: kulturni identitet i kulturno-civilizacijska uporišta," *Tokovi istorije* 3–4 (1997), 7–28.

28. Jozo Tomasevich, *The Chetniks* (Stanford, Calif.: Stanford University Press, 1975); Ivo Žanić, *Prevarana povijest*, 204–30; Riki van Boeschoten, *From Armatolik to People's Rule: Investigation into the Collective Memory of Rural Greece, 1750–1949* (Amsterdam: Adolf M. Hakkert, 1991).

29. See Žanić, *Prevarana povijest*, for the hajduk in Yugoslav socialist imagery, and particularly on the contradictory uses of "Turk" and "hajduk" (335–39).

30. V. Nazor, *S partizanima* (Belgrade: Narodna knjiga, 1965), 107.

31. T. Čubelić, ed., *Epske narodne pjesme* (Zagreb: Školska knjiga, 1955; 2nd ed., 1965), 228.

32. Franjo Tudjman, *Rat protiv rata: partizanski rat u prošlosti i budućnosti* (Zagreb: Zora, 1970), esp. 72–83. Similar interpretations of the banditry of the Ottoman period can be found in most Marxist accounts, e.g., B. Tsvetkova, *Khaidutstvoto v bulgarskite zemi prez 15–18 vek* (Sofia: Nauka i izkustvo, 1971).

33. Milovan Djilas's memoirs are an excellent example of both attitudes; see especially *Memoir of a Revolutionary* (New York: Harcourt Brace Jovanovich, 1973) and *Wartime* (New York: Harcourt Brace Jovanovich, 1977).

34. Duška Jovanić, "Kradljivac slobode: poslednja bitka komandanta Srpske garde," *Duga* (28 Sept. 1991), 18–20.

35. See, for example, S. Meštrović, S. Letica, and M. Goreta, *Habits of the Balkan Heart: Social Character and the Fall of Communism* (College Station, Tex.: Texas A&M University Press, 1993), or Karl Kaser, "Hirten, Helden und Haiduken: zum Männlichkeitskult im jugoslawischen Krieg," *L'Homme* 3, no. 1 (1992), 155–62.

36. Georg Rosen, *Die Balkan Haiduken. Ein Beitrag zur inneren Geschichte des Slawentums* (Leipzig, 1878), 25.

37. Reinhard Lauer, "Das Wüten der Mythen. Kritische Ammerkungen zur serbischen heroischen Dichtung," in R. Lauer and Werner Lehfeldt, eds., *Das jugoslawische Desaster* (Wiesbaden: Harrossowitz, 1994), 130, 110.

38. Similar causal connections between epic violence and Serbian war atrocities are also suggested in Mirko Grmek et al., *Etničko čišćenje* (Zagreb: Nakladni zavod Globus, 1993), 23; or, though in a more nuanced form, between popular myth and political action, in Tim Judah, *The Serbs: History, Myth and the Destruction of Yugoslavia* (New Haven, Conn.: Yale University Press, 1997).

39. Žanić, *Prevarena povijest,* 107–23.

40. Svetolik Ranković, *Gorski car* (Belgrade, 1897).

41. Jovan Skerlić, *Omladina i njena književnost (1848–1871): izučavanja o nacionalnom i književnom romantizmu kod Srba* (Belgrade: Prosveta, 1906).

42. One example would be Miroslav Krleža's polemics against the romantic, backward-looking cult of the hajduk, "Morlacchism," the heroic epic, and the mythologized historiography that grew from these; for example, in his essays, particularly in "O nekim problemima Enciklopedije," *Eseji,* vol. 5 (*Sabrana djela Miroslava Krleže,* vol. 23) (Zagreb: Zora, 1966), 161–62, 167–68, and elsewhere.

43. See for example Nebojsa Popov, ed., *Srpska strana rata* (Belgrade: Republika, 1996).

44. Ružica Rosandić and Vesna Pešić, eds., *Warfare, Patriotism, Patriarchy* (Belgrade: Centre for Anti-War Action, 1994).

CHAPTER 3

1. Giulio Bajamonti, "Il Morlacchismo d'Omero," *Nuovo Giornale Enciclopedica d'Italia* (March 1797), 77–78; Franco Venturi, *Settecento riformatore,* Volume V, *L'Italia dei lumi,* Tomo II, *La Repubblica di Venezia* (Torino: Giulio Einaudi, 1990), 411–13.

2. Bajamonti, "Il Morlacchismo d'Omero," 78–79.

3. Jovan Cvijić, *La Péninsule Balkanique: Géographie Humaine* (Paris: Librairie Armand Colin, 1918), 363n; see also Grga Novak, "Morlaci (Vlasi) gledani s mletačke strane," *Zbornik za narodniživot i običaje,* vol. 45 (1971), 579–603; Branimir Gusić, "Wer sind die Morlaken im Adriatischen Raum?" *Balcanica* 4 (Belgrade, 1973), 453–64.

4. Wayne Vucinich, *A Study in Social Survival: Katun in the Bileća Rudine* (Denver, Colo.: University of Denver Press, 1975), 13–18; Vucinich, "Serbian Military Tradition," in Bela Kiraly and Gunther Rothenberg, eds., *War and Society in East Central Europe,* vol. 1 (New York: Brooklyn College Press and Columbia University Press, 1979), 290; C. W. Bracewell, "Uskoks in Venetian Dalmatia before the Venetian-Ottoman War of 1714–1718," in Gunther Rothenberg, Bela Kiraly, and Peter Sugar, eds., *East Central European Society and War in the Pre-Revolutionary Eighteenth Century* (Boulder, Colo. and New York: Social Science Monographs and Columbia University Press, 1982), 431–32; Predrag Matvejević, *Mediterranean: A Cultural Landscape,* trans. Michael Henry Heim (Berkeley: University of California Press, 1999), 202.

5. Alberto Fortis, *Viaggio in Dalmazia* (Venice: Presso Alvise Milocco, 1774), republished by Jovan Vuković and Peter Rehder, eds. (Munich and Sarajevo: Verlag Otto Sagner and Izdavačko Preduzeće "Veselin Masleša," 1974), vol. 1, 43–44.

6. Fortis, *Viaggio in Dalmazia,* vol. 2, 87.

7. Zorzi Grimani, Archivio di Stato di Venezia (ASV), *Collegio: Relazioni,* filza 69, marzo 1732.

8. Giacomo Boldù, ASV, *Collegio: Relazioni,* filza 69, 30 agosto 1748.

9. Fortis, *Viaggio in Dalmazia,* vol. 1, 44; Johann Gottfried Herder, *Ideen zur Philosophie der Geschichte der Menschheit,* in *Herders Werke,* vol. 4, ed. Regine Otto (Berlin and Weimar: Aufbau-Verlag, 1982), 393; see also Larry Wolff, *Inventing Eastern Europe: The Map of Civilization on the Mind of the Enlightenment* (Stanford, Calif,: Stanford University Press, 1994), 284–331.

10. Fortis, *Viaggio in Dalmazia,* vol. 1, 58, and 67; see also Arturo Cronia, *La Conoscenza del mondo slavo in Italia: Bilancio storico-bibliografico di un millennio* (Padua: Officine Grafiche Stediv, 1958), 331–33; Andrei Pippidi, "Naissance, renaissances et mort du 'Bon Sauvage': à propos des Morlaques et des Valaques," in *Hommes et idées du Sud-Est européen à l'aube de l'âge moderne* (Bucharest: Editura Academiei, 1980), 1–23; Barbara W. Maggs, "Three Phases of Primitivism in Portraits of Eighteenth-Century Croatia," *Slavonic and East European Review* 67, no. 4 (October 1989), 546–63; Valentina Gulin, "Morlacchism between Enlightenment and Romanticism," *Narodna umjetnost* 34, no. 1 (Zagreb, 1997), 77–100; Mate Zorić, "Croati e altri slavi del sud nella letteratura italiana del '700," *Revue des études sud-est européennes* 10, no. 2 (Bucharest, 1972), 301–12; Zorić, "Hrvat, Skjavun, Dubrovčanin, Morlak i Uskok—kao stereotipi i pjesnički motivi u talijanskoj književnosti," *Književna smotra* 24 (85) (Zagreb, 1992), 47–55.

11. Giustiniana Wynne, *Les Morlaques* (Venice, 1788), 123.

12. Camillo Federici, *Gli Antichi Slavi,* in *Collezione di tutte le Opere Teatrali del Signor Camillo Federici,* Tomo XVI (Venice: Pietro Bettini Libraio, 1819), 54.

13. *Le Nozze de' Morlacchi, ossia il Rapimento d'Elena,* Ballo eroicomico composto dal Serafini Giacomo, (Bergamo: Stampatore Duci, 1802), Walter Toscanini Collection, *libretti di ballo,* Library for the Performing Arts, The New York Public Library.

14. *I Morlacchi,* Ballo di Carattere in tre atti, composto e diretto da Antonio Biggiogero (Novara: Stamperia Rasario, 1812); *I Morlacchi,* Ballo di Carattere in quattro atti, d'invenzione di Gaetano Gioja, composto da Ferdinando Gioja (Bologna: Stamperia del Sassi, 1830); *I Morlacchi, ossia Le Nozze Interrotte,* Ballo Serio, composto e diretto dal Signor Giovanni Fabris (Milan: Stamperia di Carlo Dova, 1831), Walter Toscanini Collection, *libretti di ballo,* Library for the Performing Arts, The New York Public Library.

15. Auguste-Frédéric-Louis Marmont, *Mémoires du Maréchal Marmont, Duc de Raguse,* 3rd ed., vol. 3 (Paris: Perrotin, 1857), 26–28, 45, 52, 62, 64–65.

16. C. B. du Département de Marengo, *Souvenirs d'un voyage en Dalmatie* (Turin: Chez Botta, Prato et Paravia, n.d.), 3–5, 53–57, and 67.

17. C. B. du Département de Marengo, *Souvenirs,* 58–60.

18. C. B. du Département de Marengo, *Souvenirs,* 84–87.

19. Matthias Murko, *Das Original von Goethes "Klaggesang von der edlen Frauen des Asan Aga" (Asanaginica) in der Literatur und im Volksmunde durch 150 Jahre* (Brno: Verlag Rudolf M. Rohrer, 1937), 4, 25–26,

32–39; Ivan Milčetić, "Dr. Julije Bajamonti i negova djela," *Rad Jugoslavenske Akademije Znanosti i Umjetnosti* 192 (Zagreb, 1912), 132–49; André Vaillant, "Vuk Karadžić et l'Hasanaginica," *Revue des études slaves* 19 (Paris, 1939), 88–90.

20. Camilla Lucerna, *Die südslavische Ballade von Asan Agas Gattin und ihre Nachbildung durch Goethe* (Berlin: Alexander Duncker, 1905), 4; Goethe, "Serbische Lieder," in *Goethes Werke*, Band XII (Hamburg: Christian Wenger Verlag, 1953), 335.

21. Lucerna, 65–66; Vaillant, 90.

22. Karl Vipauz, "Zur Volkskunde: Physische Beschaffenheit der Bevölkerung," in *Die österreichisch-ungarische Monarchie in Wort und Bild: Dalmatien* (Vienna: Druck und Verlag der kaiserlich-königlichen Hof- und Staatsdruckerei, 1892), 119–20.

23. Marcell Kusar, "Zur Literatur: Die serbischkroatische Sprache und Literatur," in *Die österreichisch-ungarische Monarchie in Wort und Bild: Dalmatien*, 251.

24. Lucerna, 65.

25. Reinhard Petermann, ed., *Führer durch Dalmatien*, herausgegeben vom Vereine zur Förderung der volkswirtschaftlichen Interessen Königreiches Dalmatien (Vienna: Alfred Hölder, 1899), 251–61.

26. Maude Holbach, *Dalmatia: The Land Where East Meets West* (London: John Lane, 1908); Frances Kinsley Hutchinson, *Motoring in the Balkans: Along the Highways of Dalmatia, Montenegro, the Herzegovina and Bosnia* (London: Hodder and Stoughton, 1910); Alice Lee Moqué, *Delightful Dalmatia* (New York: Funk and Wagnalls, 1914).

27. T. G. Jackson, *Dalmatia, the Quarnero, and Istria* (Oxford: Clarendon Press, 1887).

28. Jackson, 203; Moqué, 58–60 and 101–2.

29. Hutchinson, 68–69 and 78; Holbach, 31.

30. "Dalmatia," *Encyclopaedia Britannica*, 11th ed., vol. 7, 1910, 773.

31. Jackson, 408–9.

32. H. G. Wells, *The Time Machine* (1895; New York: Dover Publications, 1995), 39.

33. John Calvin Batchelor, "Introduction," in H. G. Wells, *The Time Machine* and *The Invisible Man* (New York: Signet Classic, 1984), xxii–xxiii.

34. Maria Todorova, *Imagining the Balkans* (Oxford: Oxford University Press, 1997), 3 and 19.

35. Marijan Stojković, "Morlakizam," *Hrvatsko Kolo* 10 (Zagreb, 1929), 259.

36. Louis Adamic, *The Native's Return: An American Immigrant Visits Yugoslavia and Discovers His Old Country* (New York: Harper and Brothers, 1934), 174–75.

37. Adamic, *The Native's Return*.

38. Oddone Talpo, *Dalmazia: Una cronaca per la storia (1941)* (Rome: Stato Maggiore Dell'Esercito, Ufficio Storico, 1985), 245, 271, 281, 285, 739, 747.

CHAPTER 4

1. J. Gelcich and L. Thallóczy, eds., *Raguza és Magyarország összeköt-tetéseinek oklevéltára* (Budapest: M. Tud. Akadémia Tört. Bizottsága, 1887), 158 (hereafter *Raguza*).

2. J. Radonić, ed., *Dubrovačka akta i povelje*, I, no. 1 (Belgrade: Srpska kraljevska akademija [hereafter SKA], 1934), 325 (hereafter *Akta*).

3. *Raguza*, 381; *Akta*, I, no. 1, 338.

4. On Johannes Gazulus, see S. Jurić, "Prilozi biografiji Ivana Gazulića," *Anali Historijskog instituta u Dubrovniku* 8–9 (1962), 447–79; J. Tadić, "Johannes Gazulus, dubrovački humanista XV veka," *Zbornik Filozofskog fakulteta u Beogradu* 8–9 (1964), 429–54; B. Krekić, "Albanians in the Adriatic Cities: Observations on Some Ragusan, Venetian and Dalmatian Sources for the History of the Albanians in the Late Middle Ages," in *The Medieval Albanians* (Athens: Institute for Byzantine Research, 1998), 221–24.

5. *Raguza*, 483; *Akta* I, no. 2 (1934), 523–24; See also Z. Janeković-Römer, *Okvir slobode. Dubrovačka vlastela izmedju srednjovjekovlja i humanizma* (Zagreb, Dubrovnik: Zavod za povijesne znanosti Hrvatske akademije znanosti i umjetnosti u Dubrovniku, 1999), 223.

6. *Raguza*, 75; G. Gelcich, ed., *Monumenta ragusina*, vol. 4 (Zagreb: Jugoslavenska akademija znanosti i umjetnosti [hereafter JAZU], 1896), 148 (hereafter *MR*); J. Tadić, ed., *Pisma i uputstva Dubrovačke Republike* (Belgrade: SKA, 1935), 306 (hereafter *Pisma*); Janeković-Römer, 252.

7. *Raguza*, 53–54; *MR*, vol. 4, 118–19; *Pisma*, 214.

8. Državni arhiv u Dubrovniku (Dubrovnik State Archives, hereafter DSA), *Litterae Levantis*, vol. 4, ff. 28v–29.

9. *Raguza*, 397; *Akta*, I, no. 1, 359.

10. *Raguza*, 474; On Stefan Vukčić-Kosača, see S. Ćirković, *Stefan Vukčić-Kosača i njegovo doba* (Belgrade: Srpska akademija nauka i umetnosti [hereafter SANU], 1964).

11. DSA, *Testamenta notariae*, vol. 18, ff. 6–6v. Marinus de Gondola had eight sons. See I. Mahnken, *Dubrovački patricijat u XIV veku* (Belgrade: SANU, 1960), II, tab. XXXVI/2.

12. *MR*, vol. 2 (1882), 285; *Pisma*, 16–17, 18–20, 29–30.

13. On Ragusan patricians see Mahnken, Janeković-Römer, and D. Rheubottom, *Age, Marriage and Politics in Fifteenth-Century Ragusa* (Oxford: Oxford University Press, 2000). See also B. Krekić, "Developed Autonomy: The Patricians in Dubrovnik and Dalmatian Cities," in Krekić, ed., *Urban Society of Eastern Europe in Premodern Times* (Berkeley, Los Angeles: University of California Press, 1987), 185–215 (now also in B. Krekić, *Dubrovnik: A Mediterranean Urban Society, 1300–1600*, ch. II [Aldershot and Brookfield: Ashgate-Variorum, 1997], hereafter *Dubrovnik 1300–1600*).

14. V. Bogušić and C. Jireček, eds., *Liber statutorum civitatis Ragusii compositus anno 1271* (Zagreb: JAZU, 1904), liber I, c. 3 (now partially reprinted with a Croatian translation, Dubrovnik: Historijski arhiv Dubrovnik, 1990).

15. DSA, *Consilium Maius*, vol. 12, f. 101v; B. Nedeljković, ed., *Liber croceus* (Belgrade: SANU, 1997), 30.

16. B. Krekić, *Dubrovnik (Raguse) et le Levant au Moyen Age* (Paris, The Hague: EPHE-Sorbonne, 1961), 163n2.

17. *Akta*, II, no. 2 (1938), 272–74; see also 238, 252–57, 259–60.

18. *Liber croceus* (Nedeljković edition), 61–62.

19. *MR*, vol. 3 (1895), 232–33; *Pisma*, 100–101. On Ragusan diplomacy see B. Cvjetković, *Dubrovačka diplomacija* (Dubrovnik: Jadran, 1923); B. Krizman, *Diplomati i konzuli u starom Dubrovniku* (Zagreb: Poduzeće za izdavanje, prodaju i distribuciju knjiga, 1957); I. Mitić, *Dubrovačka država u medjunarodnoj zajednici (od 1358 do 1815)* (Zagreb: JAZU and Nakladni zavod Matice hrvatske, 1988); *Diplomacy of the Republic of Dubrovnik* (Zagreb: Ministry of Foreign Affairs of the Republic of Croatia, Diplomatic Academy, 1998); Janković-Römer, 136–41.

20. *Litt. Levantis*, vol. 4, f. 110. Already in the Liber statutorum (liber VIII, c. 48) one finds measures against those who act contrary to governmental instructions. On Sandalj Hranić-Kosača see S. Ćirković, *Istorija srednjovekovne bosanske države* (Belgrade: Srpska književna zadruga [hereafter SKZ], 1964), 177–267.

21. *Litt. Levantis*, vol. 7, ff. 57–59v; *Raguza*, 210–11.

22. *Akta*, I, no. 1, 290.

23. *Litt. Levantis*, vol. 4, ff. 51–55; *Raguza*, 142.

24. *Litt. Levantis*, ff. 85–85v.

25. *Litt. Levantis*, vol. 8, ff. 134v–135.

26. *Litt. Levantis*, vol. 17, ff. 42v–43.

27. *Litt. Levantis*, f. 45.

28. *Litt. Levantis*, ff. 47v–48.

29. DSA, *Secreta rogatorum*, vol. 2, ff. 136–136v. On dangers menacing Dubrovnik at this time because of Ottoman activities, see T. Popović, *Turska i Dubrovnik u XVI veku* (Belgrade: SKZ, 1973), 235–49.

30. DSA, *Consilium Minus*, vol. 48, f. 127.

31. *Secreta rog.*, vol. 2, ff. 157–58. This decree was confirmed in 1618. Ibid.

32. *Cons. Minus*, vol. 48, ff. 125, 229.

33. *Secreta rog.*, vol. 1, f. 28. On Akhmed-beg Kusumbašić, see Popović, 158. An interesting case involving knowledge of other languages is worth mentioning here. In April 1514, a man from Croatia, "Petrus de Zagabria," was engaged as a soldier in the Ragusan town of Ston with a monthly salary of 6 hyperpers (approximately 10 ducats) and "on condition that he be obliged whenever it might please our government to go to Hungary, Germany, Italy and other regions whose languages he says he knows." *Cons. Minus*, vol. 31, f. 254v.

34. *Secreta rog.*, vol. 2, f. 178. On December 30, 1568, the Senate discussed in a secret session "in which language . . . news that will be given to the Porte should from now on be written," but the debate was adjourned.

Ibid., f. 180. On Mehmed-Pasha Sokolović, see R. Samardžić, *Mehmed Sokolović* (Belgrade: SKZ, 1971); on Sokolović's relations with Dubrovnik, see Popović, 238–41.

35. *Raguza*, 18; *MR*, vol. 3, 72; *Pisma*, 40.

36. *Litt. Levantis*, vol. 8, ff. 160–160v.

37. See Janeković-Römer, 64, 65, 95, 107, 122–27, 159; B. Krekić, "Influence politique et pouvoir économique à Dubrovnik (Raguse) du XIIIe au XVIe siècle," in *Gerarchie economiche e gerarchie sociali, secoli XII–XVIII* (Florence: Le Monnier, 1990), 250–52 (now also in Krekić, *Dubrovnik 1300–1600*, ch. I).

38. *Liber statutorum* (see note 14 above); J. Lučić, ed., *Liber statutorum doanae Ragusii MCCLXXVII* (Dubrovnik: Historijski arhiv Dubrovnik, 1989); A. Solovjev and M. Peterković, eds., "Liber omnium reformationum civitatis Ragusii," *Dubrovački zakoni i uredbe* (Belgrade: SKA, 1936); B. Nedeljković, ed., *Liber viridis* (Belgrade: SANU, 1984); *Liber croceus* (see note 15 above).

39. *Cons. Minus*, vol. 44, ff. 133v-34.

40. Janeković-Römer, 252–53.

41. Janeković-Römer, 181.

42. DSA, *Lamenta de criminale*, vol. 2, ff. 61v-63.

43. DSA, *Lamenta de foris*, vol. 2, f. 87.

44. On the importance of the Senate, see Janeković-Römer, 100–102; on misbehavior of Ragusan patricians, see ibid., 33–37, 258–64; B. Krekić, "Ser Basilius de Basilio—a less than Commendable Ragusan Patrician (1361?–1413)," in Krekić, *Dubrovnik 1300–1600*, ch. III. See also my article "Note e osservazioni sulla vita e sul ruolo del patriziato a Ragusa e nelle città dalmatte tra il Due- e Cinquecento" (Florence: Universita degli Studi di Firenze, Dipartimento di Storia, 1999).

45. *Liber viridis* (Nedeljković edition), 261.

46. *Cons. Maius*, vol. 20, f. 141v; *Liber croceus*, f. 128 (Nedeljković edition, 264–65).

47. See B. Krekić, "Miscellanea from the Cultural Life of Renaissance Dubrovnik," *Byzantinische Forschungen* 20 (1985), 133–51 (now also in Krekić, *Dubrovnik 1300–1600*, ch. IX).

48. Janeković-Römer, 116, 184, 189–92.

CHAPTER 5

The author wishes to express his gratitude to several Stanford friends who have helped him in various ways with this chapter. Due to limited space he can mention but a few by name. They are Ivo Banac, Sima Ćirković, Dušan Djordjevich, Anne Garvey, Ferdinand Ivanek, Bariša Krekić, Sanja Medić, Thomas Emmert, Nicholas Pappas, Lynn Patyk, Alexander Vucinich, and Nicholas Vucinich.

1. For details on transhumance, see *Webster's New Collegiate Dictionary*, 8th ed. (1977).

2. The villages south of Orah—those of Zavodje, Andjelić, and Ljubomir—are more distant from the mountain *katun* than those north of Rilica. Most *katun* mountain stations are located in the Bosnian district of Foča, and a few in the mountainous Herzegovinian Gacko district. It took four days for my Orah family and its associates to reach our *katun*. Those from the villages in the northern part of the Bileća district, located closer to the mountains, could get to their *katuns* in one, two, or three days.

3. Mirko Marković, "Plemensko društvo i kultura dinarskih stočara," *Predmet i metod izučavanja patrijarhalnih zajednica u Jugoslaviji*, (Titograd [Podgorica], 1981), 247.

4. Mirko Marković, 248–49.

5. Ibid., 251.

6. Ibid.

7. Meaning the Serbs from Serbia.

8. A few additional words on Majo's misfortune may be of interest to the reader. In his final days of life, Majo and his comrades established their base in Baljci, a village near Bileća. There they were guests of the Vujović clan, a family that claimed kinship with the Vujović clan in Montenegro. Through this alleged filial link, the Vujović families of the two regions claimed common origin. It appears that someone in the community betrayed Majo by reporting his hideout in Baljci. The gendarmerie lost no time in surrounding the Vujović home, and, during the short exchange of fire, a gendarme killed Majo. The news quickly spread, and a cart was dispatched to bring Majo's body to the district courtyard where it was publicly exhibited, seated on a chair with a gun over the knees, photographed, and then buried at an undisclosed place. The gendarme, a Muslim, who killed Majo was promptly transferred from Bileća for his personal safety.

Many years later, sometime in the 1980s, I was giving a lecture in my class at Stanford on the Balkan resistance to the Turks and took a few moments to speak about the *hajduks*, patriot-bandits in the Balkans. My pupils were fascinated by these "Robin Hoods" and the tales told about them and their legendary exploits. During a discussion after class, one of the students told me with some pride that an uncle of his was a famous hayduk and that he had a photograph of him after he had been killed in battle. I expressed interest in the photo and asked the student to bring it to class. This he did, and it was a photo I could never forget: dead Majo sitting on a chair!

9. As time passed, the animal herds of individual families declined in size, and some changes had to be made in established practices. Livestock breeding, however, remained alive for a short while.

10. Both highly nourishing and undesirable grass grows in Zelengora. Nothing was done to prevent deterioration of the pastures. Undesirable grass was allowed to overtake and choke preferred and nutritious grasses, rich in protein and fat, such as Alpine timothy (*Pheleum alpinium*), bent grass (*Igrostis vulgaris*), annual bluegrass (*Poa annua*), and Kentucky bluegrass (*Papratensis*). Many once-fine pastures in the Zelengora mountains were overgrown by undesirable grasses and brush. Large areas were taken

over by mat-grass (*Nardus stricta*), which the locals call "wolf's whiskers" (*vučji brk*), a low-quality forage. Critics have also noted that the shepherds have tended to ignore the traditional grazing pattern.

11. The people of the area of Gacko, who lived at higher elevation and had more fertile soil, raised healthier animals and produced better-quality cheese. For this reason, and out of envy, the people of Rudine call them the barley eaters (*ječmonja*) and beet-eaters (*blitvonja*), both terms connoting an ox-like appetite. In the eyes of the people of Gacko (*Gačani*), their neighbors several miles to the south looked pale and starved, and so they jokingly called them "patch-ups" (*krpušari*).

12. In 1885, while exploring the area of Užice in Serbia, Josip (Josif) Pančić (1814–1888) discovered a new kind of conifer, to which he gave the name *Pinus omorica*. Josip Pančić, *Eine neue Konifere in den Ostlichen Alpen* (Beograd, 1876).

13. At one time, special numbers were used in counting animals (e.g., *jednogalo*, one; *dvogalo*, two; *trogalo*, three; *četvragalo*, four; *pigalo*, five; *segalo*, six; *sedmark*, seven; *osmak*, eight; *diviroga*, nine; and *dicma*, ten). I have not been able to establish the origin of this special way of counting. It is most likely a Vlach derivation. I have not heard it again since 1924, the summer I spent in Zelengora.

14. Every year a certain number of livestock fell victim to snakes. Consequently, in the years before World War I, Austria-Hungary gave modest rewards for killed poisonous snakes. After the war, the Yugoslav government encouraged the propagation of non-poisonous *blavor*, which destroyed vipers. St. Bolkay, Vejsil Čurčić, "O našim zmijama otrovnicama," *Glasnik Zemaljskog Muzeja (GZM)* 32: 1–2 (1920), 155–205.

15. Svetozar Koljević, *The Epic in the Making* (Oxford: Clarendon Press, 1980), 347–48.

16. The peasants could have lived better and in greater comfort, but they were slaves of tradition. When, in the early 1920s, one Spasoje Vidačić returned from Watsonville, California, where he had spent many years, he decided to build a modern cabin, modeled on the kind he must have seen in the Santa Cruz Mountains in California. Instead of kudos, he received needling from his peasant neighbors. To be sure, his cabin was better built than the other cabins in the *katun* and was somewhat better finished on the outside, but was not much different from others. His was also the only cabin that had two fairly comfortable beds, and the fireplace was an improvement on the traditional one. "The American," as they called him, stayed in his cabin only one summer. It was probably never occupied again until World War II, when guerrilla fighters made use of it.

17. Wayne S. Vucinich, *A Study in Social Survival* (Denver, Colo.: University of Denver, 1975), 44.

18. In 1962, a part of Sutjeska, an area of about 17,500 hectares, was proclaimed a national park. A small primeval forest called Perućica, of about 1,434 hectares, said to be the only one in Europe, is located here.

19. Vucinich, *Study in Social Survival*, 45.

20. Ibid., 84–85. 21. Ibid.
22. Ibid. 23. Ibid.
24. Ibid., 95–97. 25. Ibid.
26. Ibid., 86. 27. Ibid.
28. Ibid., 86–87. 29. Ibid.
30. Djordjo Krstić, *Problematika poljoprivrede donje Hercegovine* (Sarajevo, 1956), 98–99.
31. Vucinich, *Study in Social Survival,* 86–87.
32. Ibid., 87.

CHAPTER 6

1. R. J. Kerner, *The Jugo-Slav Movement* (Cambridge, Mass., 1918), 81, 94–95.
2. Johann Gottlieb Fichte, preface by Reinhard Lauth, *Reden an die Deutsche Nation* (Hamburg: Meiner, 1978), 178.
3. The three universities—Belgrade, Zagreb, and Ljubljana—are not included in this study. They became centers of their respective nationalisms, and their textbooks carried the same nationalistic themes found in their respective secondary school textbooks. See Ljubodrag Dimić, *Kulturna politika kraljevine Jugoslavije 1918–1941,* vol. 1 (Belgrade: Stubovi kulture, 1997), 245–46.
4. Viktor Novak, *Antologija Jugoslavenske misli i narodnog jedinstva, 1390–1930* (Anthology of the Yugoslav Idea and National Unity, 1390–1930) (Belgrade, 1930).
5. The developments in prewar Serbian, Croatian, and Slovenian education are discussed in Charles Jelavich, *South Slav Nationalisms—Textbooks and Yugoslav Union before 1914* (Columbus: Ohio State University Press, 1990). See also Dragutin Franković, ed., *Povijest školstva i pedagogije u Hrvatskoj* (Zagreb: Pedagoško-književni zbor, 1958), and Vladeta Tešić et. al., eds., *Sto godina prosvetnog saveta Srbije* (Belgrade: Zavod za udžbenike; nastavna sredstva, 1980).
6. *Prosvetni glasnik—Službeni list ministarstva prosvete i crkvenih poslova* (Belgrade, 1912), no. 33, 11. Dragoljub Živojinović, in his article "Serbia and Yugoslavia: Past, Present and Future," in Alex N. Dragnich, ed., *Serbia's Historical Heritage* (Boulder, Colo.: East European Monographs, 1994), 54, states:

> To the Serbs living within the Kingdom of Serbia during the early years of the twentieth century, however, the Yugoslav idea did not have a strong appeal. Serbian statesmen and intellectuals were more deeply concerned than ever before with the sufferings of the Serbs in Kosovo, the Sandžak, Macedonia and Bosnia and Herzegovina. . . . It is interesting to note that King Peter I, when talking to Serbian journalists, teachers and artists from Austria-Hungary and Turkey, insisted that it was expected of them to work for "cultural Yugoslavism" only. Other prominent Serbian politicians

(Slobodan Novaković, Nikola Pašić, Ljubomir Stojanović) shared this approach. They were aware, and admitted it, that their first aim and duty were towards the Serbs living outside the kingdom. Moreover, Serbian Army officers did not conceal their common concern for the destiny of the Serbs living under foreign domination. They did not talk about Yugoslav unity or the necessity of fighting for it.

7. *Prosvetni glasnik* 35 (1914), 172–74.

8. Charles Jelavich, "The Issue of Serbian Textbooks in the Origins of World War I," *Slavic Review* 48 (1989), 214–33.

9. There are many studies dealing with the South Slavs in the war. See, for example, Ivo Banac, *The National Question in Yugoslavia: Origins, History, Politics* (Ithaca, N.Y.: Cornell University Press, 1984); Vasa Čubrilović, *Istorija političke misli u Srbiji XIX veka* (Belgrade: Prosveta, 1958); Dimitrije Djordjević, ed., *The Creation of Yugoslavia, 1914–1918* (Santa Barbara, Calif.: Clio Books, 1980); Dragoslav Janković and Bogdan Krizman, eds., *Gradja o stvaranju jugoslavenske države*, 2 vols. (Belgrade: Institut društvenih nauka, 1964); and Ivo J. Lederer, *Yugoslavia at the Paris Peace Conference: a Study in Frontiermaking* (New Haven, Conn.: Yale University Press, 1963).

10. For contrasting views on the constitutional issue see Banac, *National Question*; Alex N. Dragnich, *The First Yugoslavia: Search for a Viable Political System* (Stanford, Calif.: Hoover Institution Press, 1983); and Momčilo Zečević, *Na istoriskoj prekretnici: Slovenci u politici jugoslovenske države 1918–1929*, vol. 1 (Belgrade: Prosveta, 1985).

11. Dimić, *Kulturna politika*, 191–224; Zečević, *Slovenci*, 15–47, 351–75; Ervin Dolenc, *Kulturni boj: Slovenska kulturna politika v kraljevini SHS 1918–1929* (Ljubljana: Cankarjeva založba, 1996), 199–259; Hrvoje Matković, *Svetozar Pribičević i samostalna demokratska stranka do šestojanuarske diktature* (Zagreb: Institut za hrvatsku povijest, Liber, 1972), 15–82; Vladko Maček, *In the Struggle for Freedom* (New York: R. Speller, 1957), 93–96.

12. Tešić, *Sto godina*, 94–97; Dimić, *Kulturna politika*, 112–27; Franković, *Povijest školstva*, 308–10.

13. Tešić, *Sto godina*, 89; Franković, *Povijest školstva*, 323; Milan Grol, "Prosveta, školstvo i nauka," in *Jubilarni zbornik života i rada Srba, Hrvata i Slovenaca*, vol. 2 (Belgrade: Matica živih i mrtvih Srba, Hrvata i Slovenaca, 1929), 386; Dimić, *Kulturna politika*, vol. 2, 117–20; Martin Mayer, *Elementarbildung in Jugoslawien (1918–1941): Ein Beitrag zur gesellschaftlichen Modernisierung?* (Munich: R. Oldenbourg, 1995), 39–55.

14. Tešić, *Sto godina*, 106.

15. Jov. P. Jovanović, "Za buduću narodnu školu," *Učitelj* 34, no. 5–6 (1920), 3–5.

16. Tešić, *Sto godina*, 96–97; Franković, *Povijest školstva*, 310; Jovan J. Babić, "Profesori i zakon o srednjim školama," *Glasnik profesorskog društva* 9 (1929), 1–3; Dimić, *Kulturna politika*, 216–25; Josip Skavić, "Naša

prosvjetna politika poslednjih godina," *Učitelj* 40, no. 1 (1927), 32–41, 97–106, 180–89; Mayer, *Elementarbildung*, 64–71.

17. Tešić, *Sto godina*, 88–89; *Učitelj* 34, no. 3–4 (1920), 66–68; Dimić, *Kulturna politika*, 226–39.

18. Franković, *Povijest školstva*, 318–23; Zečević, *Slovenci*, 346–414; Dolenc, *Kulturni boj*, 93–189; Dimić, *Kulturna politika*, vol. 2, 247.

19. Grol, "Prosveta," 384–89; Dimić, *Kulturna politika*, vol. 2, 152–60.

20. Grol, "Prosveta," 384–89; Mayer, *Elementarbildung*, 125–32. It should be stressed that in the fall of 1929, after the dictatorship was established, directives approving the consolidation of classes, the reorganization of school districts, repairs to schools, etc., were still being authorized based on the prewar education laws of 1869, 1888, 1904, and other relevant regulations.

21. Grol, "Prosveta," 384.

22. Ibid., 387; see also Vlado Petz, "Nacrt nastavnog plana," *Nastavni vjesnik* 37 (1929), 35–38.

23. Tešić, *Sto godina*, 111–16; Franković, *Povijest školstva*, 323–24, 330–45; Mayer, *Elementarbildung*, 201–5.

24. Voj. Petković, "Na početku nove godine 'Učitelja'," *Učitelj* 40, no. 1 (1930), 1; B. Vesić, "Za jugoslovensku pedagogiju," *Učitelj* 40, no. 2 (1930), 86–95, 172–79.

25. *Učitelj* 45, no. 1 (1931–32), 3.

26. Ibid., 4–6.

27. Ibid., 6–10.

28. Ibid., 12–13.

29. Ibid., 13–17.

30. Milan M. Jovanović, "O mogućnosti nacionalnog vaspitanja u srednjoj školi," *Glasnik jugoslovenskog profesorskog društva* 17, no. 1–12 (1936–37), 280–84; Dimić, *Kulturna politika*, vol. 2, 220–28; Vuj. Petković, "Skupština jugoslovenskog učiteljskog udruženja," *Učitelj* 44, no. 1 (1930–31), 50–61; "Rezolucija učiteljske skupštine," *Učitelj* 45, no. 1 (1931–32), 17–21.

31. Dimić, *Kulturna politika*, 279–94; Franković, *Povijest školstva*, 330–33; Mayer, *Elementarbildung*, 80–96.

32. "Pismo G. Ljub. M. Protića," *Učitelj* 41, no. 1 (1928), 71–72; Josip Skavić, "Pravci i težnje jugoslovenske pedagogije," *Učitelj* 51, no. 3–4 (1936), 199–205.

33. M. S. Moskovljević, "Hrvatski jezik," *Glasnik jugoslovenskog profesorskog društva* 18 (1937/38), 802–805; B. Vesić, "Jugoslovensku pedagogiju," 172–79; Živko Jakić, "Hrvatski i srpski udžbenici," *Nastavni vjesnik* 36 (1928), 131–33.

34. Stanoje Stanojević, *Istorija srpskoga naroda (sa pregledom hrvatske i slovenačke istorije) za srednje i stručne škole* (History of the Serbian People [with a Review of Croatian and Slovenian History] for the Secondary and Vocational Schools) (Belgrade: Geca Kon, 1921–22). Stanojević's criticism

of prewar Serbian historiography and textbooks is discussed in Charles Jelavich, "Milenko M. Vukičević: From Serbianism to Yugoslavism," in Dennis Deletant and Harry Hanak, eds., *Historians and Nation-Builders: Central and South-East Europe* (London: Macmillan, 1988), 113–14. In reviewing Vukičević's book, the authorized textbook for the secondary schools, Stanojević wrote:

> The author, without hesitation and without any appreciation, reviles and belittles all that is foreign and praises all that is ours, even if it is undeserved. According to Mr. Vukičević, all that is ours is good and we always were good and intelligent and brave and judicious and tender and kind and fair, whereas we always were, and today still are, surrounded by wily and dishonest and cowardly and uncivilized peoples. However, in this respect, Mr. Vukičević is not alone in this presentation of Serbia's past; he alone does not write this way. All the histories of the Serbian people are written this way [*sve Istorije Srpskog Naroda tako pišu*]. In all these books it seems that the history of the Serbian nation is a perpetual struggle between good and evil, between heaven and hell. In all these books the Serbs are always angels, whereas all the neighboring people are the progeny of hell, who do not do anything and do not think about anything than how they will destroy the nobility of mind, goodness, knowledge and heroism, which are personified in the Serbs. The entire history of the Serbian nation in these books appears as a religious epic of the battle between good and evil.

35. Stanojević, *Istorija Jugoslovena (Srba, Hrvata i Slovenaca) za srednje i stručne škole* (History of the Yugoslavs [Serbs, Croats, and Slovenes] for the Secondary and Vocational Schools) (Belgrade: Geca Kon, 1930–31).

36. Ibid., 55.   37. Ibid., 102.

38. Ibid., 127.   39. Ibid., 138.

40. Ibid., 160.

41. Živko Jakić, *Povijest Srba, Hrvata i Slovenaca za niže razrede srednjih učilišta* (History of the Serbs, Croats, and Slovenes for the Lower Grades of the Secondary Schools) (Zagreb: Narodna knjižnica, 1926).

42. Volume 2 carried the title, *Povijest Srba, Hrvata i Slovenaca s obzirom na opću historiju za srednje i njima slične škole* (Zagreb: Troškom i nakladom piščevom "Tipografija," 1929), 108.

43. Ibid., 118.

44. Ibid., 120, 131–33.

45. Jakić, *Povijest Jugoslavije s općom historijom za IV razred srednjih i njima sličnih škola* (History of Yugoslavia including General History for the Fourth Grade of Secondary and Similar Schools) (Zagreb: Narodna knjižnica, 1935).

46. Jakić, *Povijest Jugoslavije*, 110–13.

47. See Wolfgang Höpken, *Oil on Fire? Textbooks, Ethnic Stereotypes and Violence in South-Eastern Europe* (Hannover: Hahn, 1996), and "War, Memory and Education in a Fragmented Society: The Case of Yugoslavia," *East European Politics and Societies* 13, no. 1 (1999), 190–227.

CHAPTER 7

1. Ivo Goldstein, *Croatia, A History* (London: C. Hurst & Co., 1999), 111–12.

2. Ivo Banac, *The National Question in Yugoslavia: Origins, History, Politics* (Ithaca and London: Cornell University Press, 1984), 129–31.

3. Banac, *National Question*, 135–36.

4. Banac, *National Question*, 226.

5. Goldstein, *Croatia*, 96–107; Arnold Suppan, *Zwischen Adria und Karawanken: Deutsche Geschichte im Osten Europas* 8 (Berlin: Siedler Verlag, 1998), 243–56.

6. Banac, *National Question*, 136–38; Goldstein, *Croatia*, 112; Andrew Baruch Wachtel, *Making a Nation, Breaking a Nation: Literature and Cultural Politics in Yugoslavia* (Stanford: Stanford University Press, 1998), 70–71.

7. Peter Vodopivec, "Slovenes and Yugoslavia, 1918–1991," in *East European Politics and Societies* 6, no. 3 (Fall 1992), 220.

8. Vodopivec, "Slovenes," 224.

9. Suppan, *Adria*, 340.

10. Carole Rogel, *The Slovenes and Yugoslavism, 1890–1914* (Boulder, Colo.: East European Quarterly, 1977), 89.

11. Suppan, *Adria*, 341.

12. Suppan, *Adria*, 341.

13. Vodopivec, "Slovenes," 225; Suppan, *Adria*, 342–48.

14. Vodopivec, "Slovenes," 226–27.

15. Goldstein, *Croatia*, 93–106.

16. Suppan, *Adria*, 260.

17. Wachtel, *Making a Nation*, 55–59, 109–15.

18. Andrić had been a student in Zagreb, Vienna, and Cracow. During World War I, he was in Austrian internment. After 1918, he continued his studies in Graz. He later became an official in the Yugoslav ministry for foreign affairs and envoy to Berlin (1939–41). In 1961, he won the Nobel Prize for literature. Wayne S. Vucinich, "Introduction: Ivo Andrić and His Times," in Wayne S. Vucinich, ed., *Ivo Andrić Revisited: The Bridge Still Stands* (Berkeley: International and Area Studies, University of California, 1995), 1–46.

19. Suppan, *Adria*, 261.

20. Suppan, *Adria*, 261.

21. Goldstein, 108–11; John R. Lampe, *Yugoslavia as History: Twice There was a Country* (Cambridge: Cambridge University Press, 1996), 104–6.

22. Dejan Guzina, "The Ideology and Identity of Serbian Nationalism: Serbia between East and West" (The Center for Austrian Studies, University of Minnesota, conference paper, 1999), 1–4.

23. Lampe, *Yugoslavia*, 86; Wachtel, *Making a Nation*, 53–54, 70, 257.

24. Banac, *National Question*, 110–16.

25. Banac, *National Question*, 117–25; Lampe, *Yugoslavia*, 107–8.

26. Banac, 126–32.

27. Latinka Perović, "Yugoslavia Was Defeated from Inside," in Sonja Biserko, ed., *Yugoslavia: Collapse, War, Crimes* (Belgrade: Centre for Anti-War Action, 1993), 60.

28. Vodopivec, "Slovenes," 223–28.

29. Vodopivec, "Slovenes," 223, 228–29.

30. R. W. Seton-Watson to May Seton-Watson, March 22, 1923, in *R. W. Seton-Watson i Jugoslaveni: Korespondencija, 1906–1941*, vol. 2 (Zagreb: Institut za hrvatsku povijest, 1976), 103–4.

31. Suppan, *Jugoslawien*, 392.

32. Annual Report in 1929, in Public Record Office, Foreign Office 371/14.443, C 1141/92.

33. R. W. Seton-Watson, *Jugoslaveni*, 193–200.

34. R. W. Seton-Watson, *Jugoslaveni*, 320–31.

35. Goldstein, *Croatia*, 128–29; Dragiša Cvetković, *Ili rat ili pakt: Unutarnja i spoljna politika Namesništva* (Paris, 1965)—unpublished manuscript in Hoover Institution Archives, Cvetković papers, box 2.

36. Vladimir Žerjavić, *Yugoslavia: Manipulations with the Number of Second World War Victims* (Zagreb: Croatian Information Centre, 1993).

37. Goldstein, *Croatia*, 131–59; Suppan, *Adria*, 391–422; Vesna Pešić, "The War for Ethnic States," in Nebojša Popov, ed., *The Road to War in Serbia: Trauma and Catharsis* (Budapest: Central European University, 2000), 9–49.

38. Suppan, *Adria*, 391–422.

39. Vodopivec, "Slovenes," 232–34.

40. Goldstein, *Croatia*, 176–78.

41. Goldstein, *Croatia*, 178–95.

42. Audrey Helfant Budding, "Serb Intellectuals and the National Question, 1961–1991" (Ph.D. diss., Harvard University, 1998), 115–26.

43. Guzina, *Serbia*, 8–9; Laura Silber and Allan Little, *Yugoslavia: Death of a Nation* (New York: Penguin Books, 1996), 31–32.

44. Silber and Little, *Death of a Nation*, 37–38.

45. Silber and Little, *Death of a Nation*, 58–81.

46. Vodopivec, "Slovenes," 223.

47. Silber and Little, *Death of a Nation*, 48–50.

48. Vodopivec, "Slovenes," 237–38; Dušan Nećak, "A Chronology of the Decay of Tito's Yugoslavia, 1980–1991," *Nationalities Papers* 21, no. 1 (Spring 1993), 173–87.

49. Silber and Little, *Death of a Nation*, 48–57.

50. Goldstein, *Croatia*, 205–20.

51. Vodopivec, "Slovenes," 239–40. Silber and Little, *Death of a Nation*, 105–46.

52. Silber and Little, *Death of a Nation*, 25–30.

53. Pešić, "Ethnic States," 9–10.

54. David Rohde, "Kosovo Seething," *Foreign Affairs* (May/June 2000), 65–79.

55. Ivo Banac, "Sorting Out the Balkans: Three New Looks at a Troubled Region," *Foreign Affairs* (May/June, 2000), 152–57.

56. Rado L. Lenček, "Preface," *Nationalities Papers* 21, no. 1 (Spring 1993), 8–9.

CHAPTER 8

1. There is no scholarly survey of the entire history of the Macedonian question in the nineteenth and twentieth centuries. Among the most useful works in English are H. R. Wilkinson, *Maps and Policies: A Review of the Ethnographic Cartography of Macedonia* (Liverpool: University Press of Liverpool, 1951); Elisabeth Barker, *Macedonia: Its Place in Balkan Power Politics* (1950; reprint, Westport, Conn.: Greenwood Press, 1980); L. S. Stavrianos, *Balkan Federation: A History of the Movement Toward Balkan Unity in Modern Times* (1944; reprint, Hamden: Anchor Books, 1964).

2. No comprehensive bibliography on the Macedonian question has been compiled thus far. For the most extensive bibliography on the modern history of Macedonia and the Macedonians see Mihailo Apostolski et al., eds., *Istorija na makedonskiot narod*, 3 vols. (Skopje: Institut za nacionalna istorija [INI], 1969), 2, 439–53 and 3, 477–88.

3. This study does not deal with the formation, the "construction," of the Macedonian national identity. I have written on that subject elsewhere (see, for example, "Macedonianism and Macedonian Nationalism on the Left," in Ivo Banac and Katherine Verdery, eds., *National Character and National Ideology in Interwar Eastern Europe* [New Haven, Conn.: Yale Center for International and Area Studies, 1995], 219–54, and "The British Foreign Office and Macedonian National Identity, 1918–1941," *Slavic Review* 53, no. 2 [Summer 1994], 369–94). In connection with this discussion, I would stress that the Macedonian identity formed in a long, complicated, at times confusing, but continuous process of national development and affirmation. The process began with the first Slav and thus anti-Patriarchist, anti-Greek, and anti-Turkish cultural strivings in the second quarter of the nineteenth century and culminated, more than a hundred years later, during World War II, with the proclamation of the Macedonian state in the communist-led Yugoslav Federation. It was stimulated by the political, economic, social, and cultural changes that took place in the Ottoman Empire throughout the nineteenth century. However, it also represented a Macedonian reaction against the well-known designs of the newly established Balkan national states—Bulgaria, Greece, and Serbia—to annex and rule their homeland, Macedonia. Or, more precisely, it was a Macedonian reaction against and rejection of the well-organized and financial campaigns of the neighboring Balkan nationalisms, both before and after they partitioned Macedonia in 1912–13, to impose their respective national ideologies on them; that is, to Bulgarianize, Greekocize, or Serbianize them. By the same token, the determined efforts on the part of the three states to destroy all

signs of Macedonian particularism, patriotism, and nationalism obviously hindered the normal and natural development of Macedonian national identity, and help explain the weakness and slow development of Macedonian nationalism. (On the development of a Macedonian national consciousness and the formation of a Macedonian identity see the works cited below in notes 51 and 52.)

4. For a concise and clear definition of the Macedonian question see Wilkinson, *Maps and Politics*, 4–7; L. S. Stavrianos, *The Balkans Since 1453* (New York: Holt, Rinehart and Winston, 1958), 517–21; Rossos, "Macedonianism and Macedonian Nationalism," 220–22. See also Blaže Ristovski, *Makedonskiot narod i makedonskata nacija*, 2 vols. (Skopje: Misla, 1983) 1, 163–87, 235–62, 263–80.

5. A. J. P. Taylor, *The Struggle for Mastery in Europe 1848–1918* (Oxford: Oxford University Press, 1954), 246, 252.

6. Krste P. Misirkov, *Za makedonckite raboti* (Sofia: Liberalnii Klub, 1903), facsimile edition (Skopje: Institut za makedonski jazik, 1974), 114, 122–26; Ristovski, *Makedonskiot narod*, 194–96; Blaže Koneski, *Kon makedonskata prerodba: Makedonskite učebnici od 19 vek* (Skopje: INI, 1959), 8–10; Rossos, "Macedonianism and Macedonian Nationalism," 223–24; Victor A. Friedman, "Macedonian Language and Nationalism During the Nineteenth and Early Twentieth Century," *Balkanistica* 2 (1975), 84–86.

7. See especially Fikret Adanir, *Die Makedonische Frage. Ihre Entstehung und Entwickelung bis 1908* (Wiesbaden: Steiner, 1979), 42–72; Lj. Doklestić, *Srpsko-makedonskite odnosi vo XIV vek* (Skopje: INI, 1969), 133–72; M. Arnaudov, *Ekzarkh Iosif i bŭlgarskata kulturna borba sled sŭzdavaneto na Ekzarkhiata* (Sofia, 1933); I. Vanchev, *Novo-bŭlgarskata prosveta v Makedoniia prez vŭzrazhdaneto (do 1878 godina)* (Sofia, 1982), 53–131.

8. Roderick H. Davison, *Reform in the Ottoman Empire, 1856–1876* (Princeton, N.J.: Princeton University Press, 1963); Ernest E. Ramsaur, *The Young Turks: Prelude to the Revolution of 1908* (Princeton, N.J.: Princeton University Press, 1957); Niyazi Berkes, *The Development of Secularism in Turkey* (Montreal: McGill University Press, 1964).

9. On the struggle for Macedonia after 1878 in general and the interplay between the Great Powers and the Balkan states see M. S. Anderson, *The Eastern Question, 1774–1923* (London: St. Martin's Press, 1966), chs. 7–10; and the appropriate sections in G. P. Genov, *Iztochniat vŭpros*, 2 vols. (Sofia, 1925–26); M. Laskaris, *To anatolikon zitima, 1800–1923*, 2 vols. (Salonika, 1948–54); V. Popović, *Istočno pitanje* (Belgrade, 1928).

10. The Bulgarian, Greek, and Serbian claims were extensively publicized. For a representative sampling of the divergent points of view see T. R. Georgevich, *Macedonia* (London, 1918), and Jovan M. Jovanović, *Južna Srbija od kraja XVIII veka do oslobodjenja* (Belgrade, 1941) (Serbian); C. Nicolaides, *La Macédoine* (Berlin, 1899), and G. Modes, *O Makedonikon agon kai i neoteri makedoniki istoria* (Salonika, 1967) (Greek); I. Ivanov, *La question macédoine* (Paris, 1920), and Institut za istoriia pri BAN, *Makedonskiat vŭpros. Istoriko-politicheska spravka* (Sofia, 1963) (Bulgarian).

11. A good documentary survey in English of the activities of the neighboring Balkan states in Macedonia is to be found in George P. Gooch and Harold Temperley, eds., *British Documents on the Origins of the War, 1898–1914* (London: H. M. Stationary Office, 1926–38), vol. 5, 100–23. For a most balanced treatment in a Western language see Adanir, *Die Makedonische Frage;* useful works in Western languages are Duncan M. Perry, *The Politics of Terror: The Macedonian Revolutionary Movement, 1893–1903* (Durham, N.C.: Duke University Press, 1988); Henry N. Brailsford, *Macedonia: Its Races and Their Future* (1906; reprint, New York: Arno Press, 1980); Barker, *Macedonia;* Jacques Ancel, *La Macédoine* (Paris: Delagrave, 1930); Gustav Weigand, *Ethnographie von Makedonien* (Leipzig: F. Brandstetter, 1924). For the Bulgarian, Greek, and Serbian points of view see works cited in note 9. Macedonian historians turned their attention to this problem more recently. See Kliment Džambazovski, *Kulturno-opštestvenite vrski na Makedoncite so Srbija vo tekot na XIX vek* (Skopje: INI, 1960); Risto Poplazarov, *Grčkata politika sprema Makedonija vo vtorata polorina na XIX i početokot va XX vek* (Skopje: INI, 1973); Krste Bitoski, *Makedonija i Kneževstvo Bugarija, 1893–1903* (Skopje: INI, 1977).

12. A. Girginov, *Naradnata katastrofa. Vojnite 1912–1913 g.* (Sofia, 1926), 4–5; V. Čorović, *Odnosi izmedju Srbije i Austro-Ugarske u XX veku* (Belgrade: Državna šamparija Kraljevine Jugoslavije, 1936), 322–23.

13. I. E. Geshov (Gueshoff), *The Balkan League* (London, 1915), 14, 16–19; M. Milovanović, "Istorik pregovora za zaključenje srpsko-bugarskog ugovora od 29 februara 1912," in S. Skoko, *Drugi balkanski rat 1913* (Belgrade: Vojnoistorijski institut, 1968), 379–80.

14. Andrew Rossos, "Serbian–Bulgarian Relations, 1903–1914," *Canadian Slavonic Papers* 23, no. 4 (December 1981), 403–4, and more extensively in Andrew Rossos, *Russia and the Balkans: Inter-Balkan Rivalries and Russian Foreign Policy, 1908–1914* (Toronto: University of Toronto Press, 1981), 36–46.

15. Rossos, "Serbian–Bulgarian Relations, 405; Rossos, *Russia and the Balkans,* 46–52.

16. Rossos, *Russia and the Balkans,* ch. 6, 153–78.

17. Rossos, *Russia and the Balkans,* ch. 6, 172–74, 176–78.

18. Rossos, *Russia and the Balkans,* ch. 7, 179–206.

19. Barbara Jelavich, *History of the Balkans,* 2 vols. (Cambridge: Cambridge University Press, 1983), 2 (Twentieth Century), 117–18.

20. On the Macedonian question at the Paris Peace Conference see H. Andonov-Poljanski, *Velika Britania i makedonskoto prašanje na parizkata mirovna konferencija vo 1919 godina* (Skopje: Arhiv na Makedonija, 1973); I. Katardžiev, *Vreme na zreenje: Makedonskoto nacionalno prašanje megju dvete svetski vojni 1919–1930* (Skopje: Kultura, 1977), vol. 1, ch. 1.

21. Katardžiev, *Vreme na zreenje.* See also Andrew Rossos, "Macedonianism and Macedonian Nationalism," 232–34, and Rossos, "British Foreign Office," 371–73.

22. On developments in Yugoslav (Vardar) Macedonia see Katardžiev, *Vreme na zreenje,* vol. 1, 23–83 and Aleksandar Apostolov, *Kolonizacijata*

na Makedonija vo stara Jugoslavija (Skopje: Kultura, 1966). On the situation of the Macedonians in Greek (Aegean) Macedonia see Andrew Rossos, "The Macedonians of Aegean Macedonia: A British Officer's Report, 1944," *The Slavonic and East European Review* 69, no. 2 (April 1991), 282–88; Katardžiev, *Vreme na zreenje*, vol. 1, 85–106; and Stojan Kiselinovski, *Grčkata kolonizacija vo Egejska Makedonija (1913–1940)* (Skopje: INI, 1981).

23. Public Record Office (London), FO371/11405, Kennard (Belgrade) to A. Chamberlain, April 21, 1926, Enclosure, R. A. Gallop, "Conditions in Macedonia," April 19, 1926, 1. (All British documents cited are found in the Public Record Office [hereafter P.R.O.].)

24. P.R.O., FO371/43649, Chancery (Athens) to Southern Department, 12 December 1944, Enclosure. Captain P. H. Evans's "Report on the Free Macedonia Movement in Area Florina 1944" (14 pp.) is given verbatim in Rossos, "Macedonians of Aegean Macedonia," 291–309.

25. On support given to the VMRO see Katardžiev, *Vreme un zreenje*, vol. 1, 171–83 and part 2, ch. 2; Dino Kiosev, *Istoriia na makedonskoto natsionalno revuliutsionno dvizhenie* (Sofia: Otechestren front, 1954), 493–99; and to the communist parties, Katardžiev, *Vreme un zreenje*, vol. 1, 375–76; Evangelos Kofos, *Nationalism and Communism in Macedonia* (Salonika: Institute of Balkan Studies, 1964), 69; Dimitrios G. Kousoulas, *Revolution and Defeat: The Story of the Communist Party of Greece* (London: Oxford University Press, 1965), 65.

26. On Bulgarian (Pirin) Macedonia as well as the Macedonians in Bulgaria see Katardžiev, *Vreme na zreenje*, vol. 1, 107–19; *Istorija na makedonskiot narod*, vol. 3, part 12; Dimitar Mitrev, *Pirinska Makedonija* (Skopje: Naša kniga, 1970), 126–202; Rossos, "Macedonianism and Macedonian Nationalism," 234.

27. See Zoran Todorovski, *Vnatrešnata makedonska revolucionerna organizacija, 1924–1934* (Skopje: Robz, 1997). See also Stefan Troebst, *Mussolini, Makedonien und die Machte, 1922–1930: Die "Innere Makedonische Revolutionäre Organisation" in der Südosteuropapolitik der faschistischen Italien* (Cologne: Böhlau, 1987); Barker, *Macedonia*, ch. 2; Stavrianos, *Balkan Federation*, chs. 8 and 9.

28. Todorovski, *Vnatrešnata;* Barker, *Macedonia*, ch. 2; Stavrianos, *Balkan Federation*, chaps. 8 and 9; and works cited in note 24.

29. The first Balkan Conference met in Athens (5–13 October 1930); the second in Istanbul (20–26 October 1931); the third in Bucharest (22–29 October 1931); and the fourth in Salonika (5–11 November 1933). See Stavrianos, *Balkan Federation*, 230–38, and J. B. Hoptner, *Yugoslavia in Crisis, 1934–1941* (New York: Columbia University Press, 1962), 14–15.

30. Stavrianos, *Balkan Federation*, 239–40; Hoptner, *Yugoslavia in Crisis*, 16–17. See also Živko Avramovski, *Balkanske zemlje i velike sile 1935–1937* (Belgrade: Prosveta, 1968), 18–22.

31. Stavrianos, *Balkan Federation*, 240–42, Hoptner, *Yugoslavia in Crisis*, 17; Avramovski, *Balkanske zemlje*, 23–34.

32. Stavrianos, *Balkan Federation*, 246–47; Hoptner, *Yugoslavia in Crisis*, 91, note 69; Avramovski, *Balkanske zemlje*, 237–60, 319–26.

33. Stavrianos, *Balkan Federation*, 249; Hoptner, *Yugoslavia in Crisis*, 161–62.

34. Stavrianos, *Balkans Since 1453*, 744–45.

35. Stavrianos, *Balkan Federation*, 254; Hoptner, *Yugoslavia in Crisis*, 216; Jelavich, *History of the Balkans*, 2, 233–35.

36. On the occupation and partition of Macedonia see *Istorija na Makedonskiot narod*, 3, 279–301.

37. Rossos, "Macedonianism and Macedonian Nationalism," 236–39, 251–54. See also Katardžiev, *Vreme na zreenje*, vol. 1, part 3, chs. 1 (the Comintern), 2 (KPJ), 3 (KKE), 4 (KPB).

38. Ibid. See also Andrew Rossos, "Great Britain and Macedonian Statehood and Unification 1940–1949," *East European Politics and Societies* 14, no. 1 (Winter 2000), 129; Kiril Miljovski, *Makedonskoto prašanje vo nacionalnata programa na KPJ, 1919–1937* (Skopje: Kultura, 1962), 24–109; Dimitar Mitrev, *BKP i Pirinska Makedonija* (Skopje: Kultura, 1960), 42–62; Darinka Pačemska, *Vnatrešnata makedonska revolucionerna organizacija (Obedineta)* (Skopje: Studentski zbor, 1985), ch. 1.

39. Rossos, "Great Britain and Macedonian Statehood"; Stojan Kiselinovski, *KPG i makedonskoto nacionalno prašanje* (Skopje: Misla, 1985), chs. 2–4; Kofos, *Nationalism and Communism in Macedonia*, ch. 4.

40. Stavrianos, *Balkans Since 1453*, 778.

41. See the polemical writings by representatives of the KPJ, Svetozar Vukmanović [Tempo], *Borba za Balkan* (Zagreb: Globus, 1981) (English edition: *Struggle for the Balkans* [London: Merlin, 1990]), and Slobodan Nešović, *Jugoslavija—Bugarska, ratno vreme, 1941–1945* (Belgrade: Narodna knijga, 1978); and of the KPB, Tsola Dragoicheva, *Poveliia na dŭlga (Spomeni i razmisli)* 3 vols. (Sofia: Partizdat, 1972, 1975, 1979), vol. 3, especially 309–88. On the views of the KKE, see Stojan Kiselinovski, *Egejskiot del na Makedouija (1913–1989)* (Skopje: Kultura, 1990), 54–140; Andrew Rossos, "Incompatible Allies: Greek Communism and Macedonian Nationalism in the Civil War in Greece, 1943–1949," *Journal of Modern History* 69, no. 1 (March 1997), 45–46; and Rossos, "Macedonians of Aegean Macedonia," 286–88.

42. See particularly Rossos, "Incompatible Allies," 45–46 and "The Macedonians of Aegean Macedonia," 286–88; Barker, *Macedonia*, 83–101; and Barker, ed., *British Policy in South-East Europe in the Second World War* (London: Macmillan, 1976), chs. 11–13. See also Phyllis Auty, "Yugoslavia's International Relations (1945–1965)," and Wayne S. Vucinich, "Nationalism and Communism," both in W. S. Vucinich, ed., *Contemporary Yugoslavia: Twenty Years of Socialist Experiment* (Berkeley and Los Angeles: University of California Press, 1969), 161–62, and 250–52.

43. See Novica Veljanovski, *Makedonija vo jugoslovensko-bugarskite odnosi 1944–1953* (Skopje: INI, 1998); also Slobodan Nešović, *Bledski sporazum. Tito-Dimitrov (1947)* (Zagreb: Globus, 1979); Ivo Banac, *With Stalin Against Tito. Cominformist Splits in Yugoslav Communism* (Ithaca, N.Y.: Cornell University Press, 1988), 31–32; Auty, "Yugoslavia's International Relations," 161–63; Stephen Clissold, ed., *Yugoslavia and the Soviet Union:*

A *Documentary Survey* (London: Oxford University Press, 1983), 45–47; Rossos, "Great Britain and Macedonian Statehood," 133.

44. Rossos, "Incompatible Allies," especially 43, 47–53, 61–62, 66–67, and "Great Britain and Macedonian Statehood"; Elisabeth Barker, "The Yugoslavs and the Greek Civil War of 1946–1949," in Lars Berentzen, John O. Iatrides, Ole L. Smith, eds., *Studies in the Greek Civil War, 1945–1949* (Copenhagen: Museum Tusculanum Press, 1987), 297–308. See also Banac, *With Stalin Against Tito*, 33–36; Clissold, *Yugoslavia and the Soviet Union*, 47–49; Peter J. Stavrakis, *Moscow and Greek Communism, 1944–1949* (Ithaca, N.Y.: Cornell University Press, 1989), 145–46, 149–50, 162–64.

45. Auty, "Yugoslavia's International Relations," 155, 161.

46. Rossos, "Incompatible Allies," 67–68, 73–74, 76, and "Great Britain and Macedonian Statehood"; Auty, "Yugoslavia's International Relations," 162–65. For a good survey of major developments and changes in attitudes see also P.R.O., FO371/72192, Peake (Belgrade) to Bevin, August 28, 1948 and FO371/7833, Peake (Belgrade) to Berin, June 29, 1949. See also FO 371/87833, April 14, 1949 and FO371/87470, May 5, 1950, Foreign Office Research Department, "Note on the Chief Developments Effecting Yugoslav Macedonia and Bulgarian Macedonia Since 1945," a lengthy report in two parts.

47. Loring M. Danforth, *The Macedonian Conflict: Ethnic Nationalism in a Transnational World* (Princeton, N.J.: Princeton University Press, 1995), 65–67; Barker, *Macedonia*, 127–29; Stephen E. Palmer, Jr. and Robert R. King, *Yugoslav Communism and the Macedonian Question* (Hamden: Archon, 1974), 133–35, 184–87; Stefan Troebst, "Yugoslav Macedonia, 1944–1953: Building the Party, the State and the Nation," *Berliner Jahrbuch für osteuropäische Geschichte* 1, no. 2 (1994), 103–39.

48. Danforth, *Macedonian Conflict*, 76–78; Palmer and King, 185–87. See also Stojan Kiselinovski, *Egejskiot del na Makedonija 1913–1989* (Skopje: Kultura, 1990), 141–47; Human Rights Watch/Helsinki, *Denying Ethnic Identity: The Macedonians of Greece* (New York, 1994).

49. Danforth, *Macedonian Conflict*, 68; Palmer and King, 185–88. See also Vanja Čašule, ed., *Od Priznavanje do negiranje (Bugarski stavovi za makedonskato prašanje). Stati, govori i dokumenti* (Skopje: Kultura, 1976); Human Rights Watch/Helsinki, *Destroying Ethnic Identity: Selective Persecution of Macedonians in Bulgaria* (New York, 1991).

50. See for example Palmer and King, *Yugoslav Communism*, 189–98.

51. Danforth, *The Macedonian Conflict*, ch. 6, 142–84; Hugh Poulton, *Who Are the Macedonians?* (Bloomington: Indiana University Press, 1995), ch. 9, 172–82 and 203–5; John Shea, *Macedonia and Greece: The Struggle to Define a New Balkan Nation* (Jefferson, N.C., and London: McFarland and Co., 1997), chs. 9 and 10.

52. On the ideas and aims of the *Makedonisti*, see Krste P. Misirkov, *Za makedonckite raboti* (Sofia: Liberalnii Klub, 1903), facsimile edition (Skopje: Institut za makedonski jazik, 1974). Krste P. Misirkov was an outstanding representative and, indeed, an ideologist of Macedonian national-

ism. See also Ristovski, *Makedonskiot narod.* Ristovski is the leading authority on Macedonian national thought and development. The two volumes contain previously published studies on the subject. For the original date and place of publication of these writings see vol. 2, 663–68. See also Blaže Koneski, *Kon makedonskata prerodba: Makedonskite učebnici od 19 vek* (Skopje: INI, 1959), 87–97; Marco Dogo, *Lingua e Nazionalità in Macedonia. Vicende e pensieri di profeti disarmati, 1902–1903* (Milan: Jaca Book, 1985); Rossos, "Macedonianism and Macedonian Nationalism," 223–24, 227–28.

53. Makedonska akademija na naukite i umetnosite (MANU), *Sto godini od osnovanjeto na VMRO i 90 godini od ilindenskoto vostanje* (Skopje: MANU, 1994), a very useful collection of articles on the Macedonian national liberation struggle and movements by leading Macedonian specialists. See also Slavko Dimevski, *Za razvojot na makedonskata nacionalna misla do sozdavanjeto na TMORO* (Skopje: Kultura, 1980); Aleksandar Hristov, *Sozdavanje na makedonskata država, 1878–1978*, 4 vols. (Skopje: Misla, 1985). The works of Khristo Silianov, *Osvoboditelnite borbi na Makedoniia,* 2 vols. (Sofia: Izd. na Ilindenskata Organizatsiia, 1933, 1943) and Dino Kiosev, *Istoriia na makedonskoto natsonalno revoliutsionno dvizhenie* (Sofia: Otechestven front, 1954) are still useful.

54. The literature on the VMRO in general is vast. See especially Adanir, *Die Makedonische Frage,* chs. 2 and 3; Jutta de Jong, *Der nationale Kern des makedonischen Problems: Ansätze und Grundlagen einer makedonischen Nationalbewegung, 1890–1903* (Frankfurt: Lang, 1982); Perry, *Politics of Terror;* Manol Pandevski, *Nacionalnoto prašanje vo makedonskoto osloboditelno dviženje, 1893–1903* (Skopje: Kultura, 1974); Konstantin Pandev, *Natsionalno-osvoboditelnoto dvizhenie v Makedonia i Odrinsko, 1878–1903* (Sofia: Nauka i izkustvo, 1979).

55. On the national liberation ideas of the *Makedonisti* of K. P. Misirkov's generation, see the works cited in note 51. See also Blaže Ristovski, *Dimitrija Čupovski, 1870–1940 i makedonskoto naučno-literaturno drugarstvo vo Petrograd,* 2 vols. (Skopje: Kultura, 1978), and the facsimile edition of the journal *Makedonskii golos* [St. Petersburg, 1913–14] (Skopje: INI, 1968).

56. The ideas and activities of the political right have not been adequately investigated. However, see Katardžiev, *Vreme na zreenje,* vol. 1, 171–83 and 271–96; Kiosev, *Istoriia na makedonskoto,* 512–25; Barker, *Macedonia,* 36–45; Stoyan Christowe, *Heroes and Assassins* (New York: R. M. McBride, 1935). See also the memoirs of the leader of the VMRO after 1924, Ivan Mikhailov, *Spomeni,* 4 vols. (Selci, Louvain, Indianapolis, 1952, 1965, 1967, 1973). For the most recent research and findings see Vojo Kučevski, "Za dejnosta i ulogata na VMRO na Todor Aleksandrov i Ivan Mihailov vo vrska so postavuvanjeto na makedonskoto prašanje vo društvoto na narodite (1920–1934)," in MANU, *Sto godini od osnovanjeto na VMRO,* 427–43.

57. On the ideas of the Macedonian left, see Rossos, "Macedonianism and Macedonian Nationalism," 219–54, and Rossos, "Incompatible Allies," 42–76. See also Katardžiev, *Vreme na zreenje,* vol. 2; Darinka Pačemska,

Vnatrešnata makedonska revolucionerna organizacija (Obedineta) (Skopje: Studentski zbor, 1985), 68ff; and the reminiscences of Mihailov's opponent on the left, Dimitar Vlahov, *Memoari* (Skopje: Nova Makedonija, 1970), part 2, 251–366.

58. On the federalist idea in Macedonian political thought through World War I, see Mihajlo Minoski, *Federativnata ideja vo makedonskata politička misla (1887–1919)* (Skopje: Studenski zbor, 1985).

59. On the federalist conception after the partition of Macedonia, see Rossos, "Macedonianism and Macedonian Nationalism," 238–40 and 247–54. Stavrianos, *Balkan Federation* is still a most valuable survey on the impact of the Macedonian question on inter-Balkan relations.

60. On the political right on the eve of World War II, see works cited in note 55 and Ivan Mikhailov, *Macedonia: A Switzerland of the Balkans* (St. Louis, Mo.: Liberator Press, 1949).

61. On the political left on the eve of World War II, see works cited in notes 56 and 58.

62. See the program of the young Macedonian Revolutionary Organization (MMRO) in Blaže Ristovski, ed., *Kočo Racin: Istorisko-literaturni istražuvanja* (Skopje: Makedonska kniga, 1983), 141–44; and of the Macedonian Peoples' Movement (MANAPO) in Hristo Andonov-Poljanski, ed., *Dokumenti za borbata na makedonskiot narod za samostojnost i nacionalna država*, 2 vols. (Skopje: Univerzitet "Kiril i Metodij," 1981), vol. 2, no. 74, 145 (hereafter cited as *Dokumenti*). See also Rossos, "Macedonianism and Macedonian Nationalism," 252, and Wayne S. Vucinich, "Interwar Yugoslavia," in Vucinich, *Contemporary Yugoslavia*, 247–48.

63. See notes 24 and 26.

64. See note 24.

65. P.R.O., FO371/29785 Campbell (Belgrade) to Halifax, January 6, 1941, Enclosure, "Report on the General Situation in Southern Serbia by Mr. Thomas, British Vice-Consul at Skopje."

66. P.R.O., FO371/43649, Chancery (Athens) to Southern Department, December 12, 1944, Enclosures, 13; also in Rossos, "Macedonians of Aegean Macedonia," 308. See also Rossos, "Great Britain and Macedonian Statehood," esp. 124.

67. "The year 1944 was momentous in Macedonian wartime history. By August the first Macedonian Partisan Division was formed, by November there were seven partisan divisions in the field with a total of 66,000 troops under arms." (National Archives [Washington], R.G.59, Dec. File 1945–49, Box 812, No. 868.00/4–1249, Cannon Belgrade, to Secretary of State, April 12, 1949. See the enclosed secret report entitled "The Macedonian Question, Greece and South Slav Federation," Appendix A ["An Account of Communist Relationships in the Balkans"], 21.) See also *Istorija na makedonskiot narod*, vol. 3, 442.

68. Andonov-Poljanski, *Dokumenti*, vol. 2, no. 206, 412–15 and no. 262, 540–41. See also Jozo Tomasevich, "Yugoslavia During the Second World War," in Vucinich, *Contemporary Yugoslavia*, 103.

69. Andonov-Poljanski, *Dokumenti*, vol. 2, nos. 227 and 228, 472–477.

70. Andonov-Poljanski, *Dokumenti*, vol. 2, no. 287, 604–13. On ASNOM see also MANU, *ASNOM. Ostvaruvanje na ideite za sozdavanje na make-donskata država i negoviot odglas i odraz* (Skopje: MANU, 1977), especially the contributions by A. Hristov, S. Gaber, and N. Sotirovski, 43–54, 55–74, and 75–82, respectively.

71. See Rossos, "Incompatible Allies," 47, note 19.

72. Rossos, "Incompatible Allies," 43–44.

73. Ibid., especially 42–43, 49, 58–59, 61–62, 68–69, 70, and 73–76.

74. Stoyan Pribichevich, *Macedonia: Its People and History* (University Park: Pennsylvania State University Press, 1982), part 2; Palmer and King, *Yugoslav Communism*, chs. 8 and 9; Fred Singleton, *Twentieth-Century Yugoslavia* (New York: Columbia University Press, 1976), 39–41.

75. Ivan Katardžiev, "Oživuvanjeto na idejata, imeto i dejnota na VMRO vo Republika Makedonija," and Mihalo Minovski, "Tajnata politička orga-nizacija VMRO vo Narodnata (socialistička) Republika Makedonija," both in Gligor Krsteski, ed., *Otpori i progoni, 1946–1950* (Skopje: Matica make-donska, 1994), 98–115 and 118–126. See also Palmer and King, *Yugoslav Communism*, 136–140, 189–98; Shea, *Macedonia and Greece*, 175–76.

76. "The International Position of the Republic of Macedonia and Its Sta-tus in the Yugoslav Community," in Republic of Macedonia, *Independence Through Peaceful Self-Determination: Documents* (Skopje: Balkan Forum, 1992), 5–8. See also Sabrina P. Ramet, *Balkan Babel: The Disintegration of Yugoslavia from the Death of Tito to the War for Kosovo*, 3rd ed. (Boulder, Colo.: Westview Press, 1999), ch. 3, 48–76; Vladimir Gligorov, *Why Do Countries Break Up? The Case of Yugoslavia* (Uppsala: Acta Universitatis Upsaliensis, 1994).

77. *Independence Through Peaceful Self-Determination*, 17–18; Ramet, *Balkan Babel*, 183, and Danforth, *The Macedonian Conflict*, 142–43.

78. See Sabrina P. Ramet, "The Macedonian Enigma," in Ramet and Ljubiša S. Adamovich, eds., *Beyond Yugoslavia: Politics, Economics and Culture in a Shattered Community* (Boulder, Colo.: Westview Press, 1995), 211–36; Ramet, *Balkan Babel*, 183–95; Duncan M. Perry "The Republic of Macedonia: Finding Its Way," in Karen Dawisha and Bruce Parrot, eds., *Pol-itics, Power and Struggle for Democracy in South-East Europe* (Cambridge: Cambridge University Press, 1997), 226–81.

79. Text of the report of the R. Badinter Commission in *Independence Through Peaceful Self-Determination*, 32–43.

80. See items cited in note 77, and Danforth, *Macedonian Conflict*, 142–53.

81. Ramet, *Balkan Babel*, 182–86; Danforth, *The Macedonian Conflict*, 142–53; Gligorov, *Why Do Countries Break Up?*, 88; and Alice Ackermann, *Making Peace Prevail: Preventing Violent Conflict in Macedonia* (Syra-cuse, N.Y.: Syracuse University Press, 1999). However, see especially Ivan Katardžiev, *Sosedite i Makedonija: Včera, denes i utre* (Skopje: Menora, 1998), 24–84.

82. Katardžiev, *Sosedite i Makedonija*, 69–84; Ramet, *Balkan Babel*, 186–87.

CHAPTER 9

1. Rod Nordland, "Vengeance of a Victim Race," *Time* (April 12, 1999), 43.
2. Daniel Goldhagen, "A New Serbia," *New Republic* (May 17, 1999), 17–18.
3. The proceedings published as Slavko Gavrilović, et al., eds., *Evropa i Srbi* (Belgrade: Istorijski Insitut SANU, 1996).
4. Aleksandar Despić, "An Introductory Speech," in *Evropa i Srbi*, 10.
5. Milorad Ekmečić, "Encounter of Civilizations and Serbian Relations with Europe," in *Evropa i Srbi*, 21.
6. Rebecca West, *Black Lamb and Grey Falcon* (New York: Viking Press, 1941), 1079.
7. Dubravka Ugrešić, *The Culture of Lies* (University Park: Pennsylvania State University Press, 1998), 245.
8. Tim Judah, *The Serbs* (New Haven, Conn.: Yale University Press, 1997), 47.
9. William Y. Morgan, *The Near East* (Topeka, Kansas: Crane and Co., 1913), 85.
10. Ibid., 90.
11. See Gale Stokes, *Politics as Development: The Emergence of Political Parties in Nineteenth-Century Serbia* (Durham, N.C.: Duke University Press, 1990).
12. Ibid., 306.
13. Quoted in Maria Todorova, *Imagining the Balkans* (New York: Oxford University Press, 1997), 5–6.
14. R. G. D. Laffan, *The Serbs: Guardians of the Gate* (New York: Dorset Press, 1989), 281.
15. Ibid., 281–82.   16. Ibid., 13.
17. Ibid., 14.   18. Ibid., 15.
19. Serbian National Defense League of America, *Kosovo Day in America: 1389–1918* (New York, 1918), 9.
20. For the Yugoslav Committee by Dr. Ante Trumbić, *Southern Slav Bulletin* 10–11 (10 April 1916), 1.
21. Noel Malcolm, *Kosovo: A Short History* (New York: New York University Press, 1998), 355–56.
22. Dimitrije Djordjević, "The Tradition of Kosovo in the Formation of Modern Serbian Statehood," in Wayne S. Vucinich and Thomas A. Emmert, eds., *Kosovo: Legacy of a Medieval Battle* (Minneapolis: Minnesota Mediterranean and East European Monographs, 1991), 310.
23. Rade Mihaljčić, *The Battle of Kosovo in History and in Popular Tradition* (Belgrade: BIGZ, 1989), 200.
24. See Michael Sells, *The Bridge Betrayed: Religion and Genocide in Bosnia* (Berkeley: University of California Press, 1996).

25. Jovan Cvijić, *Balkansko poluostrvo i južnoslovenske zemlje* (Belgrade: Zavod za izdavanje udžbenika, 1966), 368.

26. Miloš Blagojević, "On the National Identity of the Serbs in the Middle Ages," in R. Samardžić and M. Duškov, eds., *Serbs in European Civilization* (Belgrade: Nova, 1993), 31.

27. Ibid.

28. Ibid.

29. Radovan Samardžić, "Aristocratic Vertical in Serbian History," in *Serbs in European Civilization*, 14.

30. Samardžić, "Aristocratic Vertical," 15–16.

31. Ibid., 16, 18.

32. Aleksa Djilas, *The Contested Country* (Cambridge, Mass: Harvard University Press, 1991), 193, n. 36.

33. Branimir Anžulović, *Heavenly Serbia: From Myth to Genocide* (New York: New York University Press, 1999), 74.

34. Olivera Milosavljević, "Yugoslavia as a Mistake," in Nebojša Popov, ed., *The Road to War in Serbia* (Budapest: Central European University Press, 2000), 77.

35. Latinka Perović, "The Flight from Modernization," in *The Road to War in Serbia*, 119.

36. Miodrag Povović, *Vidovdan i časni krst: Ogled iz književne arheologije* (Belgrade, 1976), 131–32, quoted in Olga Zirojević, "Kosovo in the Collective Memory," in *The Road to War in Serbia*, 201.

37. Sabrina Ramet, "The Serbian Church and the Serbian Nation," in *Beyond Yugoslavia: Politics, Economics, and Culture in a Shattered Community* (Boulder, Colo: Westview Press, 1995), 103.

38. Nikolaj Velimirović, *Pravoslavlje i politika* (Belgrade, 1997), 6.

39. Nicholas J. Miller, "The Nonconformists: Dobrica Ćosić and Mića Popović Envision Serbia," *Slavic Review* 58, no. 3 (Fall 1999), 525.

40. Ibid., 518.   41. Ibid., 520.

42. Ibid., 533.   43. Ibid., 535.

44. Vesna Pešić, "The War for Ethnic States," in *The Road to War in Serbia*, 36.

45. See the analysis by Dubravka Stojanović, "The Traumatic Circle of the Serbian Opposition," in *The Road to War in Serbia*, 449–78.

46. Ibid., 458.

47. Robert Thomas, *Serbia Under Milošević: Politics in the 1990s* (London: Hurst & Company, 1999), 3–4.

48. Predrag Palavestra, "Major Trends in Recent Serbian Literature," in *Serbs in European Civilization*, 165.

CHAPTER 10

1. First, it should be noted that much of this text was written before the death of Croatian President Franjo Tudjman and the recent Croatian elections that followed. Thus I trust that many of the statements about "current"

Croatia may rapidly—I hope even before this chapter's publication—become matters of the past. Second, it should be noted that the positions taken by this chapter and its critics, chiefly partisans of the new statelets, are political. I believe that the horrors of the warfare that were bound to occur when Slovenia and Croatia seceded in 1991 far outweighed whatever benefits the secessionists might have hoped to achieve for their own regions; and, in fact, at present only Slovenia may be said to be doing well. Yugoslavia was a state with many flaws; but though not perfect, it was certainly not a repressive place. Politicians should therefore have done everything possible to preserve it (even if it took several years) and not have claimed that matters were hopeless and turned to destroying it. Thus the underlying issue behind the controversy over this paper is: Was Yugoslavia so dreadful that the secessions were justified, even though they were clearly going to let loose a large-scale and bloody war?

2. As Dubravka Ugrešić, one of present-day Croatia's most talented writers, puts it, following a passage on the admirable earlier Yugoslav policy of multicultural brotherhood and unity: "Today those same peoples claim that they lived in a *prison of nations*, and that it was that idea, the idea of Yugoslavism—not they themselves—which is responsible for the present brutal war." She then goes on to state:

> Other totalitarian states [communist ones implied] articulated their dissatisfaction with their regimes in strong intellectual undergrounds, both in the country and abroad. Yugoslavia had virtually no intellectual underground (apart from an insignificant number of dissidents in the early communist years). After the Second World War 'Ustashas,' 'Chetniks,' 'collaborators,' and 'anti-communists' were driven out of the country (dead or alive); some twenty years later there was an economic migration out of the country, of Gastarbeiter. The intellectual emigration was numerically insignificant. If a strong intellectual underground did exist, as everyone swears it did today [August 1993], then how is it that no one knew about it; and if it didn't exist, how can we believe that *the truth* which people craved behind the walls of the so-called *prison of nations* is the one that has now come to the surface? Perhaps the regime, that soft Yugoslav totalitarianism, was not so soft after all, perhaps it was worse than the Albanian or Romanian versions? If that was the case, how come there was so little protest? At this moment it is an indisputable and statistically verifiable truth that many intellectuals from the former Yugoslavia are *voluntarily* joining the ocean of *involuntary* refugees and knocking on the doors of other countries.

(Italics throughout the passages are D. U.'s). D. Ugrešić, *The Culture of Lies* (University Park, Penn.: Pennsylvania State University Press, 1998), 68–69.

3. That the Slovene leadership was actively working toward the destruction of Yugoslavia (or at least toward transforming the Yugoslav state into one that could not function) can be clearly seen in constitutional developments in Slovenia from 1989 to 1991 that put that republic's laws above all

federal ones. Croatia followed in Slovenia's footsteps. For a detailed description of these separatist initiatives, see R. Hayden, *Blueprints for a House Divided: The Constitutional Logic of the Yugoslav Conflict* (Ann Arbor: University of Michigan Press, 1999), ch. 2.

4. In fact what occurred in the 1990s was exactly what Tito had warned of in 1945. "Think well about this [i.e., what would have happened had the Partisans not won the war], dear brothers and sisters, and you will see that we should have been in a state of terrible chaos, in a fratricidal war, in a country which would no longer be Yugoslavia, but would be only a group of petty states fighting among themselves and destroying each other." Cited by J. Ridley, *Tito: A Biography* (London: Constable, 1994), 263.

5. In fact one might wish that Tito had occasionally administered the type of regime the current nationalists have accused him of; then many of the vicious chauvinists who broke up Yugoslavia and set off the ghastly war, such as Tudjman and Vojislav Šešelj, might have remained in jail indefinitely, instead of being promptly released to carry on once again their destructive activities.

6. I hope that with Tudjman's death and the elections of the honorable Ivica Račan and the truly reformed former nationalist Stipe Mesić this trend will be thrown into reverse and make my rhetorical question unnecessary. However, there are chauvinists in the wings who still would like to push the rehabilitation of the Ustaše to such extremes. For reason for hope about Croatia's new leadership and the positive transformation of Mesić, see B. Denitch, "Democratic Breakthrough in Croatia," *Dissent* (Spring 2000), 34. But even with hope on the political side, economics is something different. As Denitch notes:

Any fear that we [the United States] would respond quickly with substantial aid, which is essential, [was] dispelled by Madeline Albright's almost insulting "present" of U.S. $8 million upon her visit to Zagreb right after the elections. . . . It is useless to hope that the United States and Western Europe might come up with the money that one month's bombing of Yugoslavia and Kosovo cost. . . . Instead, we will almost certainly encourage the Croat government to undertake a grim policy of fiscal austerity and debt payment, to show that it is "responsible." The message will be that a move toward democratic decency in Croatia is necessarily accompanied by a drop in an already dangerously low living standard. A center-left government must betray its own base in order to be "responsible" in the eyes of the West and its financial institutions.

7. M. Ignatieff, "The Politics of Self-Destruction," *The New York Review of Books* 42, no. 17 (November 2, 1995), 17. A reading of the British SOE liaison accounts (e.g., Maclean and Deakin) and the German documents published by Hehn and the serious scholarship of objective postwar scholars based on war-time records (e.g., Roberts) make it clear that the Partisans actively fought engagements with the Germans throughout the war. F. Maclean, *Eastern Approaches* (London: Cape, 1949), Part 3: "The Balkan War"; F. W. Deakin, *The Embattled Mountain* (Oxford: Oxford University Press, 1971);

P. Hehn, *The German Struggle against Yugoslavia: Guerrillas in World War One* (New York: Columbia University Press, 1979); W. Roberts, *Tito, Mihailovich and the Allies* (New Brunswick, N.J.: Rutgers University Press, 1973). In terms of this question I was naturally seeking non-Partisan sources. But a mass of evidence about the Partisans' warfare against the Germans and Italians can be found in *The War Diaries of Vladimir Dedijer* (originally in Serbo-Croatian), appearing in a three-volume English translation published by the University of Michigan Press, Ann Arbor, 1990.

8. For example, Aleksa Djilas can write, without providing the slightest evidence—and in the case of Tito's inner thoughts and motives the evidence could not exist, since it is impossible for a person to get inside anyone else's head: "Tito was a seasoned politician who had survived the purges (*and according to some accounts participated in them*) [source?] . . . Tito's patriotism and concern for Yugoslavia's unity would increase, but would always remain subordinate to political expediency and personal power. . . . Since Tito's main concern was always to prevent any kind of all-Yugoslav opposition to his rule—and modern Yugoslav management and work forces might have become that—he *welcomed the disastrous fragmentation* [of the country] . . . Tito was no Hitler [!], nor was it even his goal to destroy Yugoslavia [!]. But since his dictatorial misrule enormously contributed to Yugoslavia's bloody disintegration, *its ruins are a monument he deserves.*" (A. Djilas, "Tito's Last Secret," *The National Times* 4, no. 5 [November 1995], 22–23 [all italics mine]). This evaluation is irresponsible nonsense. Tito's nationality policy was full of flaws, but he was dealing with an incredibly complex problem that had no simple solutions. With hindsight, we can see that he made many mistakes, especially his giving in too much to the pressure of republic nationalists at the expense of trying to develop an all-Yugoslav national consciousness and his leaving the state to a decentralized eight-person executive (who were representatives of the nationalist republics) that simply could not function. But his errors, and the results they eventually had—and, of course, many of the events that brought Yugoslavia down occurred after his departure from the scene—were errors in judgment and can in no way suggest that he did not love Yugoslavia. He was vain and, I suspect, believed that he was indispensable for Yugoslavia—and many Yugoslavs certainly believed he really was indispensable—but these weaknesses do not make an either/or and they could, and I am certain did, coexist with a dedication to and love of Yugoslavia. His whole career from 1941 until his death in 1980 belies Aleksa Djilas's mean-spirited comments, and Yugoslavia's tragedy is Tito's as well. This sort of vituperative writing, however, has become commonplace in the present post–Cold War world, where strangely (considering communism's demise) it has hit new heights of negativity and any excommunist, no matter how positive his contributions to his society may have been, has become fair game. Unlike many East European Communist leaders, Tito deserves a better fate.

9. That Milošević had previously intervened and established martial law in Kosovo did not pose any actual danger for Croatia and Slovenia (which

were republics), for Kosovo was only an autonomous region and constitutionally part of Serbia.

10. The JNA has recently had a terrible press, and if one judges it on its actions in the mid-to-late stages of the Croatian war and in the Bosnian war, that criticism is completely justified. But if we move back to Tito's last years and the 1980s, this institution, established by Tito and dedicated to his ideals, was the only true Yugoslav body in the country. And the leaders that Tito appointed and those who rose up in the army's ranks in the 1980s were on the whole a very honorable and dedicated group with true Yugoslav patriotism. They also, what is very important (though usually ignored by the army's critics), had accepted the principle of constitutional rule and the army's submission to civil authorities. This meant that the army (though making comments and trying to exert pressure) remained essentially on the sidelines throughout the crises of 1990–91 (until the actual declaration of independence by Slovenia and Croatia on June 25, 1991). Milošević tried to draw the army into the fray during the last year of Yugoslavia, but the army would not act without the agreement of the whole presidency, and thus was called on to carry out only very limited assignments. Tito had imbued his officers with a strong belief that the army had to be subordinate to civilian authority. Thus the last chance to save Yugoslavia prior to June 25, 1991, a military coup to prevent separatism, was, owing to the generals' Titoist principles, a non-possibility. Though no fan of military coups, I, taking into consideration the leadership of the army in early 1991, believe that such a coup, by preserving Yugoslavia, might have been beneficial in the long run to a majority of the peoples of Yugoslavia. This suggestion is based on an assumption that it would have been carried out efficiently, bloodlessly, and only at the last moment (i.e., a day or two before the scheduled independence day, June 25, 1991) and, then, only if it was completely clear (as it was by then) that Slovenia, Croatia, and Serbia had given up on any sort of serious discussions. It would presumably have been effected simultaneously by locally based JNA troops in at least the three major cities of Belgrade, Zagreb, and Ljubljana (and against territorial defense force centers that were stockpiling weapons to support secession), and carried out in the manner that the JNA had operated in December 1971 when Croat chauvinism was then getting out of hand. That such a JNA operation would likely have been restrained in 1991 is confirmed by the JNA's actions in Slovenia in June 1991, for the JNA (whose leadership then was still in the hands of the Titoists) obeyed orders from federal civilian authorities and never used its enormous strength against Slovenia; indeed, every skirmish that occurred in Slovenia that led to a casualty was started by Slovenes. The generals, though conservative and centrist, would, if effecting their own coup, have removed all the chauvinists (including Serb ones like Milošević) and would probably as soon as possible have restored civilian rule under a new constitution, which, though presumably respecting all the ethnicities' cultural rights in the spirit of Tito, would have produced a more centralized state that would also have outlawed and punished chauvinism and come up with

a means to deal with the economy and World Bank. Moreover, even if the army were to have been rougher or more authoritarian than I suggest, it is very unlikely that the junta would have become a permanent institution; thus, after achieving its objectives, the junta would almost certainly have returned government to civilian and constitutional rule. The army's character from late 1991 on resulted, however, from the presence of too many Serb officers (including Serbs from Croatia, Bosnia, and Montenegro). Tito for years had tried to push an affirmative-action policy to advance other nationalities, but Serbs were particularly attracted to military careers in Yugoslavia (as Southerners have been in the United States). So with this Serb presence in its leadership, and the effects of Serb chauvinism on certain younger officers during the late 1980s, followed by the breakup and the withdrawal from the army of Croats, Slovenes, and Macedonians to take up positions in the separatist republics, Serbs came overwhelmingly to dominate the army. Then Milošević, once the war with Croatia was under way, was able to bring about a purge among these Serbs, cashiering off those who were Titoists (or giving them, for example, leadership of boot camps in Serbia) and promoting the Serb chauvinists. By the time the Bosnian War started, owing to the withdrawal of the other nationalities and the retirement and reassignment of Serb Titoists, Milošević basically had a Serb national army, which in its development phase carried out many atrocities in Croatia and subsequently (under a totally different sort of leadership in terms of mindset) was able to carry out the horrors we saw in Bosnia and later in Kosovo. But I believe that scholars should not let JNA post-1991 behavior color their picture of the Yugoslav army that existed prior to that time. Moreover, if one believes that a continuing Yugoslavia would have been better than the civil wars that actually occurred, not to speak of the on-going misery in a number of Yugoslav regions, then the alternative of a military coup responding to the situation in 1990–91 should be examined seriously. And in considering this we must think of the generals of 1990 (like the half-Serb, half-Croat minister of war General Veljko Kadijević— who has only slight resemblance to Croatia's wartime depiction of him and was to be pensioned off by Milošević later in 1991) and not the Ratko Mladić(es) who emerged in the aftermath. Of course, this is all what-if counter-history, and we can never know what would have happened had such a coup been launched. But at least it can be shown that these 1990–91 JNA generals respected civilian rule to such an extent that despite the incompetence and gridlock of the presidency and the danger to Yugoslavia, they did not act unilaterally. (On the JNA's seeking and failing to get the permission of the presidency to confiscate the illegal weapons smuggled into Croatia for the Croatian territorial defense forces and the subsequent failure to receive the endorsement of the presidency to declare a state of emergency or carry out a coup, see L. Silber and A. Little, *Yugoslavia: Death of a Nation* [New York: Penguin, 1996], 103–25, 155, 161.)

11. By this statement on responsibility, I mean responsibility for the fact that there followed a war. This statement makes no attempt to assign shares

of responsibility for the horrendous atrocities by both Serbs and Croats that occurred during the war itself in Croatia.

12. One of the absurd aspects of recent U.S. policy in the face of enormously complex Balkan issues is to set deadlines (often very short ones) for agreements to be reached or for tasks to be completed involving sides that detest one another. Such matters should be handled with all deliberate speed in a statesman-like fashion. The Dayton Accords (which make up an extremely long text) suffered greatly from the fact that no side (ourselves included) could in a short time have thought through the implications of all of its hundreds of points. We next sent IFOR (Implementation Force, NATO) in, declaring these troops would be there for a term of a year, which meant that the Bosnian elections had to be held within nine months—as if conditions for an election or for a troop withdrawal could possibly be achieved in this short period. And we did not learn any lesson on such matters from Bosnia. Three years later at Rambouillet we again set an absurdly short deadline for agreement between Serbs and Kosovars and, by attaching an ultimatum to the deadline as well, basically boxed ourselves in so that NATO had to launch a war against Serbia. The issues involved in Bosnia and Kosovo are extremely complex; one hopes that soon we will learn that time limits cannot be set for such matters. Discussions, even when all sides are serious, can and should go on for months or even more, and troops will have to stay (if we care what happens in the region) until sufficiently stable conditions have been achieved, even if it takes years. After all to talk for an extra month or even six is far better than to hastily lay out certain terms that cannot work or that will cause friction, and maybe even fighting, down the road. And, as seen above, the whole Yugoslav catastrophe occurred because the Slovenes and Croats were too impatient and set arbitrary and extremely short deadlines for declaring independence, an act that was going to affect the lives of twenty-three million Yugoslavs for years to come and that the separatists could easily have foreseen was going to result in brutal warfare. The leaders of the republics, in fact, could all still be talking within Yugoslavia; major matters such as a nation's future cannot be solved in a small number of months, particularly when the negotiations are being carried out, chiefly for the galleries, by ambitious demagogues pushing their own agendas as monologues.

13. The Accords themselves, from actual post-Dayton experience on the ground, need some modifications, which may call for a new international conference. In many cases the spheres of activity for all-Bosnia should be widened. Thus, for example, primary and secondary education should be assigned to the complete state. This would allow for a common curriculum for all Bosnian children and also get rid of the narrow, inaccurate, hate-filled textbooks on subjects such as history now being used in the various entities that seek to maintain the divisions and prevent rapprochement among the different ethnicities; each of these texts must be replaced by a commission-written (possibly by foreigners) single (e.g., history) text that will recognize the achievements of all three groups and will also be critical, when relevant,

of activities by all three. On the manner in which the entities have been treating history, see R. Donia, "The Question of Tolerance in Sarajevo's Textbooks," *Human Rights Review* 1, no. 2 (January–March 2000), 38–55.

14. Though it may be hoped that the French arrest in April 2000 of Momčilo Krajišnik will be a first step toward more serious actions.

15. Matters did not end with the soldiers' retreating from the stone-throwers, but shortly thereafter Henry Shelton, chairman of the Joint Chiefs, placed restrictions on how the five thousand U.S. troops in Kosovo could be deployed, despite their being under NATO command. Shelton then visited Kosovo to make sure the risks to his troops had been minimized. "At the same time, [American] administration officials acknowledge that an overriding priority is to avoid American casualties and keep Kosovo out of the news during an election year. One administration official, who served in Bosnia, said that the driving force behind the policy now is to keep it 'off the front page.'" (J. Perlez, "Spiral of Violence in Kosovo Divides U.S. and Its Allies," *The New York Times* [March 12, 2000], A1, A6.) If such factors drive our Balkan policy, we clearly cannot and will not solve anything.

16. The thoughts of Slovenes may be quite different. They achieved their independence without a war (for the JNA's moving in to take over border posts hardly can be called a war) and they have put together a prosperous little statelet. Whether they will be able to maintain their independence or have any impact on even regional politics, only time will tell.

17. For an excellent discussion of these tolerant and selfless nineteenth-century Croat Yugoslavists, see M. Kabelin, *Vjekoslav Babukić: His Role as Linguist during the Illyrian Movement* (Ph.D. thesis, University of California, Berkeley, 1994).

18. As for their nationalist late-twentieth-century counterparts: "A law due to come into force in September [1995] is intended to rid the Croatian language of foreign words. A new State Office for the Croat language will inspect school textbooks and supervise the use of language in books, the press, media, theatre and film. Proposed penalties for violating linguistic rules include fines and imprisonment up to six months (Alternative Information Network)." *Index on Censorship* 24, no. 5 (September-October 1995), 175.

19. The exception on the animosity that existed in 1918 was to be found among the Serbs and Albanians of Kosovo, for the Kosovars strongly objected to their incorporation into this state after having been conquered by the Serbs in the Balkan Wars; but even here, it may be noted that much of that animosity also emerged in the twentieth century. The heart of Kosovo is the battlefield, where the Turks (Muslims) in 1389 allegedly defeated the Serbs (Christians). In fact, the battle was a draw, for both sultan and Serb prince were killed and the Ottomans had to withdraw their forces at battle's end; moreover, Serbia (though soon having to become a vassal state of the Ottomans) hung on as a principality for another half century. Indeed, the Albanians in 1389 were still not Muslims, and Albanians even fought on the Serb-Christian side against the Turks, while it is almost certain that the Serb epic hero Marko Kraljević (by 1389 a Turkish vassal) fought for the

Turks against the Serb forces of Knez Lazar (on Kosovo, see J. Fine, *The Late Medieval Balkans* [Ann Arbor: University of Michigan Press, 1987], 408–14). Subsequently in the Ottoman period, though Albanian and Montenegrin tribes fought one another (as tribesmen), and though Albanians served in Ottoman forces to put down Serb rebellions, and though Albanian landlords oppressed Serb (and also Albanian) peasants, the conflicts were not ethnic ones. The future ethnicities were included in larger forces (e.g., in Habsburg or Ottoman armed forces against the other), but conflicts between Serbs and Albanians within the Ottoman Empire reflected either social-economic (peasant-landlord) differences or to a lesser extent religious ones. *Ethnic* tensions began in 1878 (as Albanians organized to resist the territorial transfers mandated by the Treaty of Berlin) and have led to serious problems between the two ethnicities since that time. But 1878 hardly seems very ancient to me. In fact, French-German animosity and our own North-South differences predate 1878.

20. The animosity stirred up by the events of the past decade will obviously delay these peoples' coming back together again. That Tito was able so quickly after equal or even worse horrors to re-create a multiethnic state that functioned may give one hope. However, the speed with which Tito achieved this was facilitated by the absence of the bearers of chauvinism and hate, who were in one way or another eliminated and thus not present within the state to undercut the movement for reconciliation. Such chauvinist thugs are still present and active in the current Yugoslav lands and in many places (whether holding office or not) have great influence upon their followers. A step to overcome this nefarious influence would be to carry out the arrest of all indicted war criminals.

CHAPTER 11

An earlier version of this chapter appeared as "Containing Nationalism: Solutions in the Balkans," *Problems of Post-Communism* 46, no.4 (July-August 1999), 3–10.

1. Hendrik Spruyt, *The Sovereign State and Its Competitors: An Analysis of Systems Change* (Princeton, N.J.: Princeton Univeristy Press, 1994), 19. This is not a new idea. See Aristide Zolberg, "Origins of the Modern World Economy," *World Politics* 33 (January 1981), 253–81, which argues that the development of states preceded that of the world economy. In regard to nationalism, Ernest Gellner agrees: "our definition of nationalism [is] parasitic on a prior and assumed definition of the state" (*Nations and Nationalism* [Ithaca, N.Y.: Cornell University Press, 1983], 4).

2. Perry Anderson, *Lineages of the Absolutist State* (London: Verso, 1979), 17–18 (emphasis in original).

3. Charles Tilly, "Reflections on the History of European State-Making," in Charles Tilly, ed., *The Formation of National States in Western Europe* (Princeton, N.J.: Princeton University Press, 1975), 34–35.

4. Benedict Anderson's argument for the existence of print-capitalism is thin in the extreme. He simply accepts without further discussion the view of Lucien Febvre and Henri-Jean Martin, published in 1958, that in the first half of the sixteenth century printers conducted an international trade that constituted "a great industry under the control of wealthy capitalists" (*Imagined Communities*, 2nd ed. [London: Verso, 1991], 38).

5. John Rawls, *A Theory of Justice* (Cambridge, Mass.: Belknap Press of Harvard University Press, 1971) and *Political Liberalism* (New York: Columbia University Press, 1996). Note that Rawls does not view political liberalism, which in his view is the practical consequence of conceiving justice as emerging from a condition of fairness, as a "doctrine founded on reason and viewed as suitable for the modern age" (i.e., Enlightenment monism). He takes it for granted that modern societies contain a "reasonable pluralism of comprehensive doctrines" (*Political Liberalism*, x). Nevertheless, his view would be impossible had the philosophes not first transformed the notions of freedom (from a privilege to a condition of sound rule) and equality (from egalitarianism to equal access to natural rights).

6. For a stimulating discussion of these paradoxical necessities for universalism (all belong to the nation) and particularism (the nation differs from others) see Charles Taylor, "The Politics of Recognition," in his *Philosophical Arguments* (Cambridge, Mass.: Harvard University Press, 1995), 225–56.

7. François Furet, *Interpreting the French Revolution* (New York: Cambridge University Press, 1981), 33.

8. Leonard Krieger, *Kings and Philosophers, 1689–1789* (New York: W. W. Norton, 1970), 223.

9. For excellent comments on this point, see Maria Todorova, *Imagining the Balkans* (New York: Oxford University Press, 1997), 138, 186.

10. Once we clearly understand nationalism as an ideological phenomenon rather than a socioeconomic one, for example, it is clear why economic sanctions do not work. They attack the nation-state at a place that is not actually important to nationalists.

11. Henry Kissinger, *Diplomacy* (New York: Simon and Schuster, 1994), especially chs. 3 and 4.

12. Paul W. Schroeder, *The Transformation of European Politics, 1763–1848* (New York: Oxford University Press, 1994). Schroeder's powerful book is the most original piece of diplomatic history written in a generation. He argues that more fundamental structural change took place in the arena of international affairs during the period he covers than in the social or political spheres more commonly thought to have been transformed by the French Revolution and Napoleon. The book needs to be savored in its details, but for Schroeder's rules of the balance of power system see pp. 5–11, and for a brief summary of his analysis of the Congress of Vienna, see pp. 577–82.

13. Schroeder, *Transformation*, 580.

14. Helpful here is William H. Sewell, Jr., *A Rhetoric of Bourgeois Revolution: The Abbé Siéyès and What Is the Third Estate* (Durham, N.C.: Duke University Press, 1994), 100.

15. See, for example, Emanuel Adler, "Europe's New Security Order: A Pluralistic Security Community," in Beverly Crawford, ed., *The Future of European Security* (Berkeley: International and Area Studies, Center for German and European Studies, University of California, 1992), 287–326. Today, NATO's mission is seen less as a purely military one and more as one of promoting democracy. This is true even in Kosovo and Bosnia, where troops of the NATO armies are engaged in police-keeping activities in pursuit of a goal of multiethnic democratization. During the 1990s, several American officials argued that the goal of NATO expansion was not primarily military but rather to promote democracy in Eastern Europe. See, for example, Strobe Talbott: "the prospect of being admitted to NATO provides the nationals of Central Europe and the former Soviet Union with additional incentives to strengthen their democratic and legal institutions, . . . liberalize their economies, and respect human rights" ("Why NATO Should Grow," *New York Review of Books* [August 10, 1995], 27), and Richard Holbrooke: NATO offers Eastern Europe a chance to "enjoy stability, freedom, and independence based on . . . the adoption of Western democratic ideals" ("America, a European Power," *Foreign Affairs* 74, no. 3 [March-April 1995], 41–42).

16. Although it is true that in the Yugoslav case that once the shooting started many of those involved became motivated by crude material self-interest, from the simple looting of TVs to the creation of vast criminal empires.

17. Timothy Garton Ash, "Cry the Dismembered Country," *New York Review of Books* (January 14, 1999), 29–33, and "Anarchy and Madness," *New York Review of Books* (January 13, 2000), 48–53.

18. Warren Zimmerman, "Last Chance for Bosnia?" *New York Review of Books* (December 19, 1996), 13.

19. This is not to say that the fall of Milošević is imminent or even likely. Popular unrest or poverty does not move him; he is surrounded by men who have made their fortunes following his aggressive policies and who have a lot to lose; as an indicted war criminal his options outside of power are bleak; and his people have all the guns. But if we think in terms of the long run, it is a certainty that he will not be there forever.

Index

DATE DUE

GAYLORD

PRINTED IN U.S.A.